SISTERS IN ART

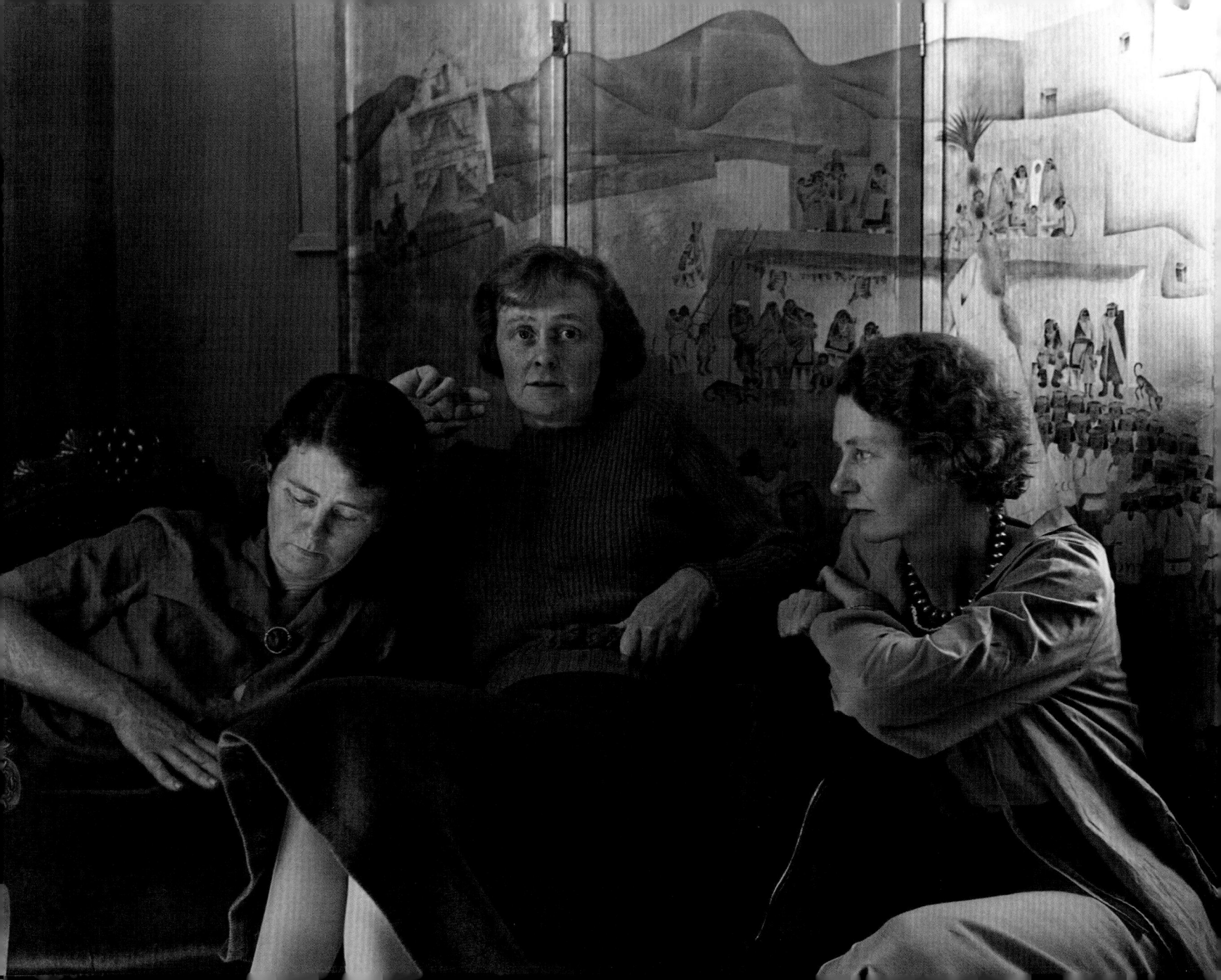

SISTERS IN ART

THE BIOGRAPHY OF
MARGARET, ESTHER, AND HELEN BRUTON

WENDY VAN WYCK GOOD

WEST
MARGIN
PRESS

Text © 2021 by Wendy Van Wyck Good

Edited by Emily Bowles
Indexed by Sam Arnold-Boyd

Copyright to archival photographs on page 221–22

Library of Congress Cataloging-in-Publication Data

Names: Good, Wendy Van Wyck, author.
Title: Sisters in art : the biography of Margaret, Esther, and Helen Bruton /
    Wendy Van Wyck Good.
Description: Berkeley : West Margin Press, 2021. | Includes bibliographical
    references and index. | Summary: "Written by the foremost expert on
    the Bruton sisters, this is the first detailed history on the incredible lives
    and contributions of California modernist artists Margaret, Esther, and
    Helen Bruton"—Provided by publisher.
Identifiers: LCCN 2021013961 (print) | LCCN 2021013960 (ebook) |
    ISBN 9781513289519 (hardback) | ISBN 9781513289526 (ebook)
Subjects: LCSH: Bruton family. | Bruton, Margaret, 1894-1983. | Bruton,
    Esther, 1896-1992. | Bruton, Helen, 1898-1985. | Artists—United
    States—Biography. | Women artists—United States—Biography. |
    California—Biography.
Classification: LCC N6537.B815 2021 (print) | LCC N6537.B815 (ebook) |
    DDC 709.2/52—dc23
LC record available at https://lccn.loc.gov/2021013961
LC ebook record available at https://lccn.loc.gov/2021013960

Proudly distributed by Ingram Publisher Services

Printed in China
25 24 23 22 21 1 2 3 4 5

Published by West Margin Press®

WEST
MARGIN
PRESS
WestMarginPress.com

WEST MARGIN PRESS
Publishing Director: Jennifer Newens
Marketing Manager: Alice Wertheimer
Project Specialist: Micaela Clark
Editor: Olivia Ngai
Design & Production: Rachel Lopez Metzger

Contents

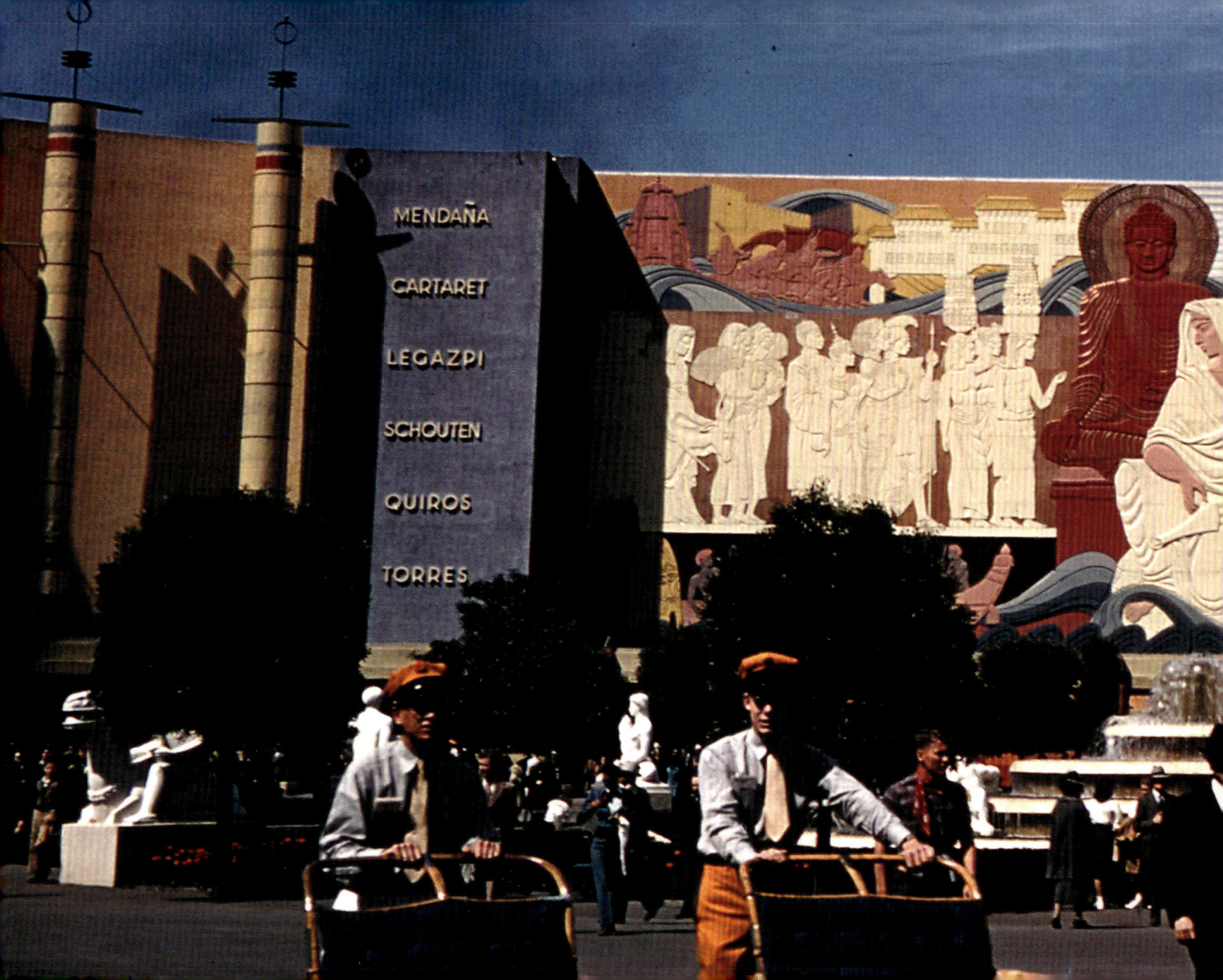

MENDAÑA

CARTARET

LEGAZPI

SCHOUTEN

QUIROS

TORRES

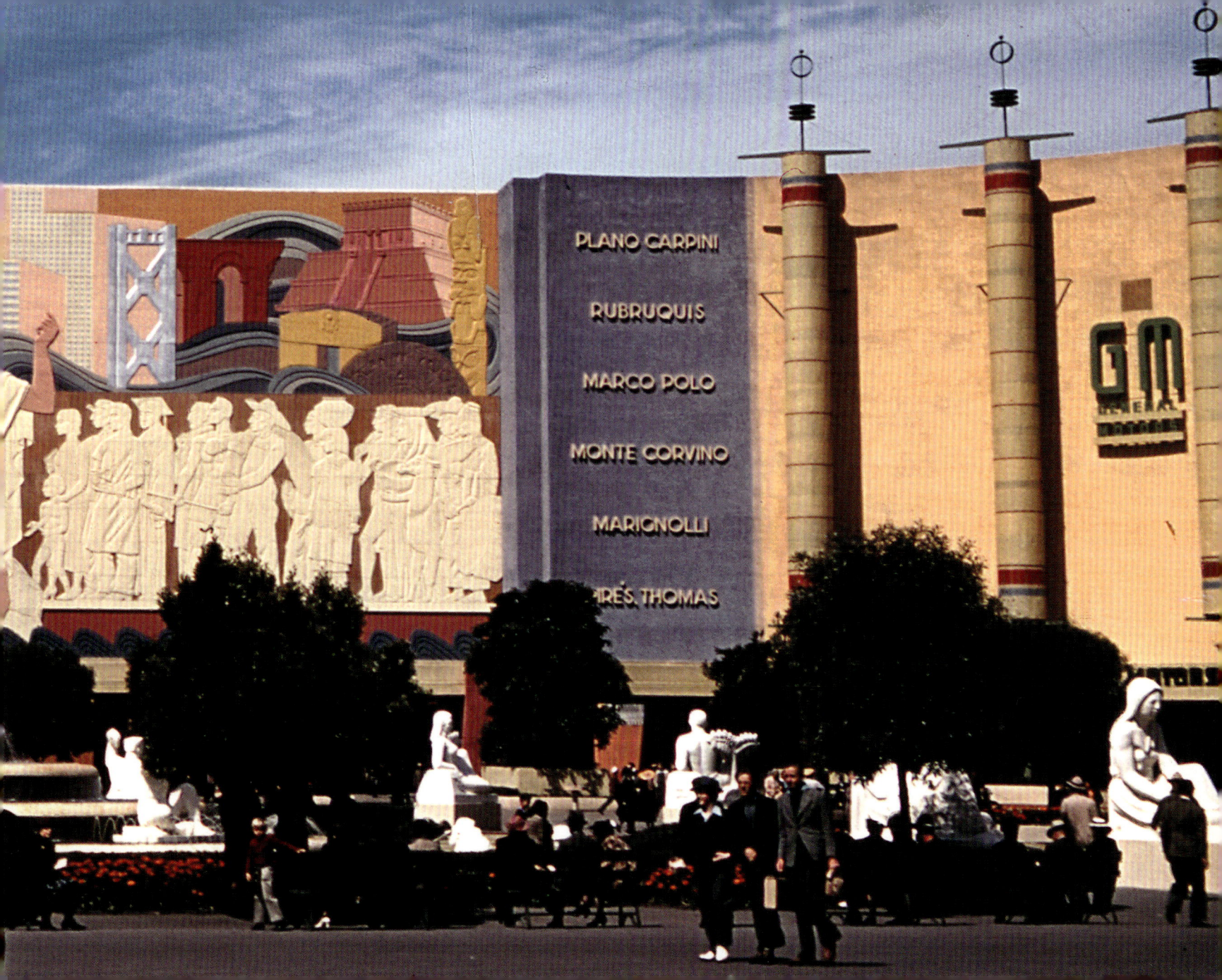

Lost in the Fire

(October 1991)

October 19, 1991, a Saturday morning, dawned clear and balmy in Northern California. The residents of the tranquil San Francisco Bay community of Oakland Hills woke up to what looked like a pleasant day. Located west of downtown Oakland, the Oakland Hills are altogether different from the urban center—a largely rural area with winding roads and superb views of the bay. Within easy commuting distance to Berkeley and San Francisco, it is an appealing location for both the edgy and the affluent, attracting professors, artists, writers, business executives, and prosperous professionals.

As is true of many hillside areas in California, this region has had its share of devastating wildfires. In 1923, 1970, and 1980, major conflagrations raged through the Oakland Hills, leaving mass destruction in their wakes. Despite the risk, the land retains its appeal; after each fire, homes were rebuilt and the hills were quickly repopulated. Since California rarely receives precipitation between May and November, the greatest danger for wildfires is in the fall. In October 1991, after five years of drought, the Oakland Hills were particularly arid.

That Saturday afternoon, a small brush fire broke out in the Oakland Hills just northwest of CA Route 24 and the Caldecott Tunnel. Oakland firefighters responded and, by evening, believed they had completely extinguished the blaze as they saw no more signs of smoke or flames. Embers covered by fallen debris, however, continued to smolder unseen. Early the next morning, dry Diablo winds moved in from the east, blowing the hot embers onto nearby dry vegetation. Fanned by unrelenting wind, the blaze spread rapidly into several new locations—canyons and hillsides not easily accessible to firefighters. Just after 11:30 a.m., the incident commander reported that the fire, now larger than one hundred acres, was "totally out of control."

Police and fire personnel were sent to evacuate homeowners in the fire's path, but many of the twisting roads were already engulfed in flames and impassable. As exit routes became clogged with evacuating cars, power lines fell across streets and ignited new fires, adding to the confusion. Many did not have time to evacuate or were unsuccessful in their attempts to outrun the blaze. As the *Los Angeles Times* reported, "Most of the victims apparently didn't realize just how rapidly the fire was moving as it swept up from a neighboring canyon and over the hilltop... And when they did, it was too late." Tragically, twenty-five people lost their lives and more than 150 were injured. Nearly 10,000 people were left homeless and the cost of the blaze has been estimated at $1.5 billion.

One of the many structures lost in the Oakland Hills fire was the home of art collectors Walter A. Nelson-Rees and James L. Coran. Nelson-Rees was a renowned geneticist at the University of California at Berkeley whose discovery of and research on the cross-contamination of cell lines in labs shook the scientific world. In addition to his work in genetics, Nelson-Rees spent many years building a premier collection of early twentieth-century California art. A knowledgeable and savvy collector who saw value in underappreciated works, he and

Coran acquired nearly 1,000 important artworks, including paintings by Albert Bierstadt, Maynard Dixon, Francis McComas, Selden Connor Gile, and Louis Siegrist. Their collection was valued at close to $45 million. In 1991, Nelson-Rees and Coran were preparing for a major museum exhibition of their paintings, and a beautifully illustrated exhibition catalog had already been printed.

Everything changed on October 20, 1991, when the paintings owned by Nelson-Rees and Coran were lost to the Oakland Hills fire. Afterwards, a devastated Nelson-Rees lamented, "I couldn't believe it. Why did our house burn? We had a metal roof, insulation. We're all so vulnerable." Art dealer John Garzoli described the significance of the tragedy: "They had No. 1 [sic] works by so many artists that can't be replaced, this is a major loss to the American art world."

Some of the artworks destroyed that day were by Margaret Bruton and Helen Bruton, artists and sisters who grew up in the nearby city of Alameda. Margaret, Helen, and their other sister, Esther, who was also a talented artist, were frequently referred to as a single unit: "the Bruton Sisters." All born in the 1890s, the Brutons were celebrities of the California art scene in the 1920s and 1930s, and each had a distinct and remarkable art career. They traveled in elite artistic circles and boldly experimented and excelled in a wide variety of styles and mediums. They were lauded by the press and won many art prizes. In 1939, at the height of their fame, they executed a masterful 8,000-square-foot mural for the Golden Gate International Exposition, the largest artwork at the fair. They were paid $20,000 for the work (more than $350,000 in today's dollars), a staggering sum to earn during the Great Depression.

The Bruton sisters were exceptionally talented, and their personal lives were complex and full of contradictions. Despite having been born into a life of privilege, they lived frugally and blended seamlessly into the bohemian art communities that embraced them. Although celebrated for their achievements, they cared little about fame and did not promote themselves nor their work. The press emphasized their lithe beauty and sharp wit, yet the sisters remained fiercely independent, prioritizing art-making over becoming wives or mothers. For each of them, art was their greatest passion.

Among the artworks destroyed in the Oakland Hills fire were Margaret's striking modernist portraits of her parents, which received rave reviews in the 1920s, and her landscape *Mining Mountains*, which won multiple prizes in the 1930s. Helen's iconic painting *Beach Picnic*, which captured the bohemian spirit of the Monterey art colony in the 1920s, was also destroyed. Given the catastrophic losses of life and property in the Oakland Hills fire, it is not surprising that little attention was given in the press to these works of art. Fire aside, by 1991, the fame and achievements of the Bruton sisters had already been nearly lost to history.

Like many women artists of the early twentieth century, the Brutons have been, for the most part, left out of the artistic canon. Despite their success in the early twentieth century, their careers were impacted by the changing post-World War II art scene, when modernism came to be associated with its male practitioners. As values shifted and their artistic output waned, the famous Bruton sisters fell out of fashion and were largely forgotten. Yet today, museums, collectors, and art historians have rediscovered and are reevaluating their work. This book examines the remarkable lives and careers of these captivating and unconventional sisters, whose endless experimentation produced an eclectic body of modern art, newly appreciated for its fearless creativity.

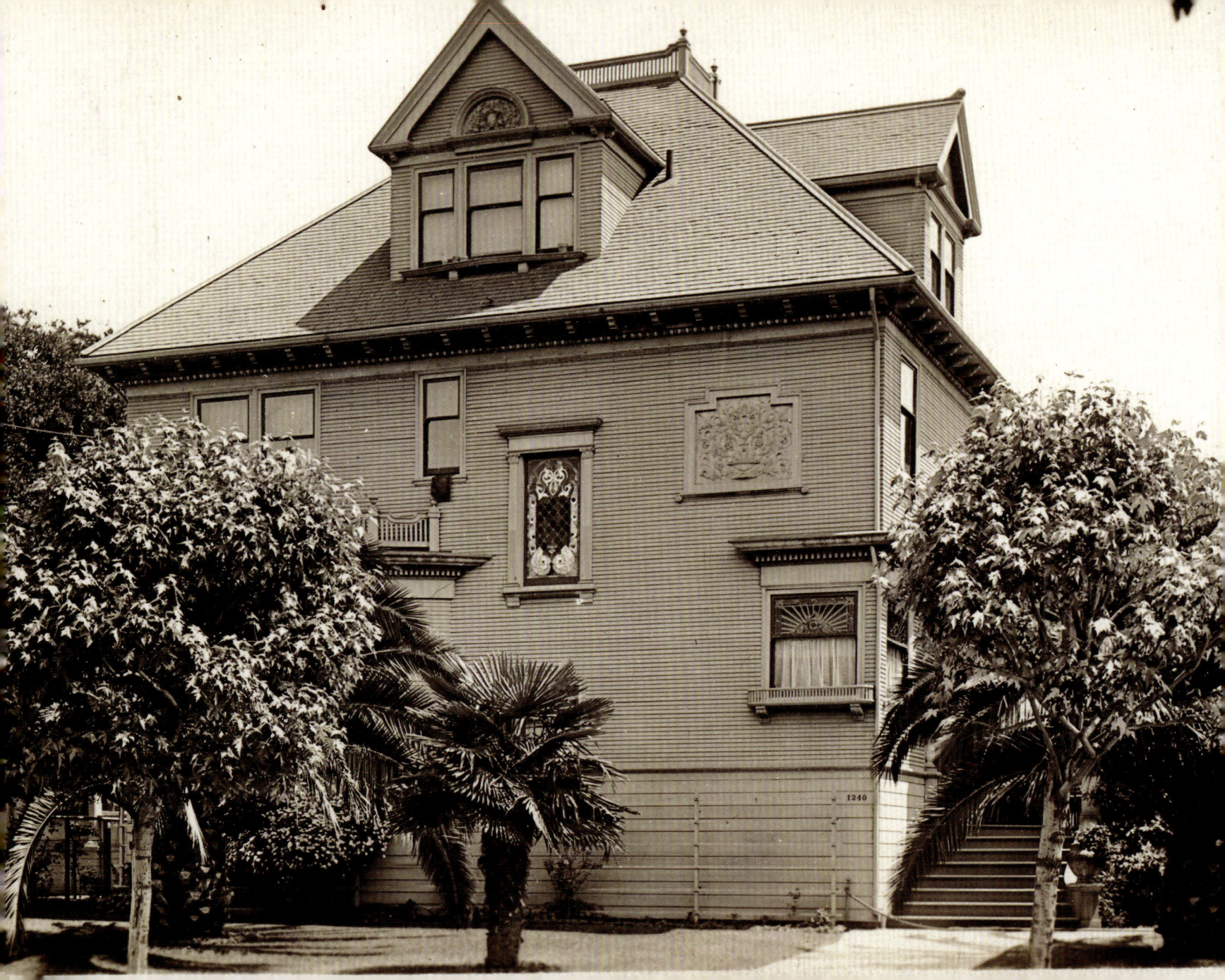

CHAPTER ONE
An Attic in Alameda
(1894–1916)

The house at 1240 St. Charles Street in Alameda, California, is a gracious Colonial Revival mansion set back slightly from the tree-lined street on a generous lot. Located in the city's coveted Gold Coast, an upscale neighborhood with a concentration of elegant homes, the house is one of the largest in Alameda at more than 4,000 square feet. On the top floor of this stately residence is a large, light-filled attic which more than a century ago was brimming with artistic dreams and creative experimentation.

The attic's first occupants were three inventive sisters—Margaret, Esther, and Helen Bruton—who used the space to sketch, paint, and sculpt. Their attic art studio was a creative laboratory of sorts for the little girls, who experimented with different materials and assisted each other with projects well into their adult years. Some critics have suggested that this studio was the birthplace of the Brutons' artistic spirit: "In the old family home in Alameda… the three Brutons, Margaret, Helen, and Esther, are working at present at fresco, pottery and prints… [in] an attic three flights up, now a studio, where Margaret has painted fresco [sic] on the plastered walls." The attic was a safe space where the sisters had unlimited creative freedom and could "valiantly experiment in new media and manners." It was so deeply connected with the sisters' artistic development and achievement that the city of Alameda designated the Bruton house a historic monument in 2012.

The sisters' father, Daniel Bruton, had this elegant home

The Bruton House in Alameda

built for his family in 1897. Born in Dublin in 1839, Bruton was an Irish immigrant whose story is the quintessential example of the American dream; he arrived in the United States as a young boy and his large family settled in Brooklyn. Despite his humble beginnings, he moved to California, became an extremely successful executive for a tobacco company, and built one of the largest mansions in one of San Francisco's most affluent suburbs.

We know little about Daniel Bruton's early years other than what appears in census records. His family's arrival in New York, sometime in the late 1840s, coincided with the onset of the Great Famine in Ireland (1845–1852) and the resulting mass exodus of Irish immigrants to the United States. There may have been another pressing reason for the Bruton family's departure from Ireland, as Daniel's father, John, supported the Irish independence movement, and the Bruton home in Dublin had become a meeting place for rebellious thinkers. Rallying for Irish independence was dangerous at the time, and John's controversial political views meant that he was banned from working for the British government. A move to the United States was likely seen as a good option by the Bruton patriarch, who needed to maintain his livelihood to support his growing family.

By 1880, John Bruton's children were industrious adults pursuing a wide variety of interests and professions in their adopted home of Brooklyn. According to census records, sons Thomas and John were "commercial travelers" (traveling

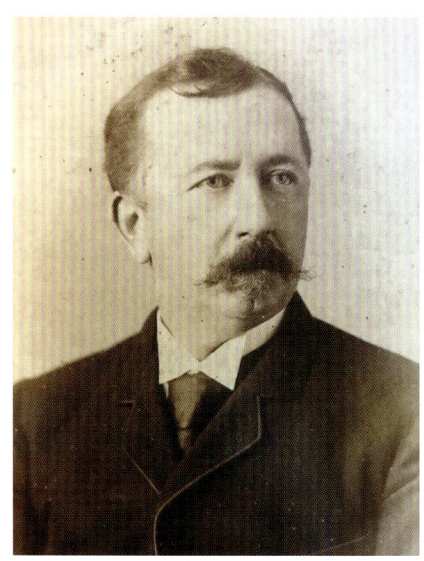
Daniel Bruton

salesmen), George was a printer, William was an artist, and Henry and James worked in tobacco. Over time, this generation of Brutons scattered across the globe, moving as far away as Chicago, London, and Australia. Daniel was hired as a West Coast agent of the Baltimore-based Marburg Brothers tobacco company and moved to California. Daniel had been fascinated with the West Coast since he was a boy, when some native Californians visited his Brooklyn neighborhood and shared glamorous tales about their home state. He first appears in the San Francisco directory in 1878, and in 1882 he was joined by his brother Thomas, who worked various jobs before pursuing a career in journalism. Gradually, other Bruton family members made their way to California, including Daniel's widowed mother, Ann.

In 1886, Daniel and Thomas Bruton left the bustle of San Francisco and relocated to the quieter, more genteel suburb of Alameda, where they rented a house near the train station. Alameda was a highly desirable place to live, boasting small town charm while being close to urban centers. Located on an island situated just south of Oakland and east of San Francisco, Alameda was within easy commuting distance to both cities by train or ferry. It was also a resort destination at the time, featuring bathhouses, ballrooms, saloons, and amusement parks that attracted celebrities like Ethel Barrymore, Al Jolson, Robert Louis Stevenson, and Jack London. Alameda's best-known resort, Neptune Gardens, was designated the "Coney Island of the West," and attracted thousands of visitors each weekend.

In 1891, Daniel's employer, Marburg Brothers, was absorbed by the American Tobacco Company, which at the time owned 90 percent of the tobacco industry in the United States, and eventually acquired the popular Lucky Strike brand. Following a promotion, Daniel made a trip back to New York to visit a friend, the physician Robert Bell. Like the Brutons, the Bells were Irish immigrants who had settled in Brooklyn. While there, Daniel developed romantic feelings for his friend's daughter, the "charming and accomplished" Helen Jane Bell. Despite their considerable age difference—he was nearly fifty-four and she was twenty-seven—Daniel and Helen were married in Brooklyn in April 1893.

Daniel Bruton returned to Alameda with his new bride and the couple moved into the house that he and Thomas were renting near the train station. When Helen

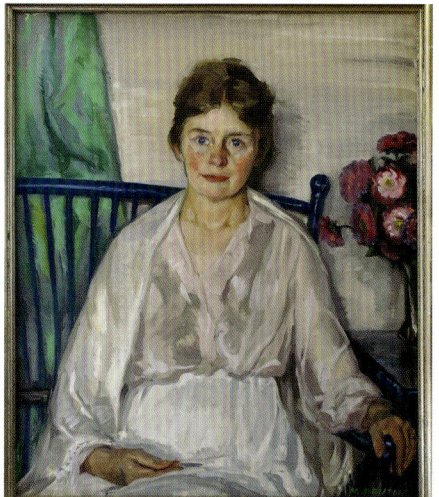
Margaret Bruton's portrait of her mother, Helen Bell Bruton

became pregnant, she returned to New York to be surrounded by her family at the birth. The Brutons' first child, Margaret, was born in Brooklyn on February 20, 1894. Named for her maternal grandmother, Margaret was always called "Marge" or "Margie" by her family and friends. Helen Bruton and her baby daughter remained in Brooklyn for almost two years; according to the local paper, Daniel Bruton didn't set eyes on his first child until October of 1895, when she was twenty months old. The Brutons' second daughter was born in Alameda on October 18, 1896. She was named Anne after her paternal grandmother, but always went by her middle name, Esther, or her nickname, "Ecky." At this point, Daniel realized that he required a proper house befitting his affluence, social status, and growing family. Construction began on the elegant mansion on St. Charles Street soon after Esther's birth. In August 1897, the *Alameda Daily Argus* informed its readers that "Daniel Bruton is having a very fine house built on St. Charles Street." Nearly three months later, the newspaper noted the family's arrival in the neighborhood. The Brutons' third child, also a girl, was born just a few months later, on February 7, 1898. She was named Helen Bell after her mother.

Daniel, Helen, and their three daughters led a comfortable existence in Alameda. Daniel was a good provider, and his daughters had every advantage and opportunity that could be expected among women of their class. As affluent young ladies, their regular attendance at luncheons, tea parties, and dances was noted in the society columns of the Alameda newspapers. The family traveled extensively, sometimes for months at a time. They vacationed at Howell Mountain, near the city of Saint Helena in Napa Valley, and at Duncan Springs in Mendocino County. They also visited their seventy-seven-acre hay ranch at Thompson's Station in Napa County, which

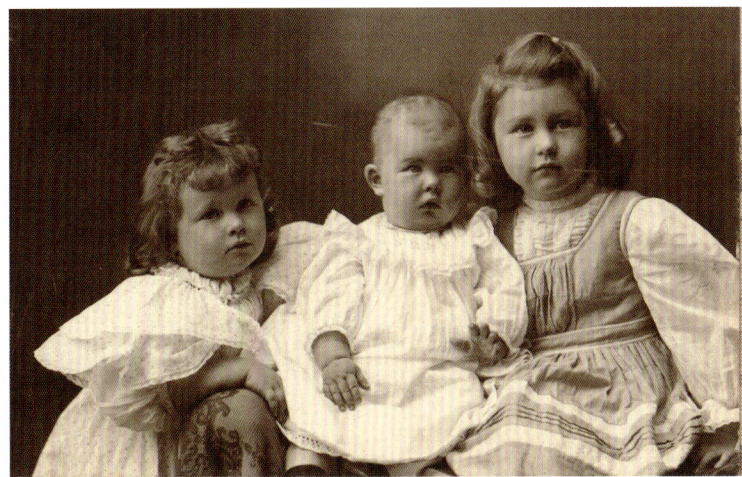

The Bruton sisters, 1898

served as home base for Daniel's mother, Ann. The Brutons spent considerable time on the Monterey Peninsula; sometimes they took the train to Salinas, and other times they traveled in an open-air, horse-drawn buggy more than one hundred miles to Monterey. The sisters had fond memories of these journeys; Helen made several drawings of her family, including their dog, riding in their carriage with a towering pile of trunks fastened to the back.

A 1906 photograph shows the elegantly dressed Bruton family posing with their horse and buggy next to the Monterey Custom House. They spent a full year in the seaside town of Pacific Grove from 1906 to 1907. The family was in Pacific Grove during the 1906 San Francisco earthquake, when one of the sisters was thrown from her bed by the shaking. The Brutons experienced more drama the following year when Helen became severely ill with abdominal pain. According to

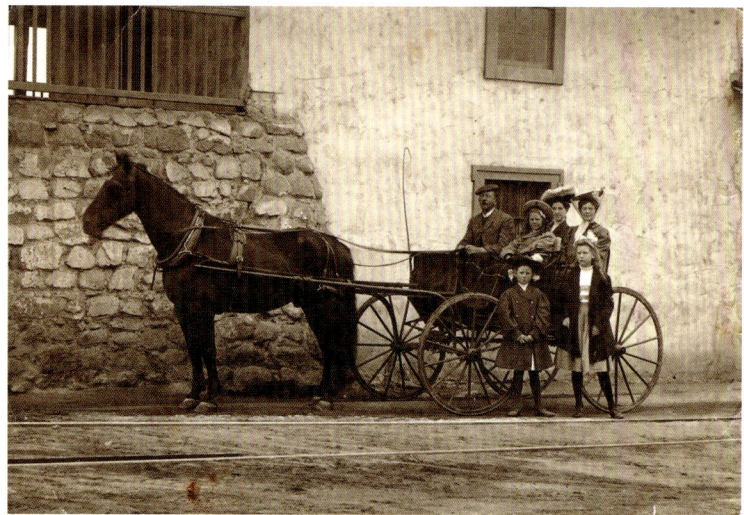

The Bruton family in front of the Monterey Custom House, 1906

family legend, she was turned away from the closest hospital—at the nearby Presidio Army Base in Monterey—because the hospital refused to admit female patients. Since there were no other medical facilities in the area, Helen was laid out on the kitchen table where a local physician performed an emergency appendectomy. Fortunately, Helen survived and seemed to suffer no ill effects from the procedure.

In May 1907, after their sojourn in Pacific Grove, the family traveled to Brooklyn to visit Mrs. Bruton's family. Although they had planned to stay only for the summer, the Brutons remained on the East Coast for an entire year. According to Margaret, she attended classes at the prestigious Art Students League in New York, even though she was only thirteen years old. When the Brutons returned to their home on St. Charles Street in April 1908, they had been away from

Alameda for nearly two years. Shortly upon their return to California, the family hosted a visit from Mrs. Bruton's younger sister, Marion Bell, who lived in Hawaii. Marion was a teacher at the Honolulu Normal School and an "amateur actress of undoubted ability." The following year, Marion married Robert C. Stackable, and the couple had one child, John Robert or "Jack," who later moved to California and eventually became one of the Bruton sisters' closest relatives.

Overall, the Bruton girls' childhood was pleasant and secure. They had a very close and empathetic relationship with each other and, surprisingly, they rarely fought. As Helen recalled, "we really got along remarkably well. It was awfully strange as kids growing up. We didn't fight the way most kids do, especially girls... but we all liked to do the same things and we'd make a lot of mess around the place. If one started in making toys out of dough... then the others would all have to butt in." This genial friendship—and their tendency to "butt in" when one started a project—was the beginning of a supportive and symbiotic relationship that would last for the rest of their lives.

The Bruton sisters' interest in art began at an early age. They made things with their hands from the time they were toddlers, including, as Esther recalled, "drawing animals with colored crayons on the window shades." Helen's first memory of expressing her creativity was in the classroom: "The earliest artwork that I can remember in school was being permitted to draw Christmas wreaths on the blackboard in colored crayon. And that set me up practically for art." By the time they were teenagers, the sisters' developing talents were being publicly recognized. Margaret received a medal in a pet poster contest in 1910 at age sixteen, and nineteen-year-old Esther won first prize in a 1916 poster contest for the Oakland Chamber of Commerce. An article about her achievement, along with her

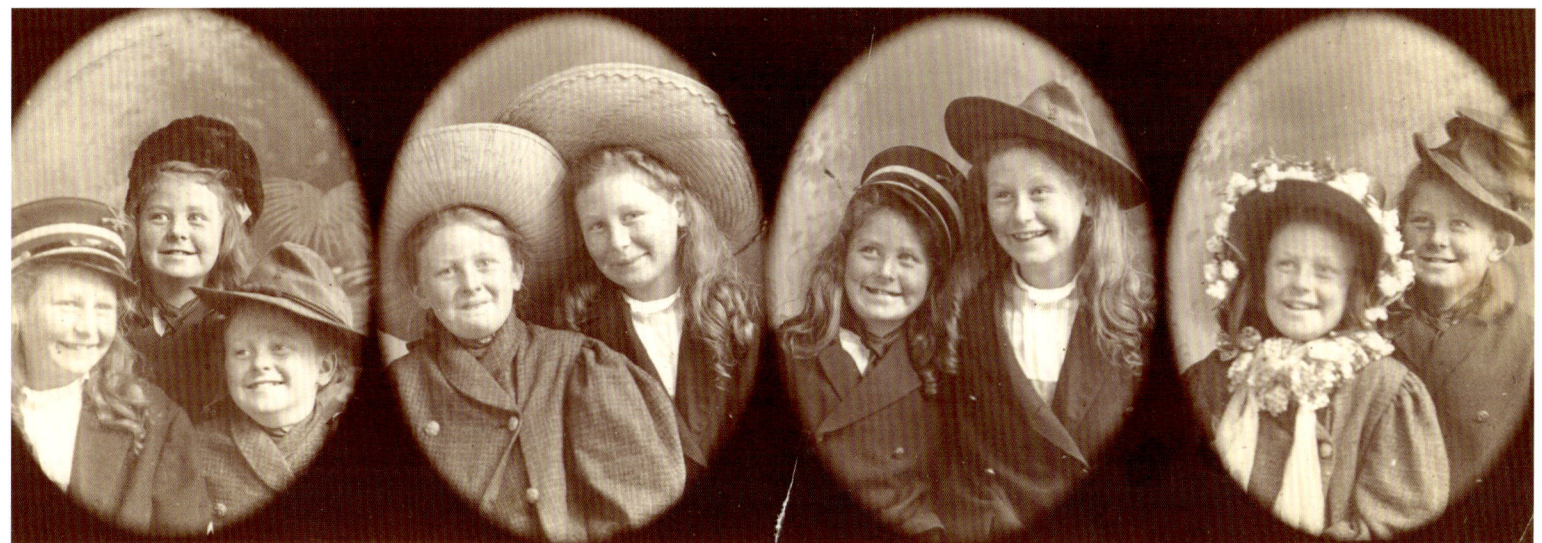

The Bruton sisters playing dress-up

photo, appeared in the *San Francisco Chronicle*.

The Brutons' collective childhood and the hours they spent in their attic art studio were formative. Their sisterly support system, combined with unwavering encouragement from their mother, resulted in a willingness to try new techniques and materials. At a very young age, the sisters felt free to take risks and make mistakes without fear of judgment or disapproval. There were artistic failures, to be sure, but they always learned from them. When their sculpted dough figures fermented and expanded beyond recognition, "the Brutons, being practical little girls, scurried around in search of more permanent and suitable materials for their purposes." The sisters' fearless, hands-on, and tactile approach to art was the beginning of what would become their unique "sensitivity to the demands of material."

Before long, all three girls wanted to become professional artists. Their father discouraged their ambitions, perhaps in part because two of his brothers had been not-particularly-successful artists by trade and both had died young. William Bruton, who contributed humorous illustrations to magazines including *Puck* and *Harper's Weekly* and illustrated a children's book, died at the age of twenty-nine. Another brother, George, a writer and cartoonist, had moved to San Francisco in 1886 in an effort to improve his failing health. He died of consumption and heart disease only a year later at the age of twenty-seven. While the financial struggles and early deaths of William and George prejudiced Daniel against the idea of his daughters pursuing art as a profession, the girls' artistic dreams were enthusiastically supported by their mother, who "encouraged them, cared for their home and fostered plans for their art studies so that each of the sisters felt free to pursue her career despite the father's opposition." Esther described their mother as a patient parent "who became resigned early in our lives to having the place messed up."

The Bruton sisters had not only many advantages in their personal lives, they also grew up in a time and place uniquely situated to accommodate their artistic dreams. In terms of pursuing their art careers, the Brutons were fortunate to be Californians. A progressive state in terms of women's rights—women in California earned the right to vote in 1911, nine years before the Nineteenth Amendment was passed—many of California's newly founded colleges and universities welcomed women students. Women artists had another benefit: whereas the well-established arts organizations in East Coast cities were male-dominated, art societies in California were just being formed and many allowed women admission from the beginning. In 1874, when the California School of Design opened in San Francisco, the majority of students were women. There were also opportunities for women to exhibit their work. In 1885, the San Francisco Art Association hosted its first annual exhibition of women's art, which was likely the first all-woman art show in the United States.

All three Bruton sisters attended Alameda High School. Early on, Margaret was encouraged to be independent, innovative, bold, and modern. In 1912, she began taking classes at the California School of Design at the San Francisco Institute of Art. The Institute, one of the country's oldest art schools, was established by a group of artists who joined together to promote the unique regional art of the West. Still in operation today, the Institute has always "embodied a spirit of experimentation, risk-taking, and innovation [and] has attracted individuals who push beyond boundaries to discover uncharted artistic terrain." Margaret studied under Frank Van Sloun, a painter of the Ashcan School—artists who used average working people as their subjects, critiqued social injustices through their art, and were considered radical for these choices. Later in life, when Margaret discussed her art education in San Francisco, she said, "Frank Van Sloun is the one I remember best, [the one] that seemed to make the most impression." It is significant that Margaret's first formal art training was at an institution dedicated to the "West Coast legacy of radical innovation," and her first instructor was an artist who rebelled against the conservative art establishment.

While at the California School of Design, Margaret primarily studied drawing. In 1913, she submitted two of her works to the annual scholarship competition sponsored by The Art Students League of New York. This was a prestigious competition, with submissions coming from students at the best art schools across the United States. Organizers remarked on the strong contributions from institutions in the West, and Margaret's submission impressed both the judges and the press. One reviewer enthused that Margaret's works were "strongly drawn, carried remarkably well, stood out in bold relief, and their well-managed values and technique suggested beautiful color and vibratory quality." As a result, nineteen-year-old Margaret was awarded one of ten coveted scholarships to The Art Students League, and departed for New York to pursue her studies in August 1913. Later in life, Helen remarked, "Mother let Margaret go to art school because all she wanted to do was draw… She shipped her off to New York all by herself." In reality, Mrs. Bruton traveled with her daughter to New York and settled the teenager to live with relatives in Brooklyn. Margaret spent the academic terms in New York and returned to Alameda for the summers.

During her second year in New York, Margaret lived at

the Three Arts Club on West 56th Street, a boarding house and club established for young women who were studying art in the city. The house was just a block from The Art Students League, where Margaret studied for the next three years. Out of all the sisters, Margaret had the most extensive formal art education, although later in life she claimed that "it nearly ruined me!" While at the League, she studied painting for the first time, and her early achievements in oils and watercolors were impressive. She would go on to have more success in this medium than either of her siblings, winning more awards than Esther or Helen and nearly all of them for her paintings.

While Margaret was studying art in New York, Esther and Helen remained in Alameda to finish high school. They rowed on the crew team, socialized with friends, and vacationed with their parents while continuing to pursue their art. Esther was already being recognized as an accomplished artist and was especially admired for her drawings; the Alameda High School yearbook identified her as one of "our future Rafaels." Helen remembered being particularly jealous of Esther because of her artistic ability and popularity in high school. Although Helen was sixteen months younger than Esther, they were in the same high school class and both graduated in 1916. According to Helen, as soon as Esther graduated, "like a bat out of hell... practically the next day, [she] took off for New York," following in Margaret's footsteps at The Art Students League.

Unlike her older sisters, Helen didn't win any art prizes as a teenager, her artistic journey less certain and her path less direct than those of Margaret and Esther. After graduating from high school, Helen spent a year at the University of California at Berkeley pursuing an art major. She was unsure about what she wanted to do with her life: "I didn't really know... what I wanted to do," she said. "I didn't feel that I was getting anywhere at the University. I didn't know enough, I didn't have any plans, so I stopped, gave up after a year." Later in life, Helen laughingly admitted that, although she considered herself "very ambitious," she was, in fact, "a college dropout." After leaving Berkeley, she remained uncertain of her artistic abilities and lacked confidence in her drawing skills. "I couldn't copy anything if my life depended on it," she recalled in a 1975 interview. "It would be a terribly bad copy." Nor did she consider herself a painter. "I never studied painting," she said, "and I don't feel that I could be considered a painter in any sense." Despite Helen's doubts about her abilities, she began to study sculpture and found her footing as an artist. But it wasn't until she discovered the medium of mosaic that her talents were fully revealed—she became a master of the technique and eventually garnered as much fame and recognition as, if not more than, her older sisters.

The Bruton sisters were fortunate to be living in Northern California during an important and influential event for the local arts community. In 1915, San Francisco hosted the Panama–Pacific International Exposition, a world's fair covering six hundred acres, including the Presidio Army Base and the newly created Marina district. The fair was designed to celebrate both the opening of the Panama Canal and San Francisco's rebirth and revitalization after the devastating earthquake that had destroyed so much of the city nine years earlier. An estimated eighteen million visitors attended the expansive fair, which featured international pavilions, exposition palaces, and state buildings; scientific and technological marvels, including transcontinental telephone calls and wireless telegraphs; sports events and music performances; and a sixty-five-acre amusement park area dubbed "The Joy Zone."

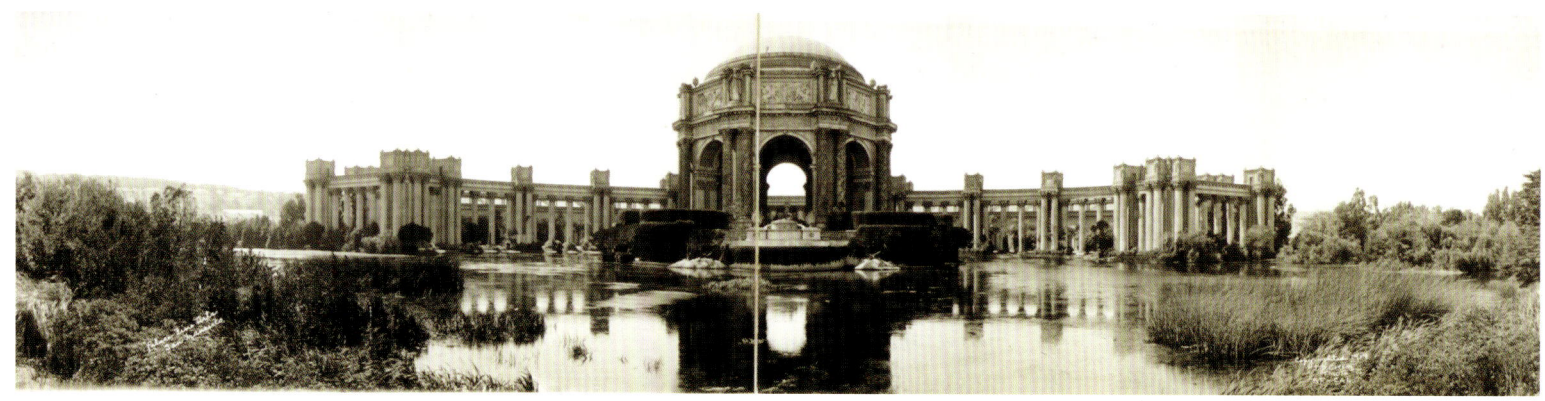
The Palace of Fine Arts in San Francisco, photo by James David Givens (1919)

Set apart from the bustle and kitsch of the crowded fair was its Palace of Fine Arts, a classically styled building with a domed rotunda and curved colonnades, facing a serene reflecting pool and surrounded by a quiet open space. Designed by renowned California architect Bernard Maybeck, it is the only structure from the Exposition still standing today and is on the United States National Register of Historic Places. For the fair, the Palace housed an astounding exhibition of more than 11,000 works of art that took nearly three years to assemble. American Realist and Impressionist painters in the exhibition included Winslow Homer, John Singer Sargent, James McNeill Whistler, George Bellows, Rockwell Kent, William Merritt Chase, and Childe Hassam. Exhibition Room 65 was devoted entirely to American women painters, and a contemporary reviewer enthused that "one who has not kept abreast of woman's work in art in this country has a surprise awaiting him in the high quality shown here." Exhibition Room 51, one of the less popular galleries, featured the works of American painters of the Ashcan School,

including John Sloan and William J. Glackens. Compared to Impressionist paintings' idealized and colorful scenes, the stark realism of Ashcan School art must have appeared harsh and even vulgar, explaining why this gallery of "extremists" earned the nickname "The Chamber of Horrors."

European artists represented in the exhibition included Auguste Renoir, Edgar Degas, Paul Cézanne, Paul Gauguin, Henri de Toulouse-Lautrec, and Vincent van Gogh. There was even a display of works by the forward-thinking Italian Futurists. The "ultra-radical" works by Norwegian painter Edvard Munch were especially controversial and caused a "bone of contention among the critics." Many Americans, as well as the judges of the show, were unprepared to view such progressive art with open minds. One critic wryly noted that although Munch "was the greatest of Norwegian painters" and had "won the Grand Prix at Rome and awards in every other European capital," he failed to make the honor list at the San Francisco exhibition.

As well as being "one of the most ambitious art exhibitions ever presented in the United States," the fine arts exhibition at the Exposition was "a vital moment in the inauguration of [San Francisco] as a cultural center on the West Coast." The exhibition marked the first time that Northern Californians from all levels of society, including local artists, could view such an extensive collection of world-class art in person. A national arts magazine enthused that interest in the exhibition was "surprisingly keen and is a very good index of the future for art enterprise on the Pacific Coast." Family photographs taken on the grounds of the Palace of Fine Arts confirm that Helen and Esther attended the exhibition with their mother. Margaret likely visited as well, and they might have attended even more than once during the exhibition's nine-month run. After viewing the modern and avant-garde works on display, the three young and impressionable artists undoubtedly would have walked away with a "new penchant for meatier subject matter and style experimentation."

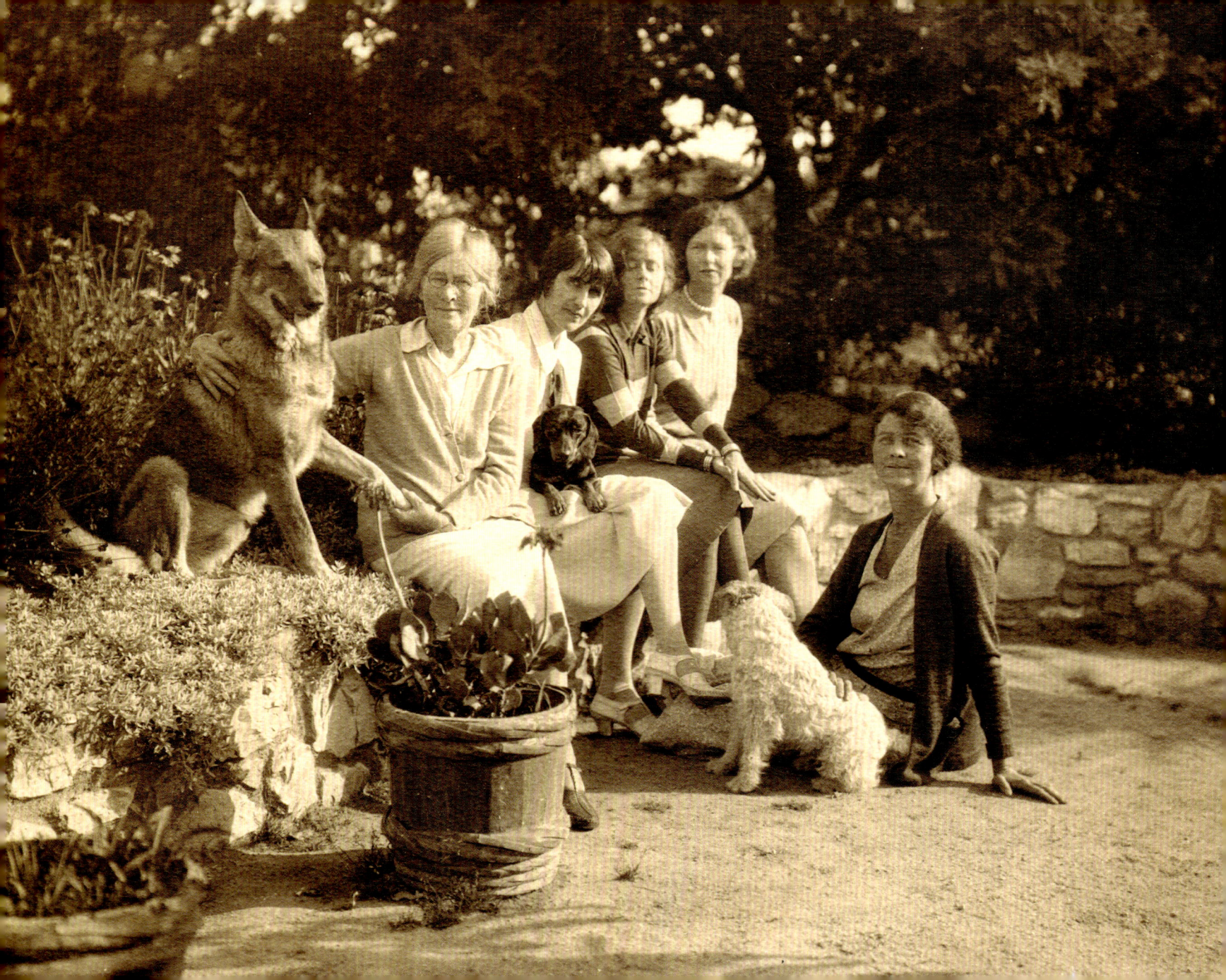

CHAPTER TWO

"The Brutons and How They Grew": Studies in Art

In 1917, while Helen was enrolled at Berkeley, Margaret and Esther were in New York, studying at The Art Students League of New York. The League, which is still in operation today, was a vastly influential organization in the early twentieth century. It was founded in 1875 by artists from New York's National Academy of Design, many of them women, who "felt that the Academy's instruction was too conservative and unsympathetic to their new ideas about art... the League consciously associated itself with a 'modern' point of view." Some of the most important artists of the early twentieth century studied or taught at the League, including William Merritt Chase, Augustus Saint-Gaudens, Thomas Eakins, and Childe Hassam. Margaret's teacher in San Francisco, Frank Van Sloun, had studied at the League under Robert Henri and Edward Hopper.

One of Margaret's first instructors at The Art Students League was Frank Vincent Dumond, an American Impressionist who taught traditional techniques and subject matter at the League for nearly six decades and was "among the most outstanding educators in American art history." Dumond had been recommended to Margaret by California Impressionist E. Charlton Fortune, one of the most accomplished women artists on the Monterey Peninsula. Perhaps because Fortune was more conservative than Margaret and a decade older, her recommendation of Dumond was not a good match for the bolder and more experimental Margaret,

The Bruton sisters with their mother and Ina Perham

who recalled that her lessons with Dumond were a "disaster" that she had to "unlearn."

Margaret had considerably more success with instructor Robert Henri. The leader of a group of nonconformist artists whose paintings challenged both mainstream academic traditions and rejected the institutional establishment—a group collectively known as "The Eight"—Henri was also associated with the Ashcan School. He eventually became a prominent art instructor—perhaps one of the most influential of the early twentieth century—and his students included American masters Rockwell Kent, George Bellows, and Edward Hopper, as well as many lesser-known women artists who went on to have a significant impact on the early twentieth-century art scene. Henri's ideas about art were revolutionary and his teaching was radical for the time. Margaret Bruton, with her background of artistic experimentation and early exposure to progressive ideas, was primed to embrace Henri's modernist painting instruction. As she was enrolled at one of the foremost schools of modern art in the nation and working with one of the school's best instructors, her painting flourished under Henri's guidance.

Henri felt that art should be based on real-life experiences and personal emotions, not idealistic visions and romantic views. He encouraged his students to experiment with new media and embrace diverse art forms that could be used in everyday life. For him, designing and fabricating textiles and furniture was just as important as painting works to be displayed in a museum gallery. Henri believed that "beauty was everywhere, there for the seeing, embodied in the stuff of everyday life... [His students] became players in a modernist experiment that aimed to fuse art, craft, and life into new and vital forms." Margaret and her fellow students embraced the idea that they could become "full-fledged artists, irrespective of the medium in which they chose to work." Henri's influence on Margaret can be seen both in her modernist painting style and in her gradual evolution from painting to decorative arts as her art career progressed.

Esther also enrolled at The Art Students League after completing high school in 1916 but had a less-inspired experience there. While Margaret was developing her modernist painting technique with Robert Henri, Esther focused on drawing and studied with George Bridgman, a Canadian American artist whose primary expertise was anatomy and figure drawing. Esther's time in Bridgman's class was not particularly productive. Helen quipped that "Esther was exposed to Bridgman briefly, but... she escaped!"

In 1917, as the United States entered World War I, the Bruton sisters went separate ways. Margaret returned to California and Esther remained in New York, where she had changed schools, moving to the New York School of Fine and Applied Art to study commercial art. While Esther was there, Frank Alvah Parsons, for whom the school was renamed in 1941, was the director. Parsons believed that art should exist for—and be seen by—not just the privileged, but everyone. "Industry is the nation's life, art is the quality of beauty in expression," he said, "and industrial art is the cornerstone of our national art." Margaret had already subscribed to these ideas while studying with Robert Henri, and now Esther became influenced by the concept that art should be useful

and a part of daily life. The New York School of Fine and Applied Art suited her better than The Art Students League had. In May 1918, at the end of her first year, Esther was awarded a prize in the school's annual exhibition of student work. After completing the two-year program, she became eligible to become a school art teacher, but instead chose to direct her efforts toward commercial art.

Helen, who had completed one year at Berkeley and taken courses at Munson's Secretarial School in San Francisco, was ready to give her full support to the war effort. Women were allowed to join the Navy for the first time in 1917, and many worked as radio operators, stenographers, nurses, messengers, and chauffeurs. In October 1918, Helen enlisted in the Naval Reserve and went to Washington, D.C., to serve as a "yeomanette." She worked as a stenographer and secretary in the Bureau of Yards and Docks, followed by secretarial positions closer to home at the Mare Island Naval Shipyard in Vallejo, California, and at the Letterman General Hospital on the Presidio Army Base in San Francisco.

Margaret, who had returned to California from New York in August 1917, was also employed at the Letterman Hospital. The hospital cared for more than 18,000 soldiers who had been seriously wounded in the war or had developed psychiatric problems. Margaret worked as an occupational therapist or "reconstruction aide," having been selected because of her "extensive art training." Her primary duty was "to teach crafts on the wards to patients who had impaired motor function or who were neurotic or mentally disoriented."

After the war, Margaret remained in Alameda while Helen, the youngest Bruton, embarked on her "first formal attempt at studying art." She traveled to New York to join Esther and, like her sisters before her, enrolled at The Art Students League,

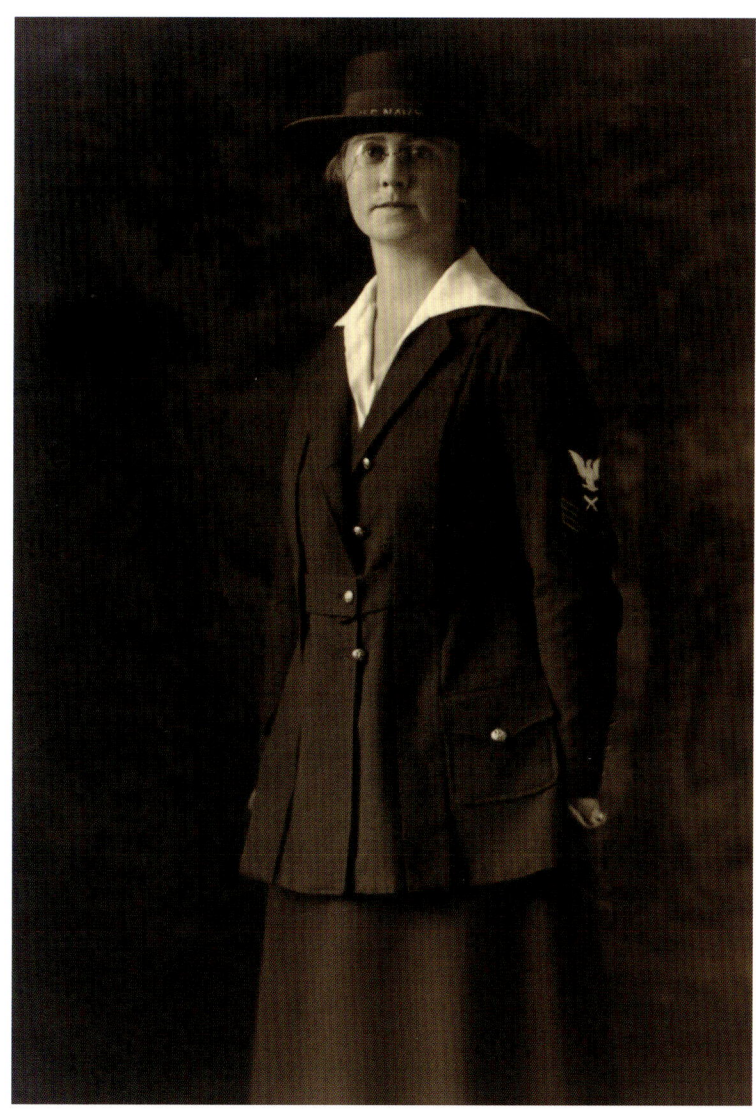

Helen Bruton in her Navy uniform, ca. 1918

studying there for two academic terms, 1920–1921 and 1921–1922. It is unsurprising that all three sisters gravitated toward New York, the city where the most modern art training of the time was most readily available. At the League, Helen decided to become a sculptor and her first instructor was A. Stirling Calder. Although he was a respected artist who had been in charge of the sculpture program at the 1915 Panama–Pacific International Exposition in San Francisco, Helen disliked his style. She did appreciate him as an instructor, saying, "He was the world's worst sculptor, but he was an awfully good teacher because he was a natural teacher, a very nice person and he didn't try to steer you in any direction."

During her second year at The Art Students League, Helen studied with the Italian American sculptor Leo Lentelli. He had studied art in Rome and Bologna before immigrating to the United States and eventually assisting Stirling Calder at the Panama–Pacific Exposition. Helen's experience with Lentelli was disappointing, as she felt he was too traditional and conservative and his "flowery" style wasn't in line with her modern sensibilities. Helen's classes with Calder and Lentelli were the extent of her formal art training until several years later. In November 1926, the *Carmel Pine Cone* announced that Helen, having returned to California, was on her way back to New York to study sculpture, although by her own account she had returned to The Art Students League to study drawing with the illustrator and cartoonist Boardman Robinson.

Although her classes at the League were mostly unsuccessful, Helen enjoyed the bohemian lifestyle she experienced while living with Esther in New York. Esther was working for the Lord & Taylor department store, illustrating advertisements for the children's department. While they likely received financial support from their parents, the young women certainly didn't lead pampered lives. "I was the housekeeper," Helen remembered. "We lived in a funny little place down in the Village." The apartment had no ventilation, so every time they cooked on the gas stove, Helen felt as if she was "in the last stages of some terrible, fatal disease."

In November 1922, Esther and Helen returned to Alameda. They reunited with Margaret, who was attending summer art classes in the seaside town of Monterey, where the Brutons had often vacationed as children. Esther was hired as a fashion illustrator for the I. Magnin & Company department store in San Francisco. Her flexible work arrangement allowed her to take extended vacations, including a four-month trip to Tahiti with her friends Ina Perham and Marie Smith. Perham, an artist from an affluent San Francisco family, became one of the Bruton sisters' closest friends. The young women departed from San Francisco in April 1924 with the intention of sketching Tahitian natives and South Pacific landscapes while walking in the footsteps of Paul Gauguin. While in Papeete, they lived next door to a hut once occupied by the legendary artist.

It was particularly daring for three young women to travel independently to Tahiti in the 1920s. Photographs from the trip show them traveling in an outrigger canoe, wading in the ocean, and posing on the beach in boldly patterned pareus with flowers in their hair. When they returned to California in August, their trip was of great interest to the local news media. An article in the *San Francisco Chronicle* included a photograph of a smiling Esther, her hair bobbed and her arms crossed confidently across her chest. She was interviewed about the trip and provided this amusing anecdote: "We watched every day from under our sun porch covered with one great leafy spread of banana leaves, waiting for something unusual to happen. And then one day it happened... We thought we saw

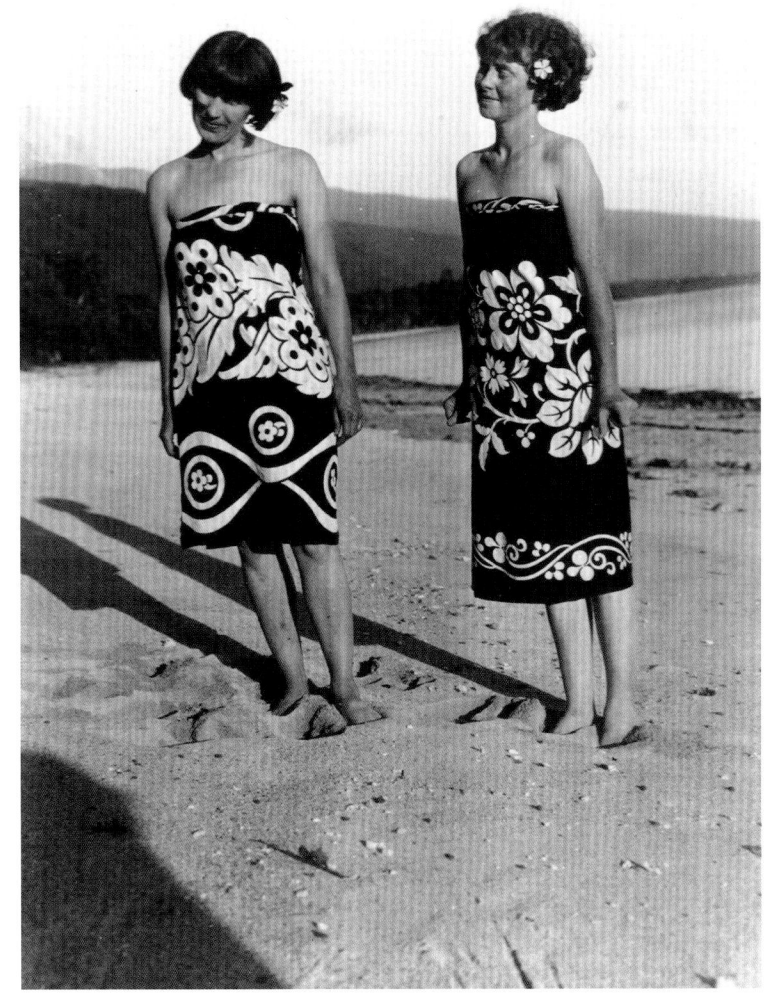

Ina Perham and Esther Bruton on the beach in Tahiti, 1924

the great Gauguin ourselves—tall, gaunt, loosely hung, with dreamer's eyes, but young... Gauguin was still in the village." Esther's story is both comical and mischievous, as she must have been aware that Paul Gauguin had been dead for more than twenty years.

When asked if the young women had found any romance in the South Seas, Esther quipped, "Tahiti is full of French girls... What chance did we have with the men there?... Such beautiful girls I have never seen before." Although they didn't date any men and saw only one artwork by Gauguin, the trip was far from a loss, as Esther fell in love with Tahiti itself. "I'm going back there someday," she said. "It's a disappointment to return to the States and see people rushing about—people who don't know how to play!" Tahiti's tropical settings did influence some of Esther's commercial work, and true to her word, she returned to the South Seas thirty years later.

By the mid-1920s, all three Brutons had taken countless classes with prominent art instructors and were well on their way to becoming professional artists. But for the serious artist of the era, no education was complete without studying in Europe, and in June 1925, Margaret, Esther, and Ina Perham set sail. A photograph of Esther and Ina shows them posed on their ship's deck in fashionable flapper dresses and hats. Their trip included sketching expeditions to the countryside of England and France, as well as to Venice and the Italian village of Positano. But the main objective for the young women was to study in Paris, which by the 1920s was the city considered to have the best art training in the world and was the center of the major avant-garde art movements. Margaret and Esther enrolled in classes at the Académie de la Grande Chaumière, located in the city's Montparnasse district. La Grande Chaumière was less academic than the other famous

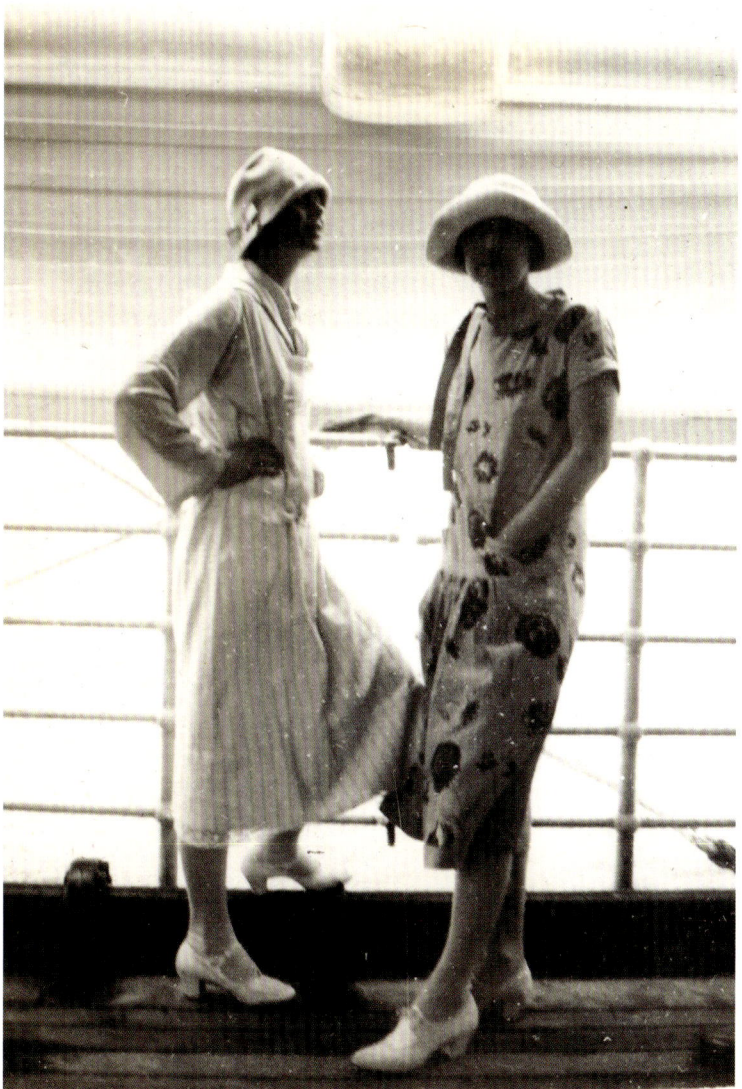

Esther Bruton and Ina Perham on a ship to Europe, 1925

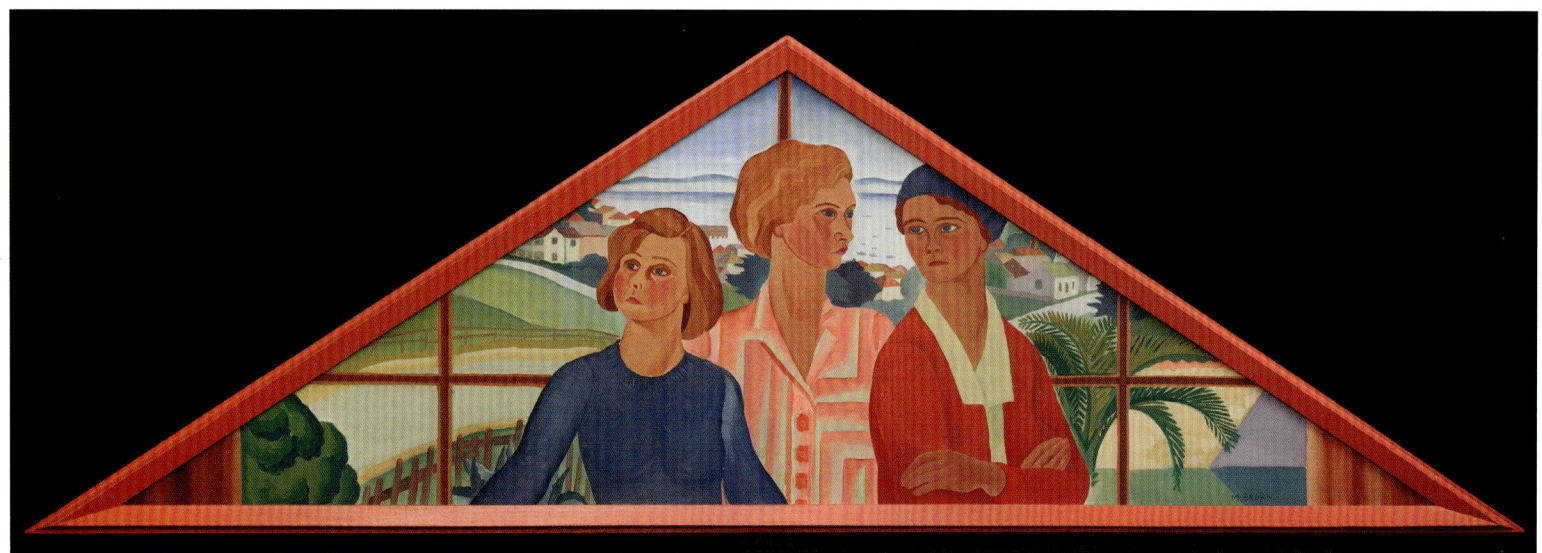

Untitled [Bruton sisters], by Margaret Bruton (1927). Published with the permission of The Wolfsonian - Florida International University (Miami, Florida)

art schools in the city, École des Beaux-Arts and the Académie Julian; its students had fewer restrictions placed on them and greater freedom to pursue their own artistic directions. In addition to the excellent art education to be found in Paris, it was an inexpensive place to live in the 1920s. The value of the French franc had plunged to nearly one quarter of its pre-World War I value. As a result, countless Americans—artists, authors, and musicians—flocked to Paris to experience a bohemian lifestyle and take part in the city's burgeoning creative environment.

While Esther and Margaret were in Paris, the city hosted the 1925 International Exhibition of Modern Decorative and Industrial Arts. This fair, which introduced the Art Deco style to the world, featured all things modern and innovative in architecture, interior design, furniture, and decorative arts. This exhibition was likely a seminal event in the lives of Esther and Margaret, as it exposed them to cutting-edge art techniques and works of art that had never been seen before. It clearly influenced the sisters' artistic development and further sparked their interest in not only modernism but also decorative arts, which would become their primary focus a decade later.

The Bruton sisters were in their twenties during the "roaring" 1920s, and, like other women of the time, they enjoyed a period of unprecedented opportunity and freedom. All American women had earned the right to vote by 1920, and the flappers of the decade symbolized women's new social and sexual liberation. At this time there was a spirit of camaraderie and cooperation between artists of both genders, and "there was not so much conflict between male and female practitioners of the arts." Artist Isabel Bishop, who studied at The Art Students League in the early 1920s, remembers "there was absolutely no feeling, in those days and in that place, about my being a girl. It just didn't come up."

Yet this sense of liberation was something of an illusion, as women artists faced significant gender biases and stereotypes as they tried to work within a system in which figures of authority and influence—art school instructors, museum curators, and gallery owners—were almost exclusively white males. It was acceptable for women to pursue art as a hobby, especially when their subject matter was appropriately "feminine," such as flowers or portraits of children. But when women began to paint in a more abstract and modern style, their works were viewed with suspicion and derision. In addition, it was considered inappropriate—and in most cases practically impossible—for women to pursue art as a full-time career. Opportunities for women professional artists remained extremely limited until the government-sponsored art projects of the 1930s.

Because of gendered stereotypes, many serious women artists downplayed or even concealed their gender by choosing what name to go by professionally. Carmel artist Henrietta Shore preferred to be called "Henry" and was irritated when critics referred to her by her given name. Painter Eugenia McComas, wife of artist Francis McComas, went by the male-sounding nickname "Gene," as did San Francisco artist and art critic Genevieve Hailey, who signed her articles "Gene Hailey." Euphemia Charlton Fortune, Mary DeNeale Morgan, and many other women artists used their initials instead of their first names when signing their works to circumvent the biased consideration they would have otherwise received. The

Brutons might have felt similar pressure, as they frequently signed their works with their first initial instead of their first name. Despite these challenges, the Brutons would become part of a progressive group of women artists who each took their passion for art and made it their full-time profession.

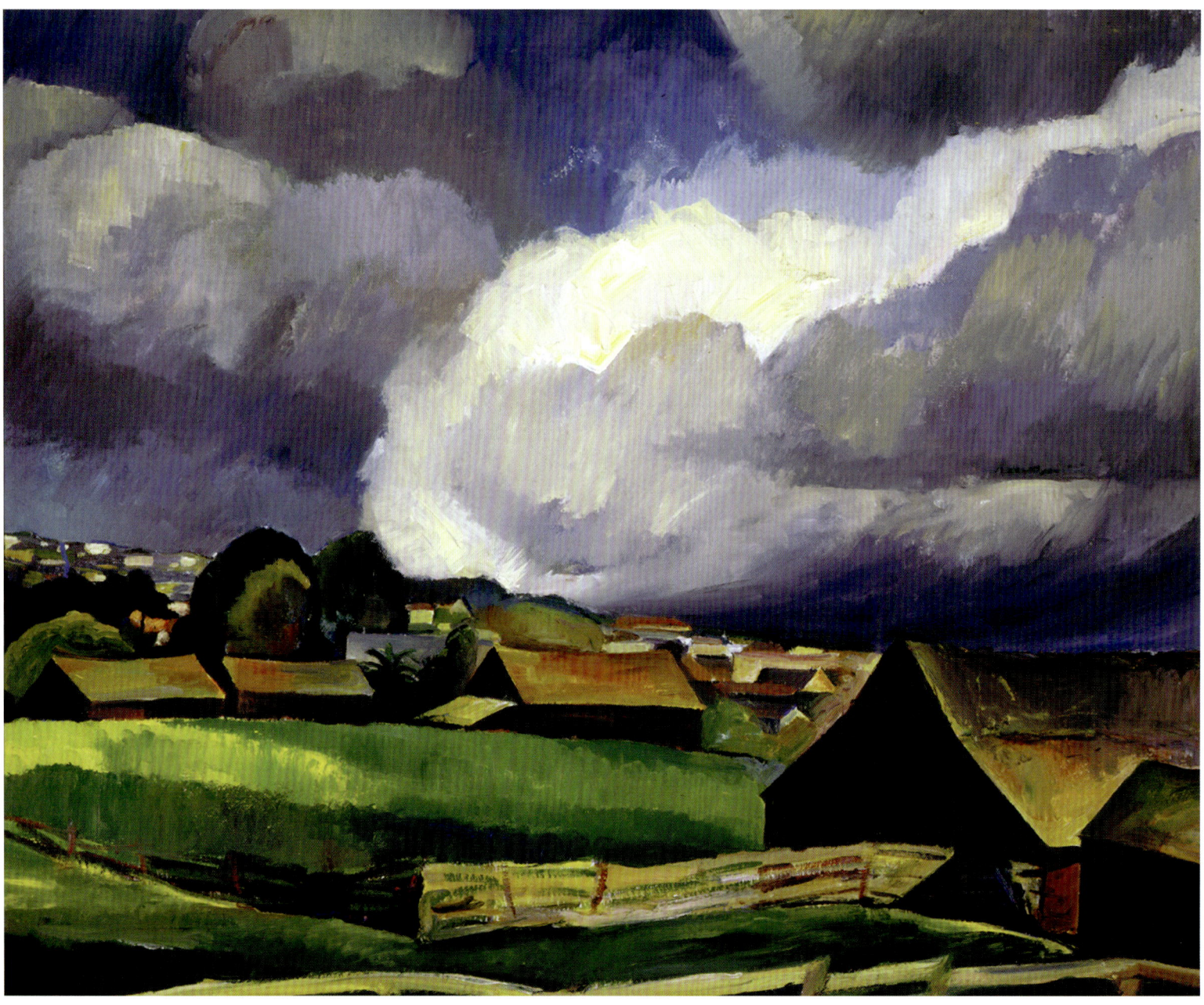

CHAPTER THREE

Margaret Bruton and "The Golden Age of Monterey"

(1921–1928)

Ever since visiting the area as children, the Brutons had been drawn to the picturesque Monterey Peninsula on California's Central Coast. The area, once secluded and relatively unknown, began to change rapidly in the 1880s with the arrival of the Southern Pacific Railroad and the opening of the expansive and elegant Hotel Del Monte, which quickly became one of the most popular tourist destinations in California. The hotel was the starting and finishing point of the peninsula's famed Seventeen Mile Drive, which wound along the nearby coastline through what is now Pebble Beach.

Artists were discovering the Monterey area's rugged coastline and dramatic vistas as early as the 1870s, when Jules Tavernier and Charles Rollo Peters established their homes and art studios on Monterey Bay. The region's temperate climate, affordable housing, and incomparable natural beauty attracted artists from San Francisco who traveled south for expeditions to paint or sketch. Many came to participate in summer art camps and classes, and some found the environs so appealing that they settled in the area permanently. By the early twentieth century, the peninsula was home to many talented artists who were achieving wide-reaching respect and recognition. The region was also a welcoming place for women artists, many of whom "never married and remained free to devote [themselves] to painting without fear of social censure... Nonconformity and eccentricity were not only tolerated but encouraged, [and]

Barns on Cass Street, by Margaret Bruton (ca. 1925).
Collection Monterey Museum of Art

women had fewer obstacles to parity with men." In 1907, the Hotel Del Monte opened its own art gallery, the first in the nation to showcase the work of California artists exclusively. Francis McComas, Ferdinand Burgdorff, and Jo Mora were some of the first to have their work displayed there. The Hotel Del Monte Gallery cemented the region's reputation as a bona fide art colony and introduced an international audience of affluent hotel guests to the best of California art.

The most prominent artist in the town of Monterey in the 1920s was Armin Hansen, the founder of Monterey's summer art school which opened in 1919. Hansen had been introduced to modern art during his travels in Europe and had embraced modernist sensibilities and techniques. He was an extremely gifted painter and etcher whose works often feature maritime themes, owing to the years he spent on a Norwegian trawler before settling in Monterey. He conducted informal classes from his home on El Dorado Street—a neighborhood where many Monterey artists resided—holding many of them outside so that his students could paint the natural beauty surrounding them.

Just south of the Monterey Peninsula, the seaside hamlet of Carmel-by-the-Sea also become a thriving art colony and home to talented artists including Mary DeNeale Morgan, E. Charlton Fortune, William Ritschel, and Ferdinand Burgdorff. Impressionist painter William Merritt Chase, who founded Carmel's summer art school in 1914, was instrumental in the village's development. Chase, who personified the Gilded Age, was known for his dislike of modern art. Enough artists lived and worked in Carmel that professional organizations such as the Carmel Art Association and the Carmel Art Institute were later formed. The Carmel art colony was well organized, held frequent exhibitions, and regularly attracted new artists.

Margaret Bruton—a young, modern painter—was understandably attracted to the art scene in Monterey. She first came to the area in the summer of 1921, expressly because she wanted to study with Armin Hansen. She attended Hansen's sketching and painting classes in the summers of 1922 and 1923, and quickly fell in love with Monterey. According to Margaret, Hansen's class "was more of a mutual association than a structured class. The students decided on locations and hired the models and paid Armin for his criticism. He was spared as much of the mechanics as possible. He was an excellent teacher in that he inspired his students without imposing any rigid formulas." Helen later called this period the "Hansenian era" because of Hansen's influence on the art students in Monterey, although she didn't feel that he influenced her or her sisters.

The founders of the art colonies in Carmel and Monterey each had a dramatic impact on the way their colony evolved. The older, somewhat stodgy Chase set the stage for Carmel's more conservative art scene, while Hansen—thirty-seven years younger than Chase—attracted younger artists interested in modernism. Another contrast was each colony's relative success overall; while Carmel's artists were flourishing, those in Monterey were struggling, as they lacked both a core group of artists and adequate exhibition space. "A great many of our local people do not realize that we have in our midst an art colony," a Monterey newspaper remarked in 1921, "and it is up to the community to patronize and preserve the valuable asset." The article went on to lament that Monterey artists had a "lack of local support" and no galleries in which to display their works.

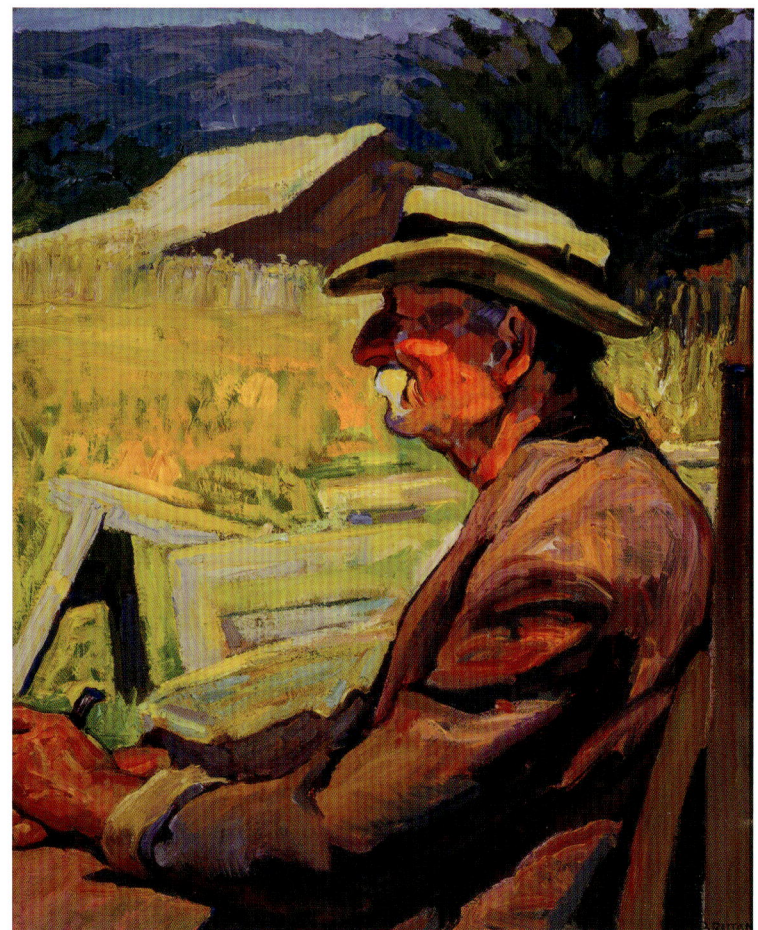

The Old Timer, by Margaret Bruton (ca. 1922). The Buck Collection at UCI Institute and Museum of California Art

Reflecting on the period later in life, Helen Bruton recalled that the Carmel and Monterey art colonies were not very aware of each other, and she observed that, for the most part, the Carmel artists were older. Hansen, however, was successful in bridging the gap between Monterey and Carmel. Active in the Carmel Art Association and a co-founder of the Carmel Art Institute, he served "as a conduit between the bohemian moderns of Monterey and Carmel's conservative art establishment." In the summer of 1921, several Monterey artists, including Margaret Bruton, were invited to participate in the Fifteenth Annual Exhibition of Carmel's Arts and Crafts Club. This exhibition was an opportunity to break down the walls between the Carmel and Monterey art communities and encourage a spirit of cooperation and mutual respect.

The city of Monterey did make several attempts to provide opportunities for local artists to exhibit their works. In September 1922, Margaret Bruton participated in the First Annual Industrial and Art Exposition in Monterey. This exhibition was touted in the local paper, with considerable exaggeration, as "one of the greatest exhibitions of paintings... ever in the history of California." Margaret was in good company, as artists in the show included local standouts such as Armin Hansen, William Ritschel, Gottardo Piazzoni, Charles Rollo Peters, Evelyn McCormick, E. Charlton Fortune, and Francis McComas. Despite the significant star power represented in the exhibition, one Monterey newspaper chose to mention only a single artist by name: "Margaret Bruton's 'The Old Timer' was in the limelight for a time last evening, when the subject—or object—of the canvas, Jim Robinson, was in the building. His friends stood him up alongside the painting and compared the two. Some said the portrait was more real than Jim himself!"

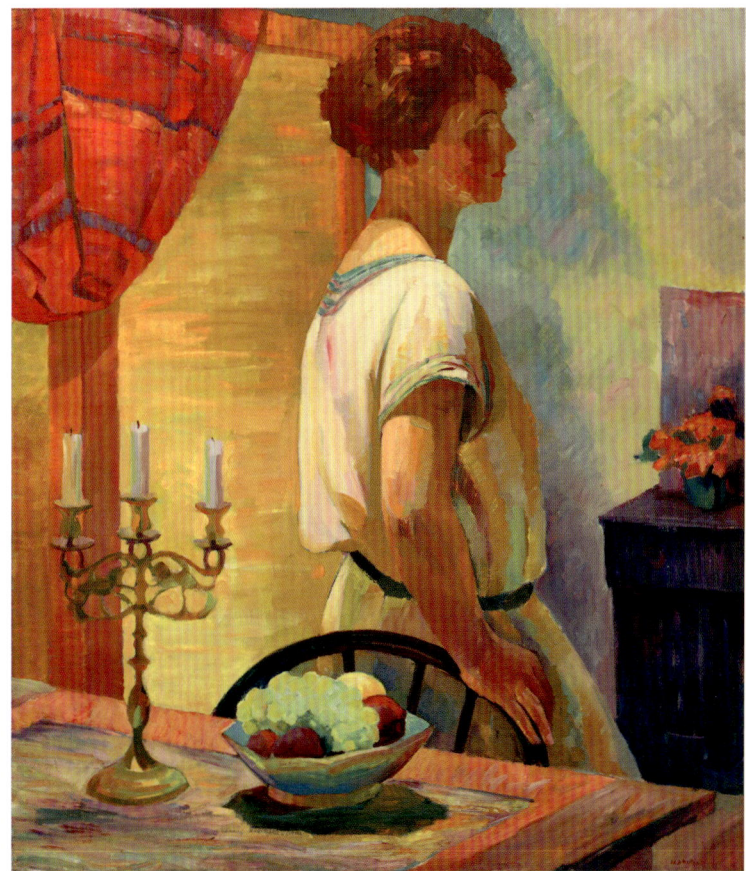

Helen at Sargent House Studio, by Margaret Bruton (probably 1922-23). The Buck Collection at UCI Institute and Museum of California Art

31

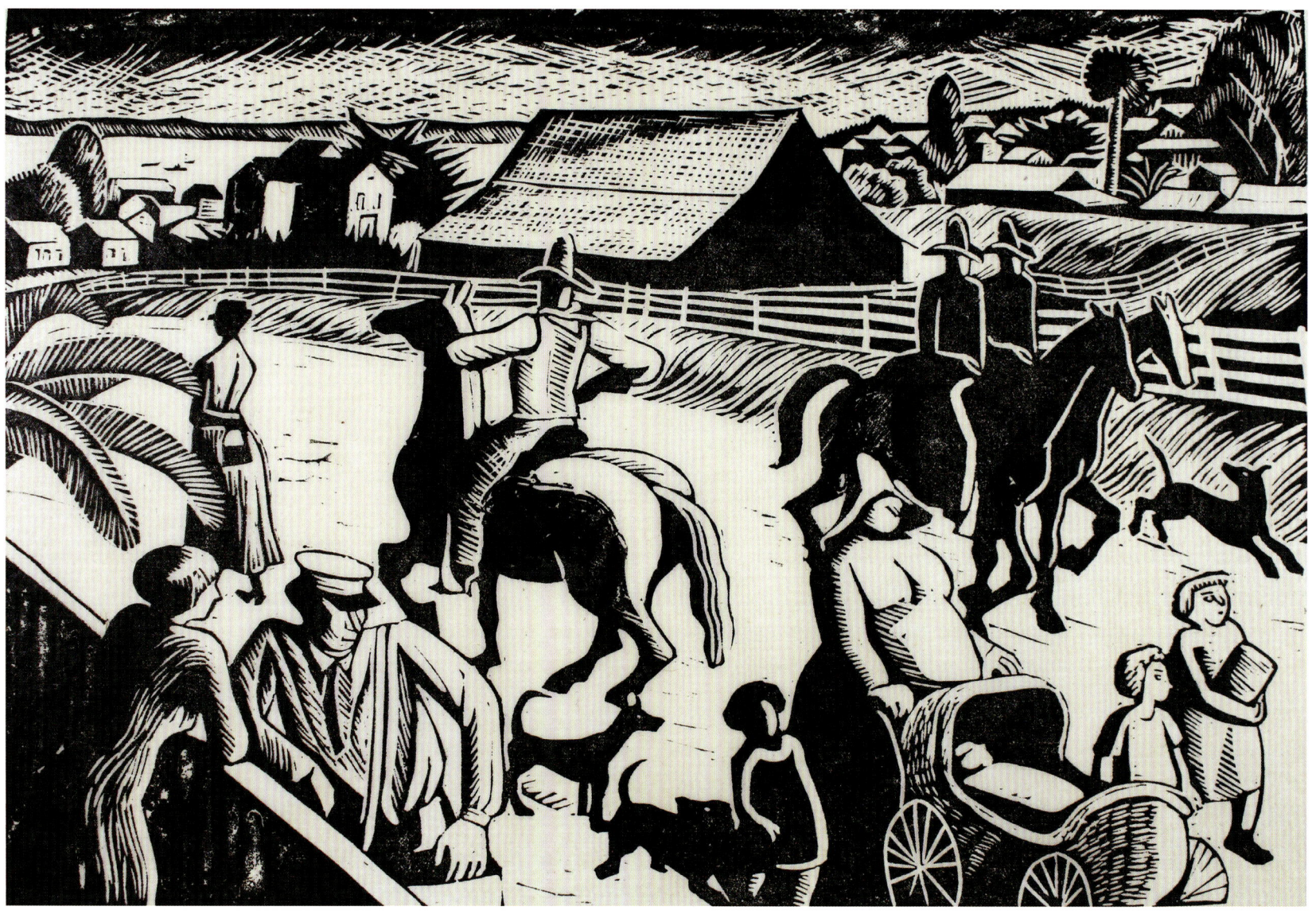

Margaret and several Monterey artists next exhibited at the Forty-Sixth Annual Exhibition of the San Francisco Art Association in December 1922. The *Peninsula Daily Herald* reported, perhaps with some bias, that "the Monterey peninsula is the workshop and the inspiration of the representative painters of the coast" and claimed that Monterey artists had "the finest works in the exhibition." After describing works by Monterey artist C.S. Price and acknowledging that "Armin Hansen dominates his gallery," the article devotes a full paragraph to the talents of the twenty-eight-year-old Margaret Bruton: "All of [her works] are quite modern: full of color and movement... This young artist has endeavored, usually with success, to depict the character and mood of her subject rather than make a slavish copy of their features." Even when she was exhibiting with more established artists, critics were beginning to take notice of Margaret's modernist art, although she was still experimenting with her style, which would develop significantly over the decade.

In 1923, after she returned from her art studies in New York, Helen joined Margaret in Monterey. Helen, Margaret, and Ina Perham lived in the attic of the "Sargent House," a large Victorian home on Cass Street owned by Judge and Mrs. Ross Sargent, who rented rooms to artists. By the following year, the Bruton sisters were spending so much time in Monterey that they built a small home there, on the corner of Cass and El Dorado Streets, in an area with a high concentration of artists. Within just a few blocks also lived Armin Hansen, Julian Greenwell, and Ina Perham. As Helen remembered, Margaret "designed that house in about one day or two flat and had the builder put it up and it was more or

Cass Street, by Helen Bruton (1924). Collection Monterey Museum of Art

less... a second summer place." Helen's linoleum block print *Cass Street* reveals just how rural the neighborhood was in the 1920s. The work features several figures in cowboy hats riding horses down the dirt street against a background of barns and open fields. As was often the case with Helen's work, she included portraits of real people—including postman Mr. Dougherty and neighbor Mrs. Soto, pushing a baby carriage— as well as several dogs.

Margaret and Helen soon became part of a vibrant artistic community known as the Monterey Group. This circle of artists was centered around Armin Hansen and began with ten of his most talented former students, although over the years various artists came and left the loosely knit group. One of these artists, August Gay, also had connections to the Society of Six, an art community based in Oakland who hiked in the Oakland Hills and painted plein air works characterized by bold colors, movement, and spontaneity. In addition to Gay, the group included Selden Gile, Maurice Logan, William Clapp, Bernard von Eichman, and Louis Siegrist.

The Society of Six artists frequently traveled to the Monterey Peninsula to paint and were considered "modernizers bringing a much-needed breath of fresh air to the regional art scene." August Gay straddled the Oakland and Monterey Groups; he brought the innovation and modernism of the Society of Six to Monterey, and the artists in both groups became connected through him. Gay and Monterey artist C.S. Price rented rooms at the old French Hotel in downtown Monterey. Popularly known as the "Stevenson House," the hotel became a gathering place where the blended group enjoyed "cookouts and beach parties... spaghetti feeds and dance sessions." Margaret Bruton later described the atmosphere at the Stevenson House:

It was a wonderful group. Lots of people would come down from the city. Lots of people would turn up that we didn't know. Rooms could be opened into each other and to the outside... [The house] was lovely because it wasn't all titillated up the way it is now with gardens and landscaping—properly. There was just lots of sun, lots of old [fishing] nets and five or ten dollars a month rent for rooms... Originally fishermen and artists had lived side by side, but gradually the artists took over, and by this time the fishermen were gone— but you couldn't get in some of the rooms because they were full of nets.

It was a time that Esther later referred to as the "crazy twenties," as the Monterey artists' jazz-age gatherings sometimes lasted until dawn.

In November 1923, an 1840s-themed costume party at Ina Perham's studio in the Stevenson House received detailed coverage in the *San Francisco Chronicle*. After a lengthy description of the event and costumes, the newspaper reported that "when dawn finally dispersed the revelers, they were revealed as the members of the artists' colony of Monterey, who had determined to revive the spirit and customs of the old days." All three Bruton sisters were in attendance; Margaret and Esther were "costumed in the manner of the hardy but gentle American women of the period," while Helen was dressed as a "small boy fresh from the Eastern seaboard." A posed photograph from that evening shows Margaret and Helen standing on either side of Armin Hansen, who is dressed as a miner, with Helen resting her hand lightly on Hansen's shoulder.

In addition to their lively parties, artists frequently gathered at the Stevenson House for spirited discussions and arguments about modern art. Margaret described the hotel as

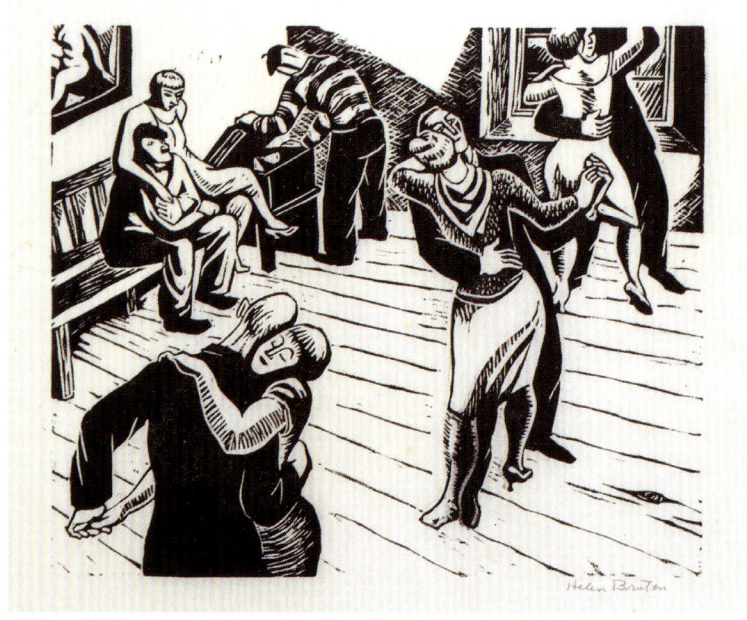

The Party, by Helen Bruton (ca. 1925). The Buck Collection at UCI Institute and Museum of California Art

"a center for lively discussions on art in general [and] shared ideas in composition and techniques." The Brutons, Gay, and Price "avidly studied reproductions of Cézanne, Gauguin and whatever others of the School of Paris they could gather." Artist Albert Barrows recalled that "some of us would wander down to Price's place on a winter evening and sit around the air-tight stove talking art and esthetics while Price would curl up in his old bear-skin on the couch and take a nap." Despite Price's quiet demeanor and love of solitude, Margaret felt that he was the nucleus of the Monterey Group.

Scottish artist William Johnstone, who spent time on the Monterey Peninsula in 1928 and 1929, frequently visited

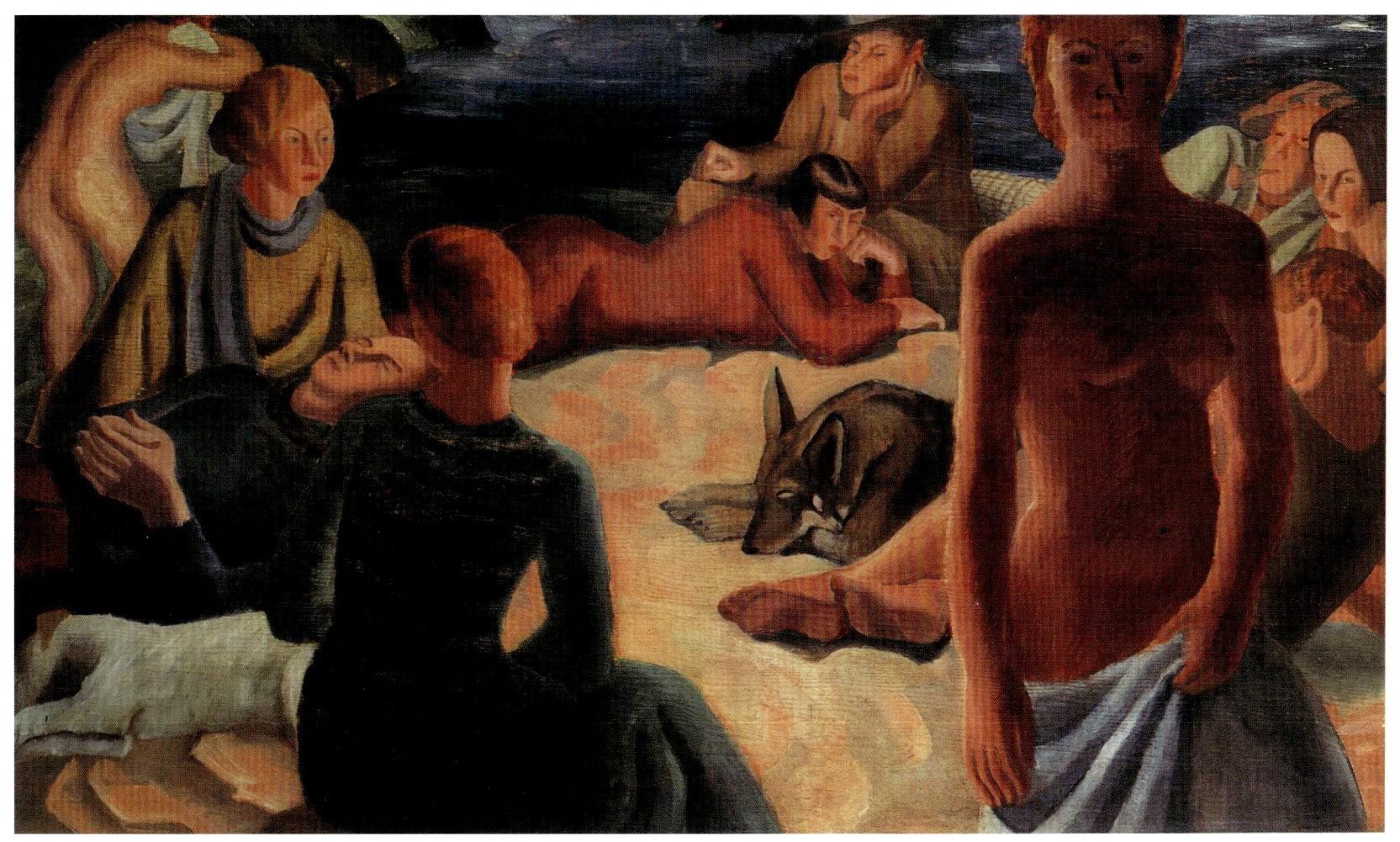

Beach Picnic, by Helen Bruton (ca. 1932)

Hansen, Price, and the Bruton sisters at the Stevenson House. He always received "a warm welcome from the artists who lived there," and the group would discuss and argue about the new movements in avant-garde art. Johnstone especially admired Esther Brutons' fashion illustrations, which he had seen in San Francisco newspapers. "Their work was brilliant," he later wrote, "far ahead of anything else I had seen at that time in this field."

Although she considered herself "on the fringe" of the Monterey Group, Helen Bruton described this time as "a very interesting, lively period" and created two iconic works that capture the youthful exuberance of the artists' social lives during the 1920s. Her linoleum block print *The Party* depicts a lively gathering at the Stevenson House. Pictured in the work are C.S. Price and Ina Perham embracing on a bench, August Gay leaning over the record player, and the three Bruton sisters dancing, each with a different partner. Awarded first prize at the California Society of Etchers exhibition in September 1928, *The Party* was praised by critics for capturing the essence of the jazz age: "'The Party' is full of the restless movement and coarse abandon of our age. One may almost hear the shuffle of feet and the click of heels on the wooden floor, the discordant grind of the phonograph, sliding up the scale as it is being wound."

Helen's large oil painting *Beach Picnic* also captures the Monterey artists at play. The work depicts a relaxed gathering on a beach, with reclining figures, two dogs, and two nude women toweling off after a dip in the ocean. Like *The Party*, friends of Helen's circle from Monterey are identifiable, including Robert Viven Howard, Ina Perham, C.S. Price, August Gay, and Flora Johnstone MacDonald, as well as Esther and Margaret. The work is impressive in its vivid color and modernist technique, as well as its humorous yet accurate likenesses. When the painting was exhibited at the Los Angeles Museum in 1932, it was described by art critic Arthur Millier as "one of the best things here... both a good picture and truthful comment, touched with unfailing humor." The reputation of this piece has held up over time. It appeared fifty years later in a 1983 exhibition of women's art at Maxwell Galleries in San Francisco, and Helen's "strong, socially symbolic" *Beach Picnic* was a favorite of at least one critic.

Despite the active social lives of the artists in the Monterey Group, they also maintained an impressive artistic output. They exhibited together for the first time in May 1925 at Carmel's Johan Hagemeyer Studio-Gallery. The show, called *Ten Monterey Painters*, featured the work of Margaret and Helen Bruton. While the exhibition received "a modest amount of publicity and a lukewarm reception" as a whole, Margaret's contribution, *Luzina*, was described as "by far the best portrait of the group." Helen also exhibited a portrait, described by a local writer as "little more than a colored drawing [yet] much is expressed by these simple means." In October 1926, the Monterey Group exhibited with artists from Carmel at a new gallery in the San Carlos Hotel, one of the few exhibition spaces in Monterey. Unfortunately, for the Monterey artists, the gallery in the San Carlos Hotel "languished and quickly closed" the following year.

The Monterey Group came together again in May 1927 to exhibit at San Francisco's Galerie Beaux Arts. The *San Francisco Chronicle* described the women in the Monterey Group as "vital painters," and Margaret's work as "pleasing to both conservative and radical." The Bay Area art criticism journal the *Argus*, however, stated that Margaret's contributions to the exhibition were disappointing, observing that her works "do not show the qualities which one knows she has." Junius Cravens, art critic for the *Argonaut*, gave an especially disparaging review of the exhibition as a whole, remarking that the Monterey artists' "zeal to be modern at all costs and to imitate the best modern foreign masters carries them beyond the point of theory... Their paintings have no special distinction unless it be unusual banality." By this point, Armin Hansen, who did not participate in the show, may have been distancing himself from the artists of the Monterey Group, many of whom were beginning to paint in a bold, non-representational style. The Brutons recalled Hansen feeling that C.S. Price's movement toward abstraction was "dangerous." In turn, the Monterey Group broke away from Hansen because they felt he wasn't modern enough. "I don't think Armin ever got anywhere with his painting," Margaret remembered. "We all felt that he wasn't at all progressive." Despite these artists' opinions, Hansen became one of the most critically acclaimed artists to emerge from the Monterey Peninsula.

Their poorly reviewed show at the Galerie Beaux Arts was the beginning of the end for the Monterey Group. A few stragglers, including Margaret Bruton and Armin Hansen, exhibited at the Hotel Del Monte Gallery in February 1928 together with Carmel artists William Ritschel, E. Charlton Fortune, and Mary DeNeale Morgan. By 1929, most members of the Monterey Group had left the area and dispersed to other locations, never to exhibit together again.

The disorganization and eventual dissolution of the Monterey Group was not a cause of concern for Margaret, as she continued to exhibit her work in other parts of California, winning numerous prizes and accolades. In the spring of 1925, at an exhibition at the Los Angeles Museum, Margaret won the $100 Hethel Prize for her oil painting *The Bar Maid*. According to the *Los Angeles Times*, the work exhibited "this aesthetic beauty, this rhythmic organization of form and color, making something that is perfect and satisfying in itself... the color

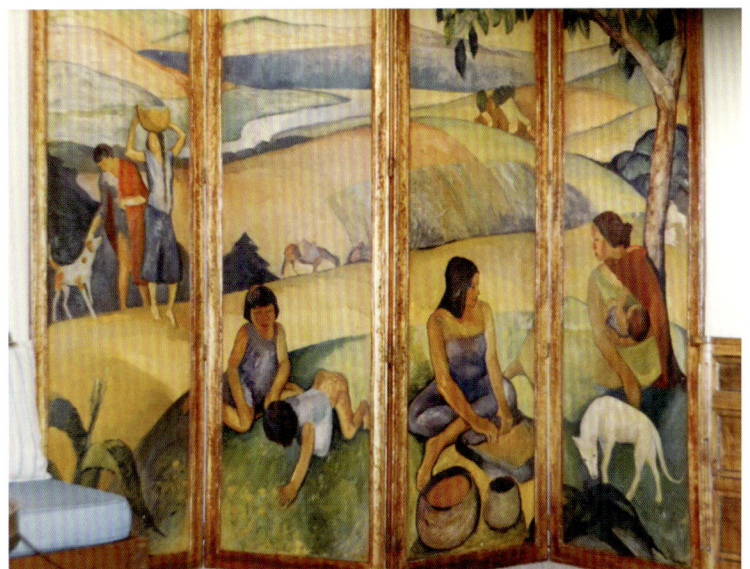

Carmel Valley, by Margaret Bruton (ca. 1925)

has rich resonance, vibrating harmony." Later that year, she was chosen as one of only five Monterey Peninsula artists "of nationwide renown" to be represented in the Pan-America Art Exhibition in Los Angeles, a show organized to showcase the work of "the best artists of North and South America."

In 1926, Margaret exhibited again at the Los Angeles Museum, this time contributing a four-panel screen called *Carmel Valley*, a landscape of golden hills with two Native American women sitting under a tree in the foreground, grinding corn and watching children play. The work was reproduced in the *Los Angeles Times*, which gave Margaret one of her best reviews. Art critic Arthur Millier raved about the screen's "happy design" and "glorious color," and proclaimed that it "captures your heart[s]... It is a pleasure to walk up and

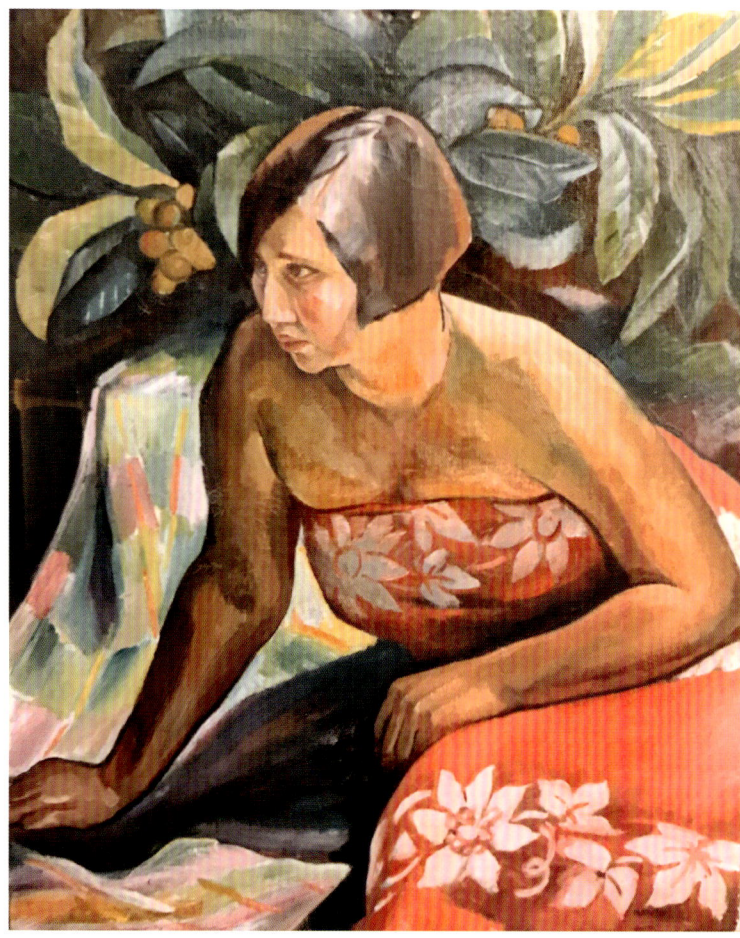

Rosie, by Margaret Bruton (ca. 1926)

see how the actual paint is laid on, the fitness of the brush stroke to the part it plays in the whole. The color is the color of a dream, but a full rich earth dream... An imagination as fine as Margaret Bruton displays here, must carry with it the will to perfection." Millier acknowledged that "this screen [with] its rich color and bold handling will kill the rest of the show" and "run away with the exhibit." Almost four years later, Millier could still recall how Margaret's *Carmel Valley* made "the neighboring paintings... appear anemic."

Following this extraordinary review, Margaret had a show at the Carmel Arts and Crafts Club in August 1926. The *Carmel Pine Cone* described her as "a painter of great originality and sense of color... She is an ultra-modernist in some aspects of her work, but her splendid imagination will delight all who see her paintings." Again, there was ample praise for Margaret's *Carmel Valley*: "Its bold handling and brilliant coloring is a delight... a fearless stroke in a bold flat method which is new and effective... Her use of color is distinguished, and put on with a sure and fluid brush."

As Margaret's reputation continued to grow, she was awarded a solo show at San Francisco's Galerie Beaux Arts in January 1927. This gallery, established by Beatrice Judd Ryan in 1925, was unique in two important ways: it was the first gallery in the city devoted exclusively to modern art and it was owned by a woman. Margaret's work continued to impress the critics; in particular, her painting *Rosie*, a portrait of a woman with black bobbed hair and bare shoulders and arms, dressed in a flowered pareu, was reproduced on three different occasions in Bay Area newspapers. It first appeared in the *Oakland Tribune*, accompanied by a glowing review of the artist and her work:

> "I wish I were more modern," said Miss Margaret
> Bruton as we sat viewing her exhibition... On this

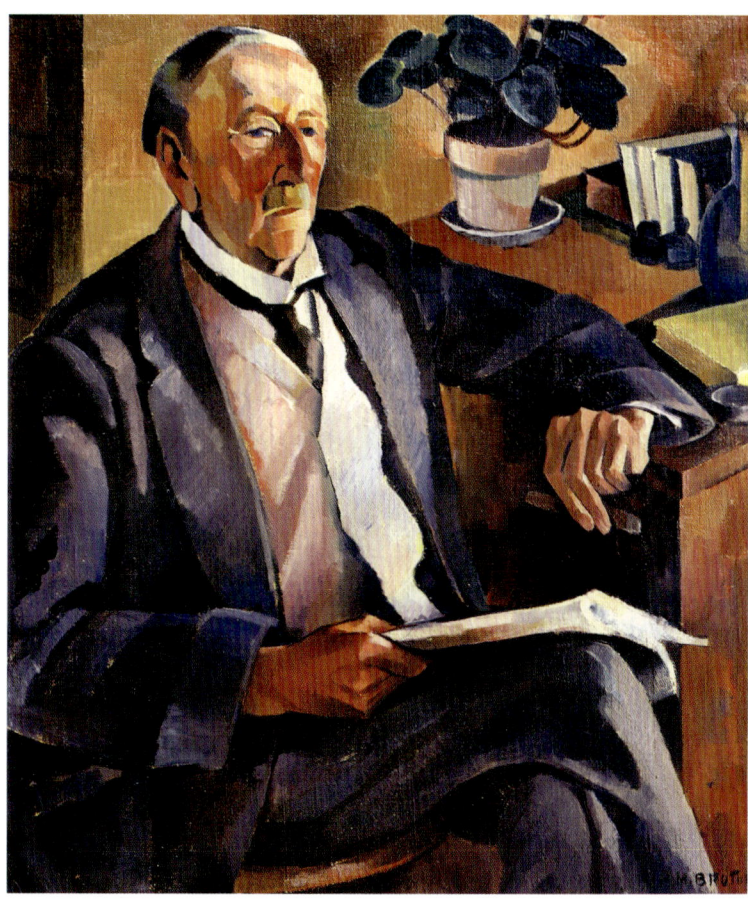
Portrait of My Father, by Margaret Bruton (1927)

point Miss Bruton and I disagree. I doubt if extreme modernism has anything to offer that would improve Miss Bruton's art. It is satisfactory as it stands now, occupying a somewhat middle position between the new and the old. She has achieved the "organization" so dear to the heart of the moderns, without their distortion. She lays her color side by side in delightful harmony without obvious effort... The exhibition, as a whole, maintains an unusually high and even standard.

Rosie was described as "strongly and crisply handled... [with] planes and colors from the modern viewpoint." The painting was awarded second prize at the Painters' and Sculptors' Exhibition at the Los Angeles Museum in April 1927—notable because Margaret's piece outperformed that of her former teacher, Armin Hansen, whose work finished third. *Rosie* was displayed again at an exhibition at the Oakland Art Gallery and was described as "one of the stronger works... suggestive of Gauguin."

The year 1927 continued to be a banner year for Margaret. In the spring, she contributed *Portrait of My Father* to the Second Annual Exhibition of the San Francisco Society of Women Artists, and again, critics appreciated her modern, inventive style. A reviewer for the *Argus*, which reproduced the portrait, raved that it "is by far the best I have seen of her. I believe it is the finest portrait of the whole exhibit. It has breadth and solidity both in lines and color. It is realistic without exaggeration and the sentiment expressed is reserved." Margaret's portrait of her father was so successful that she made a companion painting of her mother, which also received favorable reviews. Critics remarked that the "solid and convincing" portrait of her mother was "simple, forceful and altogether admirable."

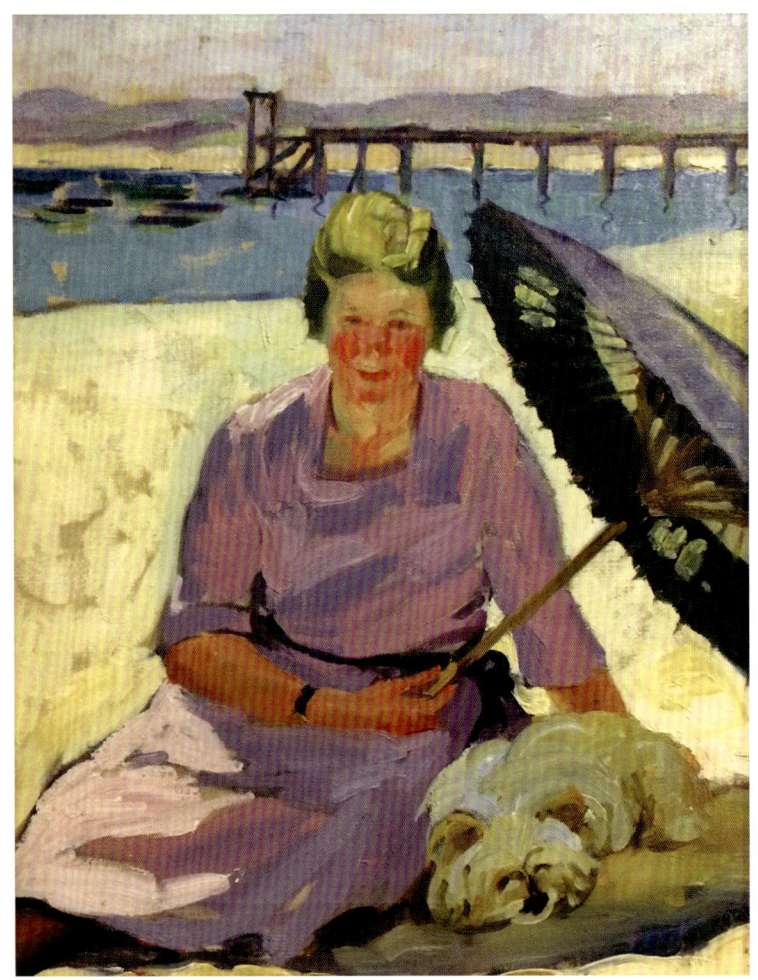

Sunning (My Mother), by Margaret Bruton (ca. 1920).
Collection Monterey Museum of Art

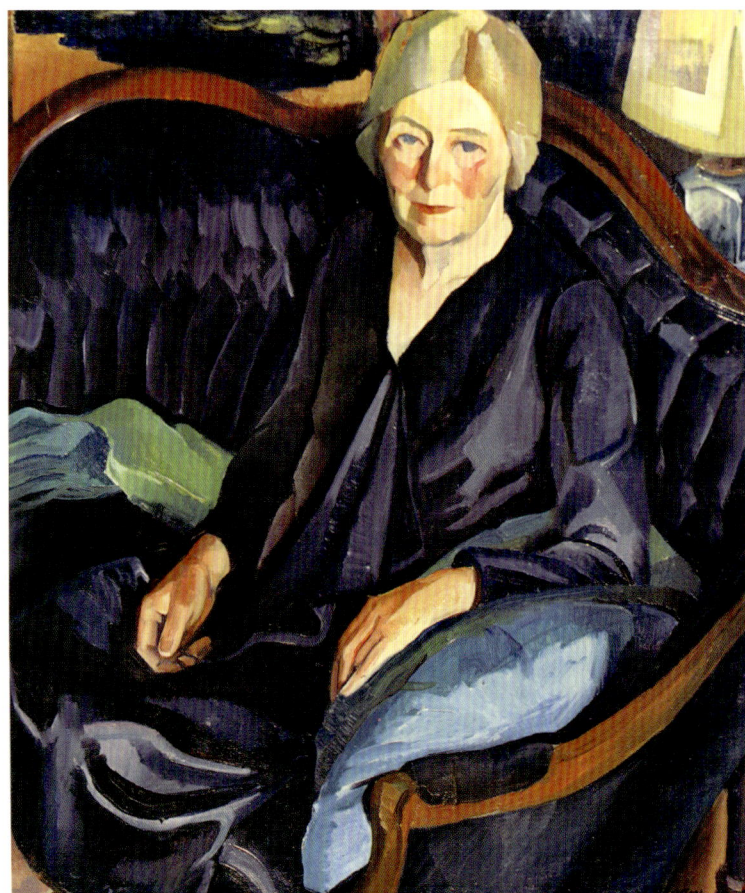

Portrait of My Mother, by Margaret Bruton (1927)

When comparing two of Margaret's portraits of her mother side by side—*Sunning (My Mother)* from around 1920 and *Portrait of My Mother* from 1927—one can discern a clear development in her style over the years. *Sunning* is a more traditional impressionistic work, with soft colors, loose brush strokes, and blurred lines. *Portrait of My Mother* is painted from a different perspective—the artist is looking downward at her subject—and the work has sharper lines and bold blocks of color. The later portrait is more modern and abstract, bringing to mind a work by Cézanne or Gauguin. In 1989, Nancy Moure remarked that *Portrait of My Mother* was "a real jewel" of portrait painting: "If Cézanne, the mentor of many of this era's artists, tilted the tables on which his still lives sat, so too did Margaret Bruton tilt the sofa on which her mother sat. How beautifully it frames her and suggests her era... How beautifully faceted are her facial planes."

Margaret's modernism was once again on display at a statewide competition held at the Santa Cruz Art League in January 1928, and her painting *Monterey Landscape* won first prize for landscapes. Critics called this work the "modern type of art, again brilliant in coloring," "impressively painted in [the] modern vein," and "'modern' in its bold masses... quite abstract in conception." Margaret's impressive output of award-winning modernist works was bound to influence other artists around her, even her former teacher, Armin Hansen. Karen Crews Hendon observes "similarities in color, shape, subject and even brush strokes" between Bruton's *Monterey Landscape* and Hansen's *Before the Storm*, a work he painted ten years later. As Hendon points out, "that the teacher can sometimes learn as much from the pupil seems to have been the case in the interaction between Hansen and Margaret Bruton."

Junius Cravens, art critic for the *Argonaut*, said that when viewing Margaret's work "one feels the force of originality working its way to the surface, strength of purpose and a striving for stability... her figure work has great interest for its simplicity and directness... she frequently attains an unusually fresh, vibrant quality." By the end of the 1920s, Margaret Bruton had established herself as an award-winning modernist, perhaps one of the most critically acclaimed in California, and she would go on to have even more success in the 1930s. Today, when celebrated artists who emerged from the Monterey Peninsula art scene are discussed, names such as E. Charlton Fortune, Armin Hansen, Jo Mora, Mary DeNeale Morgan, John O'Shea, and William Ritschel are among the first to be mentioned, despite the fact that Margaret Bruton was "quite exceptional and given equal if not more attention in the press" during the same period that these artists were active. She exhibited as frequently, won as many awards, and received as many glowing reviews as her peers, yet despite these achievements, Margaret Bruton is not as well remembered as other Monterey artists still known today.

Later in life, Helen Bruton would look back on the 1920s as the "the golden age of Monterey... it was so lovely and there was such an interesting group of artists here at the time. It was a very stimulating period." As the decade came to close, the sisters were faced with the loss of their father; Daniel Bruton passed away in their Monterey home on April 29, 1928, at the age of eighty-nine. Shortly thereafter, the Bruton women decided that a change of scene was in order—they wanted to stretch themselves artistically and find inspiration in new settings and landscapes. Margaret and Esther embarked on an expedition to Taos, New Mexico, while Helen set off on an adventure of her own.

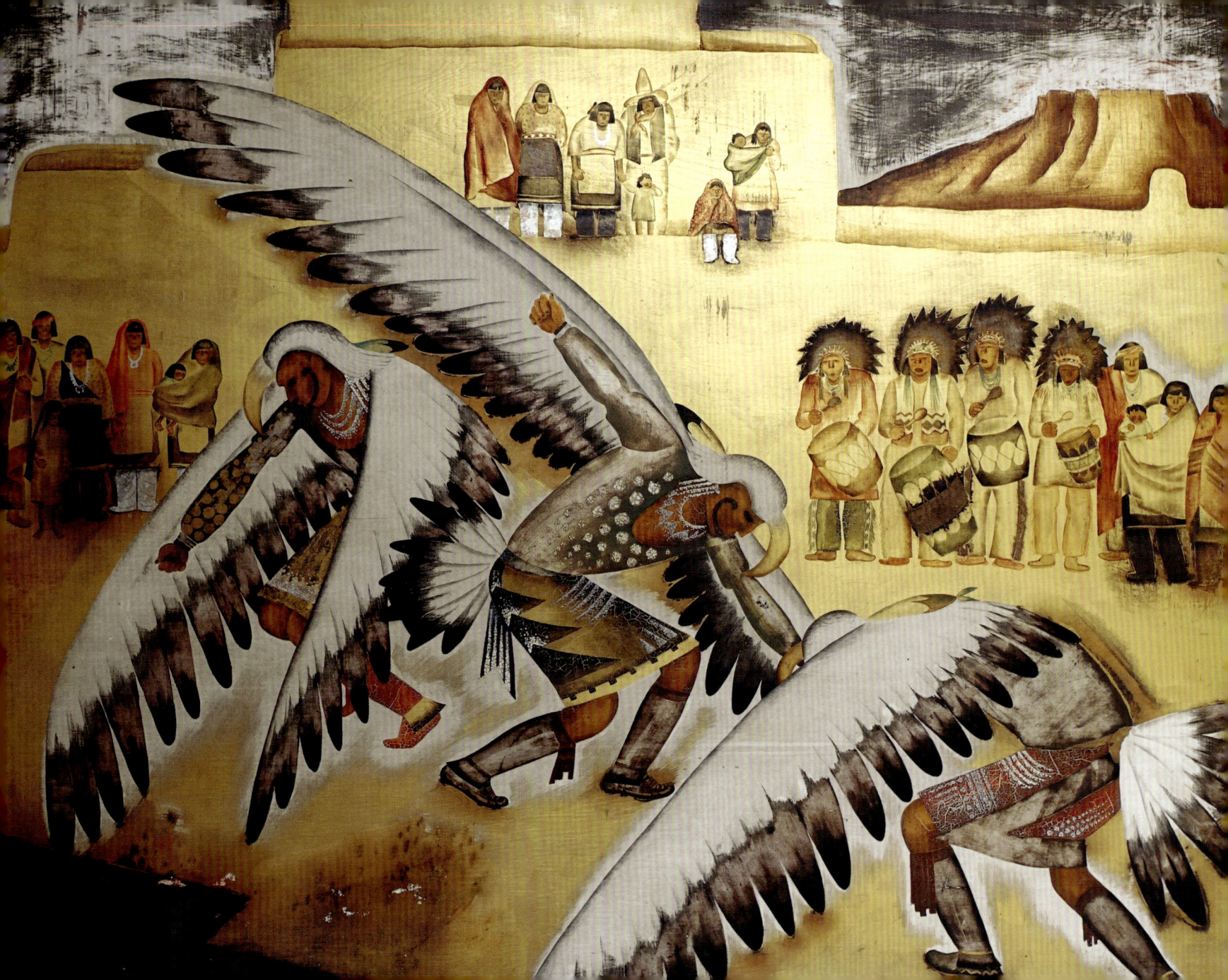

CHAPTER FOUR

"Three True Artists"
(1929–1930)

In the summer of 1929, Margaret, Esther, and their newly widowed mother left California to travel to New Mexico for an extended sketching-and-painting expedition. Esther had resigned from her commercial illustrating job at I. Magnin in San Francisco, where she had "put in at least six or seven hard years... until she couldn't stand it any longer." The Brutons were drawn to the mystique of New Mexico's awe-inspiring landscape, remarkable light, and Native American cultures. Articles from the 1920s describe the area as an ideal locale for artists: "The sun shines with its peculiar desert brightness over the flat adobe houses clustered around the plaza. Exquisite purple mists cling about the mountains, and the sky flames with the most brilliant of sunsets. The color and atmosphere make the place seem a painter's paradise." The *Saturday Evening Post* remarked on the unique quality of the light in the Taos Pueblo, saying that it "seems to rain like globules on the earth."

When the Brutons arrived in Taos, they entered a vibrant artistic circle established by American heiress Mabel Dodge Luhan. She had been the center of a modernist salon of New York intellectuals before she relocated to Taos in 1917 and married her fourth husband, Antonio "Tony" Lujan, a member of the Northern Tiwa from the Taos Pueblo. On her first day in Taos, Luhan had been overwhelmed by the spectacular landscape. "The sun made everything luminous," she wrote, "and bathed the earth and the trees in a high light... I had never seen so much color anywhere before this... Everything

Eagle Dance, by Esther Bruton (1929)

glowed and pulsated." Taos had been a thriving art colony since the early 1900s, and Luhan contributed to its popularity, inviting her creative, avant-garde friends to flee urban centers and experience New Mexico's Indigenous cultures, dramatic vistas, magical light, and fresh air. Luhan successfully enticed numerous luminaries to Taos, including D.H. Lawrence, Robinson and Una Jeffers, Willa Cather, Martha Graham, Carl Jung, Edward Weston, Dorothea Lange, and Maynard Dixon. In a letter inviting Gertrude Stein to Taos, Luhan quipped that her house was "full of pianists, painters, pederasts, prostitutes and peasants... Great material."

The summer of 1929 in Taos, when the Brutons were first there, has been described as a "legendary gathering of modernistas." At the center of this group were artists Georgia O'Keeffe and Rebecca Strand who were visiting New Mexico without their famous husbands, photographers Alfred Stieglitz and Paul Strand. During her stay in Taos, O'Keeffe experienced a spiritual and artistic awakening that forever changed her life and her painting. She claimed that Taos had "a different kind of color from any I'd ever seen... The world is so wide up there, so big." A young Ansel Adams, who was also in Taos during this time, was so inspired by the landscape and the light that he gave up his dream to become a concert pianist and committed himself full-time to photography. Mexican artist Miguel Covarrubias, an accomplished, young, commercial illustrator known for his humorous drawings and caricatures, also visited Taos that summer. It seems likely that Margaret and Esther crossed paths with these and other creative individuals with whom they shared interests. The sisters became good friends with Ansel Adams, who moved to Carmel in 1962.

By August, the Brutons were considering leaving Taos and returning home. Helen, at home in California, recounted to a friend, "Esther and Marge are still enthusiastic, but Mama is bored to death." Margaret and Esther were deeply inspired by their time in New Mexico, and their introduction to some of the cultures of the American Southwest was extremely influential, particularly for Esther. The important work born of their Taos trip would debut to great acclaim in California galleries later that year.

Meanwhile, Helen had been living in the Montgomery Block, a four-story brick apartment building in San Francisco. Originally home to writers including Mark Twain, Bret Harte, Ambrose Bierce, Robert Louis Stevenson, Jack London, George Sterling, and Emma Goldman, it attracted visual artists in the 1920s and 1930s, with its apartments and studios renting for as low as $5 per week. Its inhabitants became "part of a lively arts scene that carried over into the bars and restaurants of the surrounding neighborhood." Esther had a studio in the Montgomery Block in the 1930s, and many of the Brutons' friends and fellow artists lived in the neighborhood, including Ruth Cravath, Maynard Dixon, Dorothea Lange, Gottardo Piazzoni, Robert Howard, Ralph Stackpole, Diego Rivera, and Frida Kahlo.

By 1929, Helen had decided that she wanted to be a ceramicist. To pursue this aim, she left San Francisco in May 1929 and traveled to Southern California. Her destination was the Glendale plant of the Gladding McBean Company, a major manufacturer of terra-cotta known for their architectural and artistic tiles used on buildings in San Francisco and on the Stanford University campus. Helen had been employed as a designer by the San Jose Tile Works since 1925, and thought Gladding McBean might be interested in purchasing some of her ceramics. Her work must have impressed them, as they hired her to design a series of terra-cotta mosaic panels for the Hoose Library of Philosophy, which was under construction at the University of Southern California. She was also in the right place at the right time; the previous draftsman had left the project, and Gladding McBean needed a suitable replacement. As Helen remembered, "They were frightfully busy, and they had a great big job. They didn't have a person that could really do it to their satisfaction, so they hired me." Out of the twenty-five tile draftsmen working for the company, Helen was the only woman.

Helen first rented a room in Hollywood, which she found both stimulating and overwhelming. In a letter to her friends Ina Perham and Lucy Pierce, she wrote:

> It's all very novel and exciting, but I do have moments when the old happy-go-lucky life in Monterey seems best... At first it seemed like a madhouse to me—but I'm getting used to it, and tear into Los Angeles in the mornings now without feeling as if I was being spun around in a cyclone. Have even been driving in Lizzie [her car] this past week. Can't you see us spinning along Wilshire Boulevard with all the Packards and Rolls Royces?... I haven't seen a single notable yet—'tho the people on the street nearly all look theatrical... I haven't made any new friends, and if it were not for Kirsten, who leaves soon, and Katy, I would be quite alone in the world.

Helen's letter refers to two of her good friends: Danish

artist Kirsten Kjaer, who came to California in 1928, and Southern California artist Anna Katharine "Katy" Skeele. The three had probably met in Monterey, where each was pursuing an art career. Helen and Kirsten remained friends for the rest of their lives. "I miss you more than I can say," Helen wrote to Kirsten shortly after the latter moved back to Denmark in 1929. "Somehow, you had a way of inspiring me with confidence in myself that I need sadly." Following Kirsten's departure, Helen moved to Glendale, where she "found a quiet peaceful place" that made her feel more at home than her room in Hollywood.

Once settled in the Los Angeles area, Helen began her work for Gladding McBean and the Hoose Library of Philosophy mosaics. The Hoose Library is located inside the University of Southern California's Mudd Hall, an impressive brick building designed by architect Ralph Carlin Flewelling that incorporates Romanesque, Byzantine, and Middle Eastern architectural styles. The interior walls of the library were to include twenty-two mosaic panels representing great philosophers chosen by the director of USC's School of Philosophy, Dr. Ralph Tyler Flewelling, who was also the father of the building's architect. Each panel consisted of twelve one-foot-square painted tiles that were installed three across and four down to create the design. Helen's predecessor had completed the panels for Confucius and Buddha, and her work began with the Greek philosophers. At first, the project seemed, to Helen, to be going well:

> I like the work I'm doing—a series of twenty-two tile panels for the new philosophy building at USC. Each is supposed to represent a different philos[opher] in some incident in his life—if I can't find a definite one, I have to make up something! Have been doing Greeks

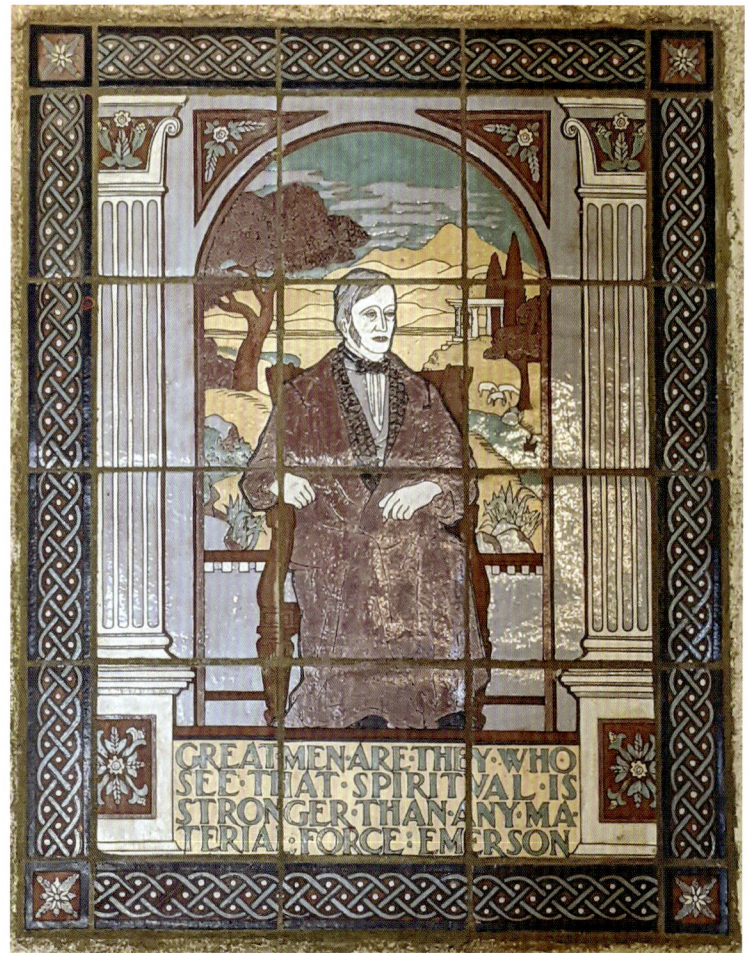

Ralph Waldo Emerson mosaic in the Hoose Library at USC, by Helen Bruton (1929)

until I'm dead sick of them—but am nearly thru with them thank God. I work them small—then they are photographed up to actual size (about three by four feet) and from that make another drawing for them to use at the factory. I suppose I shall be working at them for most of the summer I imagine.

A few months later, Helen's frustration grew. Feeling pressure to complete the project as quickly as possible, she rushed through the first panels, failing to please herself or Dr. Flewelling, who had final approval of her designs. "I'm really a bit disgusted with my own work," she wrote to Kirsten Kjaer. "It's hard and utterly devoid of imagination."

Helen was especially frustrated by the final panel, which was to be a portrait of Ralph Waldo Emerson. Helen, who loved animals, said, "all I could think of was to sit [Emerson] down under a tree on a little funny bench and I had a dog or two in it, too, because I always fell back on dogs." Dr. Flewelling didn't like this design and forbade Helen from including dogs in Emerson's portrait, saying dogs weren't dignified. Helen removed her overt depictions of dogs from the panel, but got her revenge in a subtle way: "I put the dogs up in the sky [above Emerson]—I made them like clouds drifting across, and they were all dogs racing across [the sky]... If you looked close enough, and if you knew the key, you would find the dogs." Helen completed the project in December 1929, and despite her struggles, she was pleased with what she had accomplished. "The philosophers are finished at last," she wrote. "Katy [Skeele] and Paul Rockwood and I went over to see them yesterday. They really look better than I expected, Praise God."

In 1931, shortly after Mudd Hall was completed, the building won a gold medal for design from the Los Angeles Art Association. In 2013, it was designated a City of Los Angeles Historic-Cultural Monument. Despite these accolades, Helen Bruton's significant contribution to the Hoose Library was unacknowledged and nearly lost altogether. For decades, the University of Southern California misattributed the design of the philosopher mosaics to the building's architect, Ralph Carlin Flewelling.

In November 1929, the Bruton sisters came together to spend the Thanksgiving holiday in Monterey. Thanksgiving night they attended a "darned good party" with their friends Lucy Valentine Pierce and August Gay. Esther described the evening in a letter to Ina Perham: "After dinner we gathered round," she wrote, "and Gay and I cleaned up the bunch at 'Michigan' [a card game]—then Peter won it all back at Stud Poker—and so on into the morning... We had two perfect days! Monterey was never so attractive... Helen and Gay and I and three dogs (Flash included) tramped the woods and had a grand time."

In the same letter, Esther describes a recent trip to San Francisco during which she and Helen had lunch with sculptor Ralph Stackpole. About a decade older than the Brutons, Stackpole had studied with Robert Henri in New York, had contributed a number of sculptures to the Panama-Pacific Exposition in 1915, and was an instructor at the California School of Fine Arts. Despite the recent stock market crash, the Pacific Coast Stock Exchange was increasing its profile by relocating to the former United States Treasury building, an impressively columned granite structure on 301 Pine Street. San Francisco architect Timothy Pflueger—who would later become a pivotal figure in the lives of the Bruton sisters—was in charge of renovating the building. He hired a parade of local artists, including the Brutons' friends Adaline Kent, Ruth Cravath, and Robert Howard, to provide murals, statues, and other ornamentation. Stackpole, who had befriended Diego Rivera in Paris, convinced Pflueger to hire Rivera to paint a mural inside the building.

After lunch, Stackpole took Esther and Helen to view the progress of the renovation. "It was great to see Ralph in such high spirits and looking so well," Esther wrote. "He is happy in this new Stock Exchange job and he shows it. It is the biggest job he has had yet. Times were hard for him all right last year and the year before last—he deserves the break now." Esther reported that Stackpole "has enough to keep him busy and happy for some time… The largest part, two fourteen-foot figures for the front that are to be cut in black granite, are not even yet begun. He is working on the clay models." Esther was referring to Stackpole's two massive sculpture groups, *Agriculture* and *Industry*. Exceptional examples of social realism, these commanding sculptures still stand outside the building, which today is a fitness center.

Esther's letter also mentions artist Gottardo Piazzoni, "who is busy on the library murals, so you can imagine what a happy working atmosphere there is down there with real big jobs rolling in." Piazzoni, who specialized in landscapes with "subdued, tonal colors" and "flattened, decorative forms," was working on what would become his most famous pieces, the murals for the San Francisco Public Library building. Piazzoni's murals were California landscapes painted in two series: *The Sea* and *The Land*. When the Asian Art Museum moved into the library building in 1999, these celebrated murals were removed and reinstalled in San Francisco's de Young Museum, where they are on display today.

In December 1929, the Brutons held their first group exhibition at Beatrice Judd Ryan's Galerie Beaux Arts in San Francisco. The show was a sampling of their diverse body of work, including Native American portraits by Margaret and two large screens by Esther—all inspired by their time in Taos—and about a dozen prints by Helen. Organizing a group exhibition was a fortuitous decision that resulted in unprecedented interest in the Brutons and their work. Art by one gifted woman artist was impressive, but three artistically talented sisters from one family was both a surprise and a wonder. The public became immediately curious about the Bruton sisters and their bold and inventive art. The exhibition was so successful that in February 1930 it traveled to Bullock's Gallery on Wilshire Boulevard in Los Angeles.

For the first time, artworks by all three Brutons were on view together. While often evaluated as a unit, their individual talents and achievements were also recognized: "These three sisters go their separate ways, developing along different lines, each of them retaining her marked individuality, yet all [are] motivated by an equal will for untiring effort, constant experimentation and production." *San Francisco Chronicle* art critic Aline Kistler wrote extensively about the trio, and clearly was fascinated by their striking physical appearances and engaging personalities:

It is easier to tell them apart by the characteristics of their work than it is by physical recognition… All three are stimulating, almost disconcerting. They are the sandy, Celtic type—endowed with quick wit and abrupt responses. They vary chiefly in stature and quality of temperament. The little one is Esther. She moves with quick, sure gestures. One sees in the very way she handles the canvases and prints the delicacy and care she uses in her art… Helen Bruton is taller than Esther and a bit more haphazard in her movements. She treats everything in sort of a large way, paying seemingly little attention to orderly details... Margaret Bruton, "the tall one"... seems to be the most sensitive of the three sisters. She withdraws into herself and is almost timid in her contact with the outside world... Each is a diligent worker not content to rely on mere talent. It is predicted that their work will be included among the really significant contributions of California artists within a few years.

Other critics, too, remarked on the Bruton sisters' personalities: "If Helen and Margaret are extremes of humor and pathos, then Esther is a happy combination of both." A critic for the *San Francisco Examiner* described Margaret as "the most sophisticated and erudite of them all."

Margaret's modernist portraits of Native Americans in Taos were received enthusiastically. Her painting *Taos Woman* was judged an "outstanding canvas... an exceptionally expressive work." *Augustine*, "a vividly dramatic picture... [with] many colors, subtly applied, now in harmony, and then in contrast," received an honorable mention at an exhibition by the San Francisco Society of Women Artists. The *Los Angeles Times*, which reproduced Margaret's charcoal drawing *Hopi Policeman*, described her portraits of Native Americans as "all staked on clean, modern methods of working on colors or tones that are definite, steering clear of any borderland of sentimental haze." One critic praised Margaret's ability to capture the essence of her Native American subjects without condescension or sentimentality, saying that her portraits boasted "a workable combination of aesthetics... that has been beyond the reach of most of those who attempt anything of the sort."

Esther's works in the exhibition, two painted folding screens, were also enthusiastically received by critics. Each five-foot-by-five-foot screen had three panels with scenes inspired

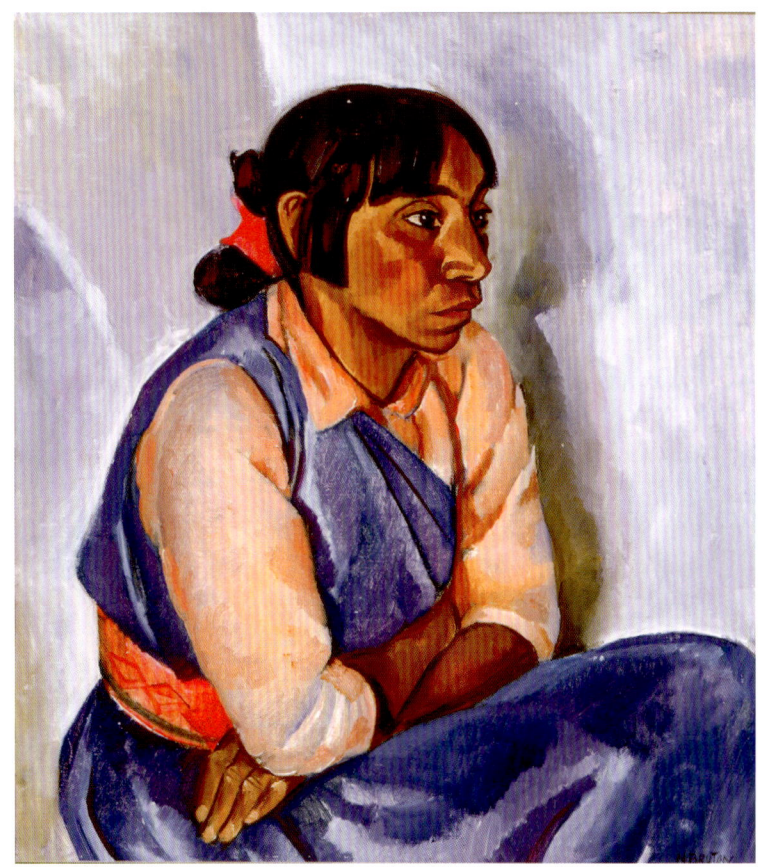

Taos Woman by Margaret Bruton (probably 1929). The Buck Collection at UCI Institute and Museum of California Art

by her travels in New Mexico. *Rabbit Hunt* features Native Americans on horseback, chasing a rabbit with their dogs through a desert landscape, and *Corn Dance* depicts a large-scale ceremonial dance taking place on a pueblo plaza. Both screens feature a golden desert landscape with pueblo buildings and a silver sky, and each is full of movement. Art critic Junius Cravens couldn't say enough about Esther's achievement with these works: "It is in two decorative screens that we see the artist in one of those revealing flashes of genius which comes now and again, at something near her full power... Both screens are so complete, so perfect, that it would be difficult to award a decision of superior merit between them." The *San Francisco Examiner* concurred, saying that the screens were "originally conceived and faultlessly made. Also, they use the American Indian themes with subtle beauty." Overall, Esther was praised for her "broad mental range" and "extraordinarily elastic mind."

Esther was aware that she had achieved something remarkable with her screens, and she planned to do more of this kind of work. "I expect and certainly hope to make some better ones in the future—and I don't mean maybe," she wrote to Ina Perham. She wanted to send the screens to New York "if no movie actress falls for them" in the Los Angeles show. She enclosed a photograph of *Rabbit Hunt* and described its coloring in the letter:

> The height of the screen is about the height of my eyebrows. What looks like white is silver leaf and the rest gold. The colors are very low... mostly the bronze color of the Indians themselves and the sorrel color of the horses—with reds and greens etc. on the trappings. The Indian parts have egg shell work in them. I should have used birds' eggs as they are thinner, but they were out of season, so I had to fall back on good old hens' eggs. I figured on selling them for about $350.00 if sold without a commission... I don't know whether that's too much or not.

In addition to her large screens, Esther painted a smaller work called *Eagle Dance*, which also incorporates gold leaf and egg shells; the work was described as "an interesting and well executed decoration." The work received an honorable mention at the San Francisco Art Association's 1932 annual exhibition, when it was described as "unsurpassed for sheer decorativeness." Later that year, *Eagle Dance* was one of thirty-five works selected for inclusion in the Oakland Art Gallery's annual exhibition.

Although Helen's contributions to the Bruton sisters' group exhibition were not considered by critics as being as remarkable as those of her sisters, her linoleum block prints were described as "capable and strong," "bold, clear, and full of humor," and "highly imaginative [and] amusing." The *San Francisco Examiner* called her "particularly gifted in illustration... a pointed talent." Helen didn't consider herself a painter and never received formal training in this medium, yet her painting *Portrait of a Poet* impressed the critics: "This expressionistic canvas... is a true artistic experiment and contains that which spells creative energy." Although the painting was judged as being technically "somewhat crude," it was "rendered with extreme simplicity, and is remarkably fine in color... imbued with that need to be born which breathes life into a work of art." Another critic called *Portrait of a Poet* "singularly interesting... [and] beautifully handled."

Los Angeles Times art critic Arthur Millier was especially impressed with the exhibition as a whole: "Collectively and individually, the sisters triumph... The high average of these California girls' work, the clarity of their style, is a real influence on the side of intelligence in Pacific Coast art... The intelligence with which they order the material and the excellence of their craftsmanship puts them on the side of the light." Another Los Angeles newspaper critic proclaimed, "For

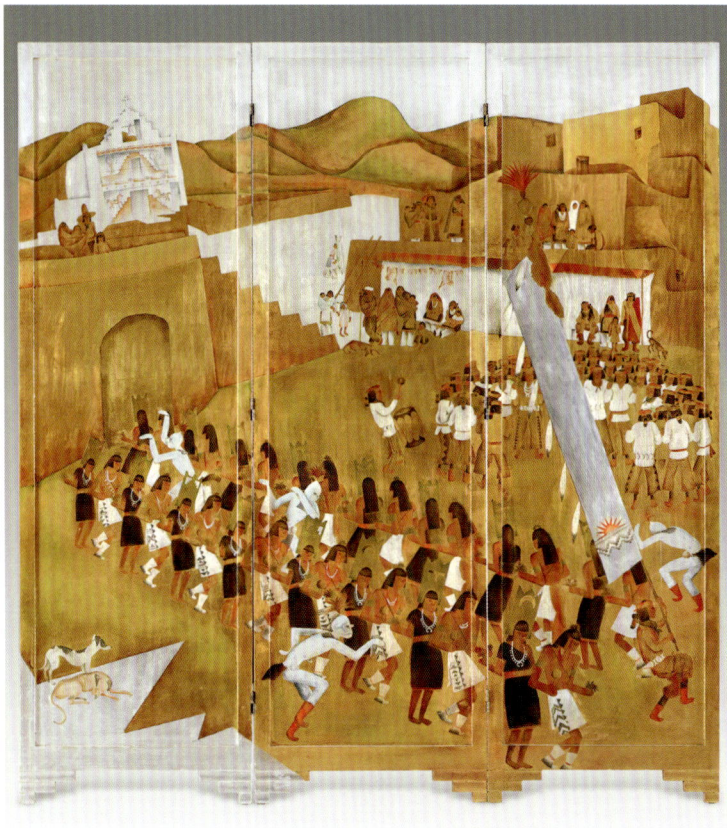

Corn Dance, by Esther Bruton (1929). Published with the permission of The Wolfsonian - Florida International University (Miami, Florida)

impressed; Maynard Dixon reportedly described the Brutons' exhibition as "positively devastating."

Several newspapers stated that the group exhibition would continue on to the Weyhe Galleries in Manhattan, although this never happened. "That business about our show at the Weyhe Galleries is a bit exaggerated to say the least," Esther explained. "We have sent some prints in and that's all. We had thought something of sending our whole show on, but on thinking it over we decided we would rather have more work to show... So we decided to let it ride for a while." Although the Weyhe Galleries exhibition fell through, a selection of their prints was displayed a year later at the Brownell-Lambertson Gallery in New York. And the Brutons did receive national attention when *Art Digest* magazine ran an article about this show, calling it "both a collective and an individual triumph."

As the Brutons continued to gain admiration from art critics, they also garnered a significant level of esteem from their peers. They exhibited regularly with San Francisco Art Association, the San Francisco Society of Women Artists, the California Society of Etchers, and the Club Beaux Arts, and were frequently asked to serve as judges in art shows and competitions.

Despite their growing fame, the Bruton sisters never took themselves too seriously. "That was the big trouble," Helen said. "It was so much fun we didn't consider that it was work." With humor and humility that was typical of them, they downplayed the importance of their wildly successful group show. In a letter to Ina Perham, Esther wrote, "Just now there is a <u>dee</u> lightful [*sic*] exhibition on at the Beaux Arts—by the three Bruton sisters! It sounds like a troupe of soft shoe dancers—we should join up with the four Marx Brothers and have a few more cocoanuts. It's just a small show of our latest stuff." Helen also

genuine vigor, see what the Bruton sisters have mustered." Months after the show closed, the *Los Angeles Times* reported that it had been one of the best exhibitions of the year, calling the Brutons "three California girls who are making a stir with their paintings and prints." Even their fellow artists were downplayed the exhibition: "The three B's had a little show at the Beaux Arts recently," she wrote to Ina Perham. "Not very exciting except for E's screens which really are lovely, and M's Taos things. [I] sold a few black and whites [prints]."

Although the reviews were outstanding, the Brutons' show was not as financially successful as they had perhaps hoped. Esther told Ina Perham that "although the sales did not mount up into four figures, we consider the show a success and well worth the trouble. I am sure it will lead to other things—in fact it already has." Even at this early stage in their careers, the Brutons were aware that the constant companion of their newfound success was the pressure to produce and exhibit their work. As Esther pointed out, "the gallery advertises and pushes a certain type of your work and expects you to keep grinding out more and more of it... It is apt to be very deadening and cramping I'm afraid." They also found the exhibition process exhausting, with Esther saying, "We are each so sick of our own work, of hauling it up and down and seeing it around that we are dying to get back and do some new stuff."

According to the 1930 census, all three Bruton sisters identified themselves as "professional artists." At around the same time, they sat for a photo shoot with the celebrated photographer Imogen Cunningham. The Brutons had known Cunningham for years and had even babysat her sons. For one of the photos, Cunningham posed the Brutons in front of Esther's screen *Corn Dance*. In the proofs from the sitting, Esther appears mischievous and playful, while Helen and Margaret are more serious, for the most part looking away from the camera. Cunningham's photographs capture the youthful trio full of promise and potential, at a moment when they were on the cusp of making it big.

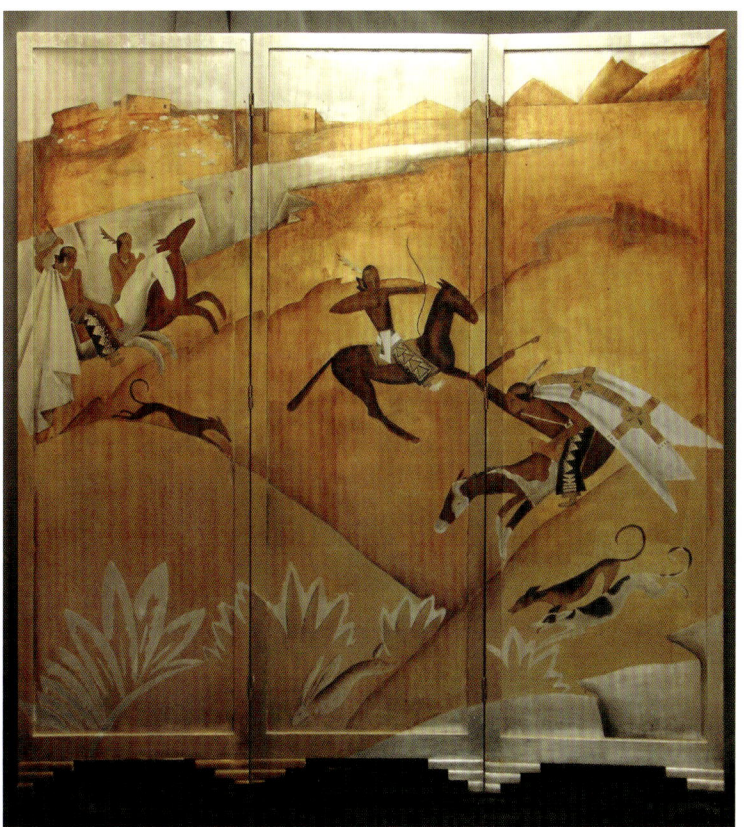

Rabbit Hunt, by Esther Bruton (1929)

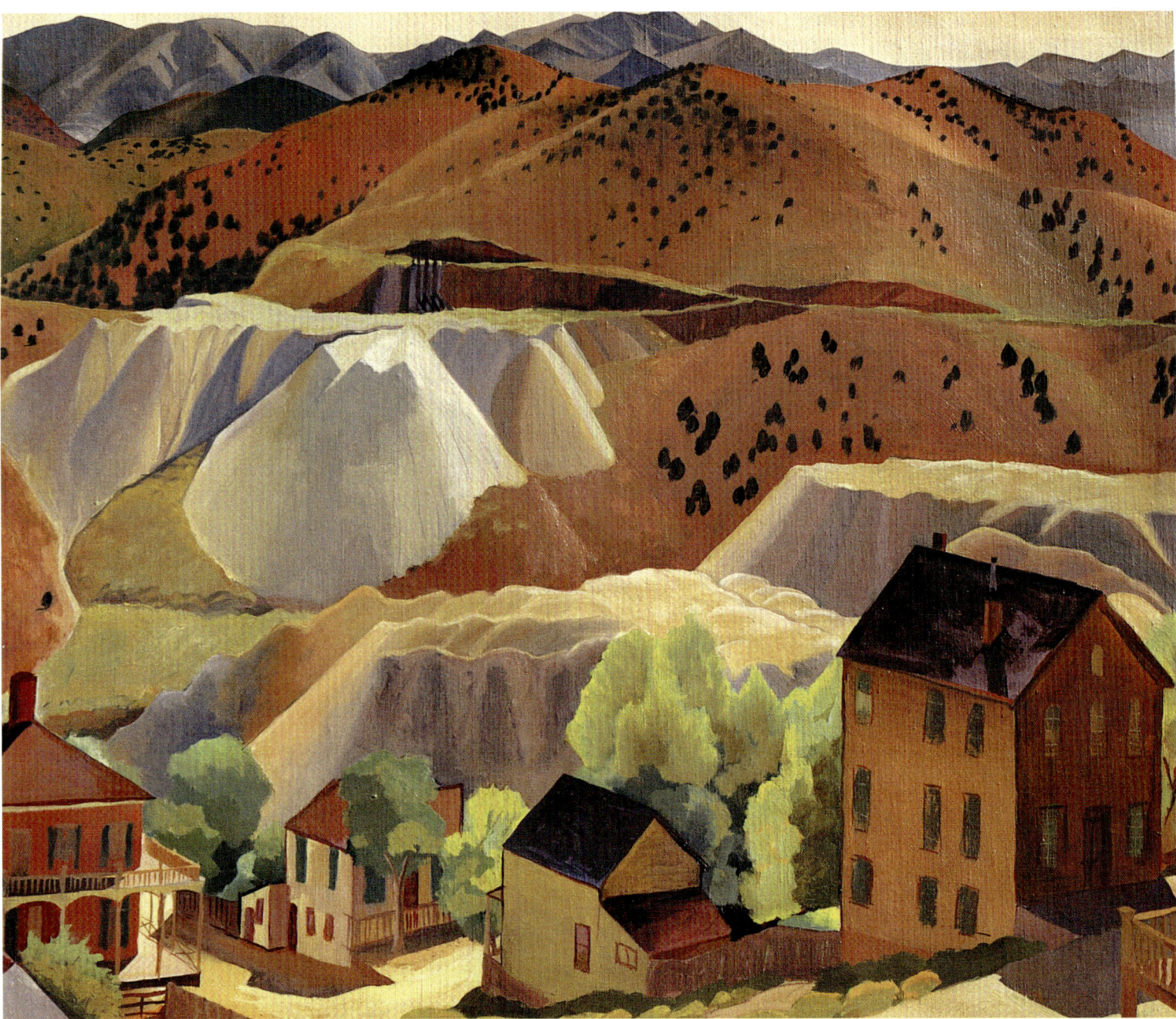

CHAPTER FIVE
"Things Got Simpler": The First Years of the Depression
(1930–1935)

By the end of the 1920s, the artists of the Monterey Group had mostly dispersed as they prepared for the economic unpleasantness that lay ahead. The Bruton sisters returned north to their home base in Alameda, C.S. Price moved to Oregon, and Ina Perham left for New York when she married investment banker Frederic E. Story. August Gay remained in Monterey, living in the Stevenson House for another decade. Despite the dispersal of their artistic community, the friendships the Brutons made in Monterey during the 1920s would be lasting ones.

The Monterey artists came from a wide variety of social and economic classes, and it is likely that the onset of the Depression and its economic repercussions played a role in the group's dissolution. Both C.S. Price and August Gay had come from a background of poverty and had "almost starved" during the Depression. Neither earned his living from painting alone; they carved picture frames and furniture to supplement their income and worked in Monterey's sardine canneries to earn extra money. To make things worse, Gay lost his savings in the 1929 stock market crash, and the Brutons "worried that he didn't have enough to eat." This was one end of the spectrum of economic conditions that prevailed on the Monterey Peninsula during the Depression; many people still maintained "considerable wealth." The women artists of the Monterey Group, for example, were the daughters of privilege. Ina Perham's family made their money in the dairy industry,

Mining Mountains, by Margaret Bruton (1933)

and Lucy Valentine Pierce's family was in the wood, coal, and grain delivery business. The Brutons, of course, were supported by their father's successful career with the American Tobacco Company.

There would have been subtle signs of the Brutons' privileged background and economic class, but the sisters were never ostentatious or showy with their wealth. "They lived a very simple life," their cousin Barbara Carroll remembers. They cared little for fashion or jewelry—their friend Lucy Pierce joked that even their new clothes looked old, and that Helen wore her dresses like a pair of overalls. For Helen, a necklace made of natural materials like date pits and eucalyptus pods was preferable to diamond jewelry, which she had no interest in.

The Brutons' wealth provided them with something much more valuable than a fancy home or elegant clothing—it gave them their freedom. The sisters attended art classes and traveled to exotic places. Money was never an issue. Correspondence between the Brutons, Ina Perham, and Lucy Pierce in the early 1930s never mentions the Great Depression, demonstrating that they were little affected by it. In fact, for these fortunate women, life went on much as before. In letters written to her husband during the worst years of the Depression, Perham describes her attendance at parties, croquet games, dog races, and multi-course dinners that included tenderloin steaks, coffee, and desserts. Even though the Depression—with its widespread unemployment and poverty—was in full swing, these affluent families clearly had free time, money to spend, and more than enough to eat.

There must have been an interesting dynamic between these wealthy women and their "starving artist" friends, especially as the Depression intensified. That being said, Gay and Price appear to have been happy to live simply. Even though Price needed money, he was "reluctant to sell [his works], as he was rarely satisfied with what he painted... One had to be a pretty good friend to acquire anything." He must have considered the Brutons good friends, as he allowed them to purchase a few of his paintings. Even so, what Price earned for the sale of one work was usually only enough to buy the paint for his next. Perhaps the wealth gap was never discussed and was of no importance to anyone, although at times, it must have been impossible to ignore.

While August Gay and C.S. Price struggled to make ends meet during their lifetimes, they are now recognized as two of the most critically acclaimed artists of the Monterey Group, although it took decades for them to establish their reputations. Price left Monterey in 1929 and moved to Portland, Oregon. Things began to turn around for him when he started working for the Works Progress Administration (WPA). Helen Bruton believed that C.S. Price "gave more to the WPA than, I think, anybody in this whole country. He was in heaven. All he asked was enough canvas and enough paints to be able to just paint continuously and hard and fast and furiously." Over the years, Price achieved national recognition for his art. He had a one man show at the Portland Art Museum in 1942, and he was included in two major exhibitions at New York's Museum of Modern Art in the mid-1940s. At the time of his death in 1950, Price was considered "the most famous painter to be developed on the Monterey

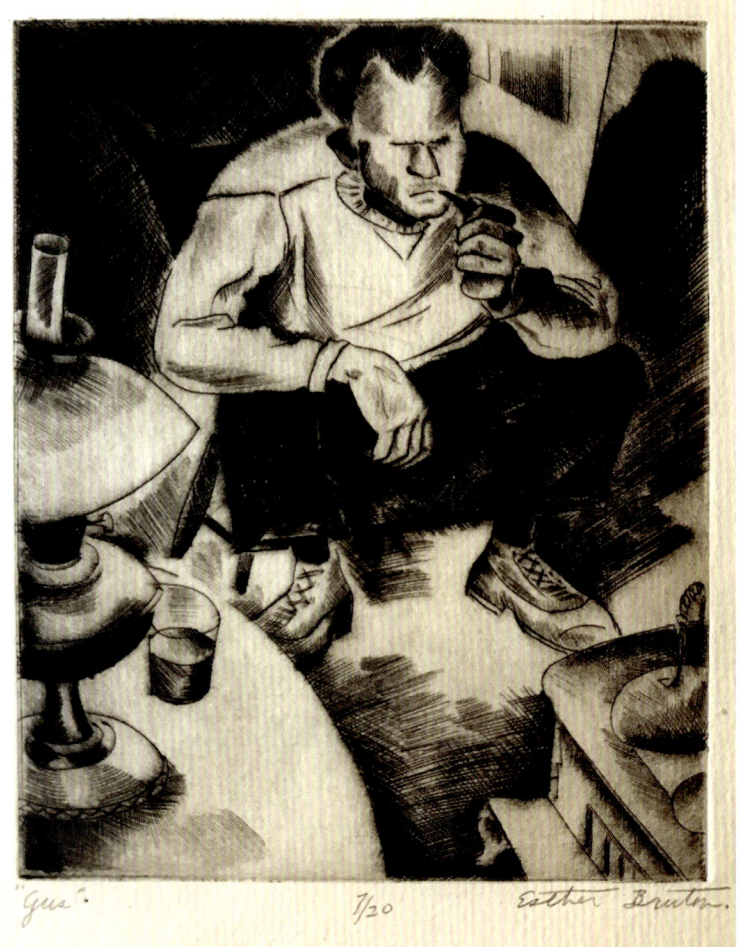

Gus, by Esther Bruton (1930)

Peninsula" and one of the "top ten in the United States."

August Gay's reputation also continued to grow over the decades. Today he is recognized as one of the most creative minds to have come from the Monterey Peninsula. Although success came largely after his death, Gay's fellow artists recognized his talent early on. "Gus was a real artist to the core," Armin Hansen said, "and lord, how he could paint. Wonderful color! Just wonderful!... The first day he came into the class I looked over his shoulder to see what he was doing, and I saw all the French masters in one canvas." The Bruton sisters, too, had huge respect for Gay. Margaret felt that he had "great sensitivity," and Helen insisted that he "was about the most talented person [in Monterey]." The art "came right out of him," she remarked. "You couldn't help but like Gay." Both Esther and Margaret drew quite different portraits of Gay.

As the Monterey Group dispersed, the Bruton sisters returned to their Alameda home, or, as their friend Frode Dann called it, their "nest." The Bay Area was their home base for the next decade, while they continued to exhibit their work on the Monterey Peninsula and throughout the country. The *Oakland Tribune* wrote of their return to Alameda:

> The Bruton sisters... have finally forsaken the fogs and heavy gray-greens of Monterey... We doubt whether Alameda will signalize the return of its three distinguished daughters by a brass band reception... But a celebration of the sort would not be inappropriate. The Brutons have been steadily increasing in artistic stature, until today they are of a caliber to redeem their home town from any suspicion of provincialism. A town with such daughters must be cultured, surely.

Once again the sisters were ensconced in their attic studio, which has been called "an exuberantly female refuge," though it was no cage: "The walls of the home were no barriers to full participation and agency in the public sphere. Their modernism... enabled them—individually and collectively—to cross those borders with style." The sisters renewed their connections in the Bay Area and became part of a circle of artists who were studying with Hans Hofmann, a renowned German American painter and one of the pioneers of the Abstract Expressionism movement who taught at Berkeley during the summers of 1930 and 1931.

In 1930, the Brutons had the opportunity of a lifetime when they were invited to a party in honor of Henri Matisse at Ralph Stackpole's San Francisco studio. Matisse, who was passing through the city on his way to Tahiti, agreed to attend Stackpole's small party of forty guests. Esther wrote to Ina Perham about the excitement of that evening, describing the dinner as "very noisy and boisterous" with "deadly cocktails" and "five gallons of red wine." "It must have sounded like bedlam to [Matisse], a good quiet gentleman (with nice bushy whiskers)," commented Esther. She observed that Matisse did not drink any alcohol and was a vegetarian, and so would not eat the chicken dinner that had been brought in from a nearby restaurant. Margaret offered to cook Matisse an omelet, and was embarrassed when it didn't turn out well. A star-struck Esther tried to communicate with Matisse using her rusty French. He "wanted to know a lot about Tahiti," she said, "and I having been there tried to tell him in my cockeyed French... [but] everything I wanted to say stuck somewhere in my gullet."

Artist Dorr Bothwell, who was also at the party, "was the star of the evening." She had just returned from two years in American Samoa, where she had lived with and learned the customs of native Samoans. Esther described how Bothwell had "both legs tattooed from knee to hip in a beautiful all over design that looks as if she had on a pair of tight little lace pants." Bothwell performed a Samoan dance for Matisse at the party. "Gee it was a thrill," wrote Esther. "[Matisse] certainly enjoyed that." It was an evening the Brutons would never forget.

While Margaret continued to garner recognition and prizes for her paintings, Esther and Helen were making etchings, woodcuts, and linoleum block prints. It is likely that Armin Hansen, who has been described as a "master-etcher" and had an etching press in his house in Monterey, introduced the Brutons to printing. Esther eventually got her own etching press sometime around 1929 after she quit her job at I. Magnin, and all three sisters began to experiment with the medium. According to Helen, they were always "butting into what the other fellow was doing... so that started Margie and me briefly etching and Esther... she did some very nice work." Esther later said in an interview that etching was "one of her first loves."

Because prints—etchings, lithographs, and woodcuts—can be reproduced inexpensively, they typically sell for prices that are more affordable than many types of art, making it possible for ordinary people to purchase them. For this reason, this egalitarian art form became increasingly popular during the Depression. The Brutons' interest in the medium was in accordance with their belief that art should be available to everyone as part of their daily lives. This is not to suggest, however, that the Brutons' prints were mass-produced; they were hand-printed rather than made by machinery, and Esther could make only about twenty prints from each etched copper plate before the plate wore out.

Esther and Helen were becoming well known not only for the excellent execution of their prints, but also for the wit and humor they used when depicting their subjects. Critics described their etchings as "truthful and sensitive... human, humorous, satirical but without bitterness." Both Esther and Helen exhibited regularly with the California Society of Etchers, which held an exhibition every September. From 1928 through 1931, Esther and Helen dominated the field at these annual competitions; for four consecutive years, one of them took home a top prize. Helen was the first to do so in 1928, when she won the competition with her print *The Party*, a work depicting a lively party at the Stevenson House in Monterey. Even at this early stage in her career, Helen was identified as "one of the most promising of the younger artists" to exhibit with the California Society of Etchers.

In September 1929, it was Esther's turn to be honored when she won a prize for *Circus II*. The work was seen as having "charming humor" and being "an evident piece of sophisticated art." It was praised for its "seriously and splendidly organized design in which nothing unnecessary has been employed... [It is] an example of true artistic expression." In 1930, Helen's etching *Soiree*, described as "replete with humor [and] skillfully executed," won honorable mention. The work depicts "a gathering of the intelligentsia... amusingly brought to attention by the delineation of various types from the long-haired poet to the Oriental mystic." In the same competition, Esther won first prize for *Top of the Tent*, another view of the circus as seen from the perspective of its high-flying performers above the crowd and featuring tightrope walkers balancing, trapeze artists flying through the air, and elephants performing below them. It was one of the few prints in the exhibition that was "contemporary in feeling." When describing Esther's work, the *Argus* said, "One seldom sees cuts with more charm... Esther Bruton attains an age-old quality in her blocks that suggests a bygone

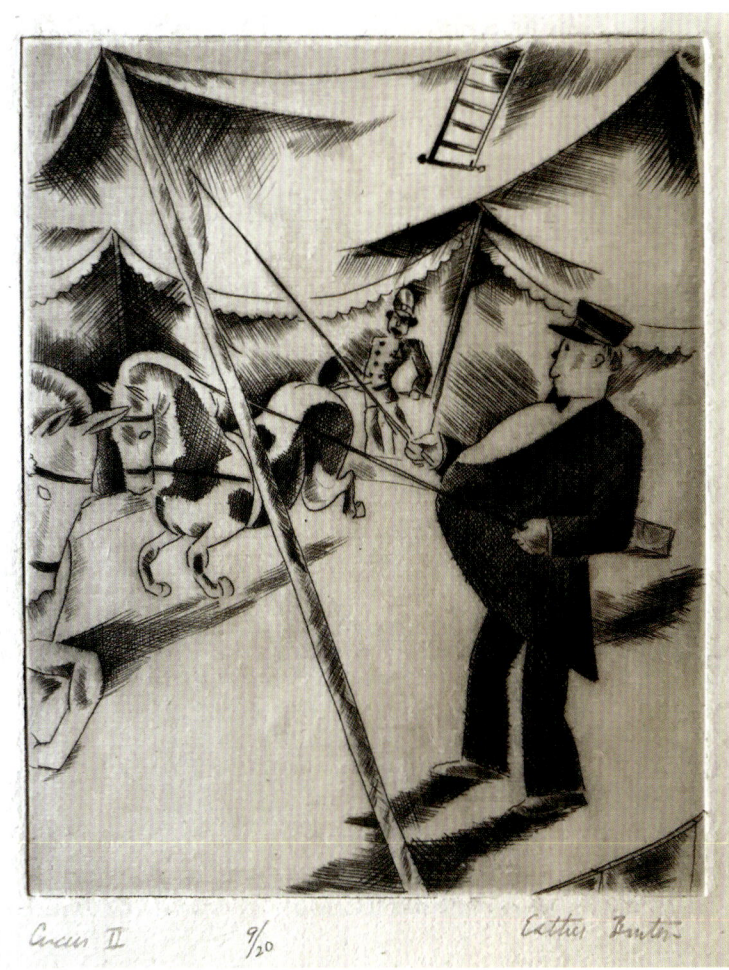

Circus II, by Esther Bruton (1929)

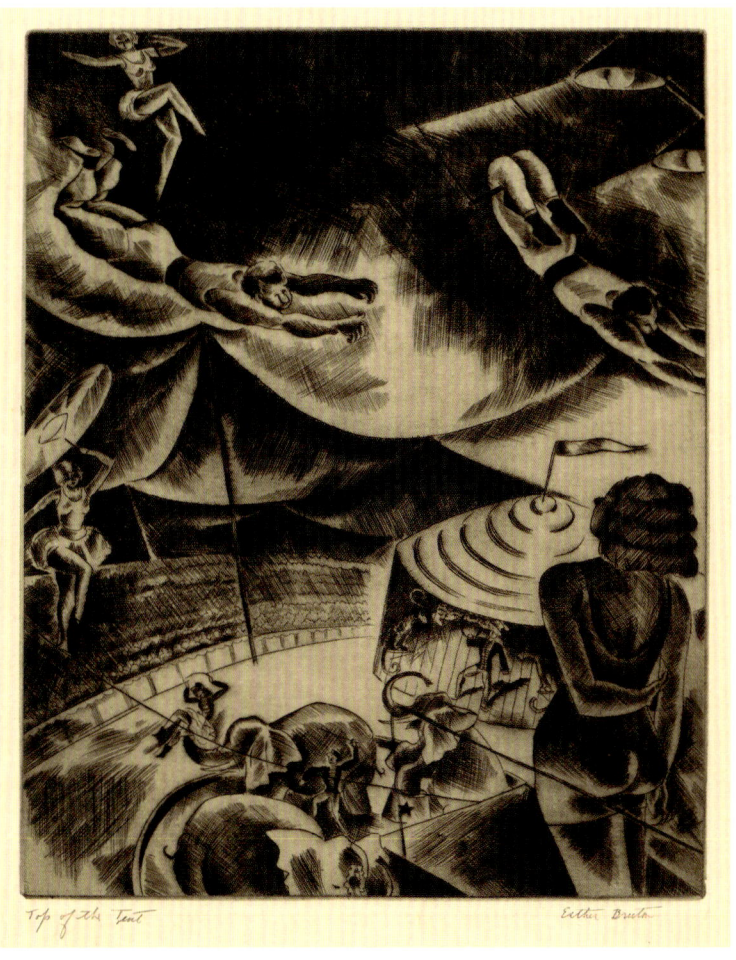

Top of the Tent, by Esther Bruton (1930)

day, without in any way imitating the masters of the past."

The following year, in September 1931, Helen won first prize in the California Society of Etchers exhibition for her print *Sunday Night*, a New York subway scene notable for its "acrid humor." In a review of the show, Esther and Helen were praised for providing a "spark of hope for the future of the society. With characteristic whimsy and humor they succeed somehow in setting their honorable craft on its feet... in considering the show as a whole in retrospect, one is inclined to sum it up with 'Thank God for the Brutons.'" During this four-year period, Esther and Helen were dominant figures in the field of California graphic arts. Their prints were also exhibited in cities across the country, including Honolulu, New York City, and Los Angeles, and were praised in national publications including the *Art Digest*, the *Christian Science Monitor*, and the *New York Times*.

All three sisters received exposure when their prints were featured in the April 1930 edition of *Touring Topics*, a magazine published by the Automobile Club of Southern California that promoted travel by car and introduced readers to scenic destinations they could visit. The article "Western Wonders" featured a seven-page spread of the Brutons' prints, including scenes of Taos, San Francisco, Monterey, and Carmel. The accompanying text described the sisters' prints as "alive and sparkling, with marked individuality... [The artists have a] rare sensitivity for essential beauty in whatever they behold, and with it technical capacity to give it expression."

Esther and Helen continued to exhibit their prints well into the 1930s. When they showed a selection of their pen drawings and lithographs at the Southard Print Room in Los Angeles in 1933, Esther included a selection of her works depicting "life among the darker Southerners." The *Los Angeles Times* remarked,

> The Bruton humor does not slapstick the weakness of men, nor does it crusade for anything unless it be for that happy comic spirit which finds laughter a natural part of any good life. Life along the Mississippi, in catfish lunch counters or in the teeming Negro quarters of New Orleans, is amusing to them because it is full of gusto. These young women laugh in their art because life is good, and we laugh with them. Their humor consists in a truthful seeing of man's unconscious attitudes of body and mind... Best of all... not a stroke is put to paper without purpose, without playing its part in orderly design.

These works were exhibited again the following year in San Francisco, when they were described by the *Oakland Tribune* as "some clever Negro character sketches by Esther Bruton." Like most artists of the time, the Brutons depicted the Black community according to racist stereotypes and caricatures, and occasionally the sisters made insensitive or racist comments in their letters. Yet at times they also exhibited more enlightened views. While spending time in Natchez, Mississippi, Esther completed a portrait series of African Americans realistically portrayed in dignified poses, without any hint of caricature or condescension. As for Helen, during a visit to San Jose in 1929, she "spent one very happy evening at the Negro church at a revival meeting... When they started up the [hymn] 'Old Time Religion'—which I really knew, I just bellowed. They invited me to come again."

During this period, Helen and Esther were having so much success with their etchings and woodcuts that they decided to try their hand at book illustrating. They spent the summer of

1930 in the mountains above St. Helena, California, preparing a portfolio of their work to present to publishing houses. That fall, Helen and Esther left sunny California to spend a bitter winter in New York, during what was perhaps the worst winter of the Depression. As Helen recalled, "it was the year they were selling apples on the street there. So we trudged around and trudged around with our portfolios and we knew the name of every art director in every publishing house... We got tired of wearing out shoe leather."

The sisters contributed a number of drawings to *The Forum* magazine, but their big break came when they were hired to illustrate *Bird Life at the Pole*, a satire of Richard Byrd's expedition to the South Pole written by Wolcott Gibbs, a regular contributor to the *New Yorker*. Esther and Helen had only ten days to complete nine drawings. The book, published in 1931, tells the story of Commander Christopher Robin (the Richard Byrd character) who leads an exhibition to the South Pole on the battleship *Lizzie Borden*. Unfortunately, the ship makes a wrong turn and ends up at the North Pole. The Brutons' sense of humor shines through in their illustrations, which were credited as having been done by "Bruton & Bruton." One drawing depicts the *Lizzie Borden* as the ship prepares for departure. Christopher Robin sits dockside, playing a grand piano. His female companion, dressed in stilettos and furs, perches on the piano as a crane lifts an enormous crate of "Elizabeth Arden Beauty Preparations" onto the ship. Other questionable items are shown being carried on board, including golf clubs and a crate of FLIT, an insect repellent popular at the time.

The humor and frivolity of *Bird Life at the Pole* was a welcome salve to Depression-era readers. The book was widely reviewed in the press, and earned "a tremendous vogue, to which the Bruton's humorous illustrations contributed greatly." Their drawings were reproduced in the *Pittsburgh Press*, the *Daily Oklahoman*, and the *Los Angeles Times*. The *Philadelphia Inquirer* called the book a "grand and clever spoof... one of the cleverest books we have encountered in many months... The illustrations well match the mood of the text." The Brutons must have been especially pleased by the review that asserted, "The illustrations are funnier than the text."

While she was in New York, Helen sketched scenes of the Depression around her, including women selling apples on the street and men camping in Central Park and washing their clothes in a stream. Yet she didn't feel that she was making any political or social statements with her art, nor did she consider herself a social realist. In fact, Helen never identified with any particular school of art and never tried to emulate any other artist. She also didn't feel that she had been strongly influenced by any of her instructors. As she said later in life, "It was just *people* that interested me... I didn't ever develop a style." Although Helen seemed to view her self-proclaimed "lack of style" as a failure, it was, in fact, evidence of her independence and open-minded spirit. The artist Alice Neel, a contemporary of the Brutons, described herself in a similar way: "I never followed any school," she said. "I never imitated any artist... I believe what I am is a humanist. That's the way I see the world and that is what I paint." Unlike Neel, however, Helen saw these qualities as weaknesses rather than strengths.

After that winter in New York, Helen was ready to go home. As for Esther, she "decided she would rather go hungry in San Francisco than in New York." In hindsight, Helen believed that if they had persevered, she and Esther could have become professional book illustrators. Instead, they returned to California, where the Depression was also in full

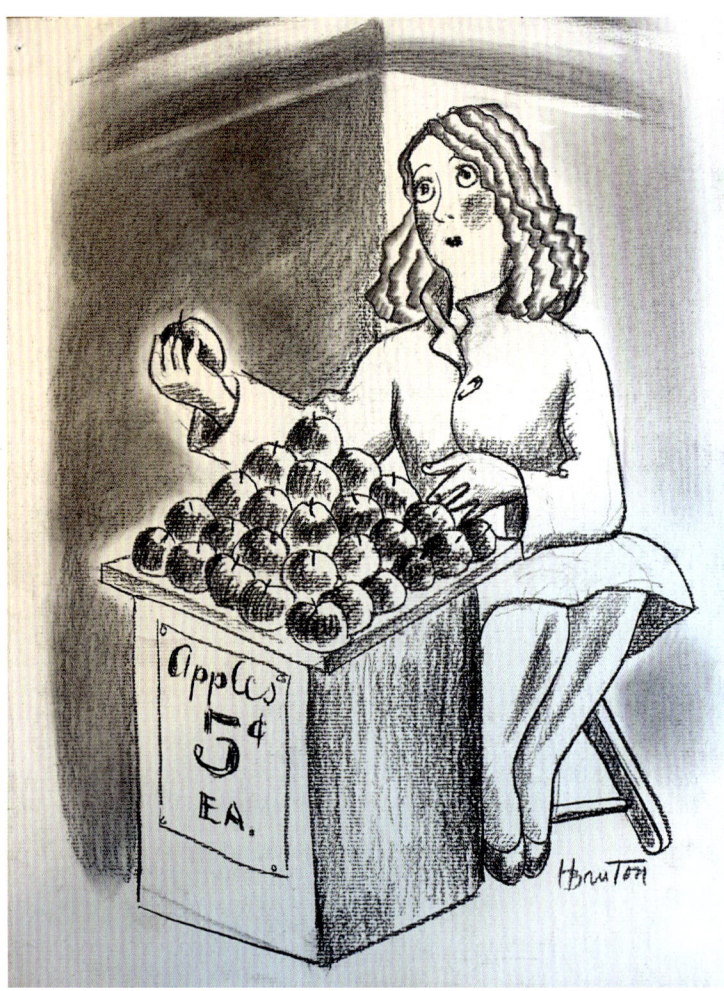

Sketch of woman selling apples, by Helen Bruton (ca. 1931)

force. Helen recalled seeing "the freight trains go by on the railroad tracks running by the highway near San Jose, and [they] would be full of people riding on the roof... They didn't know where they were going." The early years of the Depression, prior to the establishment of government-funded programs including the Works Progress Administration (WPA), were particularly difficult for artists. Times were so tough that the Galerie Beaux Arts in San Francisco held a special exhibition in which artists offered to trade their artwork for everyday necessities. Artists on the "barter list" included Gertrude Partington Albright, who hoped to trade a painting for a vacuum cleaner; Maynard Dixon, who needed a child's secondhand bike; Helen Forbes, who hoped to procure a "good sized mirror [or a] Siamese kitten"; and Margaret Bruton, who offered to trade one of her paintings for "merchandise, edible or wearable." Margaret was financially secure during the Depression and didn't need to barter her work, but it is likely that she participated in this exhibition in support of her fellow artists. It is also possible that she was attempting to draw attention away from her family's affluence in order to fit in with her colleagues whose circumstances were much worse than hers.

Despite the economic crisis, artists continued to produce and exhibit their work. All three Brutons were invited to participate in the 1932 *Black and White* show at the Denny-Watrous Gallery in Carmel, consisting of etchings, lithographs, prints, and photographs of local scenes by local artists. The Brutons' co-exhibitors included luminaries like Pedro Lemos, Mary DeNeale Morgan, John O'Shea, William Ritschel, and Henrietta Shore, as well as their Monterey friends Armin Hansen, Julian Greenwell, and August Gay. The sisters' work must have made a favorable impression, as the gallery invited

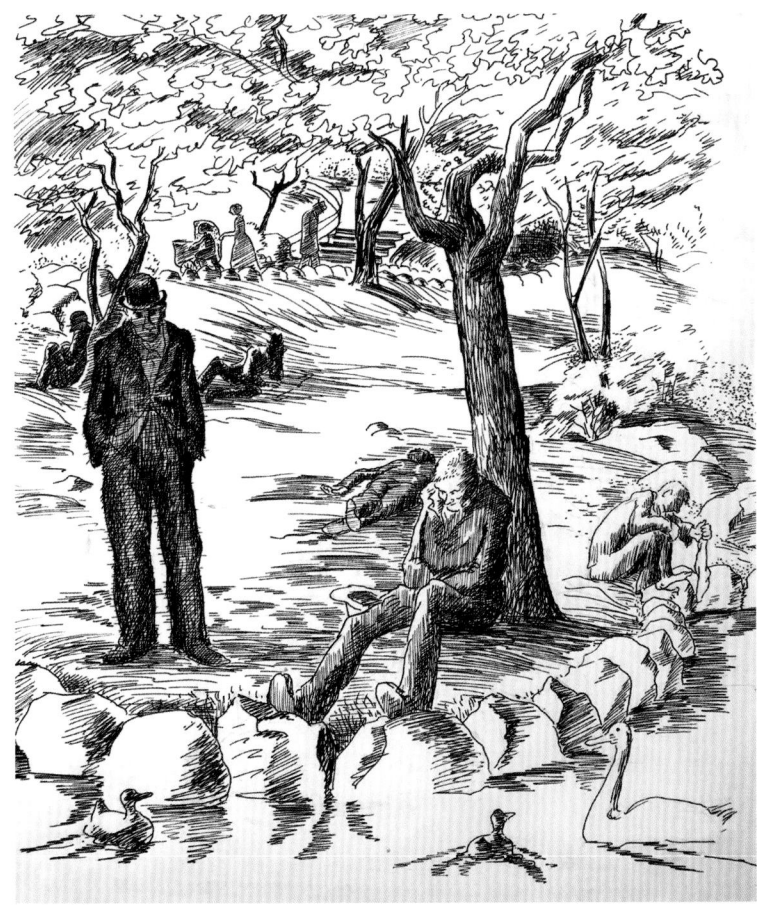
Sketch of Central Park, by Helen Bruton (ca. 1931)

them back for a show of their own just a few months later. The *Carmel Pine Cone* stated that Helen's works in the Brutons' later group show were "drawn with acrid humor and appreciation," while Margaret's tempera paintings were panned: "She has done more appealing work, but it is not here."

In August 1932, the *San Francisco Chronicle* reported that the Brutons were "motoring through the 'Ghost Cities' of the State's old mining regions." The sisters and their mother were on their way to Virginia City, Nevada, where they lived for about six months. The former mining town had flourished from 1860—when a rich deposit of silver known as the Comstock Lode was discovered there—through the 1880s. At its peak, Virginia City had 25,000 residents, but when the Brutons arrived decades later, it had been reduced to a town of only a few hundred people. The city's abandoned historic buildings and mines and the dramatic surrounding scenery made it an appealing locale for sketching and painting. During their stay in Virginia City, the Brutons rented the sunny second floor of a brick mansion, the former residence of John W. Mackay, who had made his fortune in the mining industry. On warm evenings they slept outside on the wrap-around balcony, which provided stunning views of the surrounding countryside. The bathtub was located in a corner of the kitchen, and whenever one of the women bathed, she became an impromptu drawing model for the others. Helen's sketches from Virginia City include a number of bathtub scenes.

Ina Perham visited the Brutons in Virginia City in September 1932. In a letter to her husband, she described what it was like to live, work, and play with the Bruton trio. "Life is much as it was in Taos," she wrote, "Easy going but full of activity in the art line. We get up between 6:00 & 6:30 and are on the job [painting and sketching] at 8:00 or a little after... We go to bed at 9:00 sharp." In addition to working on their art nearly full-time, the women explored the area by taking long walks and horseback rides. Perham felt that she had experienced "the grandest vacation you can imagine... The Brutons are a wonderful outfit and I love them all... They have been wonderful to me and I mean wonderful.... They are real friends & real sports."

The Brutons felt a special connection to Virginia City. As Esther explained, "It is one of those places where we all feel we 'belong,' like Taos and Tahiti. Though it might be called 'dead,' we love it." Decades later, Helen described their time in Virginia City as "a very fertile period." She was so enamored of the desolate town that she described it as "a Garden of Eden" and was thankful that most people stayed away because they thought it was "a Hell hole." Eventually, however, the charms of Virginia City became common knowledge in the art community. The abandoned mining district became "a magnet for artists, literati, and others who wished to experience something of the fast-disappearing Wild West." As a result, by 1935 the subject of deserted mining towns was considered by at least one critic to be "a vein which now seems to be about exhausted, if not actually overworked."

All three sisters had the opportunity to exhibit their Virginia City works in a March 1933 watercolor show at Gump's Gallery in San Francisco. One critic remarked that the Brutons could make even a dreary ghost town look cheerful: "The old Virginia City ruins... do not make you sad, as ruins ought to do. Something of the richness and joy of Virginia City in its prime still clings to them." Esther's watercolor *Mansion in Ruins*, painted "in the modern manner," won third prize in the competition. The works were subsequently exhibited at the Ambassador Hotel in Los Angeles in October 1933,

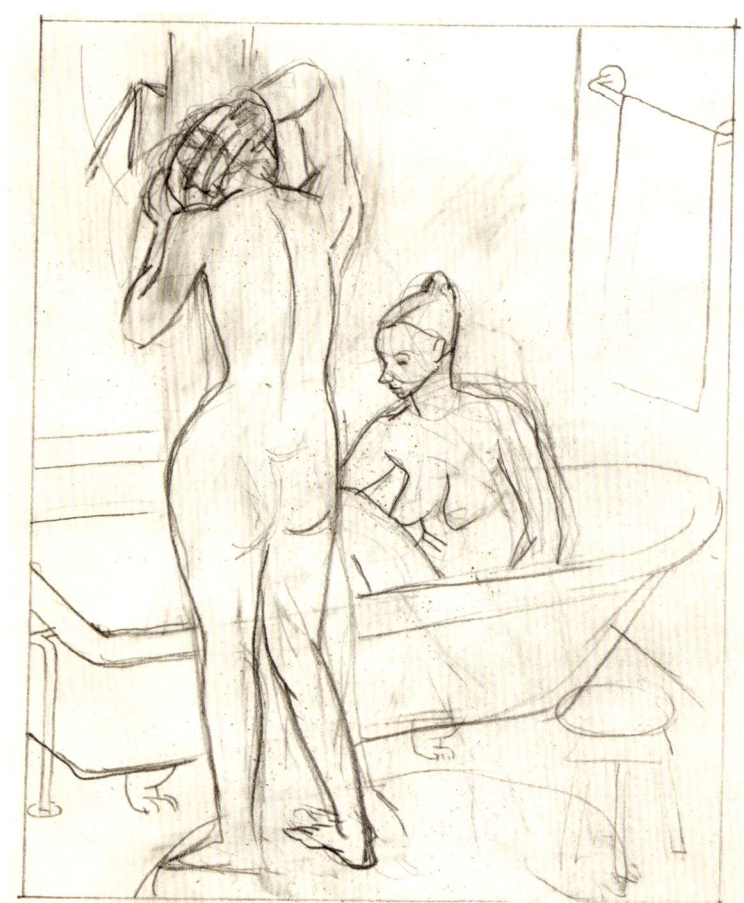

Bathtub sketch from Virginia City, by Helen Bruton (1932)

where the transformative, collective eye of the Brutons was again noted. "Life is one glad and glorious spectacle to those three California sisters," Arthur Millier wrote. "Until you have seen through their eyes you may have no idea how gay this otherwise sad old world can be." The lighthearted look of the Brutons' Virginia City watercolors must have been especially appealing to Americans struggling through the Depression.

The works that Margaret painted while in Virginia City were some of the most successful of her career. In 1934, she exhibited *On the Comstock Lode* at a show assembled by the Western Association of Art Museums; the exhibition traveled to San Diego, Seattle, Honolulu, and San Francisco. H.L. Dungan called it "the best painting I have seen of the many that have come from brushes of artists who have haunted Virginia City for the last few years. It is a picture that grows on you as only a sound work can." But it was Margaret's *Mining Mountains* that became one of her most celebrated works. Margaret started *Mining Mountains* as a watercolor and later reworked it into an oil painting. An art critic writing for the *Oakland Tribune* called it "a warm, colorful view of Virginia City's mining dumps with some houses in the foreground. A golden glow of summer heat runs through the picture." The Mackay mansion, where Margaret lived with her sisters in Virginia City, is just visible in the lower left corner of the painting.

Margaret entered *Mining Mountains* in a 1934 competition at the Oakland Art Gallery in which local artists judged their peers and voted for the best work on display. Margaret received enough votes to be included in the top ten—beating out worthy competitors like William Ritschel—and found herself in a battle for first place with Bay Area artist William Gaw. The votes were very close for several weeks in a row, and the local

newspapers kept tabs on the dramatic competition. Finally, "in the home stretch Miss Bruton forged ahead," winning the $100 first prize. Although Margaret won by a narrow margin of just seven votes, her fellow artists had judged her work to be the best in the competition, a clear indication of the respect and admiration she garnered from her peers. *Mining Mountains* won other awards, including first prize in the landscape category at the Sacramento State Fair in 1935. It went on to earn national attention in 1936, when it won a prize at the prestigious All-American Exhibition at Rockefeller Center in New York City. Margaret was one of just ten California artists invited to participate in the show. *Mining Mountains* was one of Margaret's own favorite works, and it hung proudly in her Monterey home for many years.

By the mid-1930s, Margaret Bruton was "acknowledged as one of the most distinguished artists on this Coast," and she continued to push boundaries. Her painting *Rosie* has been compared to works by Gauguin, and similarities to Cézanne have been noted in her portraits of her parents from the late 1920s. Critics observed the influence of Surrealism in her 1933 painting *Retrospect*, and she had "employed elements of the Cubist aesthetic" as early as 1928 in *Acacia*, a still life painting of a vase of flowers. When *On the Comstock Lode* was exhibited at the Museum of Modern Art in New York, the *Christian Science Monitor* said that its "numerous houses remind us of Cubist post-Impressionism."

Cubism's influence on Margaret can also be seen in *The Harmonica*, a strikingly modern depiction of a man that uses simple shapes and flat blocks of color to suggest his form, clothing, and cap. Resembling a worker during the Great Depression—a common man—he holds his robust pair of hands to his mouth and plays his unseen instrument. Margaret's

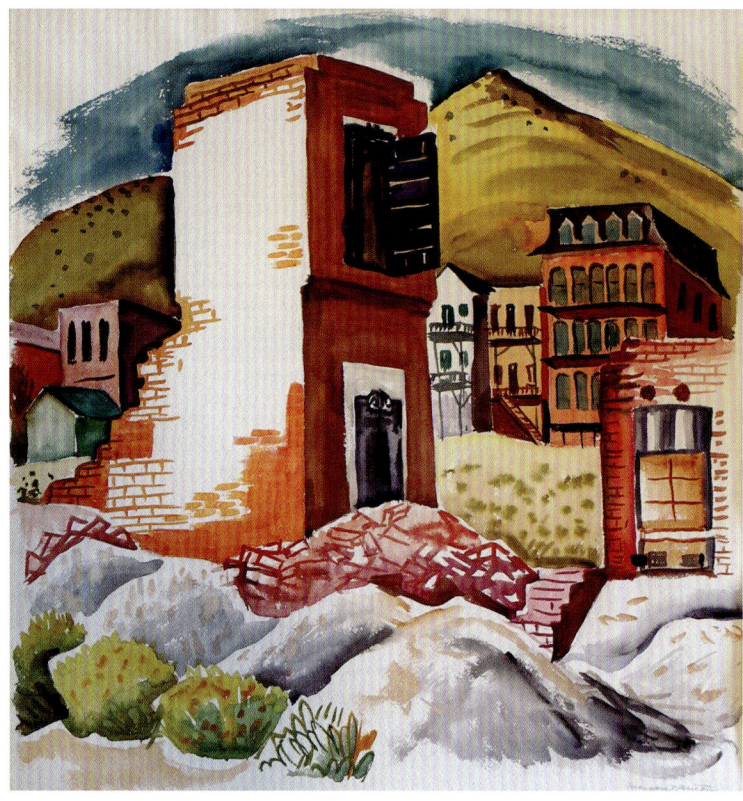
Watercolor of Virginia City, by Margaret Bruton (1932)

cutting-edge sensibilities were not missed by her peers. In 1933, she was selected to judge the "radical" works at the Oakland Art Gallery's annual competition. It is interesting to note that just as Margaret was becoming recognized for her modernist and experimental art, she was thinking about giving up painting for good.

The Bruton trio continued to receive rave reviews from art critics and attention from the media, including the *Oakland Tribune*, which profiled the sisters in a feature article in 1932. Illustrated with photos of the Brutons at work, the article stated, "The old theory that a family can have only one genius is a fallacy, according to the praise won by three Bruton sisters, whose art is now attracting attention of critics... [They] have exhibited their work in this country's leading galleries." Helen, who was interviewed for the article, summed up the sisters' collaborative philosophy and self-effacing humility in just a few sentences: "We prefer a living art that is [of] some use," she said. "While each of us has her own type of work, we find it a simple matter to work together on many of our problems... We believe that we have so far to go before we are worthy of [these] honors... we have not expected those awards which we have received."

That same year, Beatrice Judd Ryan, owner of the Galerie Beaux Arts, wrote an article about the Brutons for the *Women's City Club Magazine*. "The Brutons three, are modern in their viewpoint on art," she wrote. Ryan emphasized that the Brutons' art had matured and developed over the past decade: "A real development it is, with a serious intent... all show the same fine, gay spirit, but quite differently expressed according to their separate individualities and mediums."

Early in 1935, the Brutons had another group exhibition, this time at the Danysh Galleries in San Francisco, and the reviews were cooler. Junius Cravens remarked that "the Bruton show is neither great nor profound, but it is of sufficient weight and quality to be well worth seeing." Similarly, H.L. Dungan of the *Oakland Tribune* admired the Brutons' work while at the same time acknowledging that it wasn't "great."

> Those three amazing Bruton sisters of Alameda, who paint, etch, draw, hack, carve, mosaic, letter, and engrave... There isn't much under the sun in the way of art they don't do and do with a liberal hand—a sort of joyous abandon that is pleasing to behold. The sisters three are modern in their views on art, yet there is a primitive quaintness about it all that touches delightfully whatever emotions we have left. It is not great art, yet, but sincere, honest art, human art, with a touch of humor in it.

The article went on to say that the press and viewers "shall probably get Helen, Esther, and Margaret mixed up as to which one did what, but, no matter, it's all in the same family." This comment foreshadows a persistent problem the Brutons faced as their fame grew: the press and the public frequently thought of and described them as one person, masking their individual identities and achievements.

Despite the widespread hardships caused by the Great Depression—and perhaps in response to them—the Brutons still liked to have fun, and they threw numerous elaborate parties during the early 1930s. Their humor and creativity were always part of the festivities through witty invitations, costumes, games, and entertainment. Lucy Pierce attended one of the Brutons' holiday parties, which included "some very amusing rearranged advertisements pasted on cards—the wrong descriptions for the wrong picture—really a scream." For

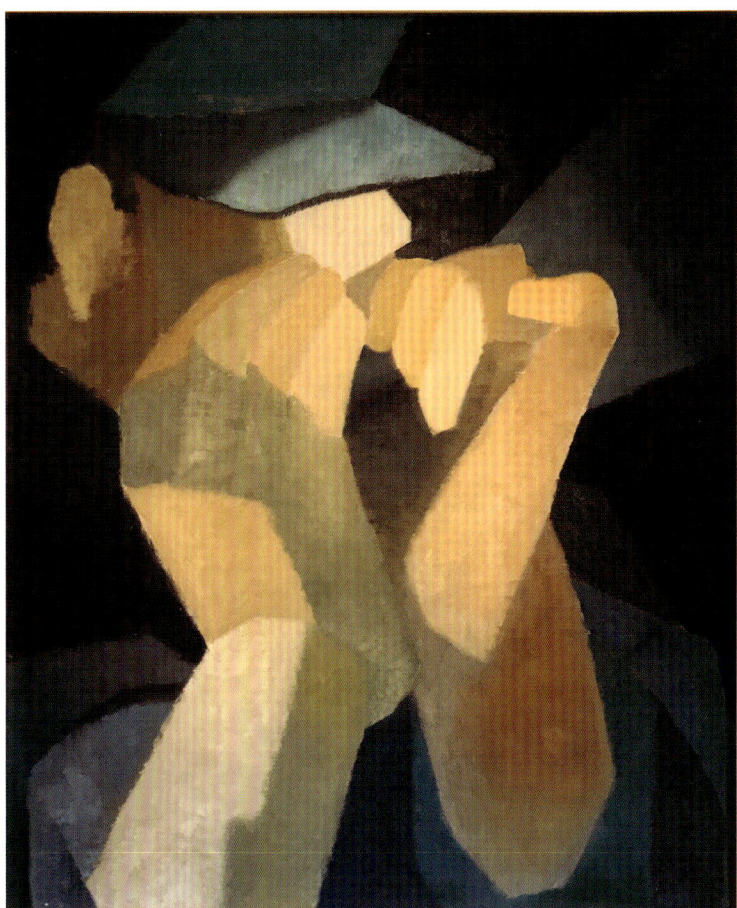

The Harmonica, by Margaret Bruton (ca. 1935)

the same party, Helen made a nativity scene for the table that included an angel over the manger blowing a trumpet made from a cigarette holder. "You know H[elen]," quipped Pierce. "She has to be funny."

In 1932, the Brutons threw a party for their friend Florence Alston Swift. Perhaps because many of their fellow artists were struggling during the Depression, the Brutons made their guests feel rich—at least for one night. A male friend, dressed as John D. Rockefeller, handed out play money as the guests arrived. The money could be used to buy items from Lucy Pierce's "spare parts shop," play blackjack and craps, or purchase stocks offered by made-up companies like "Hiccough Common, Pierce Desert Towns, and Mexico Preferred." The sisters performed in a medicine show, passing around handbills and handing out "all kinds of terrible looking pills." A surviving flyer from the party, illustrated by one of the Brutons, advertises "Dr. Rockwood's Balm of India," a potion that was guaranteed to "restore lost prosperity" and heal Depression-era ailments such as "frozen assets," "Goldman Saxiosis," and "flatulence of the wallet." Like many of the sisters' parties, costumes were part of the fun, and Helen dressed as Diamond Lil, a character created and made famous by Mae West.

Costumes, games, and entertainment were also part of a December 1935 party celebrating their friend Ina Perham. "You are invited to participate in a gala performance of Brutons' Burlesque," the invitation read. Partygoers were asked to bring a "burlesque work of art for the Grand Exhibition" to be hung in "The Bruton Museum of Art." Maxine Albro's husband, artist Parker Hall—who had painted one of the murals in San Francisco's Coit Tower the year before—contributed a tiny drawing of a topless dancer swinging her brassiere above her head.

In addition to hosting parties, the Brutons maintained an almost childlike enthusiasm for life during the Depression. Esther wrote to Ina Perham that on a trip to the San Gabriel mountains, the sisters "tobogganed like ten-year-olds" in the snow. "We knocked a few years off our calendars and a few wrinkles off our brows." In 1935, Margaret, Helen, and their mother, accompanied by their two dogs, attempted an intrepid drive to New York in their "open car of ancient vintage." Unfortunately, the car was so unreliable that they had to turn back after reaching Indianapolis.

Even international travel remained within the Brutons' reach despite the country's overall financial struggles. In late 1934, two newspapers reported that Esther had been on a trip to Mexico City and the small village of Taxco, Mexico, which had become known as an artist colony by the mid-1930s. Much like Taos, it offered a rustic environment and exposure to Indigenous cultures. Margaret visited Taxco in the winter of 1935 and 1936, and the art inspired by her time there began winning her awards in the fall of 1936. In October, her oil painting *Mexican Street Scene* won third prize at the San Francisco Society of Women Artists' annual exhibition, and the following month she won first prize for *Night Fiesta* at the San Francisco Art Association's watercolor exhibition.

While Esther and Margaret were exploring Mexico, Helen took a "world trip" on the English freighter *Silveryew*. That the Brutons traveled internationally, entertained, and continued to make art full-time during the height of the Depression is a clear indication of the family's wealth and privilege at a time when many Americans struggled to put food on the table. It is likely that the family owned stock in the American Tobacco Company, the firm that Daniel Bruton worked for, and the tobacco industry fared extremely well during the 1930s. Lucky Strike cigarettes were one of the few luxuries that even the most destitute Americans refused to give up. Sales remained strong during the worst years of the Depression, with the American Tobacco Company's stock price actually increasing by 11 percent between 1929 and 1931. Later in life, at least one of the sisters must have felt guilty about the family's connection to the tobacco industry, as among their papers are a number of handmade, strikingly modern, and strongly worded anti-smoking posters.

The Brutons were also carried through the Depression with their steady income from an apartment building in San Francisco they managed themselves. They "depended largely" on this income but were also generous landlords. They were on a first-name basis with their tenants and reduced the rents as the Depression worsened. A letter from Helen to Ina Perham in 1932 indicates that their obligations as landlords created a great deal of work. "The trouble with us," Helen said, "is we're really in the real estate business. It's a life-sized job for one person, and no job for an artist. Maybe we can get out from under some day."

When asked later in life how they survived the Depression, Margaret replied, "We were very fortunate," while Helen elaborated that she and her sisters "certainly weren't rolling in wealth ever, but we lived so simply that just things got simpler, that's all." The Brutons had survived—even thrived—through the early part of the Depression. As the 1930s pressed onward, the worsening economic climate would bring unexpected challenges and opportunities for the talented trio.

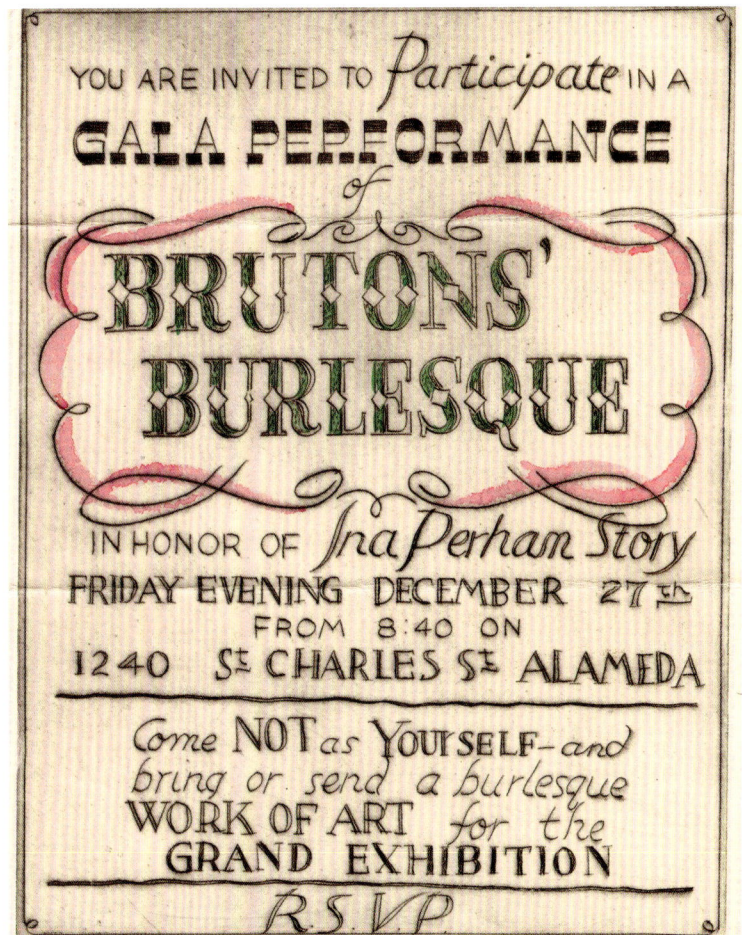

Invitation for the "Brutons' Burlesque" party (1935)

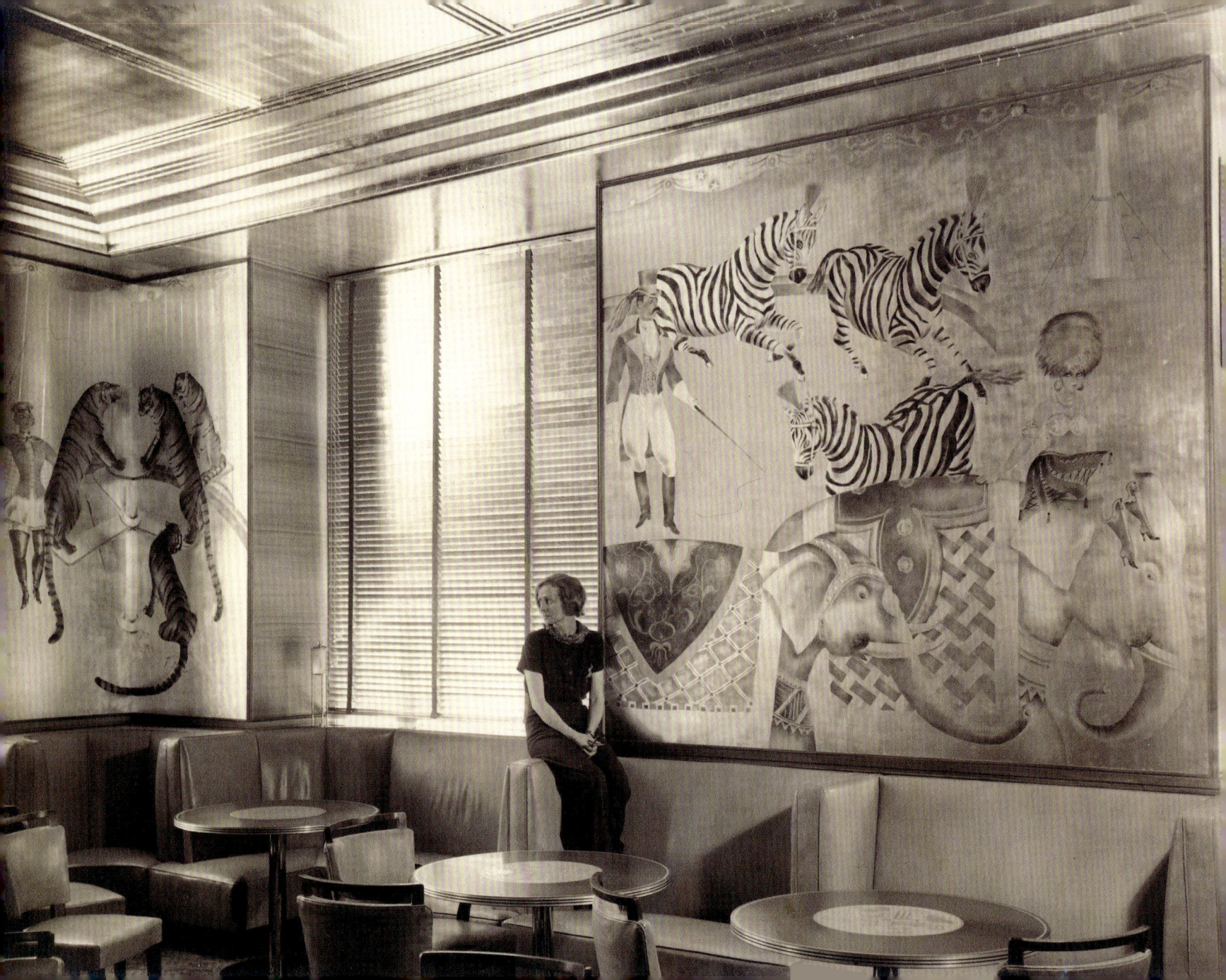

CHAPTER SIX

Esther Bruton: "An Extraordinarily Elastic Mind"

(1935–1939)

By 1935, all three Bruton sisters were in their late thirties and none had married. Photographs from this period reveal that they made a striking group, and people who knew them remarked that they made an impression when they entered a room. A reporter for the *Christian Science Monitor* described them as "blonde and buoyant," and their friend Ruth Cravath remembered them as "blonde and slender and tall." At 5'7", Esther was sometimes referred to as the "little one," while Margaret and Helen were considerably taller. Their statuesque beauty turned heads, but the Brutons' self-confidence, self-possession, and personalities left even bigger impressions. Beatrice Judd Ryan, owner of the Galerie Beaux Arts in San Francisco, described them as "tawny-headed women of Celtic background [with] a wit, sparkle and zest for life and work." The sisters were also somewhat bold in their attire, frequently wearing pants—and evidently did so "with an air"—instead of skirts or dresses, a rather daring move for women in the 1930s.

Artist Jay Hannah—a friend of August Gay's—once described the sisters as "wild women," although he failed to share any details about what this meant or how he came to this conclusion. The Brutons loved to have fun, although just how "wild" they were is a matter of speculation. There are many examples of frivolity and a few glimpses of excess in the sisters' correspondence. In a 1929 letter, Helen mentions "one very wild night with my author friend," and later that year she mentions waking up one morning feeling "lower than a snake,

Esther Bruton in the Cirque Room, 1935

after two late nights out, and early risings."

Remarkably, there is no evidence that these attractive, smart, and talented young women were involved in any serious or long-term romantic relationships, at least until Esther married at the age of forty-four. Helen and Margaret never tied the knot, and none of the sisters had children. The dearth of information about their personal lives might lead one to suspect that they were lesbians or bisexuals who, given the time period, would have felt pressure to conduct their relationships in secrecy, but there is no clear evidence of their sexual identities. Friends and relatives acknowledge that the sisters "were extremely private" and rarely discussed their personal lives, and no diaries or love letters have been uncovered.

There are, however, a few glimpses into Helen's love life. In 1983 at eighty-five years old, Helen revealed to her much younger cousin Peggy Stackable that her first love was a boy from her high school who died in a tragic accident. Her second romance came at the end of World War I, when she fell in "love at first sight" with her supervisor while working as his clerk at Mare Island Navy Yard. But when Helen opened his mail, she discovered perfumed love letters from women in other towns he had left behind. Any hope of a romance was dashed completely when he asked her to buy a gift for his child, confirming that he was already a husband and a father. Helen claimed that this unrequited love affair in her early twenties was "the last time she was in love." Nearly a decade later, in 1929, Helen's friends took her to a concert at the Hollywood

Bowl and tried to set her up with the San Francisco artist Paul Rockwood. Helen admitted that she "was a bit in love with [Rockwood] myself, under the spell of a marvelous night and a beautiful concert, but I haven't been able to sustain the feeling, so I'm afraid it didn't take."

Regardless of their romantic experiences and sexual orientation, the Brutons had many good reasons to reject marriage. Thanks to their father's money, all three women were independently wealthy and didn't need a husband to provide them with financial security. Their cousin Barbara Carroll has stated that "they were raised to be very independent and do what they wanted to do... No one was going to tell them, 'This is the path you take, a young woman is supposed to do this and get married and start having children.'" The sisters clearly enjoyed and appreciated their independence. As single women they were free to travel and pursue their art full-time, without the distractions, obligations, and responsibilities associated with husbands and children. Another factor in their individual decisions to remain single may have been that the sisters—in particular the eldest, Margaret—already felt deeply responsible for the support and care of their widowed mother. When possible, they brought their mother along on their trips, and when she became too ill or physically comprised to travel, one sister always stayed home to care for her. It is also possible that the close bond between the sisters may have been intimidating to potential suitors. One of their male friends said of the Brutons, "Wish it were possible for a fellow to fall in love with one of them. But, it is not. Possibly because they are too self sufficient. They are first of all 'The Bruton family.' Who wants to fall in love with a family?"

The decision not to get married and have a family was unconventional for women of the period—and it was a choice many serious women artists made. A number of women within the Brutons' own circle never married, including Lucy Pierce, E. Charlton Fortune, Mary DeNeale Morgan, Helen Forbes, Marjorie Eaton, Henrietta Shore, Evelyn McCormick, and Isabel Hunter. Jo Nivison, the wife of Edward Hopper, remarked in a 1932 letter that "for the female of the species, it's a fatal thing for an artist to marry, her consciousness is too much disturbed. She can no longer live sufficiently within herself to produce." Other women artists—including Ina Perham, Katy Skeele, and Esther Bruton—waited until they were in their forties to marry, perhaps, in part, because of the decreased likelihood that they would become pregnant. These women were likely "acutely aware of how motherhood (although not fatherhood) was castigated in the mainstream art world, and realistic about the demands that children would make on their lives and careers." Mosaicist Jeanne Reynal, for one, said "I have not regretted being childless." Marrying young and raising children certainly would have derailed the Brutons' flourishing art careers. It seems to have been a compromise not one of them was willing to make.

By the early 1930s, Esther Bruton had received numerous favorable reviews and awards for her artwork. At this time, she turned her focus toward a series of large-scale commercial commissions. One of her biggest opportunities came shortly after Prohibition was revoked in December 1933. With Americans once again able to drink alcohol in public, many hotels began to update and refurbish their bar areas. In November 1934, the Fairmont Hotel in San Francisco hired architect Timothy Pflueger to redesign their cocktail lounge, and he provided Esther with one of her most important and successful mural projects.

One of the murals in the Cirque Room at the Fairmont Hotel, by Esther Bruton (1935)

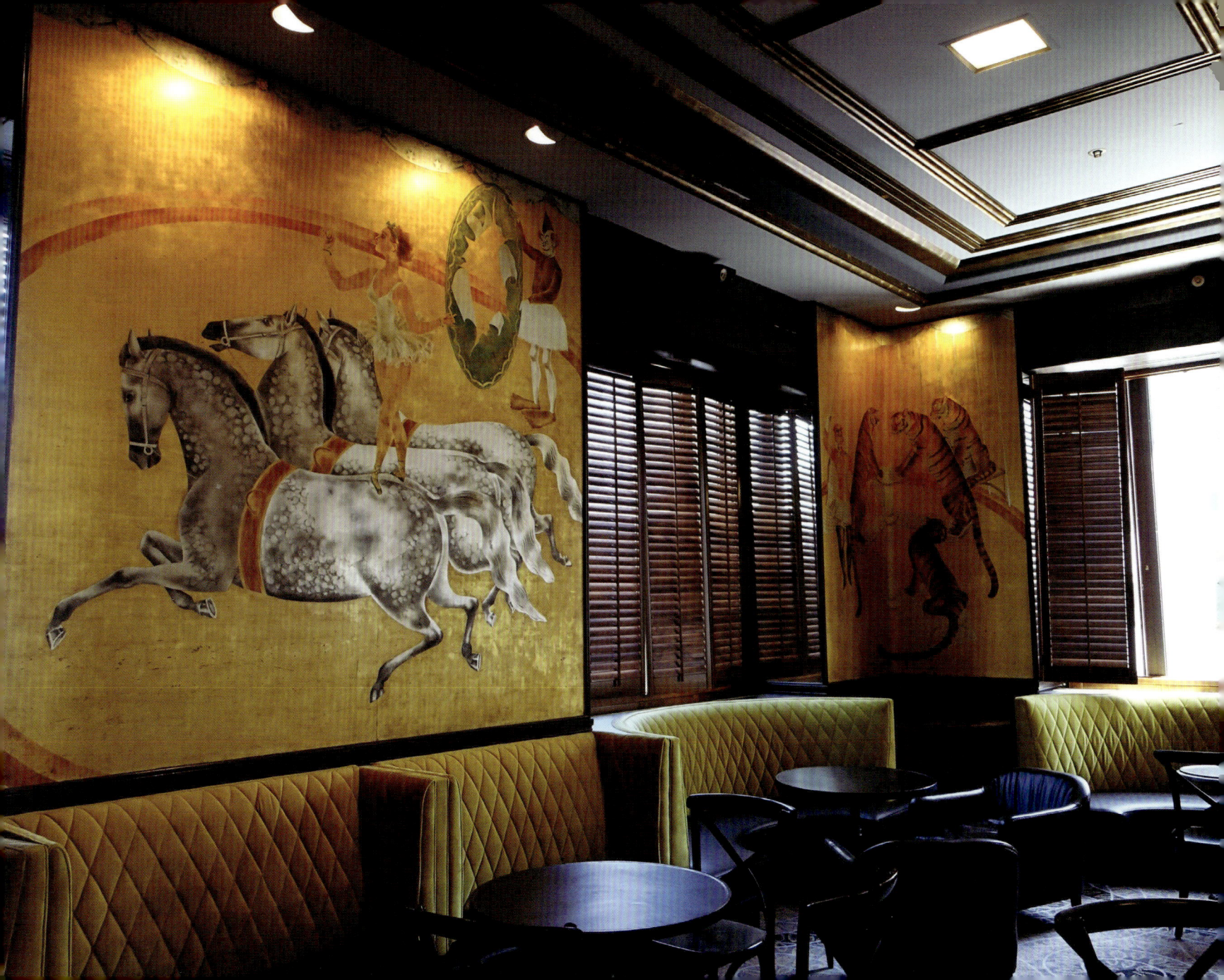

Pflueger, a San Francisco native, was known for his Art Deco style. He and his partner, James R. Miller, designed several landmark buildings in the downtown area. He was known for his fanciful design of some of the Bay Area's most decorative and beloved movie theaters, including the Castro Theater in San Francisco, the Oakland Theater, and the Alameda Theater. Many of Pflueger's buildings incorporate artwork such as murals and sculpture, and he worked closely with the Bay Area art community. When Pflueger first discovered the Bruton sisters' art, he "immediately saw in the work of the three sisters more imagination, more talent and greater facility of adaptation than he had encountered for a long time." Pflueger collaborated with the Brutons on a number of projects during the 1930s, and over the years they developed a productive professional relationship. "He was such a favorite with artists," Helen recalled. "He was really interested in using artists' work... but he let you do what you felt was the thing to do... He didn't have a preconceived picture in his mind that he wanted to transfer to your mind."

Pflueger and Miller's design for the Fairmont Hotel's cocktail lounge was an Art Deco masterpiece that caused an instant sensation in the press. The playful and lavish space literally sparkled with a silver-leaf ceiling, silvered Venetian blinds, gold moldings, and mirrored octagonal columns. Modern metal tables, leather upholstery, and a sleek, semi-circular bar added to the luxurious appearance. In addition to these decadent materials and surfaces, Pflueger wanted to decorate the lounge with large murals. He hired Esther Bruton, one of his favorite artists, to paint them. On January 8, 1935, Pflueger wrote in his day book that "the decision on Bruton paintings is unanimous, so go to it."

It is not clear how a circus theme was chosen for the lounge's murals, although it seems likely that Esther had a hand in the decision. The circus had long been a favorite

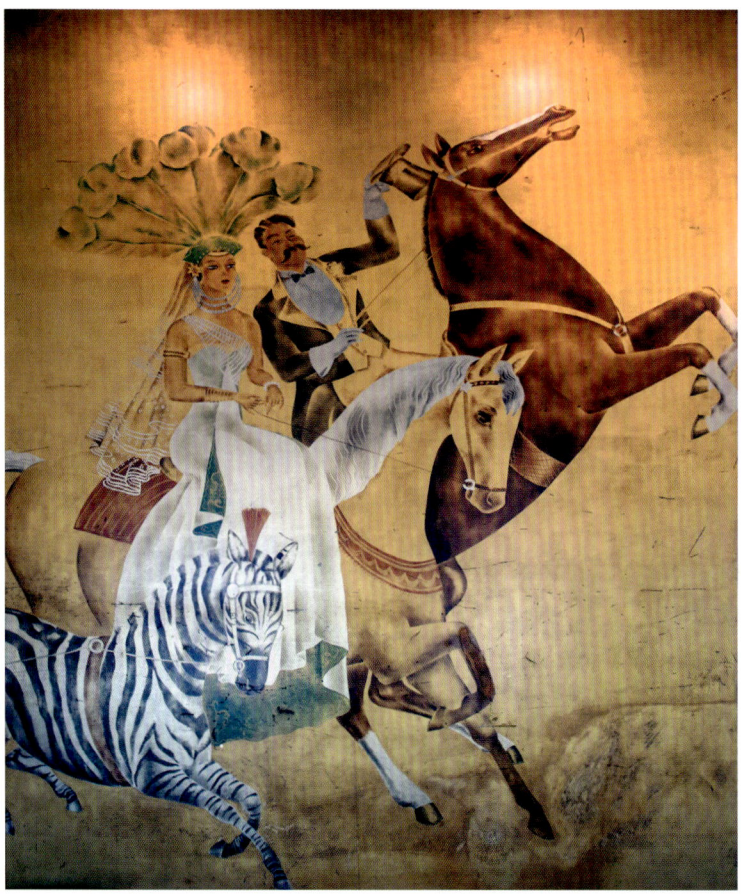

One of the murals in the Cirque Room at the Fairmont Hotel, by Esther Bruton (1935)

One of the murals in the Cirque Room at the Fairmont Hotel, by Esther Bruton (1935)

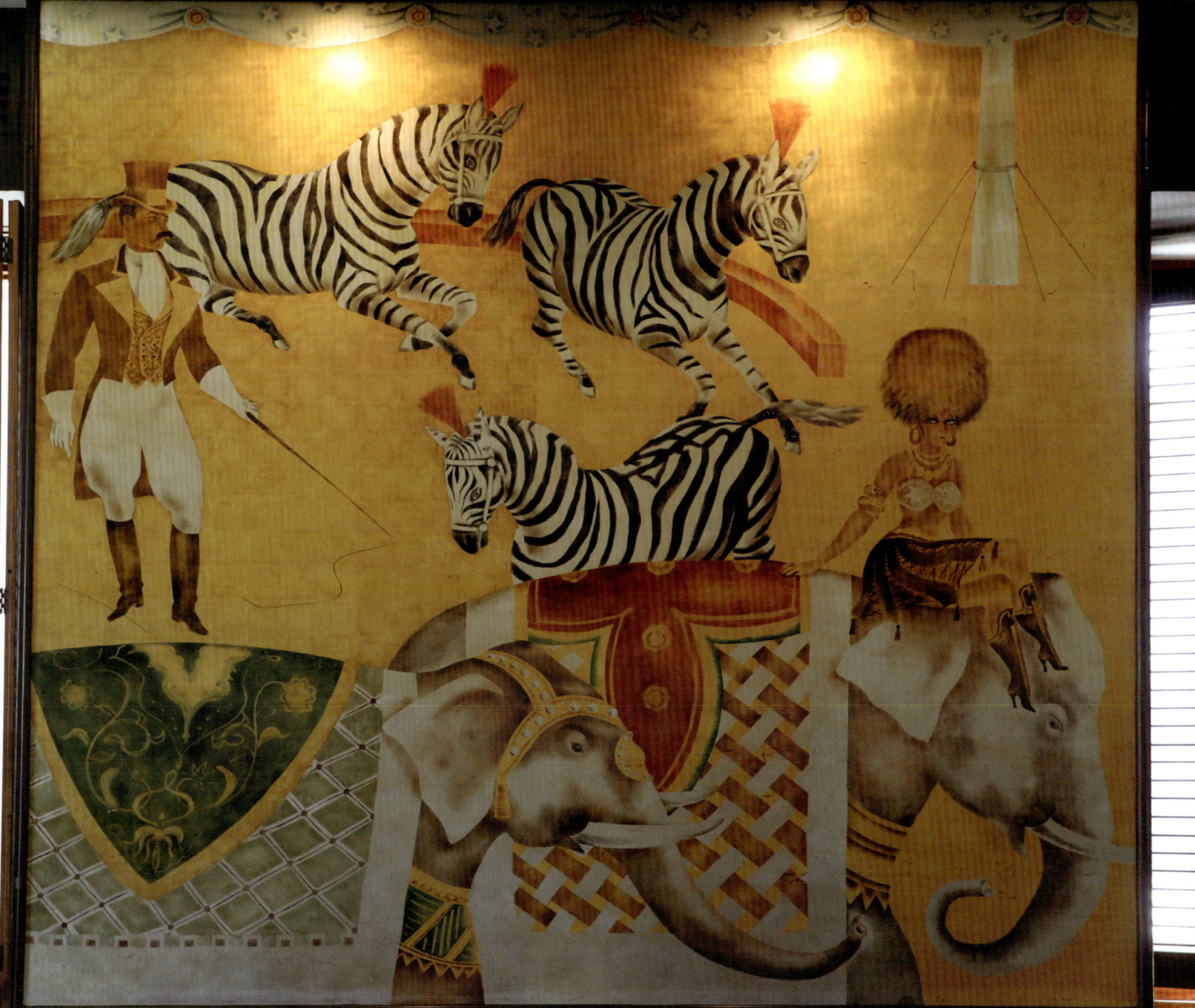

subject of hers, and she turned to this theme regularly in many of her woodcuts and etchings. Esther had never worked on a project of this scale—nine large wall murals—but she drew from her past successes and rose to the challenge. Perhaps her most important artistic decision was to use gold leaf, a medium that she had successfully used as the background in her two Taos screens. Gold leaf sheets are very small and extremely thin—so light that they easily float away—and must be applied to an area that has been treated with an adhesive while using special tools. Esther needed extra help using this tricky medium on such an enormous scale, so she hired some professionals to assist. Unfortunately they "did such a terrible job on the first day, and wasted so much gold leaf" that Esther fired them. As was frequently the case with the Brutons, she then called on one of her sisters to help, in this instance Margaret, who "did a very workman-like job of it, in half the time, I'm sure, and [using] half the gold leaf." Esther painted brightly colored figures on the gold background, including flying trapeze artists, acrobats, a ringmaster, and performing circus animals such as tigers, horses, zebras, giraffes, and elephants. Her murals made a luxurious and elegant statement that melded perfectly with Pflueger's lavish vision for what was called the Cirque Room. Helen considered it a lovely room and thought that Pflueger's design had been executed with finesse and discretion.

Credited as being one of the first bars in San Francisco to open after Prohibition, the Cirque Room made its debut with an elegant dinner dance on May 10, 1935. From the start, Esther's work was the center of attention. Junius Cravens of the *San Francisco News* attended the opening party and devoted the majority of his article to praising Esther's murals, saying,

> The Fairmont Circus Lounge... is an artistic
> achievement. This has become possible partly because

Timothy Pflueger... procured a real artist—and just the right real artist—to design and execute the decorations. The Circus is a subject made to order for Esther Bruton... in rendering [the murals] she has proven her creative strength by dominating her subject and utilizing it merely as a medium rather than an objective. The result is one of the best mural jobs that has yet been done in the Bay Region—a mural which decorates a room without overpowering it and seems to belong there. Aside from their artistic merits, Miss Bruton's decorations are delightfully humorous caricatures of the Circus scene. The artist appears to have had so much fun doing them... they are rendered with admirable restraint and in excellent taste.

An article devoted to the new bars and lounges in San Francisco said that "nothing can increase the pleasure of drinking a perfect cocktail but if anything can, the work of Miller and Pflueger, architects, and Esther Bruton, the mural painter, have done it... If this room cannot persuade you to two cocktails it will, at least, tempt you to linger over one." Esther's murals were such a hit that the bar named a cocktail after her using her nickname: the "Ecky." Yet, even before the bar opened to the public, at least one newspaper erroneously reported that "the Bruton sisters painted the new cocktail room." Although Margaret had assisted with the gold leaf, the murals are unquestionably Esther's creation and the result of her unique vision. Margaret and Helen have always insisted that "the entire credit for this work belongs to Esther."

The Cirque Room remained extremely popular over the years, especially with socialites and celebrities. When the lounge closed in 1959, its furniture was put in storage and its doors were boarded up. In a 1975 interview, Helen lamented that the murals are "all gone now." Miraculously, and unbeknownst to Helen, they had survived. In 1981, the Fairmont Hotel restored and refurbished the lounge to look almost exactly as it had in the 1930s. The former owner and president of the Fairmont, Richard Swig, tracked down the Bruton sisters and invited them to participate in the renovation. "We were lucky we didn't lose those paintings," he said. The Bruton sisters "were thrilled."

Esther earned another commercial commission when she was hired to paint murals for the Hawaiian Pineapple Company's 1936–1937 advertising campaign. Although she had not been to Hawaii, Esther drew upon her memories of Tahiti to paint several scenes depicting native people in exotic tropical settings. Her murals were featured prominently in several magazine advertisements, providing the backdrop for tableaus of elegantly dressed adults—including Hollywood actors Eleanore Whitney and Johnny Downs—sipping glasses of Dole pineapple juice. These ads appeared in popular magazines such as *Woman's Home Companion*, *Ladies Home Journal*, and the *Saturday Evening Post*. Over the years, a number of other respected artists were hired to provide illustrations for the Hawaiian Pineapple Company, including Millard Sheets, Miguel Covarrubias, Cassandre, and Georgia O'Keeffe. At least one of Esther's murals from the Hawaiian Pineapple Company's advertising campaign survived; a folding screen entitled *The Three Graces* depicts three Hawaiian women bathing in a stylized lagoon. The figures are embraced by circular patterns on the white and gold water, and more patterns cover the surfaces of the surrounding rocks and foliage, giving the work an exceptional depth and richness.

Also in the mid-1930s, Esther was hired by the California and Hawaiian Sugar Refining Corporation of San Francisco—

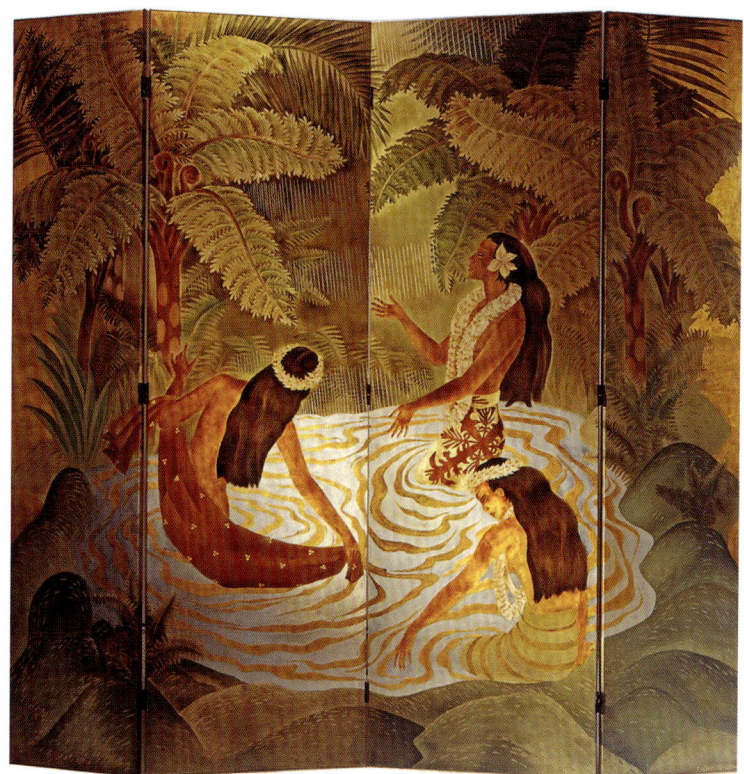

The Three Graces, by Esther Bruton (1936)

known today as C&H—to provide illustrations for a brochure with the title *Behind Your Sugar Bowl: The Story of Sugar in Words and Pictures*. The pamphlet is a feel-good history of the sugar industry that describes the process of how sugarcane is grown, harvested, transported, and refined into sugar. Its text was written by Neill C. Wilson, a minor novelist who wrote books about the Old West, and its black-and-white photographs were taken by Roger Sturtevant, a respected photographer who belonged to a Bay Area photography circle that included Edward Weston, Johan Hagemeyer, Imogen Cunningham, and Cunningham's husband, Roi Partridge. At some point, Esther posed for Sturtevant. His photograph of her captures the pensive young artist with bangs and bobbed hair, wearing a chunky beaded necklace.

Behind Your Sugar Bowl avoids entirely the labor abuses associated with the sugar cane industry and instead provides a glowing description of Crockett, California, the company town that was home to the C&H sugar refinery. The pamphlet boasts that "sunshine and blue water combine to make Crockett's setting one of tonic healthfulness and beauty." Esther's sweet and colorful illustrations enhance the idealist text in the pamphlet and would be appropriate for a children's book. The frontispiece features her painting of cheerful, well-dressed field workers in natty bandanas chopping sugar cane. A white, castle-like factory appears in the distance. Her illustration of a sugar cane press makes the powerful machinery look like a child's toy. Within this sanitized overview of a complex and controversial industry, Esther Bruton's drawings are appealing, technically impressive, and typical of Depression-era artwork that idealizes the heroic worker and glorifies American industry.

Esther continued to work regularly during the late 1930s.

Perhaps due to the praise and publicity her Cirque Room murals had received, Esther was hired to add her artistic flair to another cosmopolitan hotel bar. In 1937, she was hired to paint murals for the Golden State Hotel in San Francisco, which was adding an inviting lounge area as many hotels did following the end of Prohibition. She created California-themed murals of "daring modernistic design" for Tier's Cocktail Lounge. Esther described the project in a letter to Ina Perham:

> I finished the Golden State bar murals... and the joint is open this Saturday "amid a blare and blast of publicity" according to the new prop[rietor]... The murals are early S.F. and environs—Montgomery Street waterfront—volunteer fire department—stagecoach—Indians—vaqueros—and so forth—sounds wild and is.

When Tier's Cocktail Lounge opened in September 1937, the *San Francisco Examiner* announced that its murals—"done in delicate tones and blend[ing] effectively with the newer, simpler trend of the modern furnishings"—were "quite widely acclaimed."

When Lee Randolph, director of the California School of Fine Arts, viewed Esther's murals at the Golden State Hotel, he wrote her a flattering letter. "I was so thrilled by the beautiful effect you have achieved that I felt impelled to write you this note," he said. "The decorations inside the bar are so full of wit, gay color, and charm. One of the [hotel] managers... agreed with me that of their kind nothing better could be found in the world anywhere. Certainly you should be congratulated for having produced something of such beauty and value." Despite this lavish praise, it doesn't appear that these murals exist today. The works were likely torn down or painted over during a later renovation of the hotel, which today is called the Hotel Union Square. In 1976, Helen reported that Esther's murals had been "wiped out... by tobacco smoke... [they were] too delicate." Fortunately, three of Esther's technical blueprints for the murals survived, and these give us a good indication of what the murals would have looked like. Her work depicting the volunteer fire department is a humorous and chaotic scene of firefighters rushing down the street, pulling their engine behind them as spectators look on. A second mural features vaqueros galloping aside a herd of cattle, while a third mural depicts the Wells Fargo stagecoach being attacked by Native Americans wearing feathered headdresses and wielding bows and arrows.

Shortly after Esther completed the murals at the Golden State Hotel, she and Margaret departed for a spontaneous three-week road trip through the Southwest. Esther wrote an eight-page letter to Ina Perham describing their adventures. In addition to visiting three national parks—Zion, Bryce, and the Grand Canyon—they attended an "inter-tribal ceremonial" in Gallup, New Mexico, where they ran into their friend Maxine Albro. Esther described the Native American gathering as "purely Indian—no fat Rotarians in ten-gallon hats. The dances were beautiful and plentiful—the spectacle as a whole thrilling. There was a large exhibit of hand crafts and so forth—some of the finest I've seen." She went on to provide a detailed description of the rest of the trip, revealing not only her adventurous spirit, but her sincere, ongoing fascination with Native American culture:

> From there we headed up into the Navajo and Hopi country. We were camping so made out o.k.... The Hopi mesa villages were terribly exciting. That whole county thrilling... Camped one night atop Oraibi mesa

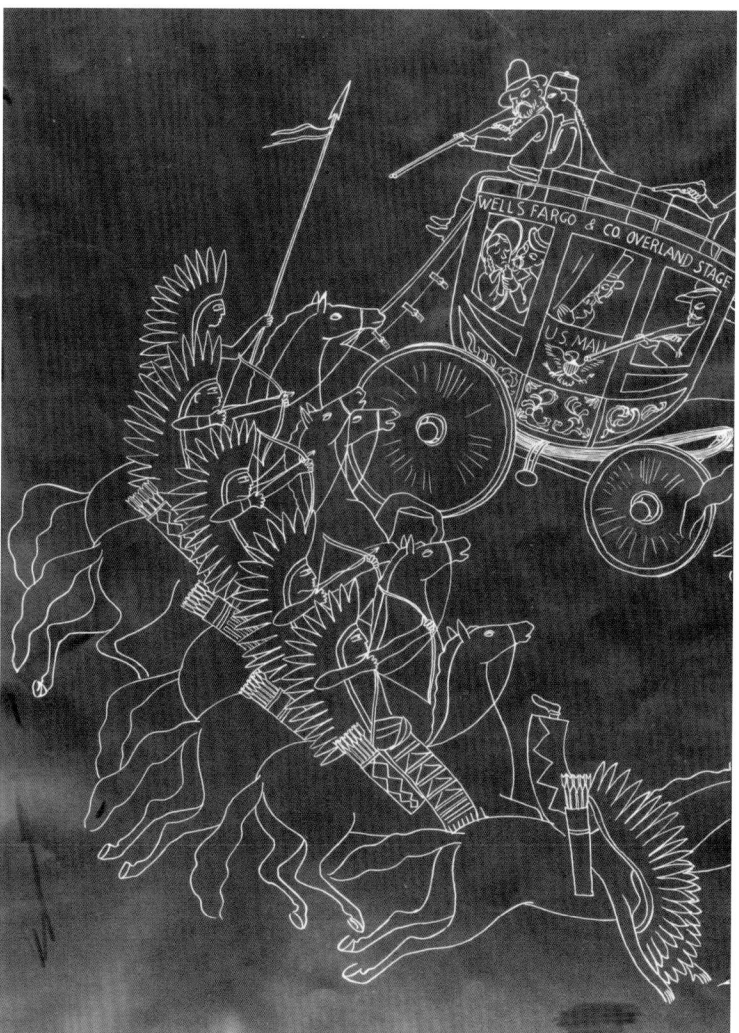

Preliminary drawing for a mural in the Golden State Hotel, by Esther Bruton (1937)

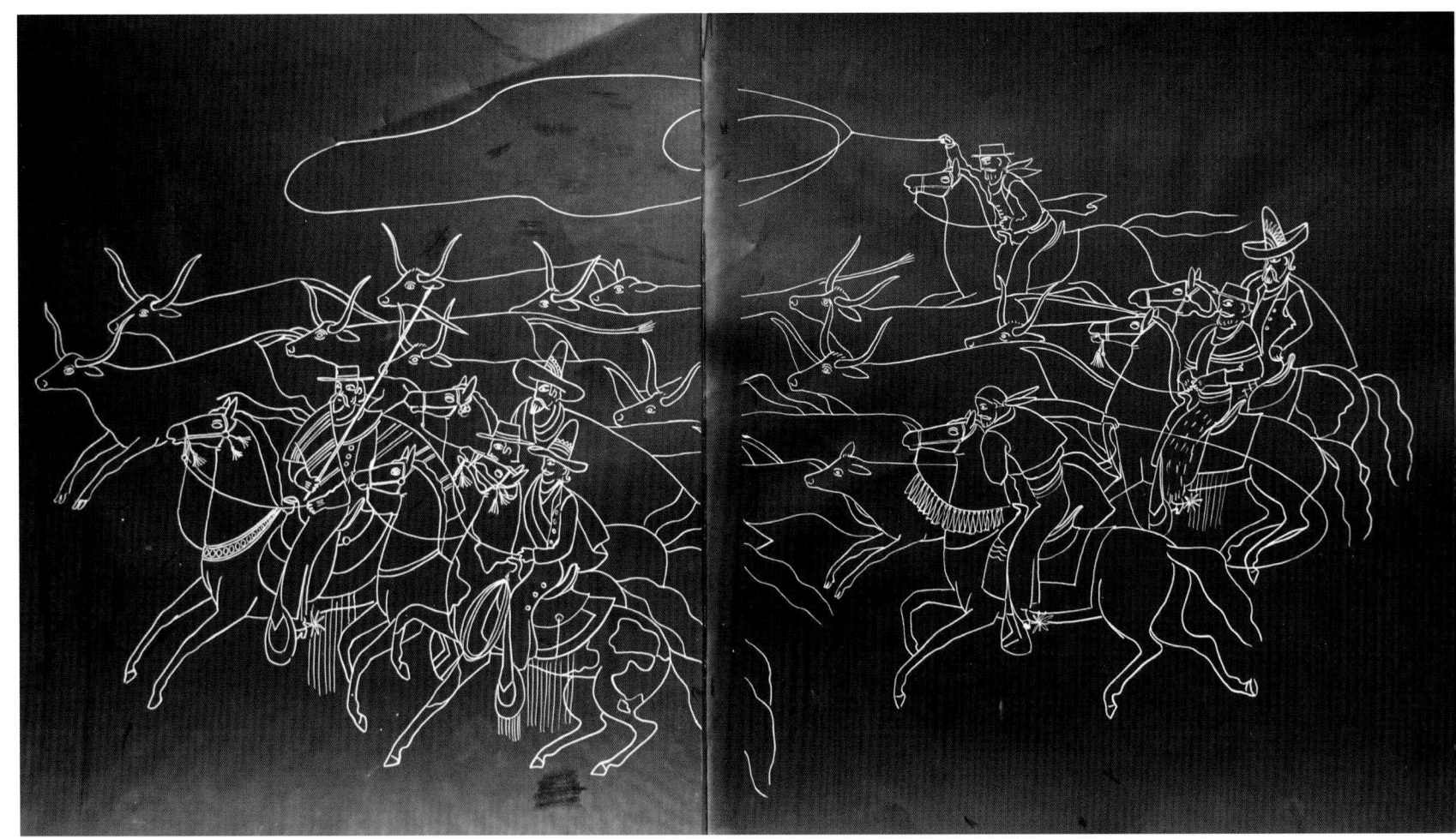

Preliminary drawing for a mural in the Golden State Hotel, by Esther Bruton (1937)

with a clear view out all over the world. Came quite unexpectedly on two dances. One was in Walpi, it was the old Hopi Butterfly Dance and ninety young people danced. Thrilling indeed to see the dance in that old village way up in the sky.

Esther's passion for the American Southwest is evident in this letter. "How I love that desert country," she wrote. "One snoot full of that air which is like wine and I purr. I see I shall soon end up in the desert—the writing is on the wall." Esther never did move to the Southwest; she lived the rest of her life in California.

By the end of the 1930s, Esther was a famous mural painter. She was hired for another large project, this time at the luxurious I. Magnin department store, which was under construction in downtown Los Angeles. Architect Myron Hunt designed the Art Deco marble building, and the interior, with its sumptuous furniture, finishings, and decorations, was the work of Esther's friend and colleague, architect Timothy Pflueger. Obviously delighted with what she had achieved in the Cirque Room, Pflueger again hired Esther to paint a series of large murals, this time in the "sports salon" of the department store, the section which sold casual menswear. Instead of using the gold leaf that had worked so well for her in the Cirque Room, Esther selected silver as her background. The murals were painted on "pewter colored Chinese paper with metal leaf applique and color." Another reporter described the works as "painted on luminous metal foil, depicting the various California sports to which the floor is dedicated."

Photographs reveal that Esther painted three large murals on the curved wall of the sports salon. The mural on the left is a scene that resembles the Northern California coastline, with windswept trees, a rocky shoreline, and two young women standing in the water, attempting to catch leaping fish in their nets. The center mural is a desert scene with a man and woman in their Western finery on horseback, riding through a cacti-covered landscape. The mural to the right is a tropical scene, with two women in bathing suits playing with a dog on a shell-covered beach surrounded by a bamboo grove. The connection between these murals and "California sports" is somewhat tenuous, but nevertheless they are beautifully done. Her stylized depiction of foliage and water on the two outer murals shows the influence of Asian prints and screens. Esther's humor comes through in her depiction of the riders in the center mural. The overdressed cowgirl, her blonde curls peeking out from an oversized sombrero, looks straight ahead with wide eyes as if she's uncomfortable or even terrified. The cowboy, smirking and with his chin lifted arrogantly, is unaware of his partner's distress. A photograph of Esther's murals appeared in *Vogue* magazine. The flagship I. Magnin department store on Wilshire Boulevard closed in the early 1990s. It is unknown whether Esther's murals have survived subsequent changes to the building.

In the midst of her frequent commercial commissions, Esther still had time to star in one of the most fascinating San Francisco social events of the 1930s. The "Parilia Ball," which took its name from a pagan spring festival originally celebrated in ancient Rome, was a fundraiser for the San Francisco Art Association. The first Parilia was held in 1927 and then not again until 1934, after Prohibition was repealed, when it was held annually until 1939. Part pageant and part bacchanalia, the Parilia was one of the wildest and most extravagant parties of the year, incorporating elaborate props, lavish sets, and exotic entertainment. Each year a different theme was selected,

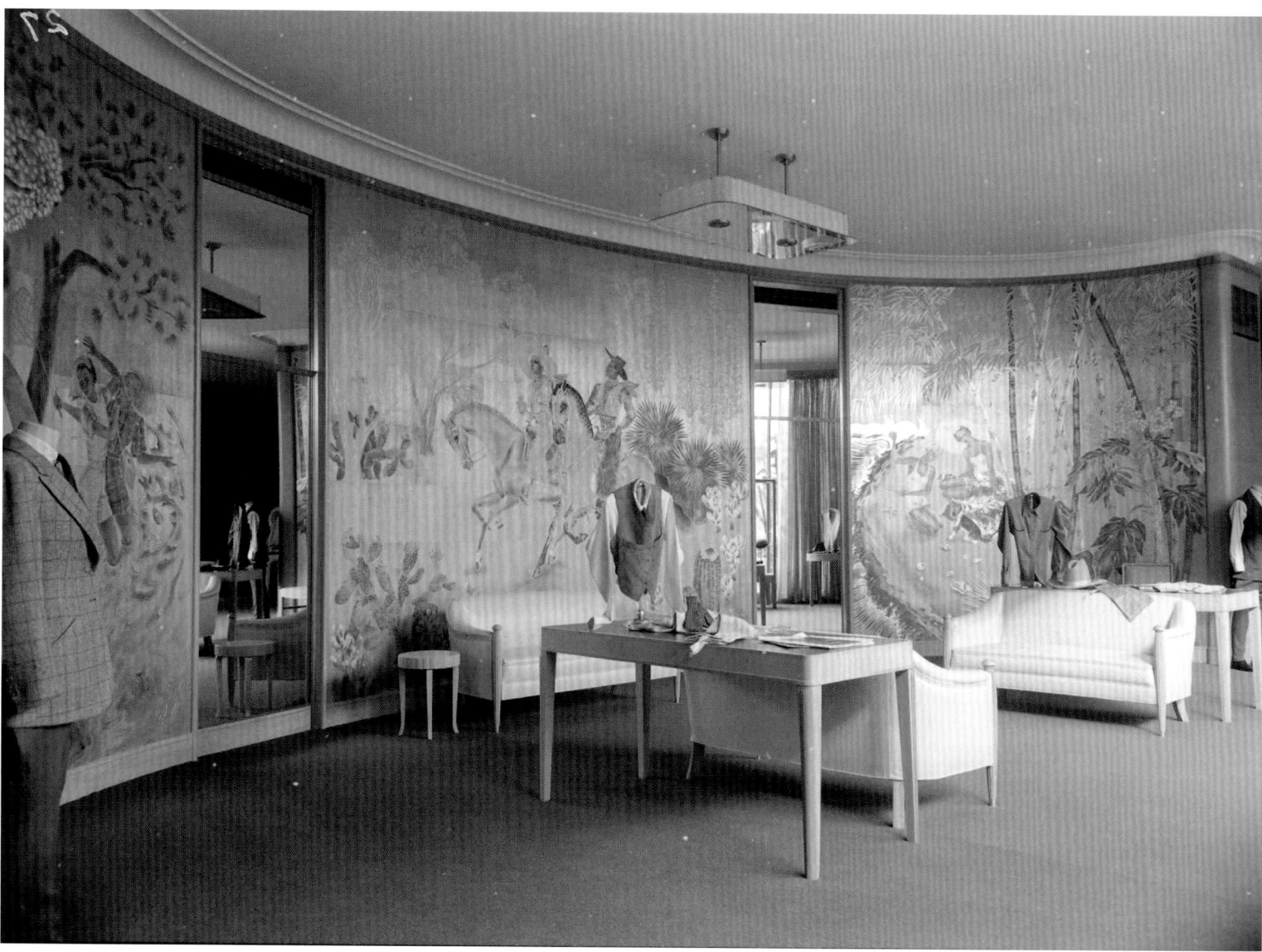

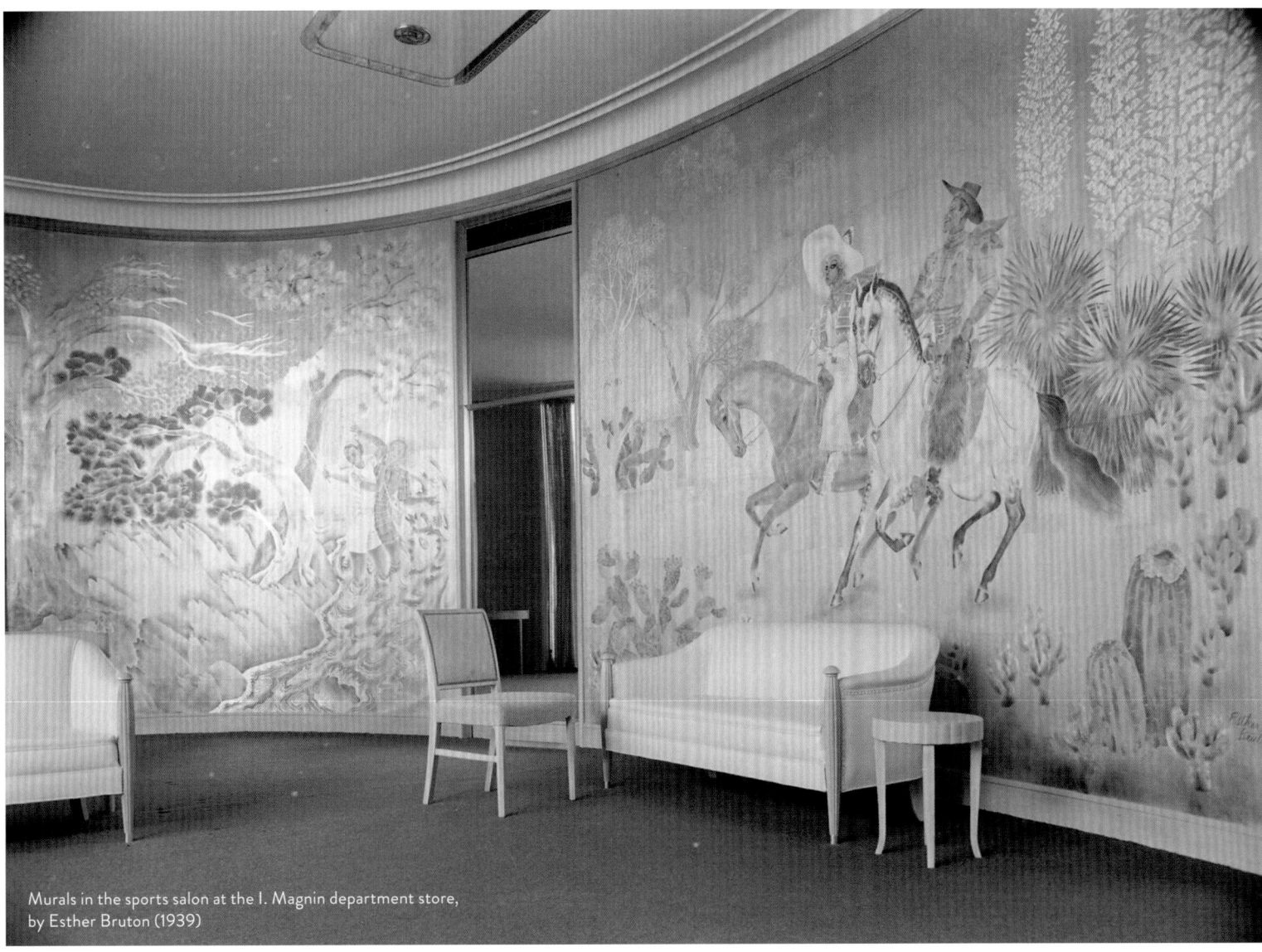

Murals in the sports salon at the I. Magnin department store,
by Esther Bruton (1939)

along with a king and queen to preside over the festivities. Hundreds participated in the pageant and thousands attended the event, which sold tickets at a variety of price points; the wealthy could purchase box seats or reserved tables, while those with a more limited budget could obtain floor tickets for a somewhat affordable $2.50.

Costumes were mandatory at the Parilia and many were creative, exotic, and risqué. Newspaper articles frequently commented on the "bizarre and scanty" outfits. The barely clothed revelers became such an issue that by 1938, the organizers insisted that the Parilia was "going in for more modesty, less nudity this year." With the repeal of Prohibition, the overconsumption of alcohol at the Parilia Ball was inevitable, and the annual parties typically got out of control. A "menu" for one of them is two pages long, detailing the selections of beer, wine, champagne, and hard liquor; the only food items available were ham-and-egg sandwiches and hot dogs, which were listed almost as an afterthought on the bottom of the second page.

The day after the 1934 Parilia, the cleanup crew had to "remove a few dozen 'bodies' from beneath boxes, behind curtains, and from under tangled decorations." The 1937 party made the front page of the *San Francisco Examiner* with the headline "13 injured, 15 jailed in Parilia." In their defense, party-goers explained that the auditorium drinking fountains had been turned off so that the liquor concessions could do more business. The following year, the newspaper reported further debauchery with the sarcastic headline, "Parilia tame, only 21 drunks land in jail."

Each year, two respected Bay Area artists were crowned king and queen of the Parilia Ball. Esther was selected as queen of the 1936 Cambodian-themed Parilia, which was held in San Francisco's Civic Auditorium. Timothy Pflueger was in charge of the event and, having just worked with Esther on the enormously successful Cirque Room, it is likely that he recommended her to be crowned "Queen Naga." The king of the Parilia was another of Pflueger's favorite artists, Victor Arnautoff. He and Esther were identified by the *San Francisco Examiner* as "prominent and popular younger artists of San Francisco."

At the 1936 Parilia—depicting the "Fall of Angkor Wat"—Bruton and Arnautoff rode into the pageant on a life-sized mannequin of a white elephant and sat on thrones before an enormous green Buddha that had been sculpted by artist Robert Howard. A cast of more than eight hundred danced, performed ceremonies, and marched in processions in front of nearly 9,000 spectators on a stage as wide as a city block. Junius Cravens called it "one of the most resplendent pageants that has been staged anywhere in our time… adjectives seem inadequate in attempting to describe it." The costumes were as racy as ever, consisting of "beads and very little more." Helen later recalled the Parilia Balls were "one of the most interesting goings on of that decade… They were terrific. They were artist parties, of course. The trouble is that they got so rowdy toward the end." The Parilia Balls of the 1930s were the perfect antidote to a society recently released from Prohibition, yet still struggling through the deprivations of the Depression. What better way to forget your troubles, at least for one night, than to don a racy costume, drink heavily, and escape into an elaborate fantasy world?

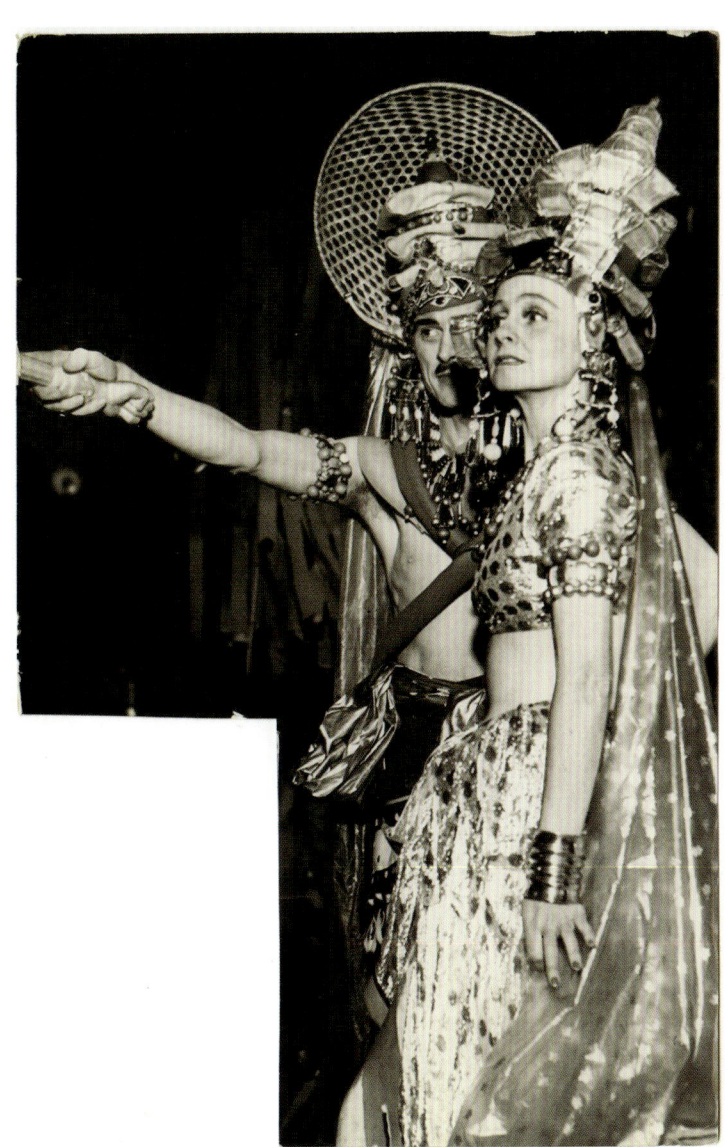

Esther Bruton as "Queen Naga" and Victor Arnautoff as the king of the 1936 Parilia Ball

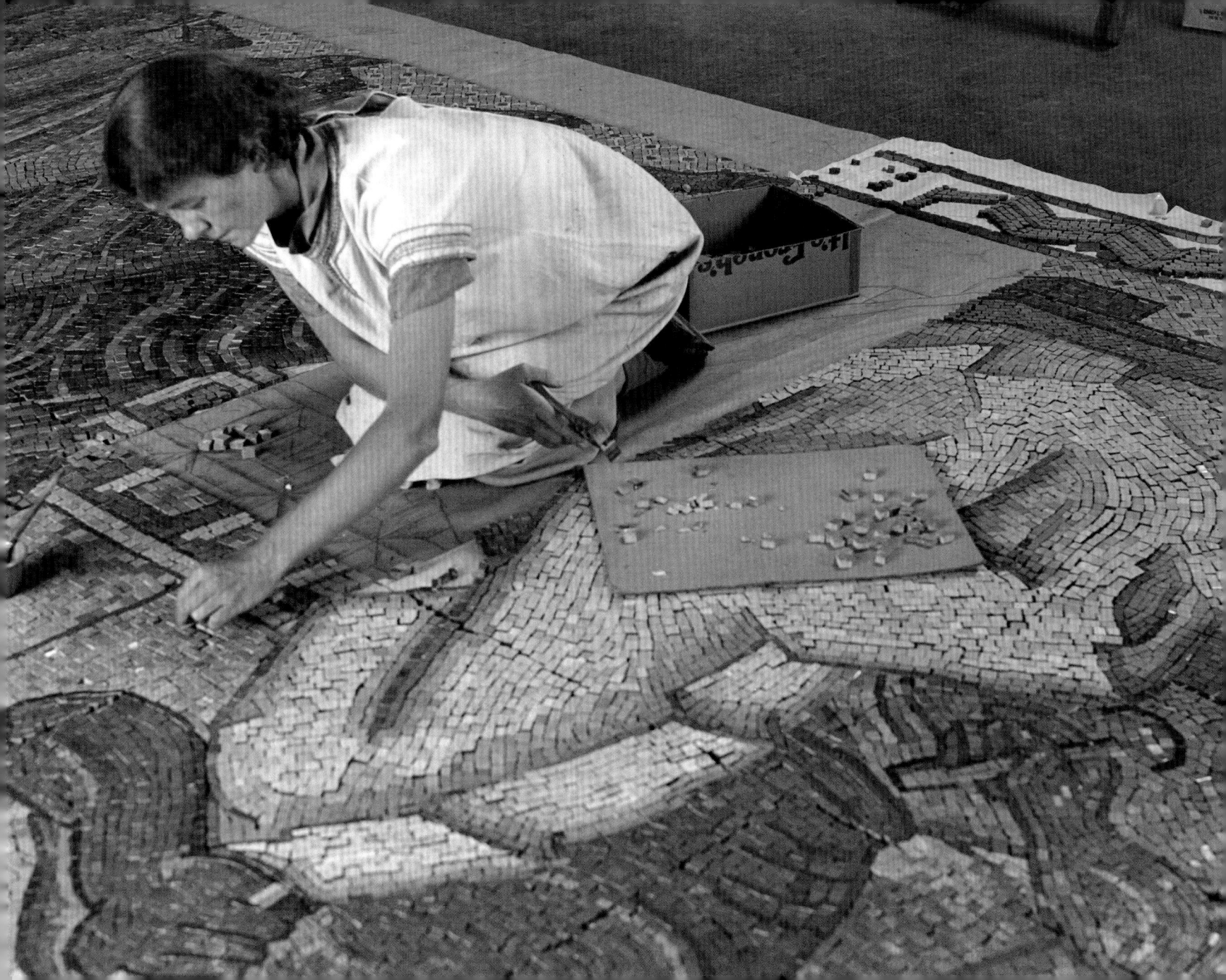

CHAPTER SEVEN

Helen Bruton and the "Modern Mosaic Revival"

(1933–1939)

When she first went to Monterey in the early 1920s, Helen Bruton was working as "a polite lady sculptress" in a studio on Pacific Street once occupied by William Merritt Chase. She had some modest success at first. In 1925 she won an honorable mention at the San Francisco Art Association exhibition for her series of bas-reliefs *The White Doe, Nos. 1, 2 and 3.* She felt that she hadn't accomplished much in sculpture, although she still liked "to fiddle around and squeeze things out of clay." Despite the prizes and awards she had won for her prints, by the mid-1930s Helen was becoming frustrated with the very technical etching process. "By the time I would get a plate scratched it would be practically ruined anyway. I'd make so many proofs and really mess it up generally." Helen was ready for a new challenge, which came when she was selected to participate in the New Deal art programs of the 1930s.

The federal government's Public Works of Art Project (PWAP), launched in December 1933, provided support for artists who were unemployed during the Depression. The program served the dual purpose of providing work for artists while at the same time beautifying public spaces for the enjoyment of all Americans. The PWAP lasted just five months but was followed by a parade of other relief programs for artists that went by various acronyms, including the Treasury Relief Art Project (TRAP) and the Federal Art Project (FAP), the latter falling under the jurisdiction of the Works Progress

Helen Bruton in the studio working on her mosaic for UC Berkeley, photo by Imogen Cunningham (1936)

Administration (WPA). Along with the PWAP, the WPA, which was launched in the fall of 1935, employed thousands of artists and resulted in tens of thousands of artworks, including hundreds of murals in schools, post offices, government buildings, and other public places. The art funded by these government programs had a different feel from the modernist art that had come before it. In the face of mass unemployment and, in some cases, even starvation, "the aesthetic preoccupations of the 1920s seemed effete and irrelevant... There was a great movement back to representational and realistic art for social propaganda and for the depiction of the American scene." Although their projects required approval from program organizers, artists had a surprising degree of freedom to choose their own subject matter and designs.

The PWAP and WPA also provided unique opportunities for women artists. The programs "were required to follow an equal opportunity policy in hiring... Women artists were hired without discrimination." This was the opinion of artist Lee Krasner, who observed "there was no discrimination against women that I was aware of in the WPA." Not only could women make a living from their art—in many cases for the first time—they also found themselves at the helm of large-scale commissions, supervising male workers, and coping with complicated logistics. Many women artists who participated in WPA programs looked back on that time as a golden age of opportunity. Painter Helen Lundeberg called the WPA "a great thing for most artists... [My WPA] project saved the day. It gave me enough to live on, and also made just being an artist okay." Women artists, including the Brutons, were the beneficiaries of an enlightened period in art when women "felt a great sense of camaraderie and equality with their male colleagues."

Dr. Walter Heil, director of the de Young Museum in San Francisco, was selected as the regional director of the PWAP for Northern California, Nevada, and Utah. In December 1933, Heil held a meeting to assign projects to sixty Bay Area artists, including Helen Bruton. Helen was the only Bruton hired for the PWAP—only one family member at a time could participate—but she always intended to share the job with her sisters. Despite reports to the contrary, there were very few projects that the Brutons shared equally; there was always one sister in charge. Of their working arrangements, Helen stated in 1964, "We didn't often collaborate actually, but one would always be sort of standing by, to help if necessary. Marge would always help me if I needed her and vice versa. And the same way with Esther." Although Helen was in charge of the PWAP project, she relied on her sisters' help and was more than willing to share her minimal weekly payment with them. As she said, "I was the only one that was officially on the payroll... We divided that in three, so we didn't exactly get wealthy over it, but we thought that was the fairest way to do it."

One wonders how Helen Bruton proved that she was in need of financial assistance when she applied for government relief programs. She could certainly have demonstrated that she had no income—she and her sisters were all unemployed artists at the time—and she could have made the case that she was the head of the household for her family of four women, including her widowed mother, but her true financial need might have been more difficult to assess. The family still had considerable assets, including an elegant home in Alameda, a house in Monterey, an apartment building in San Francisco, and other financial reserves—it is possible that these were not taken into account. The WPA itself acknowledged that there were no clear guidelines for providing assistance. In some cases "extreme destitution had to be shown before persons would be certified either for direct relief or for WPA employment," while in other communities "there was a more liberal interpretation of need." Perhaps the youngest Bruton felt just a little guilty about taking money out of the pocket of another artist who needed the financial support more than the Bruton family. But it seems likely that for Helen, the chance to get back to work and do something big in the art world was an opportunity she wouldn't want to miss.

Helen's first assignment came in 1934, when she was commissioned to create exterior murals for the Mothers Building at the San Francisco Zoo. Built in 1925, the Mothers Building was originally part of the Fleishhacker Pool complex; it was later donated to the city of San Francisco and became part of the zoo's grounds. The ornate Italian Renaissance-style stone building, designed by San Francisco architect George W. Kelham, was built as a quiet retreat for mothers and their small children visiting the nearby pool, providing restrooms, nurseries, and refreshments. Artists Helen Forbes and Dorothy Puccinelli had been selected to paint murals inside the building, and Helen Bruton was assigned to create artworks for the exterior of the structure. Helen consulted her sisters for ideas, and as they discussed different designs, Margaret came up with the idea of using mosaic, since the medium was durable and the murals would be exposed to the elements.

At first, Helen "hardly knew what [Margaret] was talking about—that's how sophisticated I was at that time." She explained that "except for some little experiments that I had made, like a bird pool or a little thing like that, I hadn't done anything big in mosaic." Despite her lack of experience with the medium, Helen agreed that making a mosaic mural was a good idea. In fact, mosaics were especially well suited to New Deal projects, which often called for artworks to be installed outside where the public could enjoy them. Mosaics also complemented the architectural spaces they decorated, and were complex enough to keep a team of workers occupied for weeks. Helen identified two arched panels under the Mothers Building loggia—each space measuring thirteen feet high by six feet wide—that seemed like ideal locations for the mosaic murals. Little did the Brutons know that Margaret's suggestion of working in mosaic would send the sisters on an entirely new creative path; before long, they would be recognized as some of the most accomplished mosaic artists in California.

What Margaret had in mind for the Mothers Building murals was quite different from the technique Helen used for the philosopher mosaics at USC, where she painted her designs on large square tiles which were installed in a simple grid pattern. Instead, Margaret suggested that the sisters use tiny pieces of tile to create a complex design in the manner of traditional mosaics from ancient times.

Helen's murals for the Mothers Building were "some of the earliest, if not the first, public mosaics to be executed in San Francisco." At least one critic of the period credited the Brutons with playing a key role in the "modern mosaic revival," stating that they were "the only ones so far in this country who are attempting to adapt the ancient medium to modern motifs." Helen confirmed, in a 1975 interview, that she and

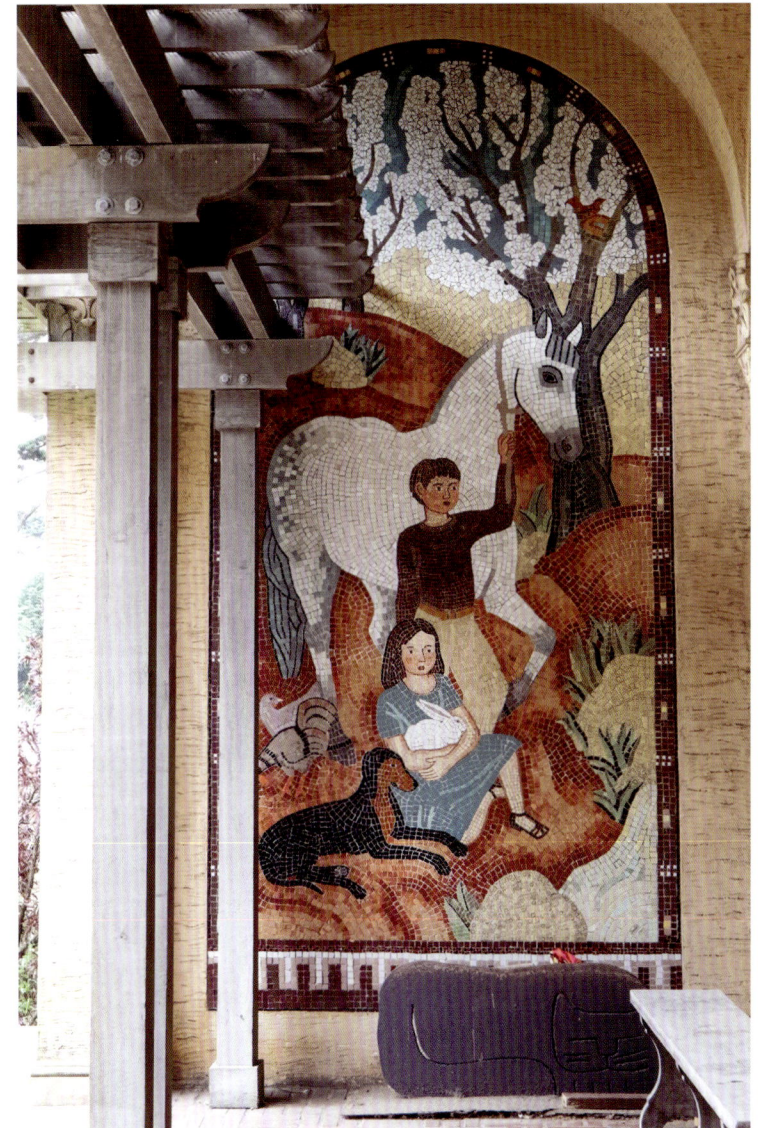

Children and Their Animal Friends mosaic at the Mothers Building at the San Francisco Zoo, by Helen Bruton (1934)

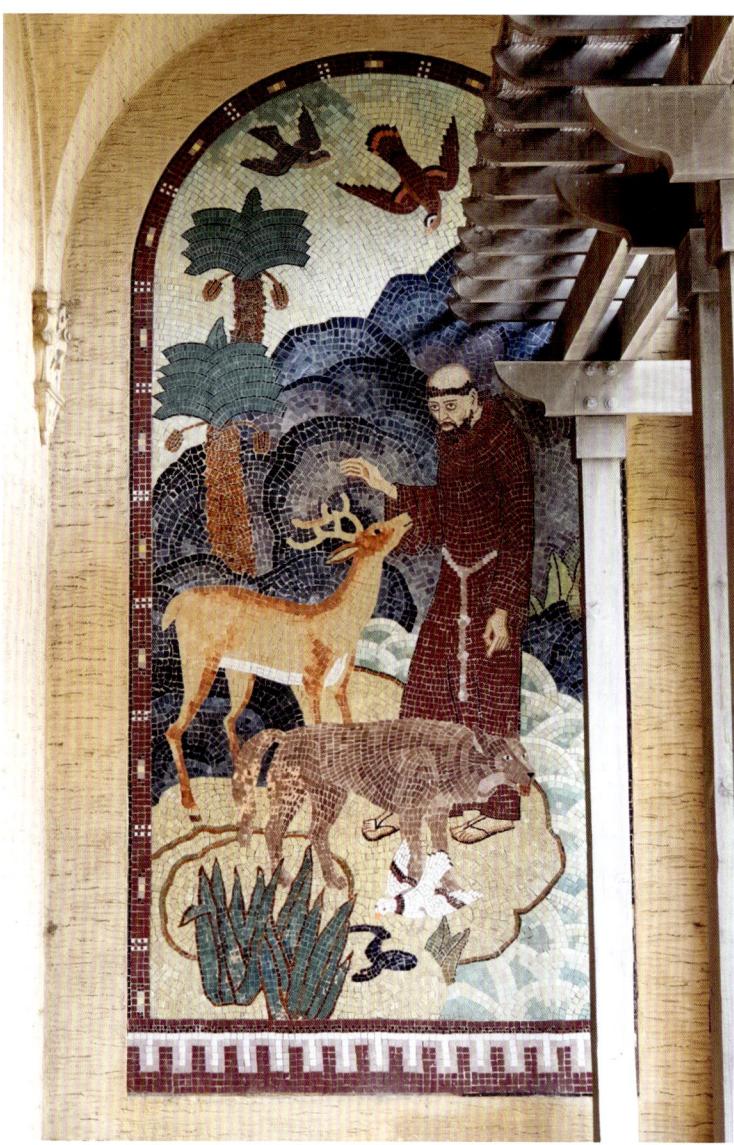

her sisters were the first artists to reintroduce the art form and use it in a modern context: "Nobody at that time was doing anything very much with mosaic." *The Van Nostrand Reinhold Manual of Mosaic*, a survey of the craft that discusses its history and techniques developed through the centuries, identifies Helen as "among the earliest pioneers of the [mosaic] revival" and recognizes her for "her role in reintroducing an awareness of mosaic in the United States."

The Brutons worked independently from Forbes and Puccinelli, who were painting inside the building; there was no consultation about unity of subject matter or style. Unsurprisingly, given that the Mothers Building was located in the zoo, both art projects focused on depictions of animals and children. Although "somebody else, probably Esther or Margaret, might have suggested the subject matter," the designs of the two mosaics were Helen's. One of them, *Children and their Animal Friends*, depicts a boy and a girl with a horse, dog, and rabbit. The second, *St. Francis*, features the patron saint of animals—for whom the city of San Francisco is named— surrounded by a deer, a wolf, a snake, and birds. Both are "gentle harmonious scenes [that] exemplify the hopeful nature of the New Deal."

The sisters had never attempted a large-scale mosaic project before, but their inexperience was strangely freeing according to Helen: "[We were] almost more fortunate in having to start from scratch than in having a rigid technique from which to break away." The Brutons found much-needed advice and guidance from their assistant, Italian master mosaicist Antonio Falcier, whose experience included mosaic work at Hearst Castle in San Simeon, California. As Helen said, "if it hadn't

St. Francis mosaic at the Mothers Building at the San Francisco Zoo, by Helen Bruton (1934)

been for Mr. Falcier, I don't know what we would have done, because he gave us pointers that we would have been quite helpless without."

The first hurdle in the mosaic process was gathering the right materials. In Depression-era California, it was almost impossible for American artists to procure the Venetian tiles used in traditional mosaics, so the sisters had to work with materials that were available. They found what they needed at the Solon and Schemmel Tile Company, also known as S&S, in San Jose. The company made a beautiful commercial terra-cotta tile, but the color of the product varied from lot to lot, frustrating craftspeople and architects when they tried to match tiles for a large project. This resulted in a fair amount of waste and seconds, a downside for S&S but a boon for the Brutons, who bought at a discount the tiles the company couldn't sell. The tiles' subtle variations in color, unacceptable to those seeking perfect uniformity, gave Helen's designs depth and complexity. The tiles used in St. Francis's brown robe, for example, vary from "fawn color" to "strong ochre" and even "deep Mars violet." Dorothy Puccinelli, working on the painted murals in the building's interior, remarked that "Helen's mosaics made with these carefully selected cast-offs have great richness and quality as well as fine design." *San Francisco Examiner* art critic Ada Hanafin concurred, saying, "The juxtaposition of little cubes, of similar but not quite identical color quality, endows the individual tones with a vibrancy and variety." Although their colors were ideal, the S&S tiles were too thick to be cut with tile nippers into the small pieces the Brutons required. To solve this problem, they went to a nearby marble works and had the machinists grind down the backs of the tiles to half the thickness.

Before the sisters worked on any large-scale project—

whether it was Esther's murals or Helen's mosaics—they did a considerable amount of preliminary work and technical planning. Although the intricacies of their process are unknown, it appears that they would start with a number of sketches followed by a small collage or painting to get the general feel for the layout and coloring of the finished work. This would be followed by an extremely detailed technical drawing or blueprint done on a small scale which they would use to execute a full-sized work. Surviving blueprints show that the finished works were nearly exact copies of the preliminary technical drawings. The quality of the Brutons' work didn't happen by chance—it was the result of exceedingly careful planning and organization.

For the Mothers Building mosaics, once the preliminary drawings were complete, the laying out of the individual tiles began—a time-consuming, physically demanding, and laborious process that also required copious amounts of space. Fortunately, the Brutons could work in their expansive attic studio in Alameda. The process would begin with the artist creating two identical cartoons, or full-sized drawings, based on the smaller technical drawing. These large drawings were cut into smaller, more manageable sections, and one copy of each section was placed on the floor recreating the mural drawing jigsaw-puzzle-style. The complexity of a project of this size is difficult to comprehend; a preliminary drawing of one of the mosaics reveals that each large mural was divided into almost ninety different sections, an extremely large jigsaw puzzle indeed. The design was then filled in with mosaic tiles, adhered face-up on the pieces of paper using Falcier's recipe for a paste made from flour, water, molasses, and vinegar. Helen described this process as "concentrated hard work," although she admitted she could have made it easier on herself by

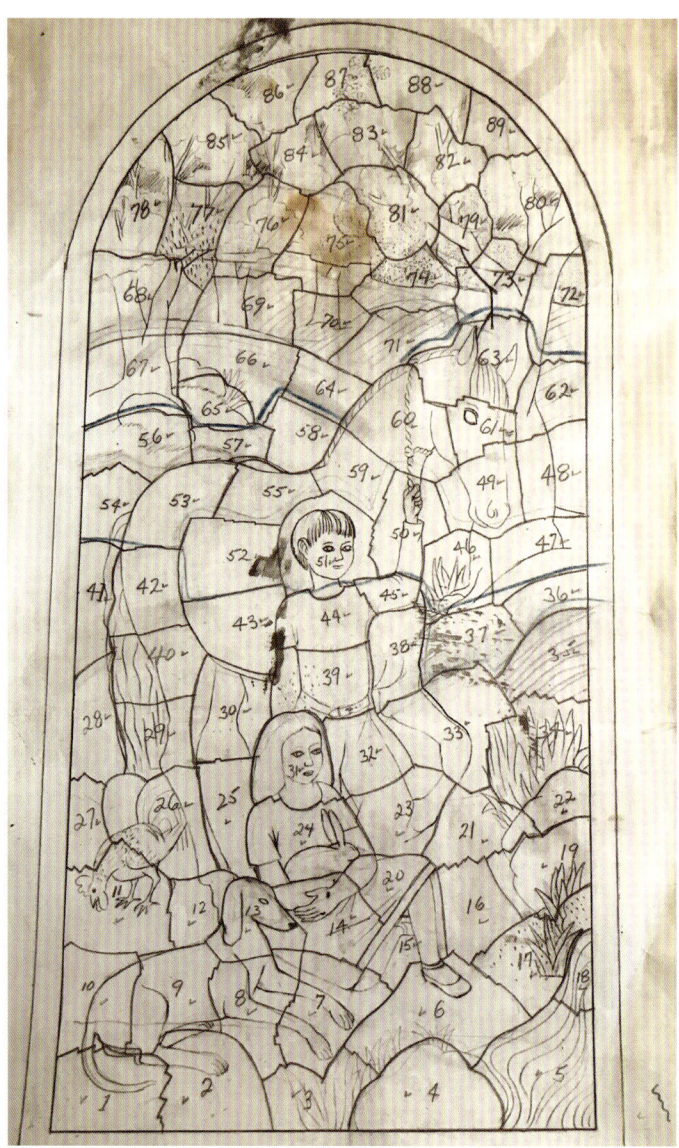

delegating more, rather than feeling a "jealous personal interest in the way each stone [was] placed."

Once the tiny ceramic pieces were glued on the paper and Helen was satisfied with the overall design of the two murals, Herbert and May Fleishhacker, the couple who donated the Mothers Building to the San Francisco Zoo, visited the Brutons in their Alameda attic studio to review the designs. As Helen remembered, Herbert Fleishhacker wanted "to see that there was not going to be anything offensive slipped in" before the mosaics were placed on the building that bore his name. Once the mosaics had received their final blessing from the Fleishhackers, the duplicate drawings were glued on top of the tiles to hold them in place. The surface paper was opaque and once it covered the tiles, it became difficult to identify the different sections. When the glue on the top paper was completely dry, the "sandwiched" mosaic was turned over, and the bottom paper was soaked off so that the sections could be attached to the wall.

Once assembled, the transportation and installation process for each of the two mosaic murals took about five days. For two exhausting weeks, Antonio Falcier met the sisters at 6 a.m. every morning to help them transport mosaic sections to the ferry in Alameda and travel across the bay to San Francisco. In addition to Falcier, Helen was assigned two male assistants to help with the installation of the mosaics. This was Helen's first time supervising a male staff, and she admitted that "it made me nervous because I wasn't used to delegating work and... [I didn't know] very much about mosaic myself." A woman in charge of male assistants was an untraditional arrangement at the time to be sure. She worked well with Leonard Meuman, whom she described as a "terribly nice, gentle, young man

Preliminary drawing for *Children and Their Animal Friends* (1934)

who was completely unsophisticated as far as art went—he was almost as bad as I was!" But there was another male worker—she couldn't remember his name—who made her feel uncomfortable. Helen said that he "was a nice enough man but I simply could not... work [with him]—he made me nervous." Although the details are unknown, it is entirely possible that this male worker was difficult to work with because he resented the fact that a woman was in charge of the project and, by extension, of him. Rather than confronting the assistant himself, Helen told the supervisors of the project that she didn't need an extra assistant, and he was reassigned elsewhere.

Fortunately, Helen's sisters were there for moral support, as was Falcier, who was on the job site every day, mixing plaster, helping with heavy lifting, and generally keeping the project on track. Once wet plaster was applied to the wall, Falcier showed the sisters how to place the sections of the mosaic starting at the bottom and working upward. It was essential that "the section that you were mounting was square enough in shape so that it didn't sag or settle too badly at one side or another, and begin to throw the thing out of whack." Once each section was set in the plaster, the paper attached to the face was peeled off and the mosaic was wiped clean and polished. Helen estimated that the entire project was completed in a surprisingly quick three months, although, in her words, "it knocked off a couple of years off my life getting it up there on the wall." The finished works have been described as "representational but not naturalistic" for their bold designs around perspective, shape, and color. Both mosaics at the San Francisco Zoo are signed "Bruton 1934." Given the extensive assistance she received from her sisters, perhaps Helen thought using just the family surname as a signature was only fair. Yet despite the help they provided,

Margaret and Esther never took credit for the Mothers Building mosaics or considered them their own artworks.

The decision to create the Mothers Building murals in mosaic was wise; the medium is quite durable, even when exposed to the elements. When Helen went to see the murals in the 1960s, she was pleased to discover that they looked as good as they did. "I can't see that there's been any deterioration at all," she said at the time. Even today, almost ninety years after their installation, Helen's mosaics at the Mothers Building remain in good condition. The only tiles showing any wear are on the St. Francis mosaic—some tiles and grout are missing and the tiles making up the wolf's tail and one of his hindquarters have lost their glazing. In contrast to the overall sturdiness of Helen's mosaics, the building's interior murals by Forbes and Puccinelli, which were painted in egg tempera, have been damaged by water and are in need of extensive conservation work.

Before long, Helen was hard at work on a second mosaic project. The Bay Area administrators of the WPA's Federal Art Project were always on the lookout for buildings in need of exterior embellishment, and one of the ones they selected was the Old Art Gallery on the University of California, Berkeley campus. The building, which was the former powerhouse for the university, was designed in 1904 by John Galen Howard, Berkeley's supervising architect during the first decades of the twentieth century. Helen was recruited for the project by her friend Florence Alston Swift, a Berkeley artist and wife of photographer Henry Swift, who had been hired for the project. Tapped to create mosaics for the niches on either side of the entrance of the building, they became the first women to make public art for the Berkeley campus.

Swift took the lead on the Berkeley murals project, choosing the performing arts as the theme in consultation with Berkeley art history professor Eugen Neuhaus. Helen recalled not having much say in the mosaics' subject matter: "It was more or less decided, I think, by Mrs. Swift, and maybe Mr. Neuhaus." Swift and Bruton collaborated on the style and color schemes for their respective murals and worked independently in their own studios. Florence Alston Swift's mosaic personifies the fields of music and painting with two standing women playing violins and a seated woman holding a palette and paint brushes. Helen Bruton's mosaic represents sculpture with a man straddling a large, white sculpture in progress and holding a chisel and hammer. Dance is represented by three female figures dancing in a row.

The artists included buildings from the Berkeley campus in the background of their works and used real people as models for some of the figures. Swift's seated woman is a portrait of Helen Wills Moody, a Berkeley alumnus and international tennis champion who was also an artist. At least one historian has remarked on the dancing women's "similarity to the slender Bruton sisters," although Helen claimed that the figures were not intended to be portraits.

It is tempting to assume that Helen's choice of women to represent dance and a man to represent sculpture demonstrates her acceptance of the "gendered divisions of the art world," where sculpture is "a genre under male control," yet such an assumption is completely unwarranted. Helen Bruton would never have suggested that sculpture was a male-dominated field; she once considered herself a sculptor, and some of her female friends—including Adaline Kent, Cecilia Graham, and Ruth Cravath—were sculptors. The figure of the male sculptor in her mosaic was modeled after Robert Boardman Howard, a sculptor and painter who was the son of the building's architect, John Galen Howard. As Helen explained, she used

him as a model not because of any conscious or unconscious gender statement, but because she felt he "had significance in relation to the building."

Artists hired by the WPA were encouraged to represent the "American scene" in their artwork by depicting the nation's beautiful landscapes or its valiant workers employed in agriculture or industry. Although it never occurred to Helen to depict the American scene in her Berkeley mosaic, both her and Swift's works exhibit the social realism one expects from WPA art—Swift's women have 1930s-styled clothing and hairstyles, and Bruton's muscular sculptor resembles the glorified and heroic worker commonly seen in Depression-era murals. Beyond this, one art historian has noted the possible influence of Diego Rivera in the "neutral earth colors... and the broad, heavily outlined eyes of the figures." Helen's mural also shows the influence of early Byzantine mosaics, which she had been studying at the time. Early Byzantine art—dating from the third through the seventh centuries—is characterized by a movement away from the Classical naturalism perfected in Greek and Roman art and toward more abstract, universal, and two-dimensional representations. Helen perfected the Byzantine style in her early mosaics and would continue in this vein for decades.

Helen Bruton's mosaic mural at Berkeley is approximately fifteen feet square, consists of more than 80,000 tiles, and took nine months to complete. The mosaics were dedicated in a ceremony held on October 31, 1936. Later that year, the mosaics were filmed by Paramount Pictures for a documentary about Federal Art murals across the United States, although their footage was cut from the final film. The works were warmly received and described as "rich in color... every play of sunlight or shift of shadow changes them to the enjoyment of the beholder." Junius Cravens remarked that "the murals will be an outstanding adaptation of the ancient art of mosaic to present-day uses... They will be a noteworthy addition to the campus scene."

Almost as soon as the Berkeley mosaics were completed, there was talk of their ultimate destruction. Just a week after the dedication ceremony, the *Oakland Tribune* speculated that "both [mosaics] will tumble soon, no doubt, when the wreckers get busy, for the buildings must come down on a date not far distant. This wreckage is a prediction of our own, but the building is not one to stand long. Time and nervous human activity will sweep it away." Over the years there have been some close calls. In the mid-1960s it was rumored that the building was scheduled for demolition, and the mosaics—which are attached directly to the brick—would have been destroyed in the process. "They undoubtedly will pull it down," lamented Helen in 1964, "and yet it seems a pity that they don't save that one building, as a record of that original brick era." At times, the mosaics have been neglected and obscured by vegetation. But despite the *Oakland Tribune's* dire predictions, the Old Art Gallery has been spared. The mosaics survive today as an important legacy of the Federal Art Project and a premier example of 1930s social realism. Many feel that Helen's mural at Berkeley is one of her "finest mosaics," high praise for an artist who specialized in this medium and was one of its foremost practitioners.

Having completed two large and successful mosaic projects, Helen was recognized as an authority in the field, and in October 1936, she was asked to contribute an article about mosaic to the *San Francisco Art Association Bulletin*. Writing about art was a chore for Helen, and she rarely welcomed requests for articles. She managed to pull together an essay called "Mosaic as a Modern Expression," which she wrote

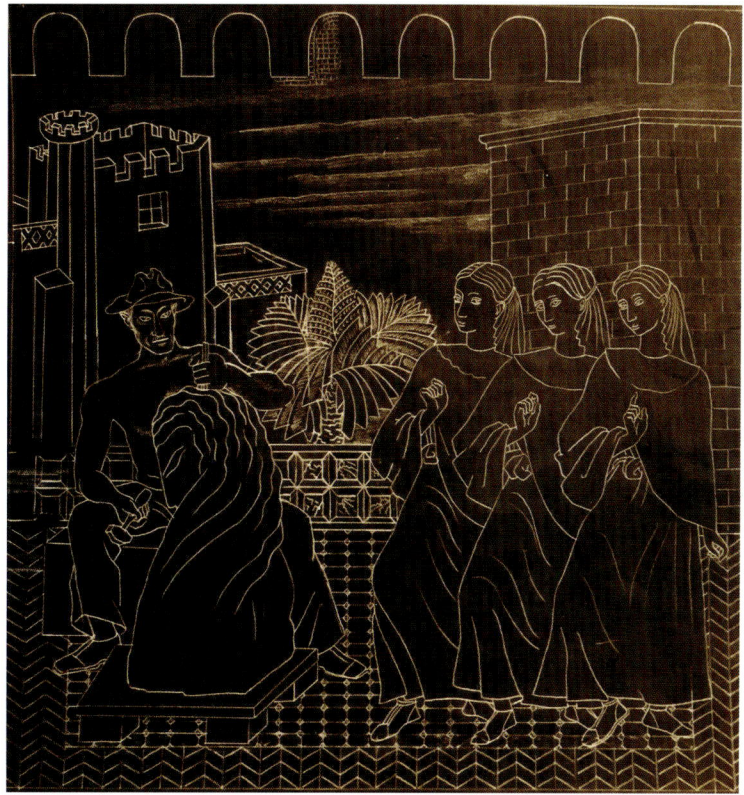

Preliminary drawing for *Sculpture and Dancing*

while in Twenty-Nine Palms, a city just north of Palm Springs, California. "I'd much rather tell you about Twenty-Nine Palms than to try and write anything about mosaic," she confessed to her readers. "It is really a great trial to have to sit still and wrack my brain for something to say... However, I shall shut my eyes and hold my nose and try and swallow it—or rather spit it out." The article eventually took on a more serious tone.

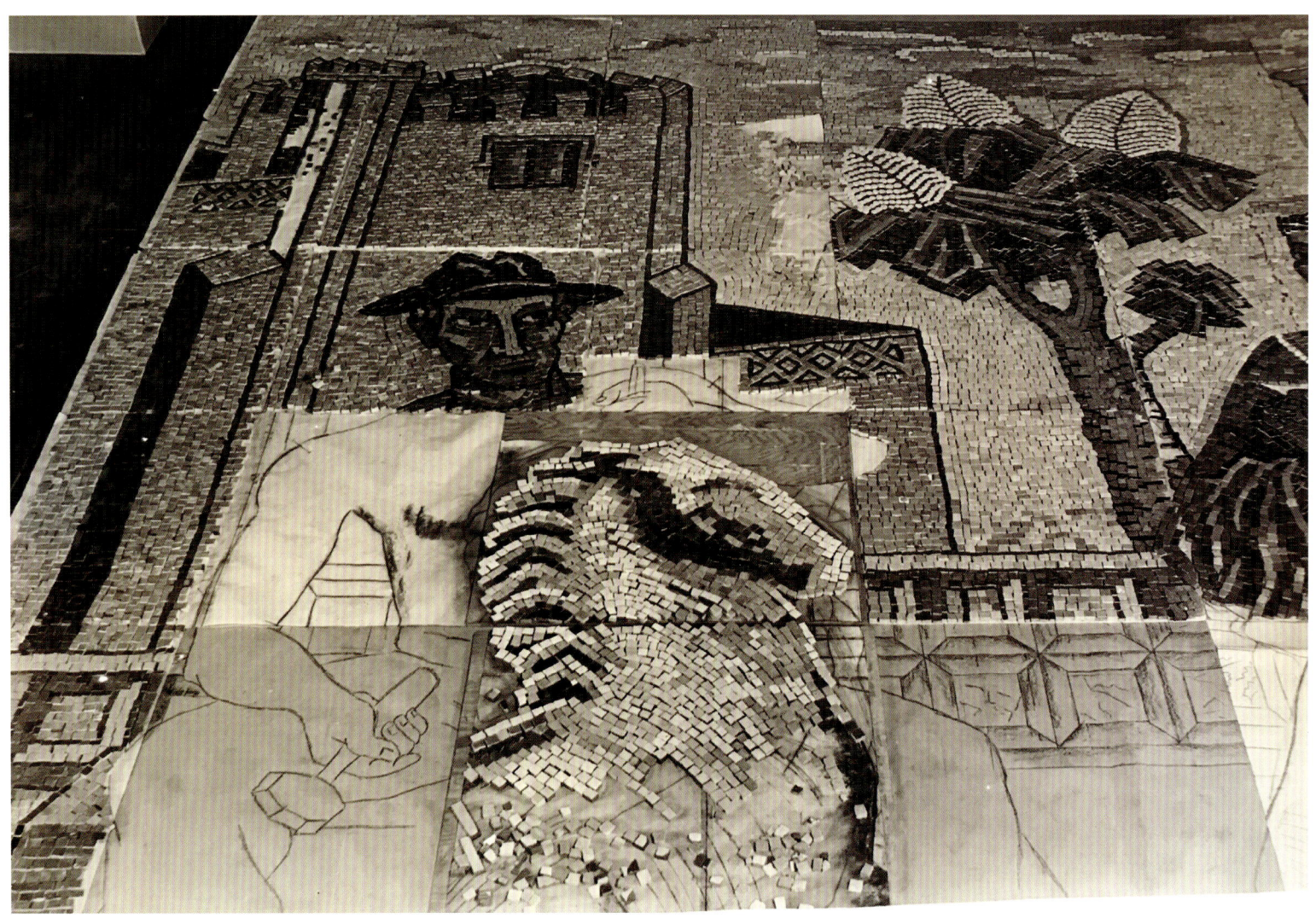

Above: *Sculpture and Dancing* in progress on the studio floor
Right: *Sculpture and Dancing* mosaic at the Old Art Gallery at UC Berkeley, by Helen Bruton (1936)

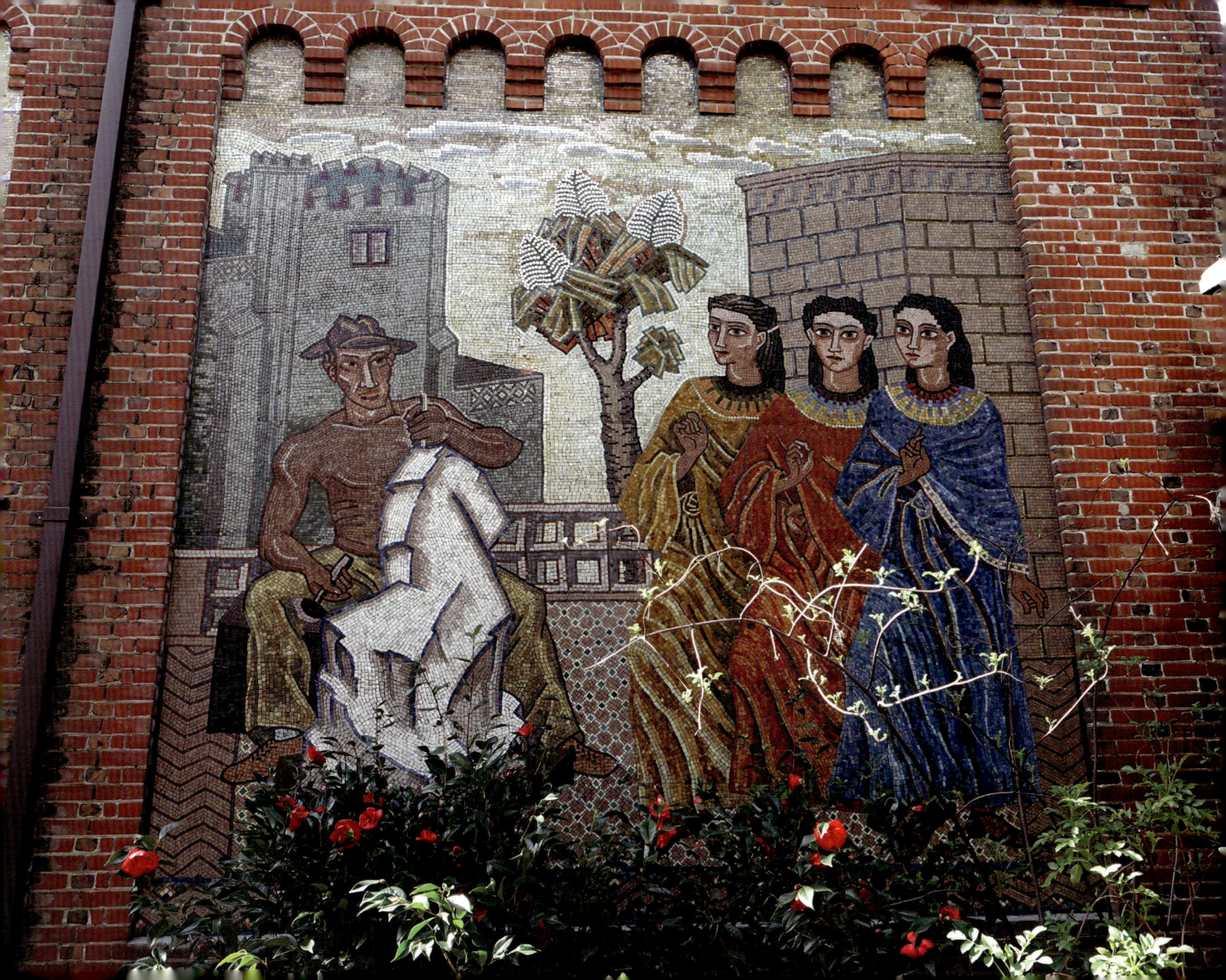

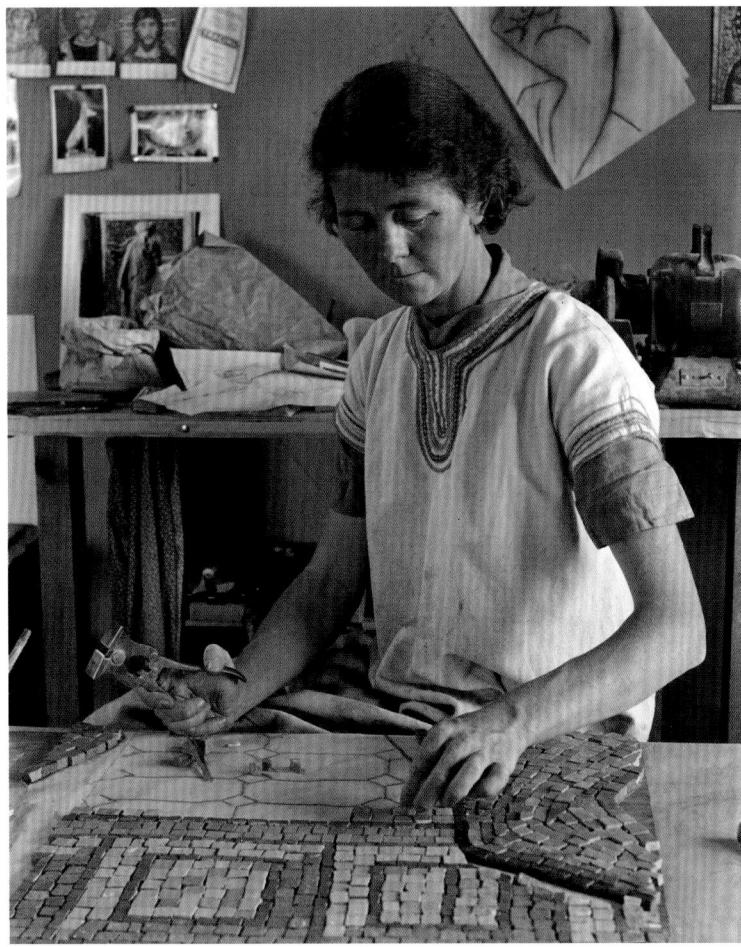

Helen Bruton in the studio working on her mosaic for UC Berkeley, photo by Imogen Cunningham (1936)

"As a medium for modern expression," Helen wrote, mosaic "has endless possibilities." She cautioned, however, that mosaic could be overused, and "we shall need to use both good judgment and restraint lest we overplay our parts." Helen also expressed her view that women were better at mosaic than men, claiming that women view this detail-driven work as "an enlarged kind of beadwork, and generally want to start right away," whereas men "seem to be numbed by the thought of the tedious labor involved." Unfortunately, Helen was reinforcing a particularly persistent stereotype that women are more suited to decorative arts and crafts that involve detail, repetition, and monotony, whereas male artists are more interested in broader concepts and abstract ideas.

Helen continued to pursue government commissions, and her third was funded through the Treasury Relief Art Project (TRAP) in 1939. This project was the design of two terra-cotta bas-relief sculptures, each five feet high and three feet wide, for the interior walls of a new post office in Fresno, California. Helen was asked to design and make one of the works, and Oregon sculptor Emma Lu Davis was assigned the other, with both on the given theme of "rural delivery." The two artists, working independently in different locations, were unsuccessful at agreeing on a unified look or design for the project. Helen felt that the two women's initial sketches were "pretty different in feeling" and were not "striking anything like a similar note." A few weeks into the design phase, Davis was dropped from the project and Helen became responsible for both works. "I feel a little sad, for Miss Davis's sake," Helen wrote at the time, "[but] I do think in this particular case it is better to leave the responsibility and the decisions to one." Helen was paid $1,400 to create both works.

Helen executed the panels in clay, from which molds

were made. The molds were used to fabricate the pieces out of terra-cotta at a pottery works in Alameda. The relief known as *RFD-1*, an address indicating a "Rural Free Delivery" postal route number, is of a boy wearing overalls and a large straw hat holding a daisy and leaning against a mailbox. A dog rests at his feet, and a chicken, a rooster, and a stalk of corn balance the composition. *RFD-2* depicts a young girl by a mailbox holding a letter in her hand. A tree is seen behind her and a basket of produce is by her sandaled feet. Although Helen claimed there was "really no story" to the murals, she seemed to have a sentimental view of what they represented:

> What I wanted to do was a small boy and girl that would be just that—you, I or anybody when we were a small girl or boy, waiting by a rural mail box. The daisy doesn't necessarily infer "she loves me, she loves me not," altho [sic] lots of people will like to think so, and that's o.k. too. He might be waiting for the mail man to bring the ice skates his pa ordered from Sears, Roebuck for his birthday. And the little girl might have her grandma's pension check or just a letter from her Uncle Willy.

These wholesome works aptly reflect both the assigned "rural delivery" theme and life in the predominantly agricultural region surrounding Fresno. The reliefs, installed in 1940, may be seen today at the former post office building, which now serves as the Fresno Unified School District Education Center.

Ambitious in her attempts to obtain federal funding, Helen applied for yet another mural project for a post office, this one located in Merced, California, a city seventy miles southeast of the Yosemite Valley. Her proposal was inspired by

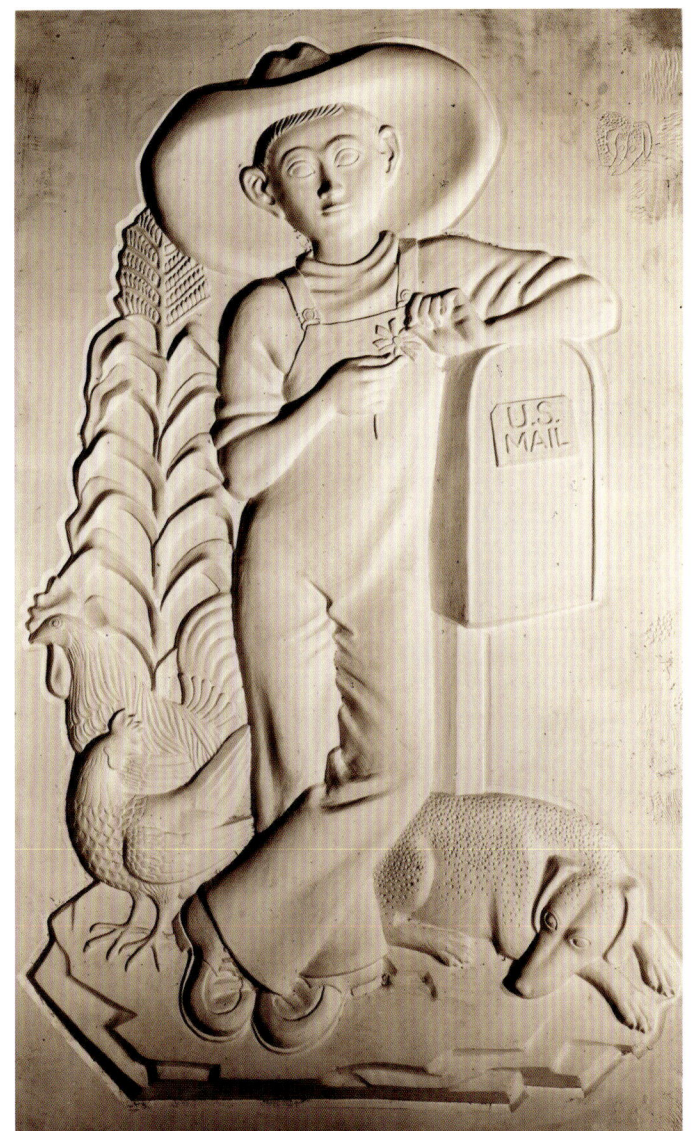

RFD-1, by Helen Bruton (1940)

Lafayette Bunnell's *Discovery of the Yosemite*, a firsthand account of the 1851 invasion and destruction of Native American settlements in the Yosemite Valley, and her work made strong political statements about the mistreatment of Indigenous peoples in Central California. Helen's preliminary drawings depicted American forty-niner James Savage and his battalion entering the Yosemite Valley, as well as Chief Tenaya and the Ahwahnechee people preparing for the anticipated attack. Helen believed that the Native Americans of the area had been blatantly mistreated, and she made her sketches reflect this. In the end, her designs were rejected. Helen Forbes and Dorothy Puccinelli, the artists of the murals inside the Mothers Building, were given the commission and created murals more in line with what administrators had in mind for the post office.

This wasn't the first commission that Helen had lost, and it certainly wasn't the last. In fact, she had a full envelope labeled "Jobs that didn't jell." Like many artists, when any one of the Bruton sisters was competing for a commission, she would prepare a significant amount of preliminary work. As Helen explained, "I'd break my heart over trying to please somebody and I never could, a number of times. And that was always because the person wanted you to do what was in his head." Despite the fact that many of them were rejected, Helen enjoyed doing preliminary sketches—sometimes more than working on the final project. When asked which WPA art project she considered her most successful, Helen replied that she had the most fun preparing sketches for a job she didn't get: the Merced Post Office. She said that she'd "work like everything to get a job, but I didn't care—it didn't matter if I didn't get it. I enjoyed doing it... The pile of scrap that I have left over from those jobs, much of it is far more interesting, I'm sure, as far as art goes, than what's on the wall." For Helen, preliminary work was

all about freedom and creativity. She "was always happiest in the process of giving birth to a project than in seeing it finally 'approved' by the architect or client and finished."

When Helen did get a commission and her plans were approved, she would begin to feel the pressure to achieve what she had promised. "You are supposed to deliver," she said, "and it's supposed to look like that drawing." Working on a commission could be stressful, and Helen didn't like "the fact that you have to please somebody else, especially if it's an architectural job and you have to please a client." Toward the end of her life, Helen felt immensely relieved that she no longer needed to make art with the intention of fulfilling someone else's expectations.

In 1937, in between her Berkeley mosaic and the terra-cotta reliefs for the Fresno Post Office, Helen received a coveted commercial job when she was paid $1,200 to create two large mosaics for the exterior of the Golden State Hotel in San Francisco. Esther was working inside the same hotel, where she had been hired to paint the murals in the cocktail lounge. Photographs from the period show that the hotel had a wide, Art Deco-style facade with two sets of doors and illuminated columns. Helen's mosaics, each measuring seven and a half feet wide and twelve feet tall, were installed on opposite sides of the entrance. *City* features a larger-than-life woman with dark skin draped in a striped robe. Her right arm steadies a basket of flowers that she holds on her shoulder while her left arm is to her side, an orange poppy—the California state flower—in her hand. She stands barefoot on a brown mound of earth, with modern stone skyscrapers behind her on one side and green mountains and a bright yellow sun on the other. On the opposite side of the hotel entrance, *Country* depicts a shirtless male field worker holding a large bunch of purple grapes in his left hand and a knife in his right. A basket of harvested grapes sits at his feet. Small stone buildings with tile roofs, fields with white flowering trees, and green hillsides fill the background. When asked about the significance of the mosaics, Helen responded, "They are just symbolic of the West. They don't tell a story."

While installing her mosaics at the Golden State Hotel, Helen was interviewed by the *San Francisco News*. Both the article and its accompanying photograph of Helen, dressed in dirty overalls and wearing work gloves and a bandana around her head, captured her during a phase of the project that was particularly tricky and required enormous concentration. Helen's frustration and lack of patience with the interviewer is evident. "I can't talk to you very much," she said to the reporter as she pounded the wall to smooth the tiles. "I have to fight this thing. Sometimes it... makes... me... mad!" Helen also emphasized to her interviewer that she didn't want to be known exclusively as a mosaic artist: "'If anyone tells me I should devote my life to mosaics I'll never do another. I'll do tombstones instead,' she warned. 'I don't like... any... set things,' she muttered pounding again." At various points in her career, Helen seemed frustrated to be identified as a "mosaic artist"; in fact, she emphasized that mosaic was of no particular interest in and of itself—it was merely another medium of artistic expression.

Like most of Helen's works, her mosaics for the Golden State Hotel feel both ancient and timeless—they could be from centuries ago or they could have been made just yesterday. The figures are classical in posture and bring to mind Egyptian hieroglyphs, yet at the same time they are fresh and modern in their simple treatment of color, pattern, and form. As Helen explained, "the very limitations of [mosaic] demand

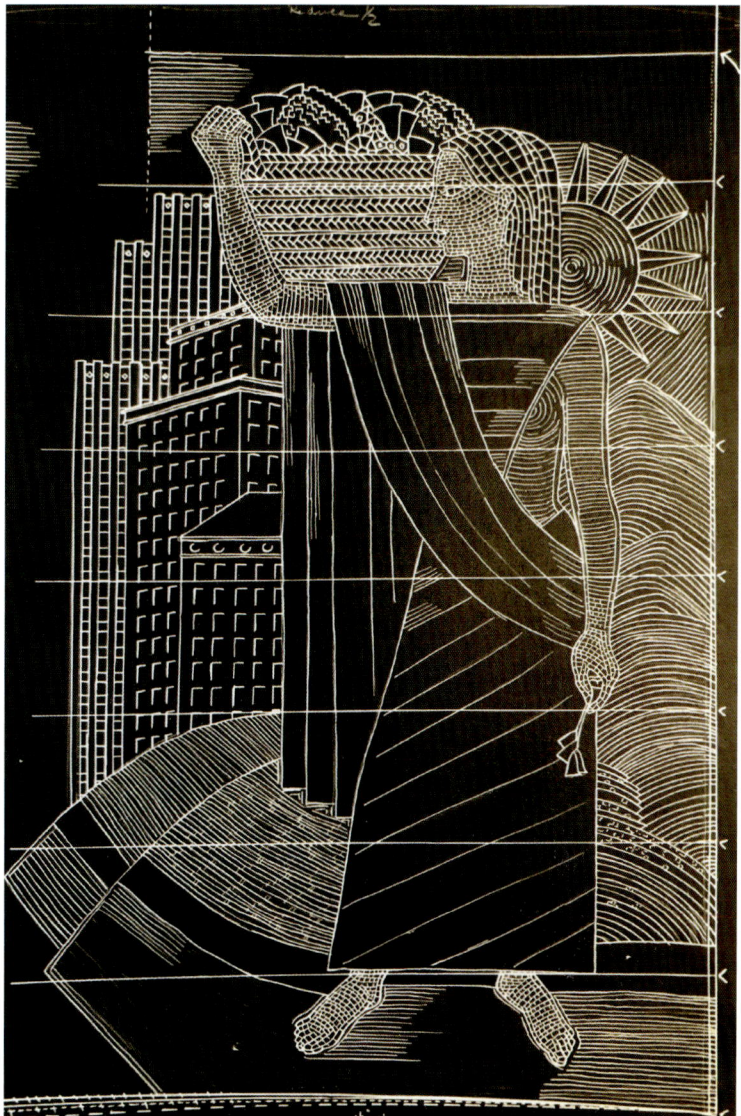

Preliminary drawing for *City* mosaic

99

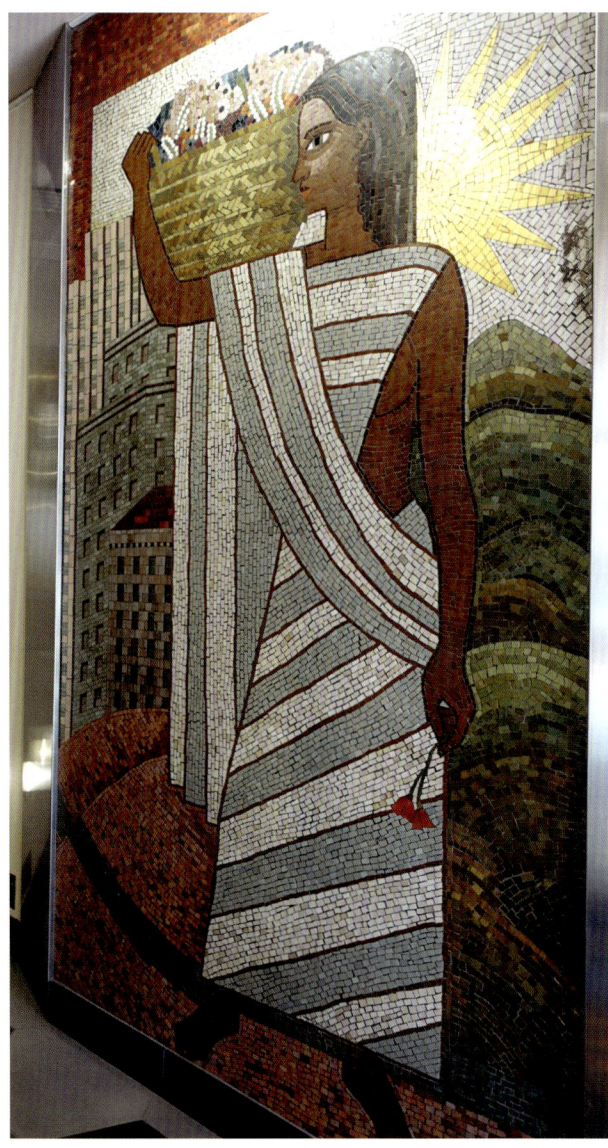

a simplified and formal treatment." In other words, mosaics have the unique ability to appear ancient and "formal" while at the same time feeling modern and "simple." Mosaicist Jeanne Reynal, a contemporary of the Brutons, agreed, saying "mosaics do not belong to a time but a human need of exceptional duration."

In 1974, the hotel went through a renovation, and both extremely heavy mosaics with thousands of individual pieces making up their surfaces were successfully removed from their original locations on the exterior of the building. Remarkably, both murals were saved, although for a while, the mosaic depicting the male field worker—which Helen nicknamed "The Grape Picker"—was in storage. Helen wrote to the owner of the hotel, expressing her concern for the work. "As the artist who created it," she wrote, "I can't help but feel a certain amount of personal interest in its preservation." She asked if the hotel would be interested in selling the mosaic; given its wine country theme, she thought someone in Napa Valley might purchase it. In the end, the hotel elected to keep both mosaics together.

Today, the entrance to 114 Powell Street, now the Hotel Union Square, is much humbler. Helen's mosaics stand across from each other in a narrow hallway just inside the entrance. Unfortunately, their current location does not allow the viewer to step back and admire these large, beautiful pieces from a distance. However, it is both remarkable and fortunate that the trouble and expense to save these mosaics was taken when it would have been much easier and less expensive to demolish them.

As Helen worked on her assignments for the WPA, many other government-funded art projects were underway in the Bay Area. Twenty-five artists, including the Brutons' good

City mosaic at the Hotel Union Square, by Helen Bruton (1937)

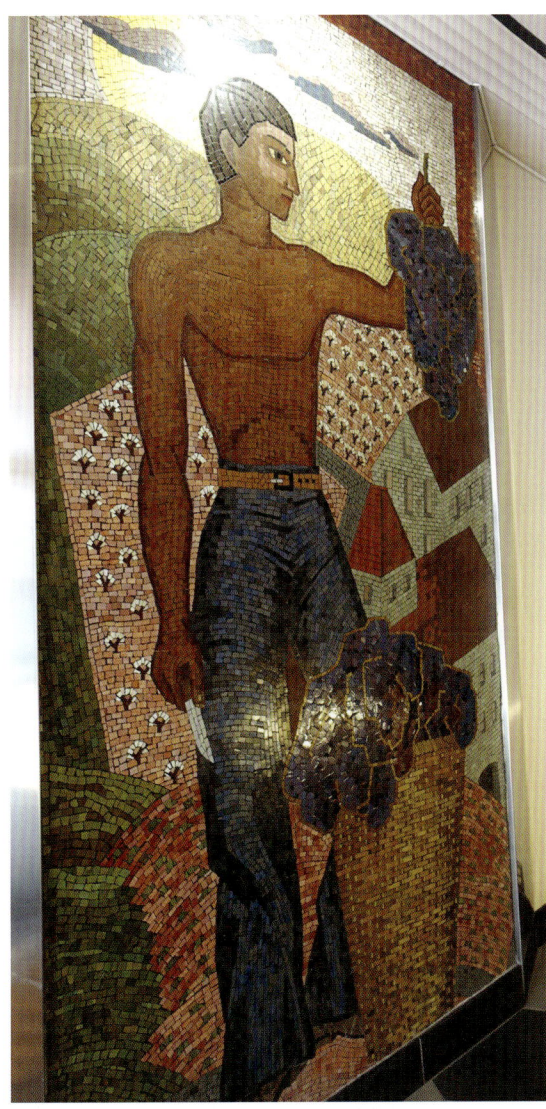

Country mosaic at the Hotel Union Square, by Helen Bruton (1937)

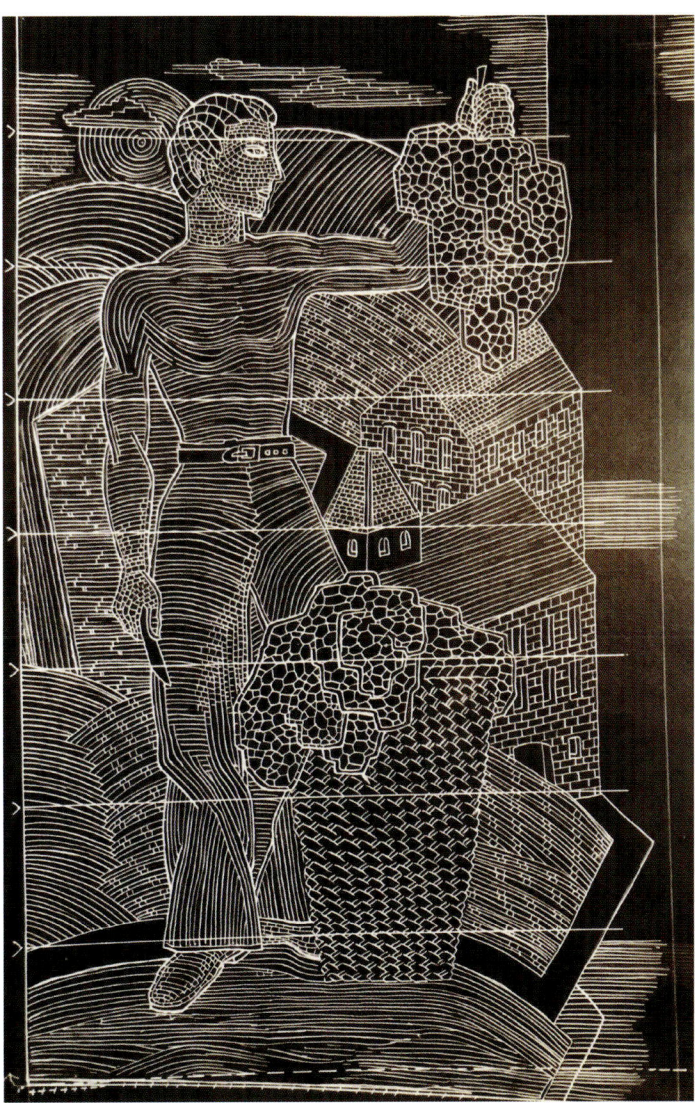

Preliminary drawing for *Country* mosaic

friends Victor Arnautoff, Maxine Albro, Lucien Labaudt, and Ralph Stackpole, were painting murals on the interior of San Francisco's Coit Tower as part of a WPA project. Labaudt immortalized the Brutons in his Coit Tower mural *Powell Street* along the walls of the curved stairway that leads to the second floor—the trio is shown together near the top of the staircase, elegantly dressed and walking a dog.

In addition to paying artists to make art, the WPA hired writers to conduct research and write about art. The California Art Research project, active from 1936 to 1938, employed forty people to research and write biographies of local artists. According to editor Gene Hailey, the project aimed to overcome "the absence of adequate information on both the early day California artists who made their residence in San Francisco... and younger artists... whose works have not been given the attention they deserve by critics, or by the museums or by the general public." The project was an important undertaking that has provided one of the most comprehensive sources of information about early-twentieth-century California artists. Many of the artists included would likely have been forgotten entirely without this valuable resource. The project grew to become twenty volumes featuring one hundred artists. Each Bruton sister has a biographical section in Volume 16. In Hailey's biographies of the Brutons, she described them as "the modern artistic counterpart of the famed Bronte sisters in literature... They are a part of the prestige now accorded women artists in California. They are dominant among western artists nationally recognized in art and publishing circles."

For decades, *California Art Research* has offered the only comprehensive biographies of the Bruton sisters. Yet some of the material written about the Brutons is inaccurate, and these errors have been subsequently reprinted in biographical

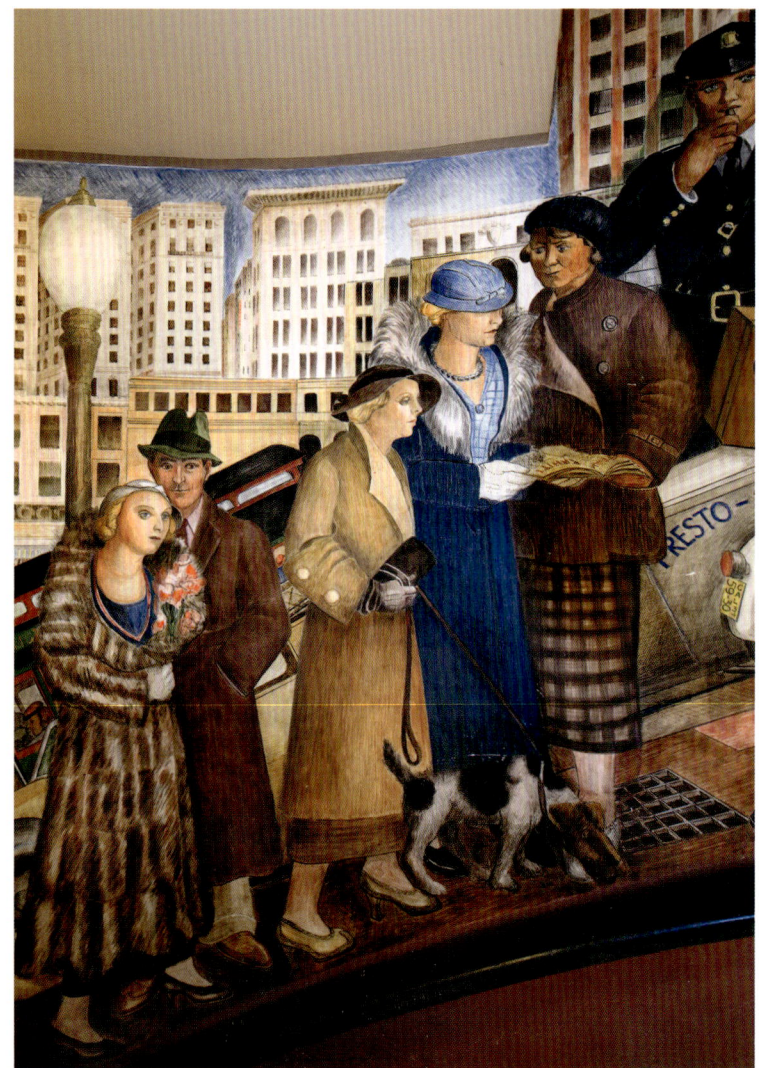

The Bruton sisters (three figures to the right) were included in Lucien Labaudt's *Powell Street* mural at Coit Tower in San Francisco (1934)

dictionaries, monographs, and articles over the years. After her biography was first published in 1937, Helen made dozens of amendments on the printed pages, perhaps with the hope that the errors would be corrected in a later edition. Fifty years later, Ellen Schwartz prepared an updated, microfilmed version of the *California Art Research* volumes, but unfortunately only the bibliographies were brought up to date. The original artist biographies were untouched and the errors about the Brutons remained. Helen remarked in 1983 that the biographical sketches "were not accurate... They so often get things twisted around that we get discouraged."

Another WPA project of the 1930s was an attempt to publish a series of essays written by artists who had participated in government-funded programs. Joseph Allen, director of the Northern California Federal Art Project (FAP), asked Helen to contribute an article about mosaic. Helen hated writing about art, and she suggested that Allen contact a different mosaic artist who "would give you much better technical information than I could." She also reiterated her belief that mosaic was nothing more than a medium. "When it comes right down to it," she explained, "the same thing holds true for any medium, it's the design that counts and the feeling with which it is carried out. I honestly can't think of anything more to say." Because of her busy schedule and lack of enthusiasm, Helen made only a half-hearted attempt to write an essay, and her article was brief and uninspired. In a penciled note on Helen's submitted manuscript, FAP Director Holger Cahill wrote, "This is hardly important. Let's see other mosaic articles." In the end, the project directors selected Jean Goodwin, a WPA artist from Southern California specializing in mosaic murals, to write the article instead. One can venture that Helen didn't mind that her article was passed over; she

was much more interested in making art than writing about it. Goodwin's essay, "California Mosaic," is well written and rightfully acknowledges the accomplishments of Helen Bruton. This collection of essays about WPA-era art remained unpublished for decades; the articles were finally edited and included in the 1973 book *Art for the Millions*.

Later in life, Helen described the 1930s as "a very happy and busy time—when one was ready to face any dragon that raised its head." When Helen and Margaret were asked how they felt about the art programs of the WPA period, Margaret replied, "I think they were wonderful. I think they gave the artists a terrific boost." As Helen recalled,

> Although there is a great deal that isn't of much value done, and lots of stumbling around in art, and lots of near misses... there's enough done... to make it really very worthwhile... So many young artists were so thrilled at the opportunity to just get their teeth into a real project... They were very earnest and very sincere about it... [and they] were enthusiastic over the opportunity that it gave them.

New Deal art programs provided Helen Bruton and her sisters with an unprecedented opportunity to create art on a large scale, and changed the momentum and direction of Helen's career entirely. As she said later in life, the WPA "provided the opportunity to work on sizable projects, and started the drift toward large-scale, more architectural efforts. One of these seemed to lead to another." The experience of working for the WPA increased Helen's confidence and prepared her to take on what would be one of the most celebrated projects of the Bruton sisters' careers.

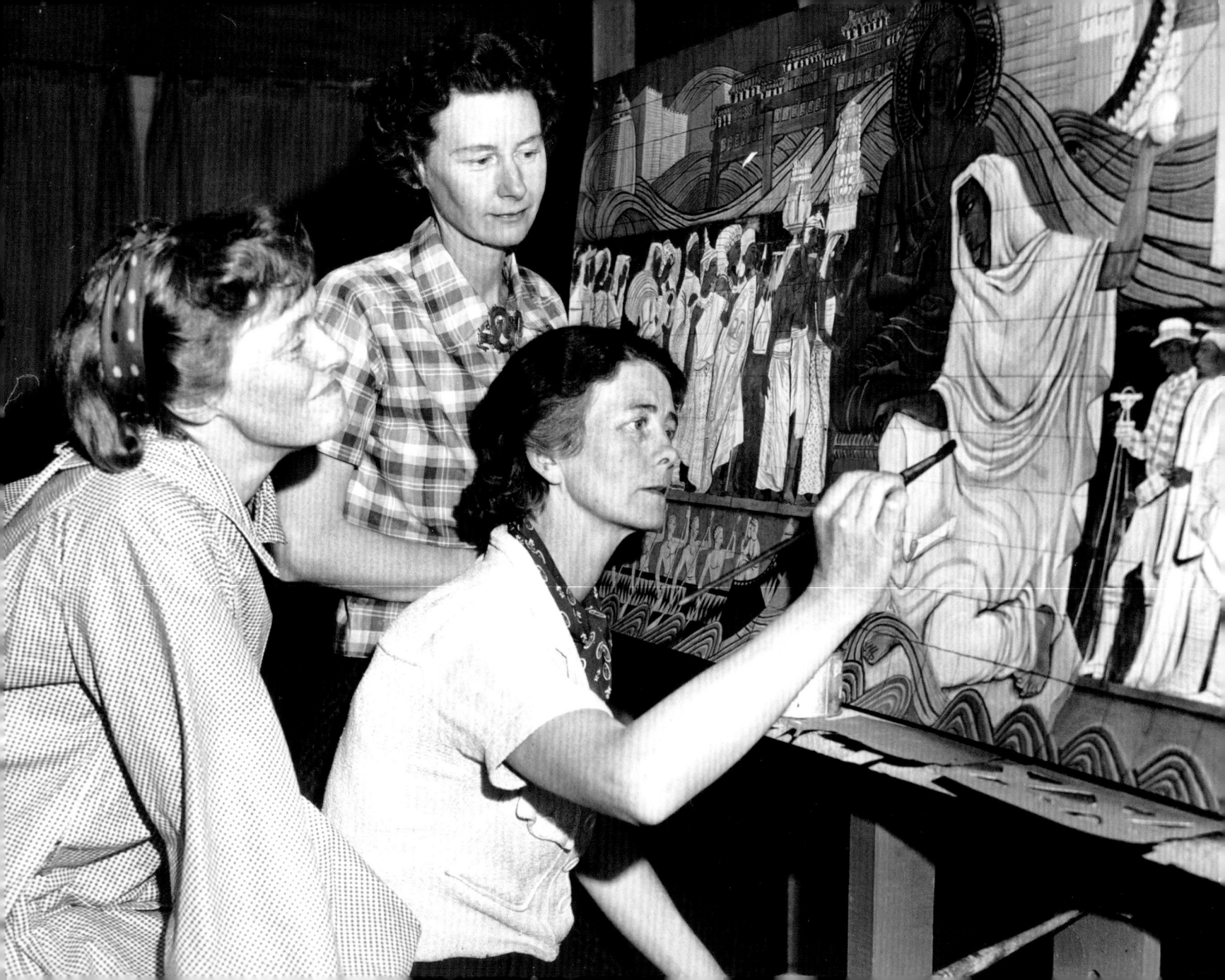

CHAPTER EIGHT
"A Beautiful Array of Special Problems": The Golden Gate International Exposition

(1938–1940)

San Francisco's Golden Gate International Exposition debuted to great acclaim in February 1939. Visitors were transported to a world of exotic architecture, splashing fountains, fanciful sculptures, and colorful murals. Nicknamed "The Magic City," this world's fair held surprises and wonders around every corner, including the Court of Pacifica which featured an eighty-foot-high sculpture—the tallest at the Exposition—called *Pacifica* that stood before a one-hundred-foot-tall metal curtain that "gave off melodious sounds as it fluttered gently in the breeze." And forming the backdrop of these enormous and grand components was the Bruton sisters' masterpiece—their 8,000-square-foot mural, *The Peacemakers*. This astounding mural dominated the Court of Pacifica as one of the largest and most critically acclaimed artworks at the Exposition.

The intensely challenging and ultimately rewarding process of creating *The Peacemakers* was a highlight of the Brutons' careers. Though the sisters were by nature modest and humble, later in their lives they still expressed their pride about this remarkable artistic and technical achievement. The mural also reflected the trio's status in the art world by the end of the 1930s; the sisters' artwork was so highly respected and so well known that they were selected to envision, design, and execute the largest artistic component at the fair and were paid

The Bruton sisters planning their mural for the Golden Gate International Exposition, 1938

an astounding $20,000 for their efforts, the "largest of the contracts" for the fair. Their impressive commission, more than $350,000 in today's dollars, was widely reported in the national press. The sisters themselves said they were "flabbergasted" by the amount they were paid.

The concept behind the 1939 Golden Gate International Exposition was to celebrate the recent completion of the two bridges spanning San Francisco Bay: the Golden Gate Bridge, which, when completed in 1937, was "the longest single suspension span in the world," and the Oakland Bay Bridge, which had opened in 1936 and was at the time called "the largest structure of its kind in the history of man." By 1939, the weary nation was nearly ten years into the Great Depression. Its organizers intended that the Golden Gate International Exposition would publicize these two immense feats of engineering and celebrate American industry and ingenuity. They envisioned a fair that was grand, awe inspiring, and "in keeping with the magnitude of the projects it was to celebrate."

Many locations in San Francisco were considered for placement of the fair, but an unlikely site was selected: the Yerba Buena Shoals, a ridge of land under the midway point of the Bay Bridge. Engineers determined that dredges and pumps could fill the area with quarried rock and sand to create a man-made island for the fair. The construction of the island took eighteen months and was followed by the addition of roads, infrastructure, and electricity to illuminate the fair in dramatic fashion after dark. In an effort to make the Exposition "the most beautiful World's Fair in history," hundreds of thousands of plants and trees were planted on the island. An astonishing $1,000,000—more than $18,000,000 in today's dollars—was designated for art, including statues, murals, bas-reliefs, and architectural embellishments.

The subtitle of the fair's name, "A Pageant of the Pacific," aptly encapsulated a symbolic mission of the event: to create cultural bridges between East and West and encourage peace and cooperation among Pacific nations. To this end, although the architecture of the fair tended toward modern and Art Deco styles, the structures also incorporated Asian and Mayan elements in an effort to combine the "mysticism of the East with the vision and vigor of the West." The selection of the trans-Pacific theme resulted in "a new mood in decorating" that had wide-reaching effects in California design for decades to come, even influencing some of the Brutons' later work.

The fairgrounds were organized into numerous "courts," including the Court of the Moon, Court of the Seven Seas, Court of Flowers, and Court of Reflections. Among the six architects hired to design the buildings at the Exposition was Timothy Pflueger, who had previously worked with Esther Bruton on the extremely successful Cirque Room at the Fairmont Hotel and who had recommended her as the queen of the 1936 Parilia Ball. Pflueger was put in charge of the Court of Pacifica, and he selected a diverse group of notable Bay Area artists to be a part of its creation, including Maynard Dixon, who painted two small murals, and Ralph Stackpole, who sculpted *Pacifica*, the eighty-foot-tall female figure that was designated the "theme sculpture" of the Exposition. At the center of the Court of Pacifica was a multi-tiered fountain surrounded by sculptures by Sargent Johnson, a prominent African American sculptor from the Bay Area, and four women artists—Ruth Cravath, Cecilia Graham, Adaline Kent, and Helen Phillips. Pflueger's plan for the Court of Pacifica was enormously successful. The *San Francisco Chronicle* praised the "surpassing quality" of his design: "One wishes the entire Fair might have been carried out in the spirit of the Court of Pacifica."

Pflueger clearly admired the Bruton sisters and entrusted them with the creation of the enormous mural that would be the focal point for his Court of Pacifica. Pflueger originally hired the Brutons to create two murals: one representing the countries of the East, and the other representing the West. Each mural was to be a staggering 144 feet by 57 feet. To Pflueger's dismay, fair organizers made the architects cut their original budgets by 40 percent, and he was forced to eliminate one of the murals from the Court of Pacifica. Helen remembered that the sisters "professed to be very sad about it, but we were really much relieved because it meant that there would be only one wall... and that was really all that we could possibly cope with."

Expectations were high for the Brutons as they planned and designed what was being called "one of the most significant murals ever conceived" and the "theme piece" for the fair. The local arts community seemed confident that the sisters were up to the challenge, with the *Argonaut* stating that "it is the general feeling among the artists' colony that this large commission has been placed in excellent hands... [The Brutons] seem to possess the ability to work together in perfect harmony of style." Several newspapers printed photographs of the trio, posing pensively with pencils and brushes gripped in their hands as they hovered over the plan for their mural,

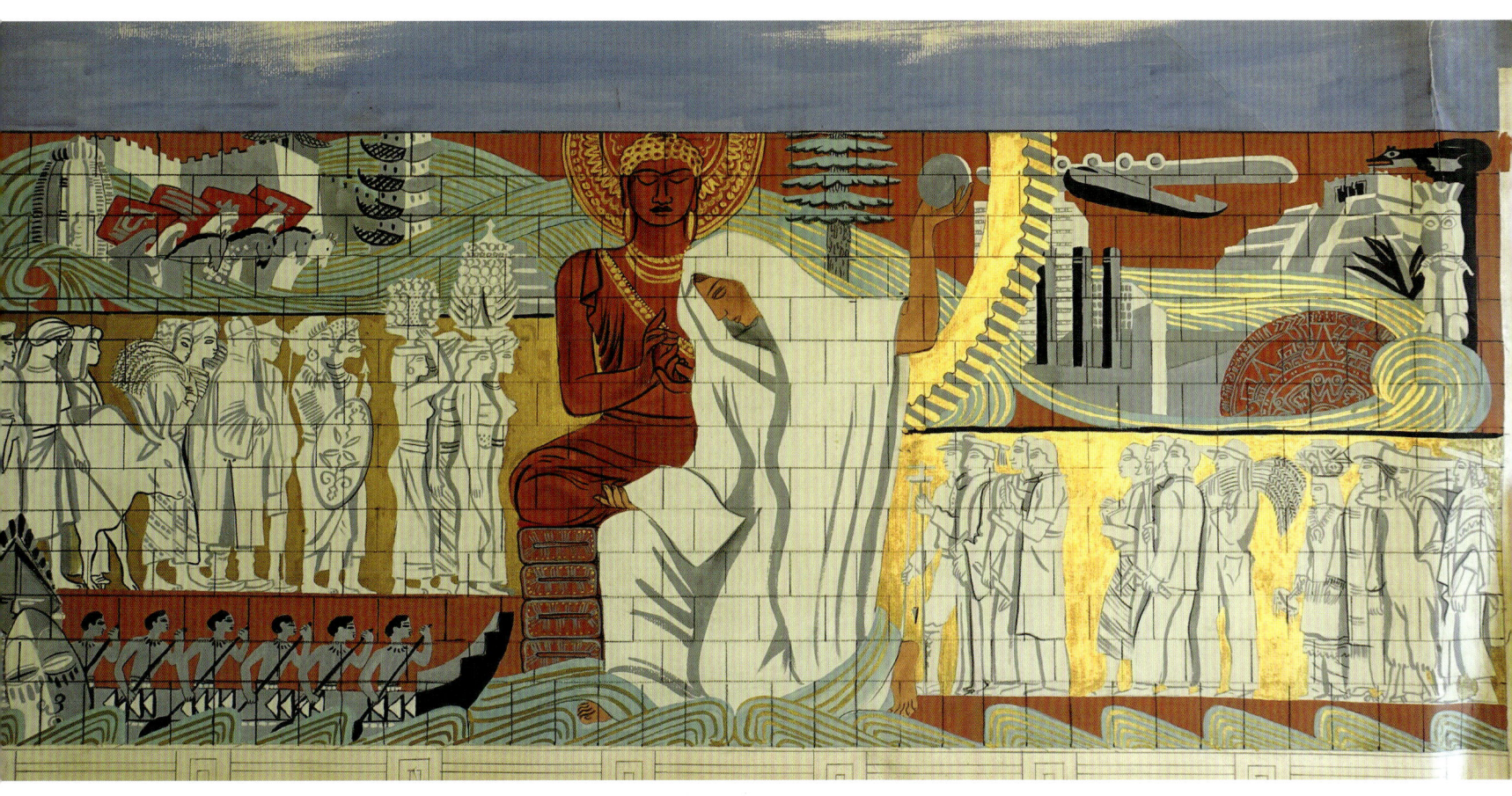

Early watercolor for *The Peacemakers* mural

brows furrowed. In one photo, Helen and Margaret manage to maintain serious expressions while Esther is clearly on the verge of laughter, as if finding all the attention both unwarranted and absurd.

Helen was of the opinion that "working out the technical parts [of the mural] was really awfully interesting"—this optimism and dedication would have been necessary as a number of obstacles stood in the sisters' way. Choosing the appropriate materials was a major challenge, as was the enormous size of the work. A painted mural on the large exterior wall would lack the depth required to complement the dramatic architectural surroundings. A bas-relief made of plaster or cement would be too heavy to manipulate easily. In short, the sisters were faced with what their friend and fellow artist Dorothy Puccinelli called "a beautiful array of special problems."

As Helen recalled, "We spent weeks and months not only experimenting and finally arriving at a medium, but also fooling around with the designs." Finally, the Brutons came up with an ingenious and elegant solution. They started with standard four-by-eight-foot plywood panels and covered them with Masonite, a thin, flexible board made of engineered wood that could be layered to create a thickness of between one and four inches. Large shapes were cut with a band saw, mounted on plywood with waterproof glue, and then carved by hand. Although the sisters had assistants to do the band saw work, they did all the hand carving themselves using sharp, thin-bladed knives. Their attic studio in Alameda couldn't possibly accommodate a project of this scale, so the sisters rented studio space in an old furniture factory in Fruitvale, a neighborhood of Oakland. Despite the challenges of this laborious process, Helen described the experience as a wonderful time and "the most interesting job I think that I've done." She told Timothy Pflueger in a letter, "I'm always wobbly at the start of a job; fortunately I was able to conceal my trepidation over the idea of tackling [*The Peacemakers*]. When we once got rolling I was all right, and didn't even lose a night's sleep over it." The sisters worked from 9 a.m. to 5 p.m., Monday through Saturday, for nine months to complete the mural. They were assisted by a young woman named Eleanor Pickersgill, who remained friends with the Brutons for many years. The finished mural consisted of 270 hand-carved four-by-eight-foot panels—more than 8,000 square feet.

Since the commission had been reduced to only one mural, the Brutons had to include representations of both East and West in a single design. They carefully planned out the mural in advance and gave a detailed description of what it would look like in an early press release. As Helen described it, "one side was… the countries of the Eastern shore, the countries of Southeast Asia, China, Japan, and [the other side] is symbolic of the Western shore, the countries of South America, North America, Western types, American Indians." The background of the work includes art and architecture from the two realms. On the right are iconic monuments and artifacts from ancient Mesoamerica: the Gate of the Sun at Tiwanaku; a circular Aztec calendar stone; and a step-temple that combines elements from El Castillo at Chichen Itza and Pakal's Tomb at Palenque. Representing North America are a totem pole by Pacific Northwest Coast Native Americans and a tower from the Bay Bridge. The architecture represented on the Eastern side includes a section of the Great Wall of China, buildings from a Japanese imperial palace, and a Southeast Asian temple spire that appears loosely based on Ankor Wat.

The Peacemakers, by Margaret, Esther, and Helen Bruton (1939)

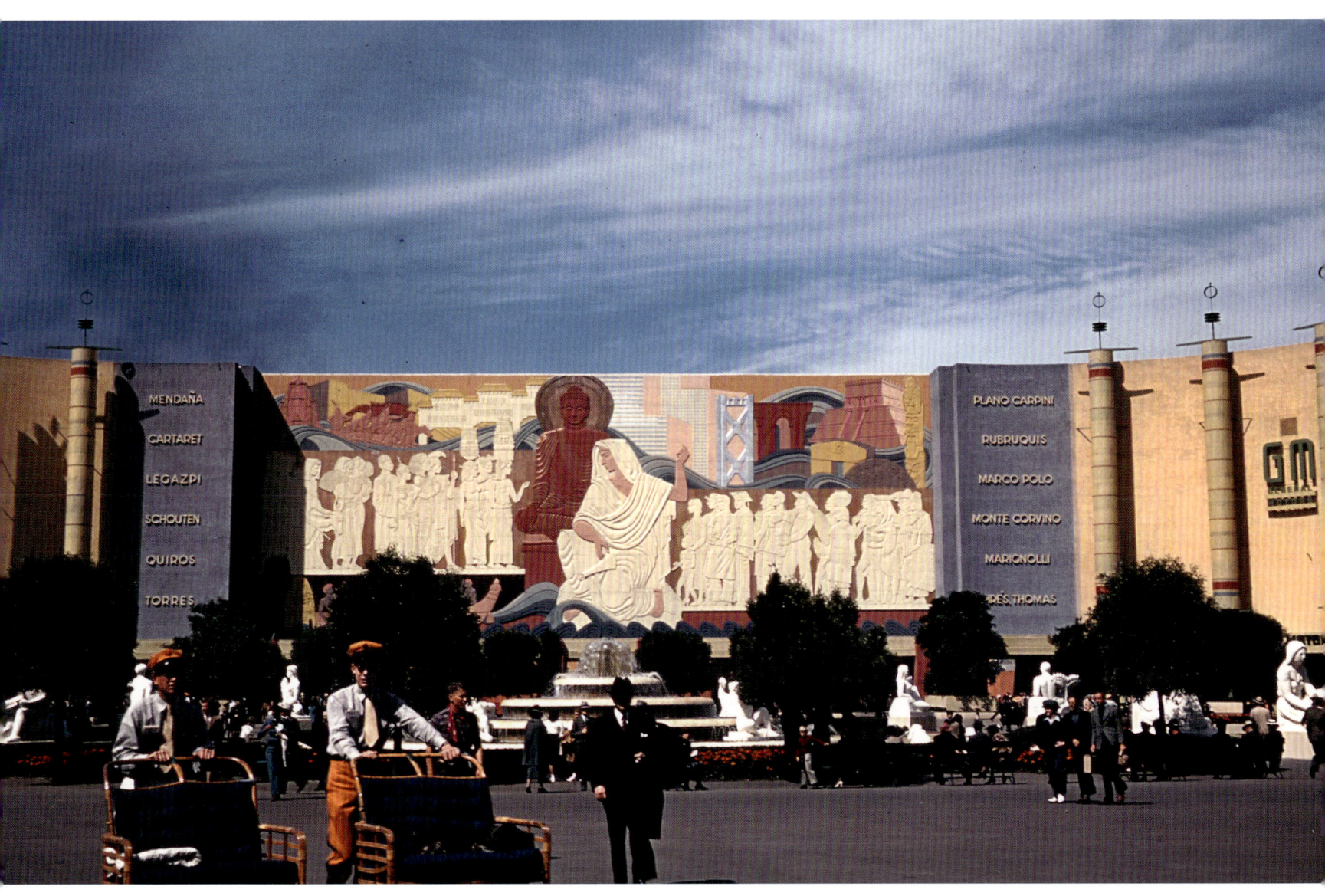

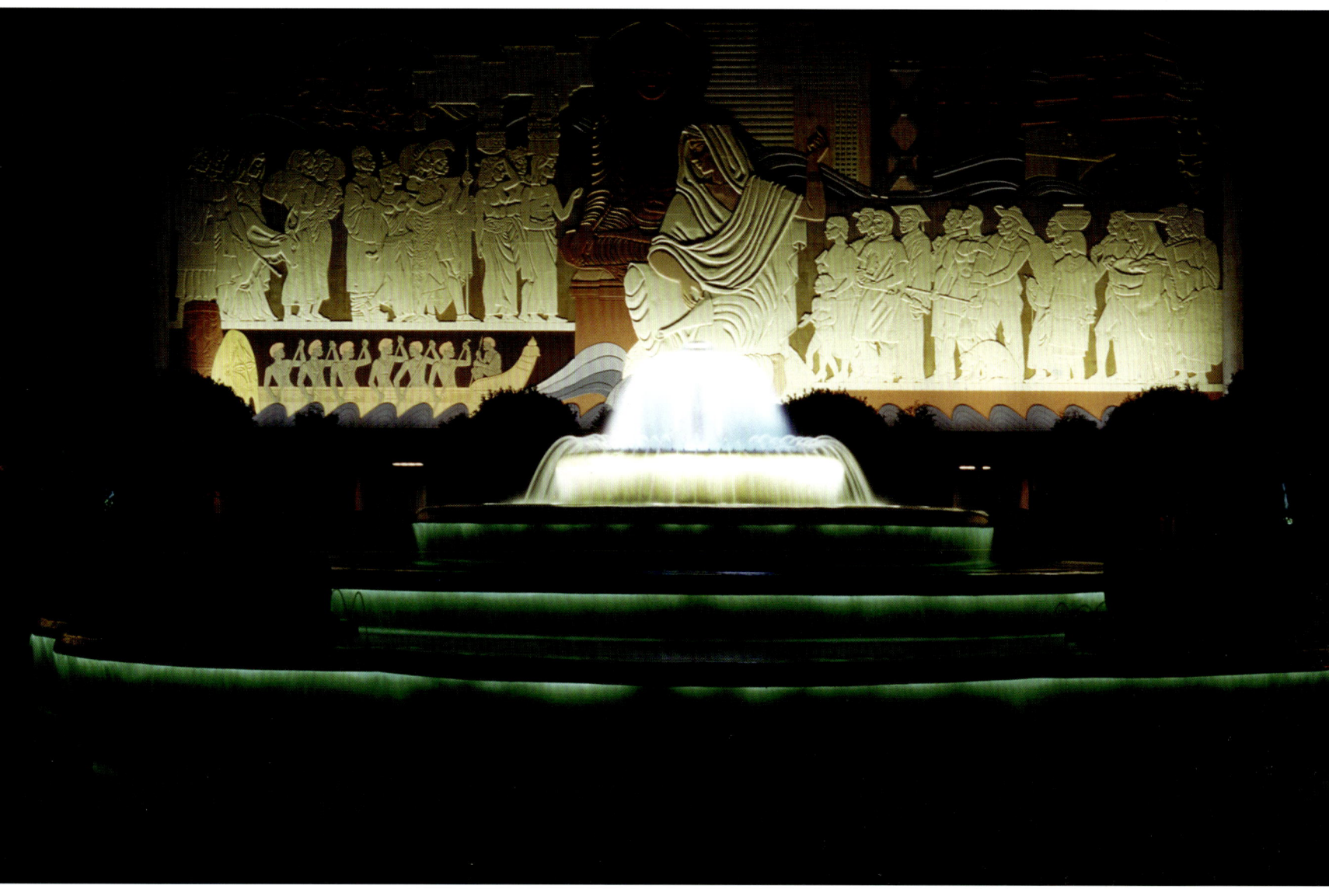

At the center of the mural stand two commanding figures: a forty-foot-high Buddha representing the East ("the Orient") and a woman kneeling in a robe representing the West (the "Occident"). According to early plans, the Bible verse from which mural derived its title—"Blessed are the peacemakers, for they shall be called the children of God"—was to be inscribed on the unfurled scroll in the woman's right hand, though in the final piece the scroll was left blank. The waves of the Pacific undulate throughout the mural, uniting its elements, with the waves on the Eastern side also being ridden by a canoe with seven men aboard. The official fair guidebook described the figures in the friezes on either side of the two central figures as symbolizing the "slow march of mankind toward peaceful ideas of East and West." The mural was painted simply in blocks of muted colors. When illuminated with spotlights at night, the relief work created stunning shadows that accentuated the carved forms.

At least one present-day critic suggested that *The Peacemakers* mural was clumsy and naive in its attempt to honor Eastern cultures. Architectural historian Andrew Shanken pointed out that the figures representing the East are depicted as either primitive—such as bare-breasted natives rowing a canoe or carrying fruit and spears—or violent, like the "marauding horsemen" charging toward the Great Wall. The Court of Pacifica and *The Peacemakers* "makes clear just how much the Pacific, understood as a region, was a European invention tied to the heroic colonial project of civilizing, if not possessing, the Other." Yet the worldview expressed in the mural was not unique to the Brutons; in fact, it "perfectly expressed the attitude of the fair" and was in harmony with the other art and architecture on view.

The Peacemakers (as seen at night), by Margaret, Esther, and Helen Bruton (1939)

The Brutons themselves recognized that the design for their mural and its message might be considered naive. Helen admitted that "exacting scholars will find plenty to criticize," but the sisters' intention was to send a message of world peace to the people, not to please the experts. The usually subdued Margaret vigorously defended their vision to the press: "Some critics have scoffed at our idea as far-fetched," she told the *Christian Science Monitor*, "But—is it? ... Regardless of outward differences of race, creed, and customs, we must continually strive to keep before us the realization of the brotherhood of man." Despite their confidence in their achievement, there was still a degree of trepidation about the bold statement they had made in their oversized artwork. When asked what they would do once the mural was installed, Helen replied, "We'll have to wait as patiently as we can for the opening date, hoping that the public will like our mural, and understand it."

The sisters had nothing to fear, as both art critics and fair attendees were thrilled by *The Peacemakers*. The work was "as beautiful as it was massive," and the Brutons' inventive process for creating the mural was deemed "new and spectacular." UC Berkeley professor Eugen Neuhaus called it "unusual and bold" and an "ambitious technical experiment." He was particularly impressed with the Brutons' ingenuity and their modern approach to solving an array of technical problems. He remarked that the mural was of special interest because the Brutons' use of Masonite represented "a technical innovation which has been made possible by modern industrial technical research." Others were in full agreement with Neuhaus, proclaiming that the mural was "one of the most outstandingly successful mural decorations at the fair" and an "outstanding artistic achievement." There were, of course, a few detractors. An unknown critic wrote to Timothy Pflueger to complain about the "commercial barbarism" of both Ralph Stackpole's *Pacifica* and the Brutons' *The Peacemakers*, exclaiming, "I expect the stunning Bruton bas-relief to advertise Coca Cola any minute!" Although it's unclear why this individual considered the Brutons' work to be commercial, at the very least he described it as "stunning."

Perhaps the most impressive aspect of *The Peacemakers* was its massive size. One reporter said that "the Bruton sisters' doubly-colossal, multicolored bas-relief of *The Peacemakers* [was] too much for our meagre critical gaze to absorb all at once. We clucked our tongues admiringly and backed away..." Another writer humorously remarked that the mural "looks to be nine miles high, seventeen miles wide, and a little like something cooked up by Paul Bunyan." Today, with the mural only surviving in photographs, its scale is even harder to grasp. Helen remembered laughing about the Buddha's ears, "They were about six feet." An image of the Brutons posing with two of the panels reveals that the heads of the smaller figures in the friezes were as tall as the Brutons themselves.

The Brutons' knack for creativity and originality was noted by *California Arts & Architecture*, which imagined that "given a few sticks and stones, odd pieces of string and some old rubber tubing, they are as likely as not to turn out something that will take your breath to the last gasp." The same article describes a humiliating incident that occurred when the Brutons went along on a group tour of the fair:

> Led by a mouthy young guy who was doing a fast spiel on all points of interest, [the Brutons] paused with the rest in front of their magnificent mural... The crowd gaped, the Brutons stood happily and anonymously listening as the young guide ripped off the facts and figures of size and dimension, only to hear him top off

the recital with, "and ladies and gentlemen, the whole thing was done by three old maids from Alameda."

It is not known whether the Brutons were able to brush off this in-person incident—as well as the record of it published in a respected arts journal—with confidence and sense of humor. As all three women were unmarried and in their forties at the time, it is certainly possible that they found the "old maid" comment both embarrassing and hurtful. Nevertheless, Helen was immensely proud of what she and her sisters had accomplished: "I am convinced, and not necessarily from conceit either, that time will prove what we have done there to be as important a contribution to the success of the show as any other single feature there."

Although initially the Brutons' $20,000 commission for *The Peacemakers* seemed extremely generous, the sisters later discovered that more than half the money would be spent on the raw materials for their mural. According to their contract with Exposition organizers, they were to be paid four installments of $5,000, with the final payment made when the mural was in place. By mid-February, nearly a month after the mural's completion, they had received just two payments, or $10,000. Helen, as unofficial business manager for the Brutons, was the one who made sure the sisters were paid for their work. She explained to the Brutons' lawyer, "most of [the money] has gone toward meeting our own obligations—labor, material, and final erection costs, and we are counting on the last two payments to pay us for the year's work... It has cost us too much effort to make [the mural] a present." In a letter to the Exposition's Assistant Treasurer, Helen demanded that the sisters get paid what they were owed: "If we do not receive the balance, or at least the third part, very soon, we will be obliged to turn the matter over to our attorneys." Shortly thereafter, the sisters received the final $10,000 of their commission.

The first year of the Golden Gate International Exposition ran from February through October of 1939. When President Franklin D. Roosevelt visited the fair, he proclaimed that "the year 1939 would go down in history... [as] a year of worldwide rejoicing if it could also mark definite steps toward permanent world peace." This celebration of international harmony was happening, of course, just as war was brewing on the other side of the world. As Hitler's troops marched into Poland, it was uncertain whether the fair would open again, especially since its first year had been unprofitable. After much deliberation, the fair reopened for a second season on May 25, 1940 with a new theme: "Fun in Forty." The Exposition transitioned from a celebration of world peace and cooperation to a nationalistic emphasis on "America's role as a peacemaker in a world harried by war."

During the second season of the fair, the Brutons again collaborated with Timothy Pflueger, this time on a new and innovative program at the Exposition's Fine Arts Palace. The "palace"—in fact, a permanent hangar building on Treasure Island—housed an astonishing temporary exhibition of European art treasures, including Botticelli's *Birth of Venus*, as well as works by Michelangelo, Raphael, Rembrandt, and El Greco. The exhibition also featured contemporary painting and sculpture, textiles, ceramics, furniture, costumes, jewelry, miniature rooms, bookbinding, metalwork, and a photography exhibition organized by Ansel Adams. Yet after the Fine Arts Palace's first season, many of the important works of art were shipped back to Europe, leaving a vacant section in the warehouse-like building. Pflueger's solution was to fill the empty space with an innovative project that would put actual artists on display so that fair visitors could view them while

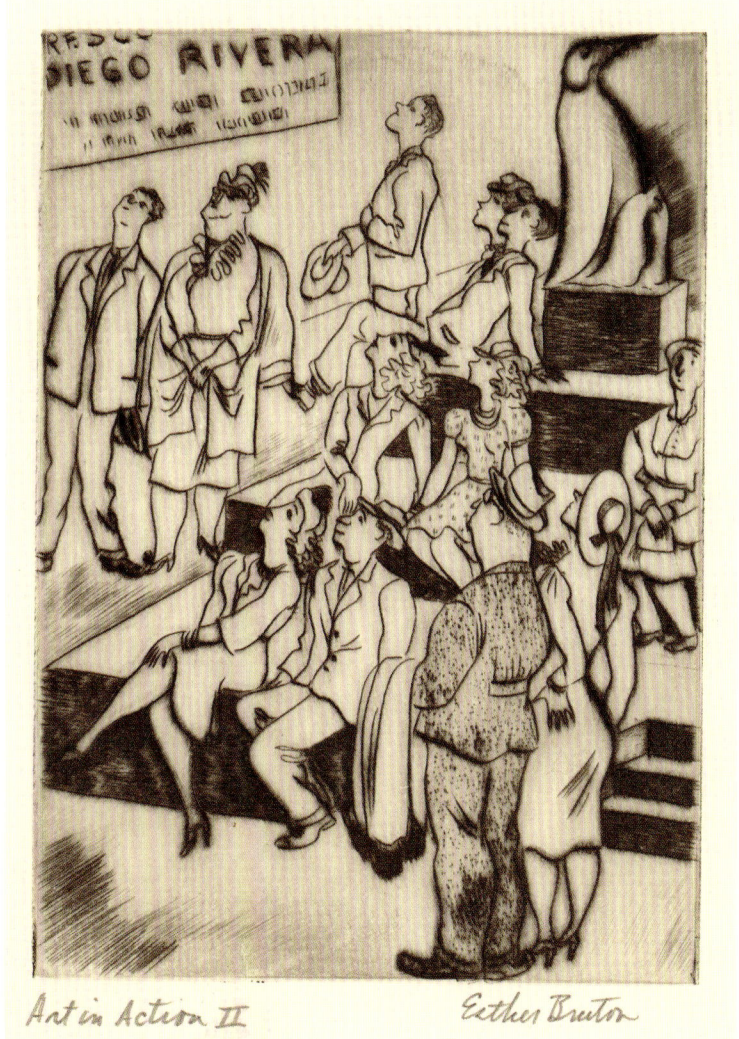

Art in Action II, by Esther Bruton (1940)

113

SAN FRANCISCO ART ASSOCIATION
BULLETIN

VOL 6 »»»»»»»»»»»»»» **APRIL 1940** «««««««««««««««« **NO 9**

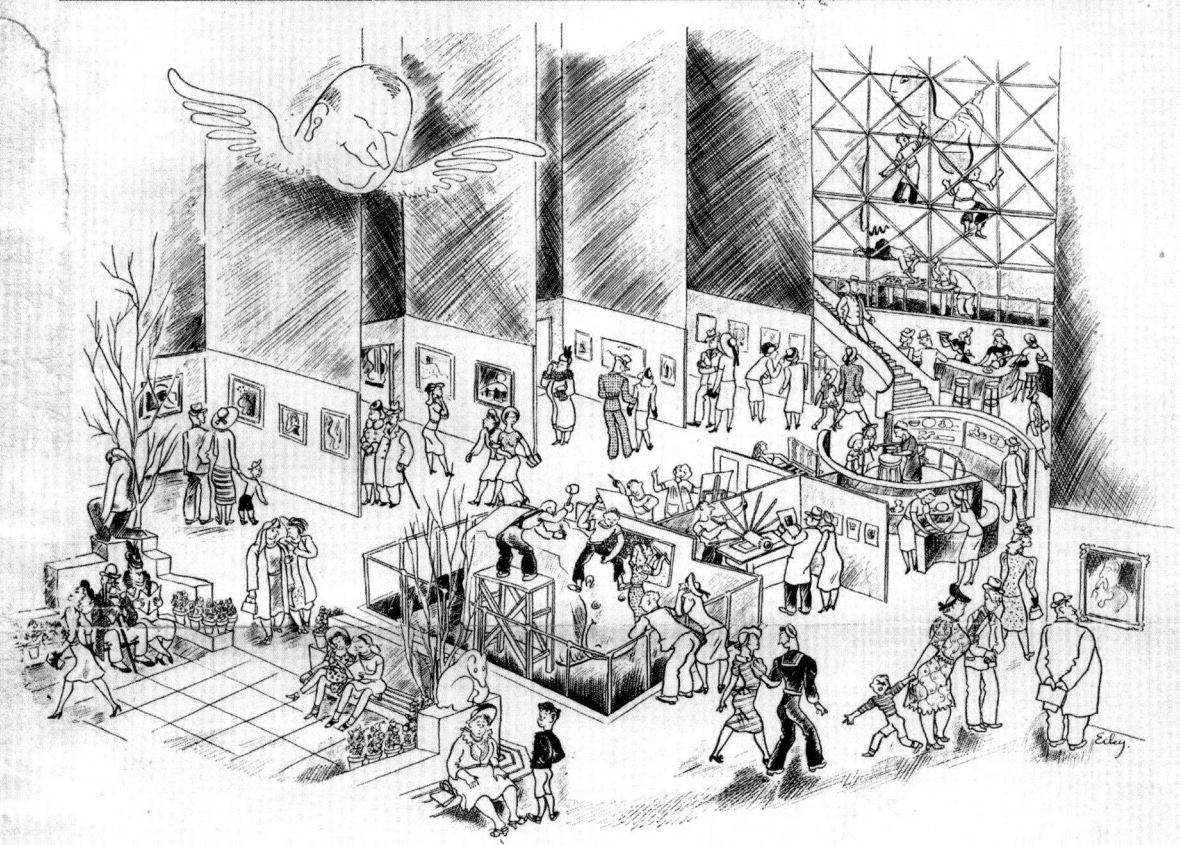

The Active Arts Section of the 1940 Fine Arts Show   Presented by ESTHER BRUTON

Fine Arts in the 1940 Fair
Active Arts Section to Present Artists at Work

By MILDRED ROSENTHAL

they worked. At the time, this inventive program, called "Art in Action" was deemed "unprecedented in the history of art display." Pflueger asked Helen Bruton to direct, organize, and run the program, which, at first, she was reluctant to do. She wrote to Pflueger, "if you still haven't got a better person… I'll do it—so help me." Eventually she agreed to take on the challenge—a headline in the *Oakland Tribune* proclaimed, "Miss Bruton in Charge."

Once Helen had fully committed to the project, she dove in with enthusiasm. She told Pflueger, "my brain has been ticking so loud these nights that I fear it must keep Ek [Esther] awake in the next room. And ideas have been hopping in and out so fast I can't hold on to them all." Helen's goal was to get famous artists to participate, hoping that name recognition would boost excitement and interest in the program. As she explained to the press, "We expect it to be quite a circus, and yet we are in no way compromising with the beauty of arrangements that is essential to the showing of fine things." She started out "aiming wide and high" when it came to selecting talent. She sent Pflueger drafts of her letters to potential participants, saying, "If these letters don't scare you off me completely, send 'em back—with whatever suggestions or changes you think necessary. And don't hesitate to tell me I'm screwy, or unsafe in such a position. But if it's o.k. with you, I'll go out after more game."

Her first draft letter was to Alexander Calder, asking if he would contribute one of his large mobiles—which he had been developing and exhibiting throughout the 1930s—for display. Her pitch to Calder included the explanation that the Fine Arts Palace could benefit from his "particular brand

Esther Bruton's drawing of Art in Action that appeared on the cover of the *San Francisco Art Association Bulletin* (1940)

of excitement." She also reminded Calder that his father, Stirling, had been one of her first art teachers at The Art Students League. Helen's next letter was to Salvador Dalí. Its casual tone suggests that she already knew the famous artist: "What are our chances of having a large, three dimensional, animated, work of art of yours[?]… It would be perfect to have you here to see personally to the execution." Her note toward the end of the letter that "the ballet was exquisite" likely refers to *Bacchanal*, which had debuted in New York the previous year and for which Dalí had created controversial costumes. Helen thought it would be a coup to get Walt Disney involved in the Art in Action program. She drafted a letter to her Alameda High School classmate Ben Sharpsteen, a director and producer who was Disney's "right hand man." She asked "Benny" if a Disney animator might participate in Art in Action, or if it would be possible to premiere a Disney film at the fair, accompanied by live symphonic music. She finished the letter by stating, "Nothing like asking for plenty. Boy! But I'm dead serious." It is unlikely that any of these drafted letters were ever sent to their intended recipients, and none of Helen's proposed ideas ever came to fruition.

Esther Bruton also had some ideas about the Art in Action program, writing to Pflueger, "We all think your court idea of art in the making really fine; the life and action will help animate that huge exhibition place." But she also hoped the decorative arts could be better represented, a hint of the direction her career would take in the next decade. "Beside [sic] the public interest in this [decorative arts] business (women particularly are very much interested) I'm thinking of the help to artist decorators of having their work incorporated into the space for living… instead of just being seen on museum walls." Esther also suggested that since there was no money to

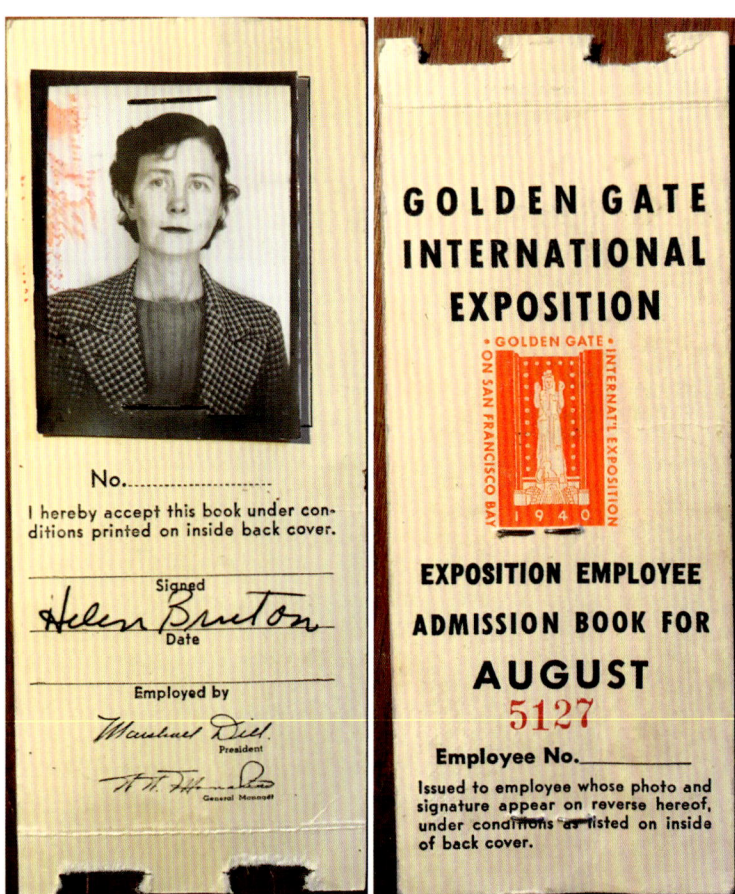

Helen Bruton's employee admission book for the Golden Gate International Exposition, 1940

pay the artists for their participation, they should be allowed to display and sell their finished works at the venue. Pflueger implemented Esther's suggestion, although he later stated that "practically none of the artists made anything out of the sale of work they did at the Exposition."

Organizing this four-month "live exhibition" of artists was an enormous undertaking, yet Helen downplayed her importance with her typical humility. She claimed that she "wasn't really running it at all. I couldn't run anything," while also stating, "I never had more fun in my life." Her memories of fun do not mean the job was without controversy: Helen often had to handle herself in uncomfortable situations while managing Art in Action. When a gentleman brought in a silver ice pitcher to ask if it might be exhibited, Helen explained that only works by participating artists were put on display and turned him down. The man was insulted, and the fact that the rejection came from a woman must have been especially galling. In a letter of complaint to Pflueger, he wrote, "I am curious to know if Mrs. Bruton's attitude is justifiable." Pflueger gave his full support to Helen, replying, "I have the utmost confidence in Miss Bruton's decisions. Her task has been an exceedingly difficult one, but I know she has approached each problem in a spirit of fairness."

Helen encouraged her artist friends to participate in the Art in Action program, and many agreed to. Helen Forbes demonstrated tempera painting, Ruth Cravath sculpted a horse's head from stone, Maxine Albro painted in oils, and Maja Albee demonstrated weaving. The Brutons' good friend Katy Skeele set up her easel and drew nearly four hundred portraits of visitors in crayon over a two-month period. Helen also asked her sisters to participate. Margaret demonstrated the "construction of murals" when the San Francisco Society of Women Artists took over the Art in Action area. Esther also joined in, constructing a mosaic bird bath she called *The Early Bird*. A Bay Area newspaper included a photograph of Esther working on the bird bath with a rapt group of spectators looking on. Intentionally or not, Helen Bruton had done a huge service for women artists. As fair visitors filed through the Palace of Fine Arts, they observed large numbers of talented and confident women artists at work, which would have been both surprising and enlightening to many in the audience. Perhaps even more than *The Peacemakers*, the live Art in Action demonstrations likely changed hearts and minds when it came to the public's perception about women's roles in the arts.

Art in Action's emphasis on women artists was noted in the press, although sometimes with some bias. One newspaper wrote that "several wild-looking female artists are modeling curious looking figures in clay or carving them out of sandstone." After a press event, the *Oakland Tribune* stated that "Helen Bruton, one of the able workers, suggested that women do all the work and added that it was hard to overestimate what was going on in the Palace of Fine Arts in the interests of art." Helen's comment seems to indicate that, in her view, women artists were largely responsible for the success of the Art in Action program. A few months later, "the three famous muralists, Helen, Margaret, and Esther Bruton" participated in a talk on women's contributions at the Exposition.

Altogether, eighty-one artists came through the "Active Arts Section"—the roped-off area of the Fine Arts Palace where the artists worked—and many were men: Glen Lukens made ceramics, Dudley Carter created wood sculptures using an ax, and Antonio Sotomayor drew caricatures, all as Robert Howard's mobile *Galaxy* (rather than the intended work

by Alexander Calder) rotated above the space. Sotomayor's caricature of Esther, which captures her vibrant personality, was later described as "a small blonde cyclone of energy, with freckles." Since there was no money to pay the artists, they received a one-dollar stipend per day, presumably to pay for their lunch, but the excitement and exposure was just as much of a draw. Ansel Adams was there too, taking photographs that later appeared in *California Arts & Architecture*. As Helen remarked, "they all had such a good time. It was just like a circus going on in the middle of this depressed pit." The "circus" atmosphere is evident in Esther's drawings of the bustling activity in the Active Arts Section. One of her humorous illustrations, which was featured on the cover of the April 1940 *San Francisco Art Association Bulletin*, depicts artists working on their various projects, spectators viewing the art, figures standing on scaffolding as they work on a mural, and a caricature of Timothy Pflueger with angel wings, floating above the chaos.

On one interior wall of the Fine Arts building, WPA artists worked on a mosaic designed by Herman Volz depicting great figures of science. On the opposite wall, artist Diego Rivera was toiling on a huge fresco he called *The Marriage of the Artistic Expression of the North and of the South on this Continent*, known today as *Pan American Unity*. This sweeping, intricate, and monumental fresco was painted on movable panels so that after the Exposition it could be installed at San Francisco's new community college, now called the City College of San Francisco. It seems that the plan to make the murals easily transferable for placement after the fair had been devised—or at least suggested—by Helen Bruton months earlier; in a February 1940 letter to Pflueger, she said, "We would have to devise a way to do [the fresco] so it could be moved successfully, and sell somebody the idea of taking it afterwards, maybe putting up some of the money."

When Rivera came to the Golden Gate International Exposition in 1940, he was divorced from his wife Frida Kahlo. The couple reunited when Kahlo joined Rivera in San Francisco while he was working on his fresco. The Bruton sisters probably knew Kahlo, and Margaret drew a portrait of her, giving it the title *Frieda Rivera*. Diego Rivera commuted daily to Treasure Island from the apartment he shared with Kahlo in the Telegraph Hill district of San Francisco. Although Helen clearly appreciated his talent, as the overseer of the Fine Arts Palace, she found working with the unpredictable Rivera intensely frustrating. Later in life, she admitted that "we had the most terrible time with him." Rivera would routinely arrive six or seven hours late to work, after most of the fairgoers who had come to see him had left. Sometimes Rivera would work through the night, resulting in his even later appearance the following day. Rivera's fame and robust ego allowed him to get away with his inconsiderate behavior, which was clearly a problem for Helen—and for the reputation of Art in Action—as the most popular "live artist" attraction was absent during the busiest hours of the fair.

Despite challenges with Rivera, Helen Bruton's Art in Action program was an enormous success. It was described as "one of the most interesting and successful innovations at the fair" and "held the greatest emotion for the public... [It was] something to boast about." The national *Magazine of Art* wrote that "the 'Art in Action' project so dominates the Fine Arts Building at the San Francisco fair that it breathes its life into all sections... Last year the collection of Old Masters stole the show. It seems fitting that this year the living artists of California should be the center of attention." Renowned war

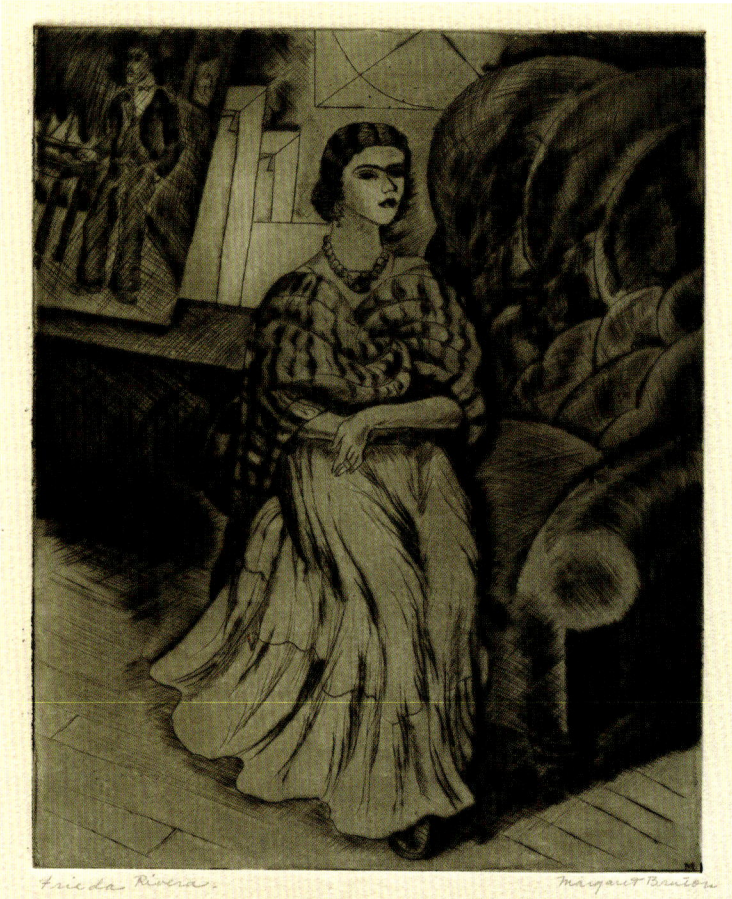

Frieda Rivera, by Margaret Bruton (ca. 1930s)

correspondent and journalist Ernie Pyle concurred, claiming that the Art in Action display was even better than the Old Masters. Pyle marveled at the "batch of artists actually drawing pictures, chiseling sculptures, carving wood and painting murals right before your eyes like performers in a circus."

His lack of punctuality aside, Rivera showed his support for Helen by praising the Art in Action program. "What a show!" he enthused. "This is the most stimulating way to create a richer understanding of the arts among the public... I am confident... that enthusiasm for the arts will grow." Grace McCann Morley, director of the San Francisco Museum of Art, hopefully claimed that Art in Action would "set a pattern for all exhibitions of the future." The program was so successful that after the close of the fair, the concept was repeated at the Society of Women Artists exhibition at the San Francisco Museum of Art.

As the fair began to wind down, the exhausted Brutons felt somewhat relieved. In a letter from September 1940, Esther wrote, "We have been so frantically busy helping 'put on a show' here at the Fair that the weeks fly by like days, and there is only one week more." Helen organized a party to thank the artists who had participated in Art in Action. The party invitation, complete with a poem, asked them to come in costume, dressed as one of the paintings from the Fine Arts exhibition:

Come as a picture from the Fine Arts Show
An apple by Cézanne - a potato by Van Gogh
An Old Master in action, a thigh bone by Dali,
But they'll be no Sanity in Art by golly.

Photographs indicate that Helen put on a party full of laughs, drinks, and singing around the piano. Many artists posed for photographs next to the paintings their costumes represented. Pflueger attended the party dressed as Diego Rivera, while Rivera appeared dressed as himself. Esther came as a portrait of Frida Kahlo, as did several other women. Helen and Margaret, who called themselves the "Picket Sisters," donned white coveralls and painter's caps, perhaps as a nod to all the hard work that had been put into the project.

On September 29, 1940, the final day of the fair, 85,000 spectators attended the closing ceremonies, which were broadcast by radio to millions across the country. Not surprisingly, given his erratic schedule and work ethic, Rivera's fresco was still incomplete at the end of the fair, and he and his assistants continued to toil away on it for an additional two months once the hangar was abandoned. On December 1, 1940, more than a thousand people returned to Treasure Island for a five-hour public viewing of Rivera's finished mural, which measured twenty-two feet high and seventy-five feet wide. Although the work ended up being almost twice as big as planned, it was nowhere near the size of the Bruton sisters' massive 8,000-square-foot mural.

The public viewing of Rivera's fresco was a "great success" as well as an unofficial "silent memorial service" for the once vibrant fairgrounds, now bleak and still. The seemingly solid and timeless Court of Pacifica—including the Brutons' *The Peacemakers* mural—stood literally and figuratively on a pillar of sand. Almost all of it was destroyed two years later. Like all world's fairs, the Golden Gate International Exposition was not built to last—its fantastical structures were simply "board-and-plaster illusions that had passed for palaces under the floodlights." Fair buildings were razed, the land was reclaimed, and life resumed its mundane rhythm and pace. One newspaper lamented, "the exhibit places, the exotic buildings, all the glamour of the Golden Gate International Exposition will be knocked down into just piles of salvageable lumber and pipes."

Twenty years later, Helen seemed accepting of the ephemeral nature of one of the Bruton sisters' greatest achievements:

> Everybody thought it was very sad, but I never missed it. We were given an opportunity to take it ourselves if we wanted it, but we couldn't imagine what we would do with it... We had to turn it down. I don't think it's too bad that those things don't last. They're made for a certain purpose and they get a little sad-looking afterward.

Yet closer to the end of her life, Helen remarked more sentimentally about *The Peacemakers*, saying, "What a pity it couldn't stay up." The Brutons' significant contributions to the Golden Gate International Exposition—their mural and Art in Action—were some of the most rewarding and successful of their artistic careers. But with the fair over and World War II on the horizon, the sisters were forced to look forward into an uncertain future, both for themselves and women artists in general.

The Bruton sisters, 1938

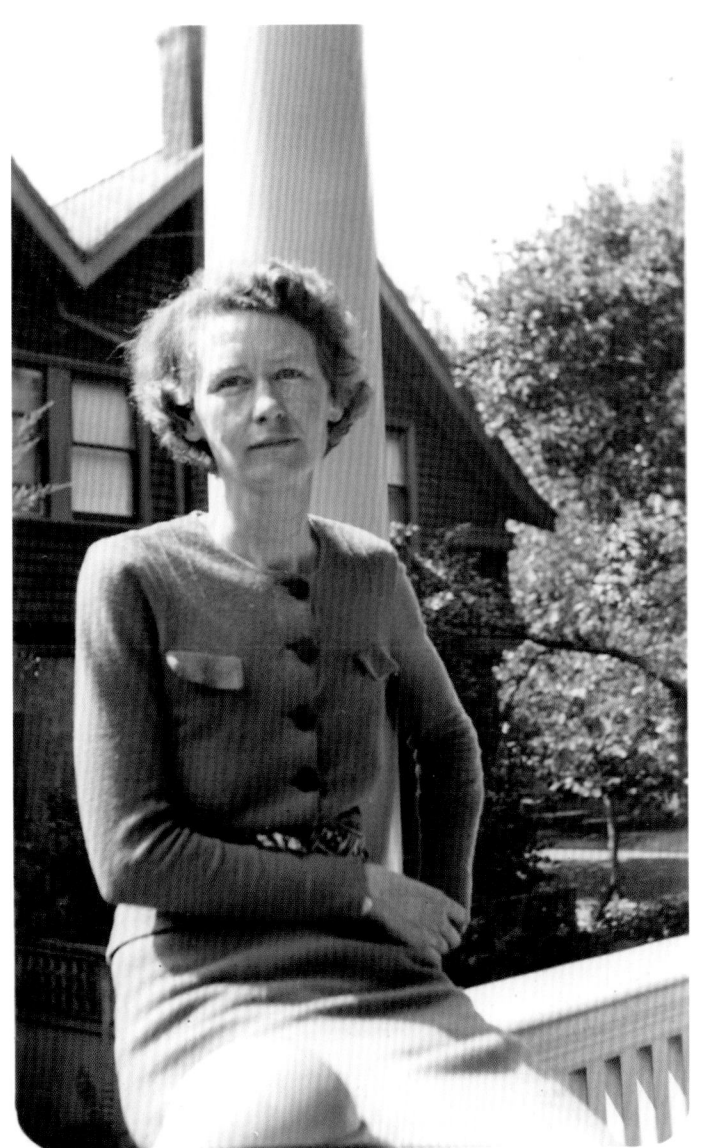
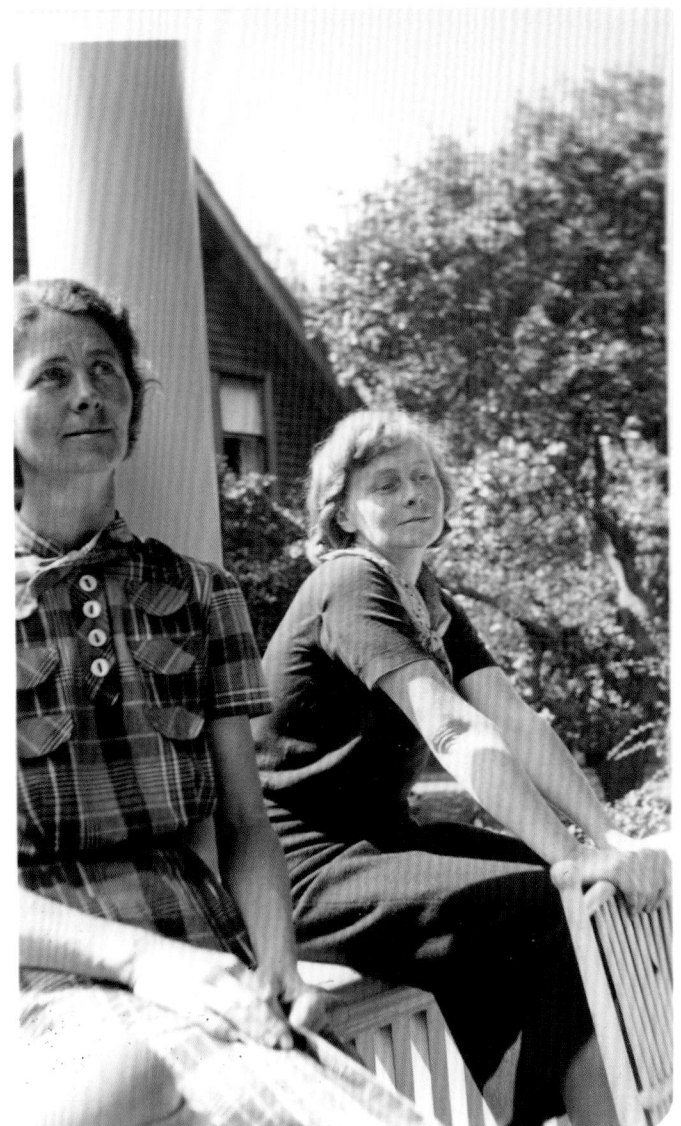

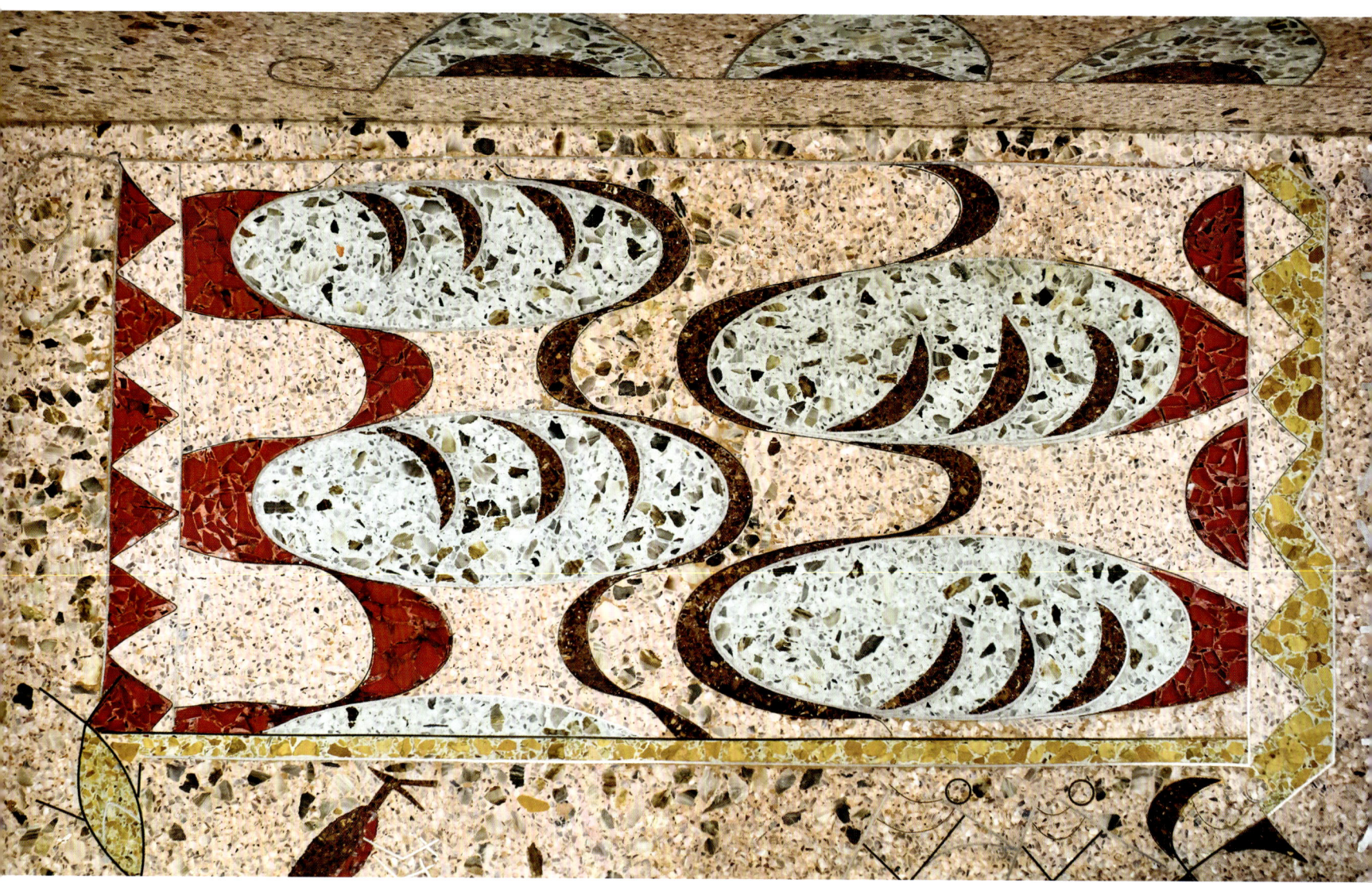

Terrazzo countertop created by Esther Bruton for her home in Ojai

CHAPTER NINE

"We Prefer a Living Art": Moving into the Decorative Arts
(1940s)

With the glory and success of *The Peacemakers* and Art in Action behind them, the 1940s brought about profound changes in each of the Bruton sisters' lives. They did what they could for the war effort, continued their artistic pursuits, and earned some important new commissions. Never ones to settle for status quo, they continued to experiment with new mediums, and their artwork developed in more modern directions. On a personal level, for the first time the trio was separated for an extended period, as Esther married and moved away and the family home in Alameda was sold.

In February 1941, the *Monterey Peninsula Herald* announced, "Their friends are extending a warm welcome to those two gifted artists, the Bruton sisters [Margaret and Helen], who have recently returned from San Francisco to again establish their residence here." A few months later, the same newspaper reported that Helen, Esther, and their mother were "motoring to New Orleans. The date of their return is indefinite." They were, in fact, on their way to Esther's wedding, which took place in New Orleans on April 4, 1941. Margaret is not in the family wedding photos and might not have made the trip because she was recovering from a mastectomy around the same time. She later referred to this procedure as her "first operation"; she had a second operation in 1976.

Esther was the only Bruton sister to marry, tying the knot when she was in her mid-forties. Her new husband, fifty-seven-year-old Carl Hooper Gilman, had been married twice before and had two grown sons. Gilman was a civil engineer whose career required him to travel extensively. He and Esther had met in Haiti in 1939, when both were on a trip to South America. They made a good match, as Carl's nomadic lifestyle was appealing to Esther. During the first few years of their marriage, they were constantly on the move as they traveled to Carl's various job sites; as Esther said, "Marry an engineer and see the world."

According to the sisters' friend Ruth Cravath, Carl "looked like a Bruton. It was very interesting. He was blond and slender and tall," just like his wife and her sisters. Gilman loved to sail, was interested in the arts, and acted and sang in amateur theatrical productions. Over the years, Esther visited the extended Gilman family in Maine several times. She was gracious and generous toward her stepchildren, playing tour guide to Carl's son when he visited California and even paying the college tuition of her two step-grandchildren. She also put her artistic talents to good use for the extended family, designing jar labels for the honey that the Gilman family produced. Carl, in turn, was proud of his wife's fame and was one of her greatest supporters. Completely unthreatened by the attention she received, he jokingly referred to himself as "Mr. Esther Bruton."

In addition to her marriage, Esther had a number of artistic triumphs in the first years of the new decade. The first occurred in 1940, when she won a national competition sponsored by the US Maritime Commission and the Federal Works Agency to make art for one of the new luxury ocean

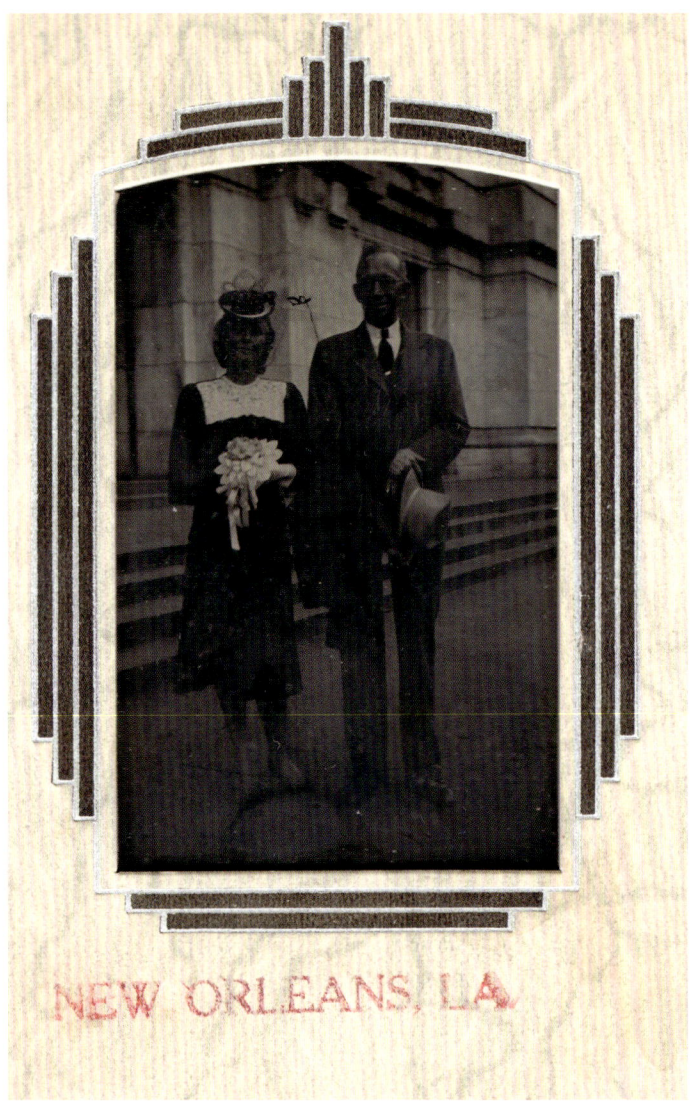

NEW ORLEANS, LA.

Esther Bruton and Carl Gilman on their wedding day, April 4, 1941

liners of the American President Line. When Esther painted a mural in the lounge of the steamship *President Garfield*, she returned to familiar artistic media, incorporating "glazed gold and palladium [silver] leaf" into her work.

Carl and Esther's first residence was in Mobile, Alabama, and the local community celebrated the fact that they now had "one of the country's most outstanding women artists" in their midst. While in Mobile, Esther painted a number of city scenes that were included in the exhibition *Ten Local Artists* at the San Francisco Museum of Art in 1942. The *San Francisco Chronicle* called the watercolors "sparkling, spirited, and sensitively created."

The following year Esther and Carl moved to Fontana, California, a town in the inland valley west of Los Angeles and not far from San Bernardino. Carl had been hired as head draftsman for the construction of a new war-effort steel factory, the Kaiser Steel Mill. The plant, which employed as many as 2,500 workers at its peak, began as a humble hog farm and was constructed in secret due to its importance to the war. As Carl's wife, Esther had access to the active construction site and found unexpected artistic possibilities within its chaos. "I usually go around looking for subjects," she once said, "but they aren't hard to find. You'll find something to paint wherever you go."

Esther painted at least fourteen watercolors documenting the transformation of the Fontana farm site into a gleaming factory. These watercolors—colorful, cheerful, and showing labor and industry in a positive light—have been aptly compared to Virginia Lee Burton's illustrations for the 1939 children's book *Mike Mulligan and His Steam Shovel*. The images' bright colors and action going on at all levels are not unlike scenes of a circus's big-top tent going up, a similarity that

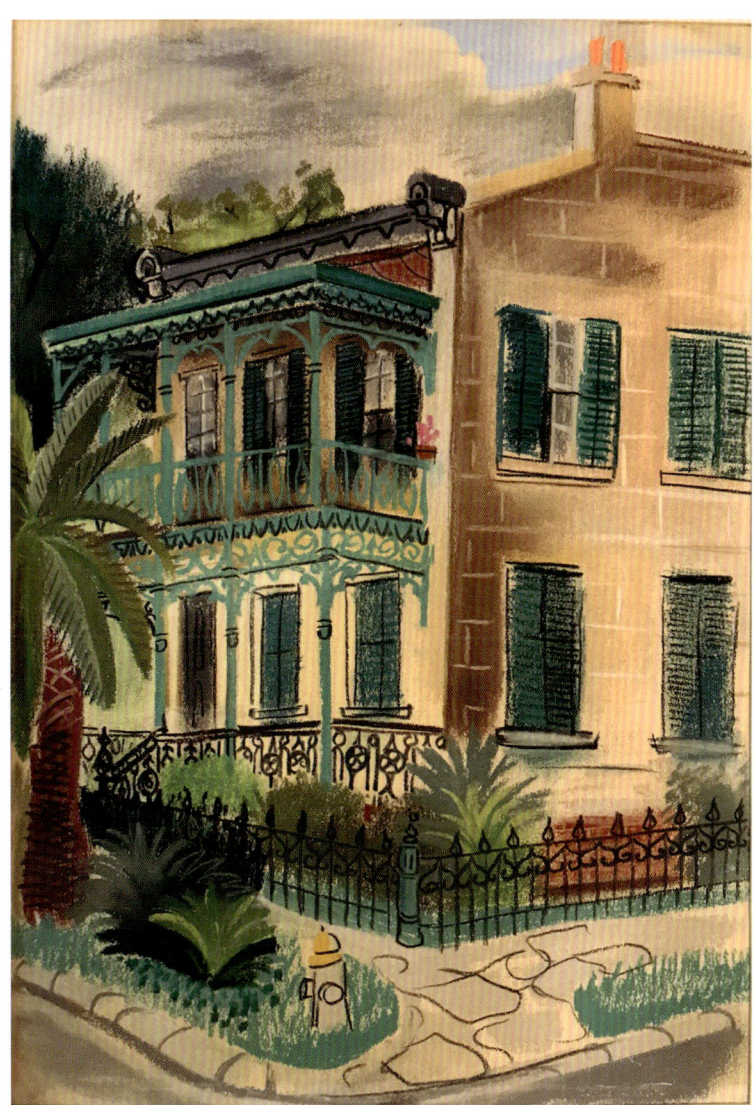

Faded Mansion, by Esther Bruton (ca. 1942)

Esther—a fan of circuses—was likely aware of, based on her statements about why she made the works:

> I guess I couldn't help doing them. I was fascinated by the pageant that was going on right under my nose—the rapid transformation of a quiet rural scene, orange groves and hog ranches, into that amazing and seething bit of industry... It was a colorful pageant too... I liked the abracadabra rapidity of the construction period, as if someone had rubbed Aladdin's lamp and it all rose up out of the orange orchards.

In October of 1943, Esther's watercolor series "From Pigs to Pig Iron" was included in a traveling exhibition organized by the Chaffey Community Art Association in nearby Ontario, California. Her works were described as "brilliant... They have enthralled art lovers... her vivid Kaiser paintings have been widely acclaimed for their vigor and strength." When the works were exhibited in a gallery in San Diego, a local art critic said they were "a revelation of the exquisite beauty of tone and form available in our frantic world, which most of us are too blind to see, until a seer makes us stop and consider. Here, fortunately, the seer is an experienced draftsman, a thorough craftsman as well as a rare spirit, and her work is full of surprising loveliness." Esther's works were also considered a valuable documentation of the war effort: "The transformation of a pig farm among orange groves into a plant producing the raw material of victory is a war epic worthy of the artist's skill... [The work] is a masterpiece of its kind." Eight of these paintings are in the collection of the Chaffey Community Museum of Art, where they are frequently on display.

After the Kaiser Steel Mill project was complete, Carl was hired by the engineering department of Convair, an aircraft

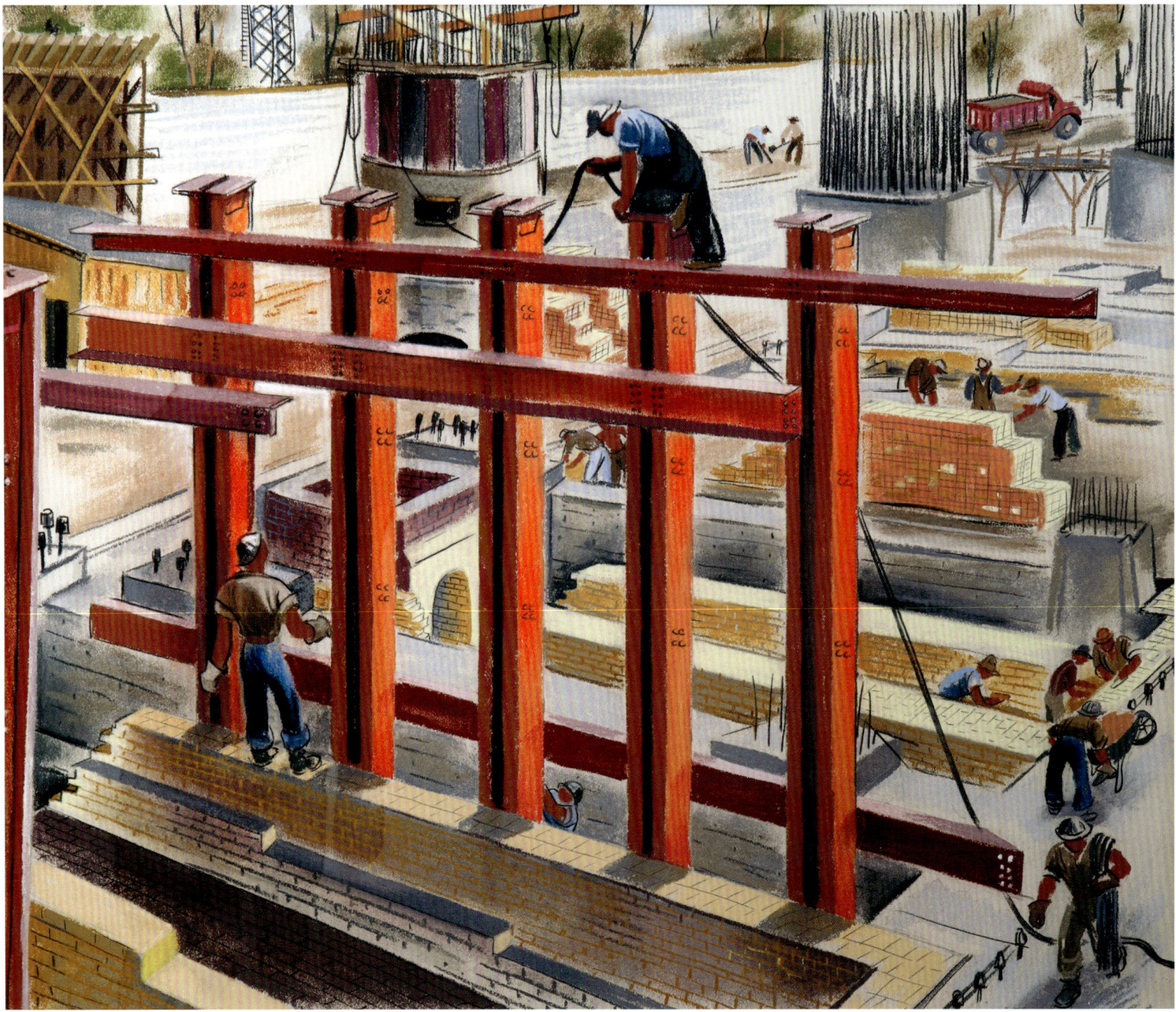

manufacturing company, and the Gilmans moved to San Diego. Esther got a job as a riveter in the Convair factory and threw herself into her new occupation. She was "just as keen about her bench-riveting assignment as she was about her painting... Her chief ambition is to make a nice countersunk rivet," one newspaper article stated. In an interview in the Convair newsletter, Esther said, "There's a certain amount of craftsmanship involved in this work." A photograph accompanying the article shows Esther dressed in coveralls with a rivet gun in her hand and a bandana wrapped around her head, looking remarkably like Rosie the Riveter.

When the war came to an end, Esther and Carl made an extended visit to Fryeburg, Maine, where they lived on a farm with Carl's son and daughter-in-law. It had been a dream of Carl's to run a family farm with his son, although after a few months he began to have his doubts about "how the two-family arrangement will work out in the long run." Esther threw herself into yet another new role, this time as a farmer's wife, and found the constant housework exceptionally tedious. "I must say I make a better farmer than farmer's wife," she remarked. "The housework I don't like nohow, and how these women are tied to it! Their whole existence is taken up by the mechanics of living." Although clearly out of her element, she maintained her sense of humor and looked on this new phase of her life as an adventure. She was particularly impressed with the domestic skills of her daughter-in-law, whom she described as "a farmer's wife by instinct, and a good one. Heck... she cans everything, even meat!"

By 1946, Esther and Carl returned to California, but Esther was tired of the chilly and foggy weather in the Bay Area. On a visit to Ojai, a small, inland town with a much warmer climate located due east of Santa Barbara, the Gilmans were taken by its rural beauty and charm. They purchased a piece of land and built an "ultra-modern" home and studio. Esther became part of a circle of artists centered around the Ojai Art Center. A 1953 article in the *Los Angeles Times* declared that "a multitude of fine work is being done in the Ojai Valley... They came to this rural community from all over, asking only to be allowed to create in their chosen field of art." The article gives some insight into this phase of Esther's life: "Mrs. Gilman works in a simple redwood studio whose large windows frame a rugged view of stony meadow and towering mountains." Esther loved having guests at her home in Ojai, which she and Carl were constantly expanding and improving. Margaret and Helen visited frequently, as did friends Imogen Cunningham and Katy Skeele.

Esther became a topic of curiosity and a minor celebrity in Ojai. She was interviewed on a regular basis, giving historians valuable insight into the personality of the mature, confident Esther Bruton, who was now nearly fifty years old. The sisters may have been bohemians during their youth in Monterey, but as they approached middle age, they were more frequently described as elegant, well dressed, and even conservative. A 1947 article about Esther began this way:

> Those who view women artists as strange bohemian creatures should meet Esther Bruton Gilman, an established artist, who is thoroughly nice and would satisfy the most conservative. She is the type of woman with wind-blown hair and a sprinkling of freckles [who] you would expect to see on a golf course. As a neighbor she is quietly cooperative, ready in an emergency, and never too busy for a friendly visit.

Girders, by Esther Bruton (ca. 1943). Collection Chaffey Community Museum of Art

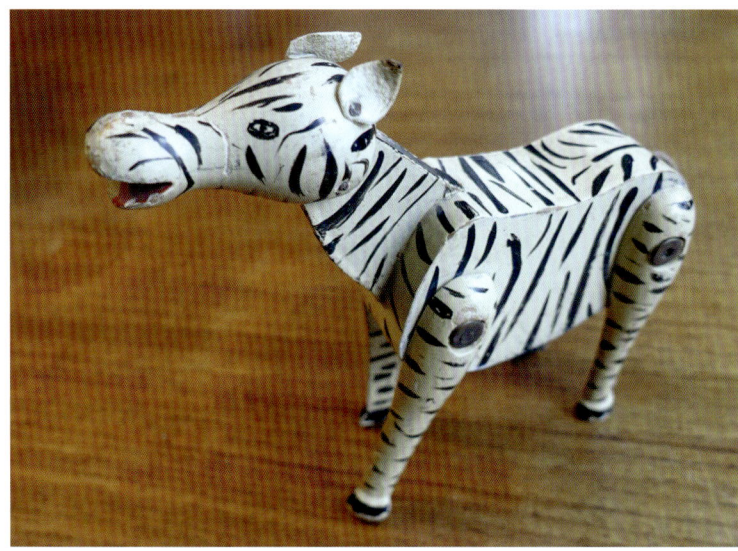
Wooden zebra toy, designed by Helen Bruton (1943)

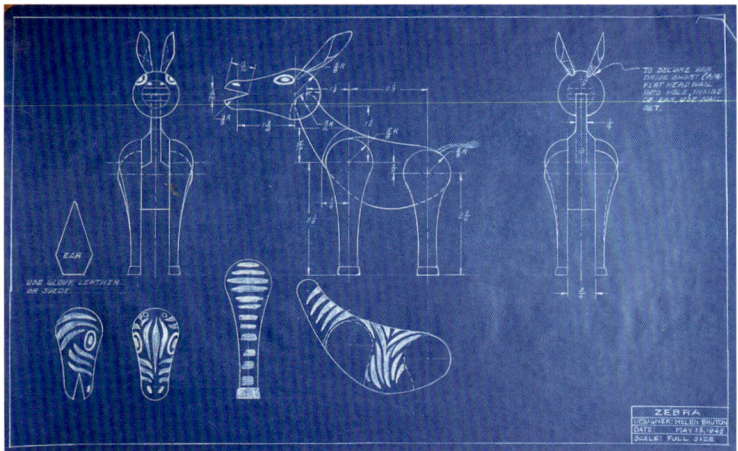
Blueprints for the zebra toy

Appearances aside, Esther was not ready to join the country club set, and continued to push boundaries with her art. One Ojai reporter focused on Esther as a working artist, describing her as "slight, unpretentious, energetic. She finds it hard to express in words her feeling about the work she does. She certainly is not an artist who brags about herself or her work. But one can see she creates beauty wherever she goes... She has won the respect and admiration of artists in other fields."

In 1947, more than a decade after completing her work in the Cirque Room of San Francisco's Fairmont Hotel, she was hired by the hotel again, this time to paint a series of murals for the hotel's new Merry-Go-Round Bar. The lounge included an actual rotating carousel, installed in the center of the room, upon which guests could sit and drink cocktails. Esther's murals in the room depicted "Golden Gate Park and Fleishhacker Zoo in 1903." The Fairmont Hotel marketed the Merry-Go-Round Bar as "America's most novel cocktail bar... and [one of] the most popular cocktail lounges in San Francisco." It was unveiled in April 1947, and from the start it was considered somewhat ridiculous: "People sitting on it... seem to feel rather silly," read one review. "But they put on a brave front and waved sheepishly to a few friends who had come round to stare." With lukewarm reviews, and after operating for less than five years, the Merry-Go-Round Bar was scheduled to close permanently in January 1952. In its final week, on Christmas Eve of 1951, a carelessly abandoned cigarette started a fire that destroyed the lounge, including Esther's murals. The former site of the Merry-Go-Round Bar is now the Fairmont's Laurel Court Restaurant and Bar. It is not difficult to imagine a carousel spinning under the room's high, circular, domed ceiling. Although Esther Bruton's works are gone, new murals have been painted on the curved walls.

While Esther was enjoying her new life as a married woman, Helen and Margaret were living with their mother in Alameda, dedicating themselves to war work, much as they had during World War I. Helen volunteered one day a week at the "Arts and Skills" unit of the San Francisco branch of the American Red Cross, demonstrating and teaching art projects to wounded soldiers. A designated "master craftsman" of the medium of mosaic, she supervised four to six other artists in the program. As was typical during wartime, women had taken over jobs traditionally performed by men. Helen and Margaret were both employed as draftsmen—Margaret worked at the Alameda shipyard and Helen at the nearby Naval Air Station, both putting their artistic talents toward work on technical plans and drawings. During this period, Helen was making technical drawings of her own, seemingly for her own amusement. In 1943 she drew a series of intricate blueprints with detailed instructions for the construction of small wooden circus animals, each measuring around six by eight inches. She even made prototypes of each animal and built a colorful circus wagon to house them. This could have been an amusing side project to distract herself from the serious concerns of the war years, or perhaps she was considering going into the toy-making business. Regardless, younger family members have enjoyed playing with Helen's wooden circus animals for decades.

In January 1944, the Brutons decided to settle permanently in their house in Monterey. With two sisters in Monterey and the third in Ojai, it no longer made sense to maintain the large family home in Alameda, and so the mansion on St. Charles Street, where the sisters spent their formative years and first experimented with art, was sold. The attic studio had been the birthplace not only of their childhood projects, but also many

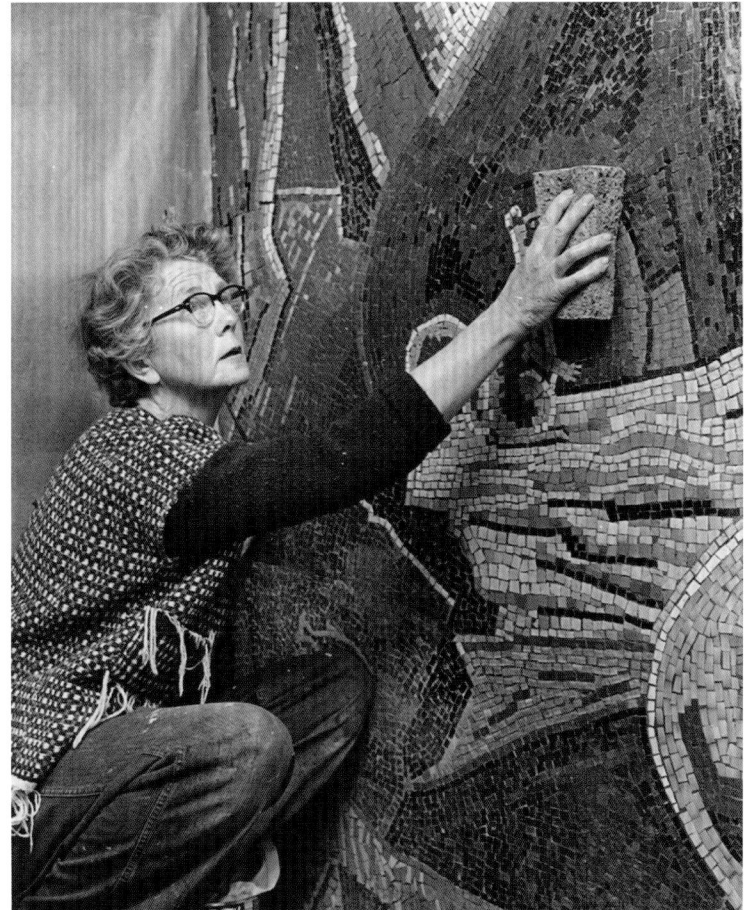

Helen Bruton working on the installation of a mosaic

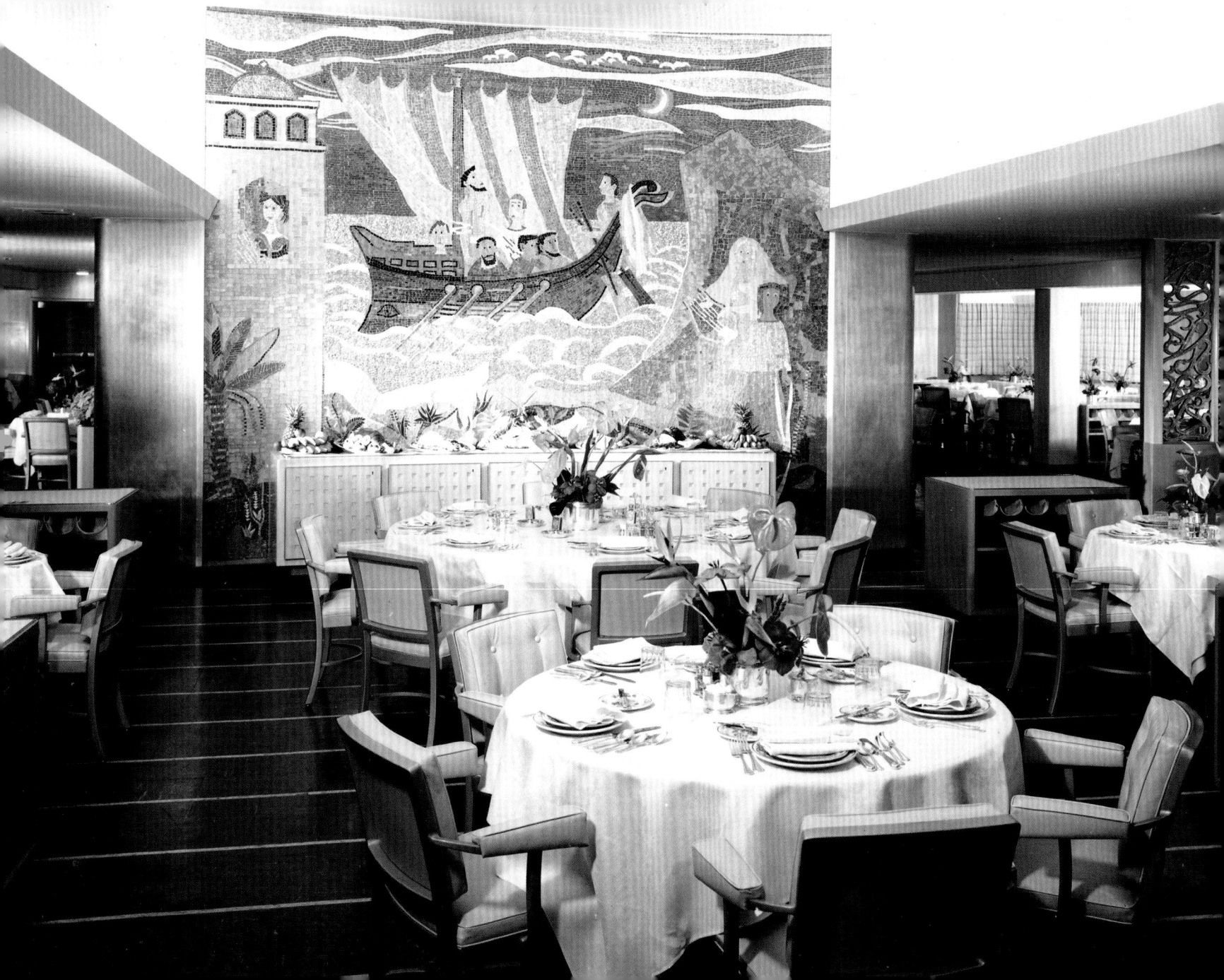

large-scale commissions they worked on as adults, including the Mothers Building mosaics. While it may have been painful to walk away from the gracious home and its countless memories, Helen and Margaret were returning to their Monterey home on Cass and El Dorado Streets, where they had lived during the 1920s—an especially exciting and productive period for them. Helen, who was still employed at the Naval Air Station in Alameda, needed a temporary place to stay in the Bay Area. In May 1944 she placed an ad in the *Oakland Tribune* that was bound to get attention: "WARNING—Anyone in Alameda knowing the whereabouts of an apartment… vacant now or soon and communicating such information to Helen Bruton… does so at their own risk… she works at Naval Air Station… can do own decorating, pinch hit for plumber or mother's helper, and needs your assistance."

After the war, Helen returned to the home in Monterey, and she and Margaret cared for their aging mother, who had a series of health problems and was eventually confined to a wheelchair. Although the sisters loved to travel, they cut back on their trips during this period, and one sister would always remain at home to care for their mother. In 1947, Helen's studio was built at 491 El Dorado Street in an area of Monterey called the Mesa, within walking distance of their home. The Brutons owned a large piece of land in the area, and in 1959 they sold five acres to the congregation of the First Presbyterian Church of Monterey, who was looking for a site to build a new church. Helen thought the church and its congregation would make good, quiet neighbors to have next door to her studio.

Once Margaret and Helen were committed to living full-time in Monterey, they became more involved in their local

Ulysses and the Sirens mosaic in the dining room of the SS *Lurline*, by Helen Bruton (1947)

community, including in a controversial matter concerning the redevelopment of the old wharf in Monterey. As the sardine industry declined in the mid-1940s, the decrepit wharf was slowly transforming from a functional fishing pier into a tourist attraction with concessions and restaurants. Many city residents opposed the plans to modify the wharf for tourism, feeling that such a renovation would effectively ruin the wharf's original character and charm. At the center of this controversy was Angelo's, the first restaurant to open on the wharf following World War II. Tensions rose when local artists Jean "Janko" Varda and Bruce Ariss painted the exterior of the restaurant—a former fish packing shed—in bright hues of blue and pink and added unusual architectural elements.

An editorial on the front page of the *Monterey Peninsula Herald* provided an excoriating criticism of the artists' design for Angelo's. "Whether one resents it as cheap, vulgar affectation, or as merely amusing," it stated, "the result is so remote from any trait in this community's true character that it offends one's sense of propriety, entirely apart from any question of art forms or good taste. Whether it's supposed to be cubist, futurist, impressionist, or vorticist is beside the point. It's NOT 'Monterey.'" Although many residents of Monterey agreed, there were others who came to the defense of Varda and Ariss. A few days later, the *Herald* published two letters to the editor, one from Helen Bruton and the other from Ed Ricketts, a friend of John Steinbeck and a Cannery Row fixture. Ricketts wrote that Varda "has dared to be free, to be original: he has expressed honestly his own individuality… the originality and courage of that group is to be commended. More power to Janko Varda and the Di Girolamos!" Helen's letter chided the *Herald* for presuming to be the arbiter of the town's taste. She pointed out Monterey's hypocrisy when evaluating the importance of historic buildings: "It was the artists long ago who first lifted up their voices in praise of the simple lines and dignified proportions of some of the old buildings, and not until they were found to have definite 'tourist appeal' did anyone else take them very seriously." Helen's impassioned and opinionated letter provides interesting insight into her views on art: "The most significant artists are always ahead of their time. It takes 'the average man' about twenty years to catch up... We should all be humble about this matter of 'taste' and appreciate that this is America, and that here, taste is still a matter of personal opinion and not ordered by directives from above." Helen couldn't resist concluding her letter with a dose of humor: "It is my personal opinion that 'Angelo's' on the old wharf is about the most vitalizing thing that has struck the town since lightning hit the oil tanks and burned for three days."

When Angelo's opened to the public in March 1946, the restaurant wisely capitalized on the controversy surrounding its colorful appearance. An advertisement for the grand opening played on the diverse opinions voiced about the restaurant: "It's artistic... It's unique... It's ghastly... It's shocking... It's spectacular... It's fantastic... It's garish... It's opening tomorrow." The ad also included excerpts from the letters written by Helen Bruton and Ed Ricketts. Angelo's went on to become an extremely successful mainstay on the Monterey wharf, popular with locals and tourists alike, and remained open for nearly forty years until it was sold in 1984.

The Brutons applied their artistic talents in support of their hometown during the Monterey Flag Raising Centennial of 1946. This enormous citywide celebration marked the hundredth anniversary of the raising of the American flag in Monterey. Notable interior designer and Monterey businesswoman Frances Adler Elkins was in charge of the project. In preparation for the enormous parade down Alvarado Street, businesses were redecorated, the street was painted gold, and store windows were adorned with decorations. Margaret contributed an "inlaid table and mobile birds" for the display in Lial's Music Shop. Margaret and Helen decorated Lial's window again for the 1946 "Yule Display Contest." They were awarded second prize for their design, which was praised for its "attractive use of brilliantly colored clay animals against a gold backdrop."

Renewed interest in travel during the postwar period brought unexpected opportunities for the Bruton sisters. As cruises became popular again, ships that had been used for troop and cargo transport during the war were in need of extensive retrofitting and renovation so that they could resume their original purpose as luxury liners. The Brutons, with their extensive experience creating large-scale murals and mosaics, found that they were in high demand. In 1947, Helen was paid $2,800 by the Matson Navigation Company to create a mosaic mural for the dining room of the SS *Lurline*, a cruise ship that was undergoing an extensive, twenty-million-dollar renovation at the Bethlehem-Alameda shipyard before resuming service between San Francisco and Hawaii. Helen chose the subject of Ulysses and the Sirens for her mural, making a preliminary sketch in pastel, as well as a collage of the work, to configure its design and color scheme. At fourteen feet by thirteen feet, *Ulysses and the Sirens* was one of the largest mosaics Helen had undertaken, and Margaret provided her with much-needed assistance during the installation. Like the mosaics she had designed in the 1930s, the *Ulysses* mosaic was also Byzantine in style, featuring two-dimensional figures and a simplified, abstract treatment of the background. The only significant development in Helen's style over the preceding fifteen years was her shift from ceramic to glass tiles in her mosaics, the latter being a material she considered "the most challenging medium available, both for color and texture." The finished mosaic on the *Lurline* was praised for its "sparkling colors—rich greens, yellows, blues, lavenders and gold, subtly combined and accented." By all accounts Helen was pleased with the piece, but it seems that despite her use of new materials, her technique hadn't evolved much beyond her 1930s style.

During this period, Margaret's art career was undergoing some dramatic changes. As early as 1932, Helen hinted that Margaret might have been struggling with her painting. "Marge had her easel set up in the sitting room," she wrote to Ina Perham. "If only she could get back to working a little again. I would be so happy." Despite the prizes she had won in the 1920s and 1930s—and her obvious talent and mastery of the medium—Margaret gave up painting altogether and began to focus on decorative arts. Family members recall her saying toward the end of her life that she hadn't painted in fifty years. According to Margaret, this movement toward decorative arts probably began around 1937, when she and her sisters participated in the *Mural Conceptualism* exhibition at the San Francisco Museum of Art. The purpose of this show was to provide "'samples' of what could be done to a wall... including decorations for large, public buildings." The exhibition emphasized collaborations between artist and architect, which would become the future path of the Brutons' artwork. *San Francisco Chronicle* art critic Alfred Frankenstein observed that the show included "many mosaics, most of them bad. The outstandingly good ones are those by... the three Bruton sisters." Later in life, Margaret identified the *Mural Conceptualism* show as "a turning point... It resulted in work

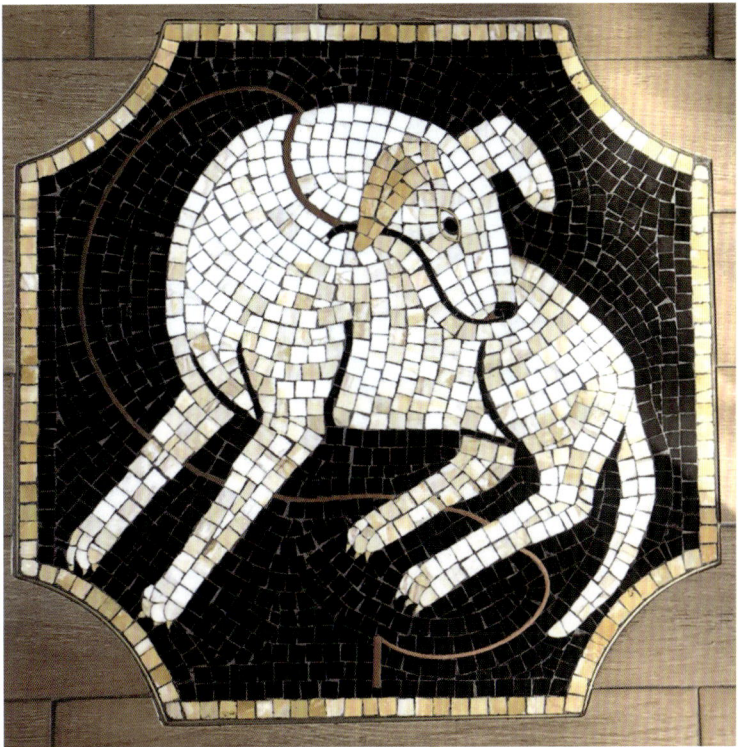

Dog mosaic, by Esther Bruton (ca. 1940s)

through architects and decorators that has kept us busy almost ever since."

One of Margaret's first forays into decorative arts may have been a work called *Carved Panel*, which she contributed to the 1939 exhibition of the San Francisco Society of Women Artists. A review of the show in the *Oakland Tribune* was overwhelmingly negative, stating that it was "so radical that it must give pause to hardy youth." The unidentified reviewer offered harsh and sarcastic judgments of many of the works—all by women artists—including Margaret's, which was disparagingly described as "French and English mustard colors along with a dash of mayonnaise." The critic clearly disapproved of modernism in general but also seemed to have a special level of contempt for women modernists in particular.

Having given up painting, Margaret discovered another medium that would occupy and challenge her for the rest of her life. She branched off from the mosaics she and her sisters had mastered during the 1930s and began to experiment with terrazzo, a technique normally used on floors. Although terrazzo derives from mosaic, it does not involve the placing of specific pieces in designated places. Instead, small chips of marble, granite, quartz, glass, or other materials are held in a composite mixture, such as concrete or an epoxy-resin binder, and poured into a location. After the terrazzo sets, the surface is ground to a glossy finish. As Esther, too, was "seeking mediums suitable for architectural work," she found that terrazzo offered many possibilities. While Margaret was in Monterey and Esther was in Ojai, both sisters began to experiment independently with terrazzo in their own studios. Again, the Brutons were pioneers in the medium, transforming it to their own purposes. Instead of using terrazzo on floors, Margaret and Esther discovered the potential to use it on tables, countertops, fireplace surrounds, and other architectural elements.

Esther exhibited her first terrazzo piece at a decorative art show at the de Young Museum as early as 1934, but she began her experimentation in earnest while decorating her Ojai home in the 1940s. One of her first attempts was a terrazzo dog with a metallic leash that she placed near the entrance of her house. The technique she developed to make her terrazzo pieces was unconventional and inventive:

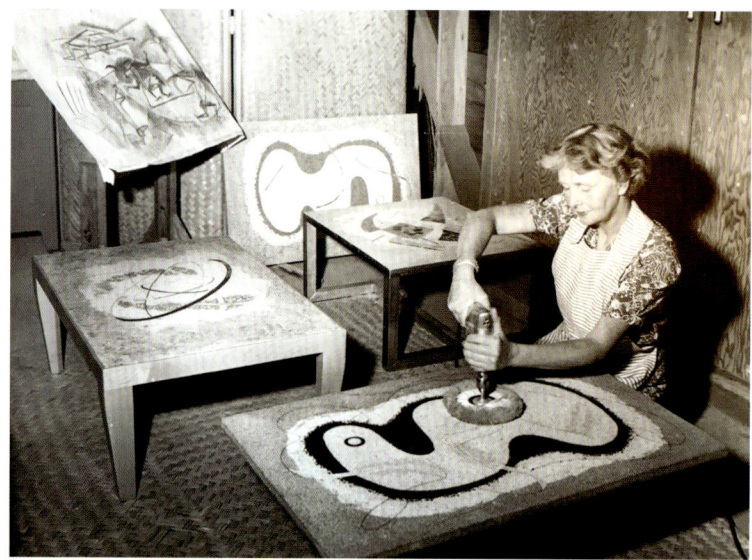

Esther Bruton polishing a terrazzo tabletop, photo by Thelner Hoover

After making her design, she uses brass strips, nails them in place temporarily, and pours a mixture of cement, coloring and granite, limestone, abalone shell, or what-have-you into the sections that have been partitioned off. She achieves a variety of colors and effects that are very interesting... A filling of cement is poured over the design, forming a solid back for the work.

No materials were off limits when Esther constructed her terrazzo pieces; she used "chicken scratch, Coca Cola bottles, road repair rock, fine native and imported marbles, and metal filings from machine shops." Since terrazzo is essentially created "upside down," the artist does not know how the piece will appear until the binding material is set and the work

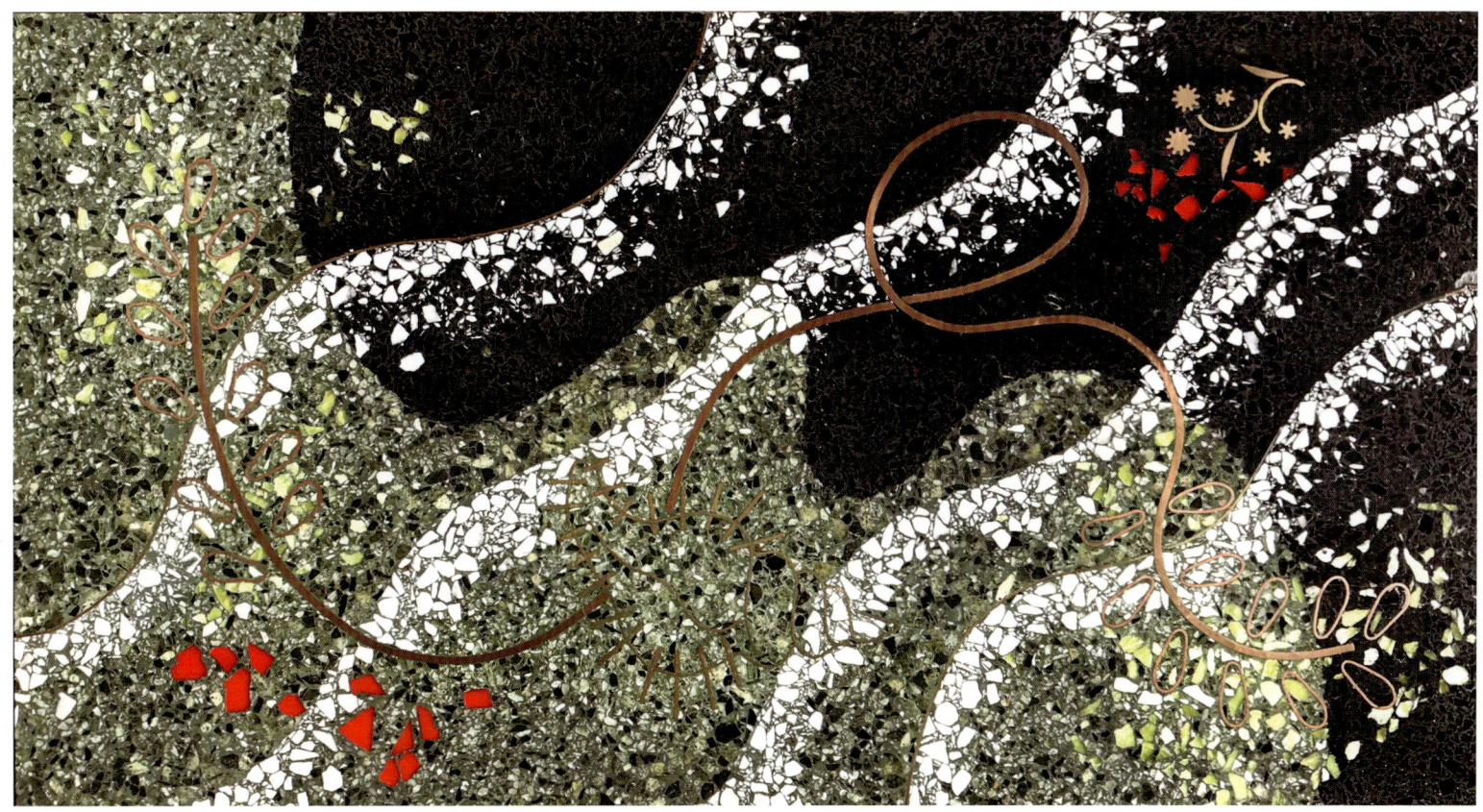

Terrazzo tabletop by Margaret Bruton (ca. 1945)

is flipped over and revealed. "We're working completely in the dark," Esther explained. "We're not sure what we'll have till it's polished, for polishing changes the colors." Esther's husband was a willing and enthusiastic participant in her terrazzo projects. "Without my husband's help it would be quite impossible for me to handle the heavy stone and forms,"

Esther explained. "He does all the heavy work and is a most wonderful helper."

Much of the work that the Bruton sisters made—whether murals, mosaic, or terrazzo—was done on a large scale and was physically demanding. The materials they worked with were heavy and often messy; photographs of the Brutons at work in their studios show them wearing overalls, smocks, gloves, and headscarves, positioned either down on their knees as they carefully placed mosaic pieces or standing while using electric sanders to smooth the surfaces of their terrazzos. Many of their large-scale projects were done when they were in their fifties and sixties, yet they seemed to have remarkable stamina and drive. They were more than willing to work eight hours a day, six days a week, in order to finish their projects on time. Yet, over time, the work took its toll; in fact, Margaret felt that the dust they inhaled while grinding the cement was causing respiratory problems for both her and Esther.

Margaret, in experimenting with terrazzo, discovered that terrazzo's smooth surfaces were very durable and especially well suited for tabletops. One critic quipped that "nothing short of a sledgehammer can harm them, but there is nothing of the sledgehammer in their design or in their technique." Margaret's tabletops frequently featured asymmetrical designs, curved edges, and biomorphic shapes. She used flattened copper or silver wire to create abstract shapes and lines, add decorative elements, and sign the piece with her initials. Like Esther, Margaret used unusual materials in her pieces. "One is apt to find all sorts of things embedded in the cement," said her friend Dorothy Puccinelli, including "metal spirals, stones, brass cog-wheels like delicately done flowers. Margaret has a gift for the successful combining of materials, a sensitive perception of textural relationships and the inherent demands of media."

Terrazzo, with its abstract forms, metallic elements, and smooth surfaces, has a particularly modern look and feel. As the Monterey newspaper enthused, Margaret and Esther's "terrazzo tables have drawn the attention of modern architects because of original designs and beautiful execution." Their tables became highly desirable to interior designers and homeowners at a time when design trends were moving toward what we now call mid-century modern. Before long, renowned interior designer Frances Adler Elkins took notice; she commissioned Margaret Bruton to make dozens of terrazzo tabletops for her clients.

Frances Elkins had an esteemed reputation as an innovative and inspired designer; she had private and commercial clients nationwide, in places like Pebble Beach, San Francisco, Chicago, and New York. To this day, she is recognized as one of the most influential and inventive interior designers of the first half of the twentieth century. From 1927 to 1947, Elkins operated her extremely successful interior design business, Casa Blanca, from the Stevenson House in Monterey; she knew the artists who lived there and was likely inspired by their spirited creativity. She hired Monterey artists including Myron Oliver and August Gay to build furniture and picture frames for her clients. At a time when many of these artists struggled to make ends meet, Elkins' commissions were a lifeline that allowed them to make a living while pursuing their own art.

Elkins would boldly fill a room with fine antiques and then add a modern piece for a dramatic contrast of form and design. This modern element could be a streamlined chair by Jean-Michel Frank, a modernist lamp by Alberto Giacometti, or a terrazzo coffee table by Margaret Bruton. In 1946, San Francisco architect Gardner Dailey hired Elkins to redecorate the interior of the Royal Hawaiian Hotel in Honolulu. The hotel had been used for military housing during World War II, and its spaces needed to be updated and refreshed. Through this project, Elkins gave Margaret a huge job, commissioning forty-seven terrazzo tabletops for the Lanai Room of the hotel.

Margaret also contributed to the Donnell Ranch, a

mid-century modern masterpiece, built in 1948 by Jean and Dewey Donnell. The Sonoma County house's grounds were designed by noted landscape architect Thomas Church and include the first kidney-shaped pool in America. The Donnells commissioned a parade of leading California artists and craftspeople to create the furnishings and decorations for their house; Margaret Bruton made the terrazzo countertops for the pool house bar.

Throughout her career, Margaret made hundreds of terrazzo tabletops. Her sister Helen felt that Margaret "did too many" and didn't get enough credit for the creativity and craftsmanship that went into each piece. It bothered Helen that Margaret would "put a terrible lot of creative feeling into the design of the table, but then it would still be a table, and they'd say, 'Oh, you make the tables.'" Margaret didn't seem to mind that she was recognized primarily for her tables; she had finally found a medium in which to work that was more commercially successful than anything she had done before. Later in life she said that she "was so pleased to think that people wanted to buy these things that I made. Nobody had been anxious to buy my paintings, and when I started making these terrazzo tables, everybody wanted them." Margaret's terrazzo work was commercially successful and well received by critics. She was, once again, winning prizes for her artwork. In 1948, she received the Decorative Arts Award for her terrazzo piece *Scylla and Charybdis* at the San Francisco Women Artists exhibition at the San Francisco Museum of Art. In the same show and competition two years later, she won the Purchase Prize for All Media for a terrazzo coffee table.

Sunset Magazine published a profile of all three Brutons in their October 1947 issue. The photographs accompanying the article were taken by Sonya Noskowiak—Edward Weston's

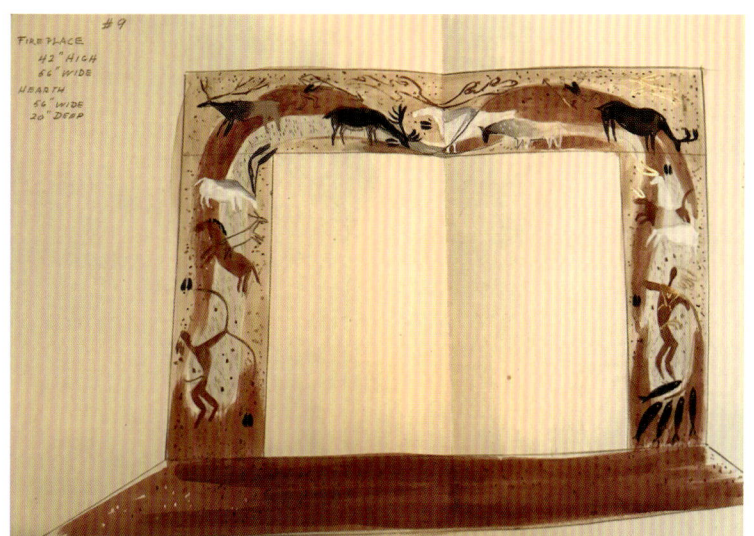

Preliminary watercolor for *The Hunt* fireplace surround

lover and a good friend of Imogen Cunningham—who was likely part of the Brutons' circle of friends. The *Sunset* article was the third in a series featuring artists who had made a significant contribution to Western arts and crafts. "Since any consideration of mosaics brought up some mention of the Bruton sisters," the article begins, "we sought them out because of their leadership. [Yet] the Bruton sisters didn't feel that they should be featured as mosaicists." Despite their indisputable mastery of the medium and innovation in various art forms, the Brutons were reluctant to have a spotlight focused on themselves and their art. This tendency to avoid publicity and downplay their accomplishments likely contributed to their gradual fading from the art scene over the next few decades.

In January 1949, Margaret wrote to the San Francisco Museum of Art asking if the museum would be interested

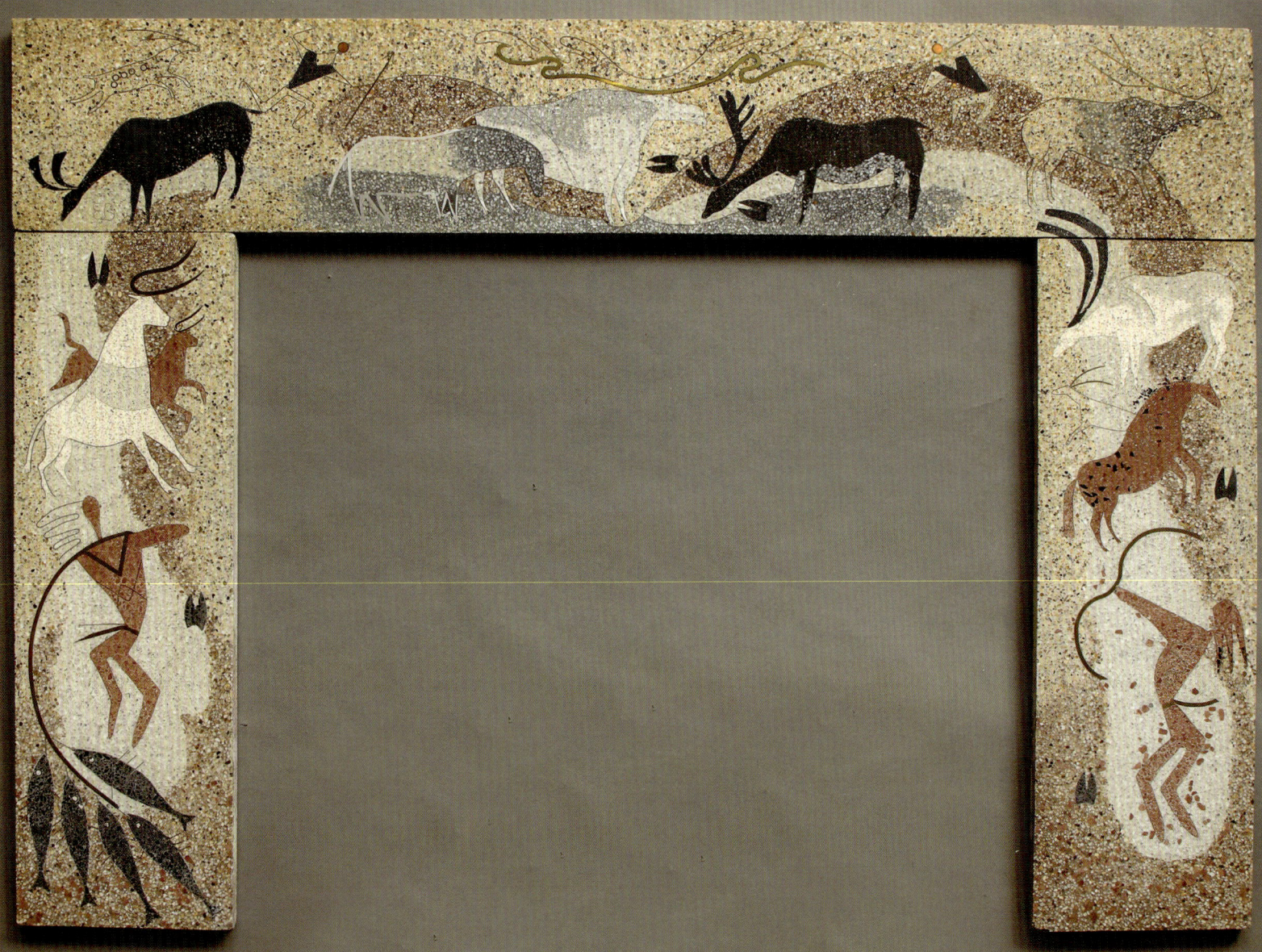

in hosting an exhibition of her and Esther's terrazzo work. Assistant Director Richard Freeman was enthusiastic about the idea, writing, "I have admired your work greatly and think you will have a very handsome show." Unfortunately, by the time Margaret received Freeman's response, Esther had already committed the sisters to a fall show at Gump's Gallery in San Francisco. Disappointed, Freeman responded, "I am more sorry than I can tell you that we missed having the exhibition of your work here at the [San Francisco Museum of Art]."

Despite missing out on a prestigious museum exhibition, the Brutons' show at Gump's was extremely popular and rivaled the success of their breakout group exhibition at the Galerie Beaux Arts which had introduced the Brutons to the world twenty years earlier. The exhibition catalog informed viewers about the Brutons' relationship with terrazzo: "For a long time the possibilities of using marble, glass and metals with cement (terrazzo) had interested both Esther and Margaret and after the war they started to experiment independently. The results proved so fascinating that they have done little else since."

The Gump's Gallery catalog correctly stated that "collaboration has been the exception rather than the rule in the work of the Brutons. They each have their own individuality and dislike being grouped." They always assisted each other on larger projects, but when only one of the sisters had been hired for a job, she was ultimately responsible for its design and execution, a fact well stated by their friend Dorothy Puccinelli:

> Since they are all sisters, all blondes, all equally expert artists and craftsmen, and usually to be found working in a state of quite unsisterly harmony on some

The Hunt, by Esther Bruton (ca. 1940s)

large commission, the average mind is incapable of disentangling one Bruton from the others... As a rule one Bruton gets a commission, designs it and executes it unless it is too big to handle alone, in which case the others act as her assistants.

Helen explained in a 1975 interview that whoever was hired for the job "would be more or less in charge and nobody [else] stuck in their two-bits worth... If it was my design, that was it." Margaret concurred, saying, "We wouldn't criticize it or want to change it or anything like that... We just helped to carry it out." Despite this, the tendency of the press and the public to view the Brutons as a single person was becoming insulting and tiresome. As the Gump's exhibition catalog and news articles of the period reveal, the sisters were making a concerted effort to set the record straight and assert themselves as individuals. Yet over time, as memories fade and first-person accounts are lost, it has become even more common for their individual works to be misattributed to "the Bruton sisters."

Most of the items featured in the Brutons' 1949 show at Gump's Gallery were for the home, such as tables, wall decorations, and patio pavers. *Ojai Valley News* described Esther's work as "somewhat modern, somewhat primitive, but wholly delightful." Esther exhibited a terrazzo fireplace surround called *The Hunt*, which was very similar to a piece she had installed in her own home in Ojai. The stylized hunters and animals depicted on both works resemble prehistoric cave drawings, while the smooth surface and abstract terrazzo patterning in the background make the pieces feel particularly modern. *The Hunt* was purchased by Mrs. Helen Woodring of Topeka, Kansas, the wife of Harry Hines Woodring, a former governor of Kansas and former US Secretary of War.

Most critics were impressed with the Brutons' mosaics

and terrazzo; their works were described as "polished, elegant, well-wrought" and were praised for their "striking individuality, ingenuity and charm." The *San Francisco Chronicle* stated that "there is nothing piddling or miniature about the size of these pieces and nothing small-minded about the designs their makers have worked out for them." The Gump's Gallery exhibition attracted an unusually large number of people, many of whom purchased works on view or ordered custom pieces. In general, Margaret and Esther's terrazzo works, described as "brilliantly fine and delicate, and rich in decorative values," received the highest praise. Helen's works, however, were not as warmly received. Critic Alexander Fried described shortcomings that included color arrangements that didn't work well, hues that had a "Victorian coarseness or heaviness," and forms with a "primitive rigidity." Helen was unable or unwilling to adjust her work to the modern aesthetic that mid-century America was seeking. This negative reception was only temporary; Helen Bruton would redeem herself admirably in the following decade.

Louisa Jenkins, an accomplished mosaicist from Big Sur, California, and a friend of the Brutons, wrote a review of their Gump's Gallery exhibition for the Monterey newspaper. Jenkins was one of the few critics to make the important observation that the Brutons' art was moving in a new direction. Instead of "monotonous rows of pictures," this exhibition featured "art in its relation to daily living." This type of work "will take an increasingly important place in the decoration of the home," Jenkins predicted. Overall, Jenkins felt the show was "outstanding both in the integrity of the work and the excellence of the display... Its effects will reach far into the future." The Brutons' movement into decorative arts, and their use of modern materials and designs, did bring them

new attention and critical appreciation in the mid-century.

The Brutons' progression from "fine" arts to "decorative" arts occurred during a period of dramatic change in the American art scene. Women artists had been given unprecedented opportunities during the anti-discriminatory WPA art projects of the 1930s, but after World War II, female roles narrowed and became even more prescribed than they had been before the war. Women were forced to give up professions and factory jobs they had taken on during wartime, and those who were wives, mothers, and homemakers were expected to return to those roles. For women artists like the Brutons, "the forties, fifties, and sixties turned out to be a period of increased discrimination. The leading galleries carried few works by women, and very few women had solo shows in major museums... Male artists... formed an unofficial old boys' club in which the work of their female colleagues was not taken seriously." The Abstract Expressionism movement, centered in New York, was almost exclusively associated with male artists including Jackson Pollock, Mark Rothko, and Willem de Kooning. The postwar art scene had become "an all-male, all-white enclave" that was "devastating for women artists, particularly for those on the West Coast."

Many women painters toiled onward, even though "their work was marginalized and relegated to the status of curious asides" and they were "dismissed as feminized versions of the 'real' thing." It's possible that the Brutons' movement into the decorative arts was a conscious or unconscious response to discrimination against women artists, but it's equally plausible that this new direction was simply a natural progression in their craft. The sisters are not known to have complained about—or even acknowledged—discrimination against them as women artists. In an interview, their cousin Barbara Carroll could not recall the sisters ever discussing the challenges they faced as women artists: "They got to do things, whatever they wanted to do, and being female didn't inhibit them. They went ahead and did what they wanted to do."

Regardless of the impetus behind this new direction in their art, the Brutons had the uncanny ability to excel in nearly every medium they attempted, and they found acceptance and success in the traditionally feminine sphere of the decorative arts. All three sisters had opportunities to be modern and inventive in the 1950s, and their art continued to mature and develop during this productive period.

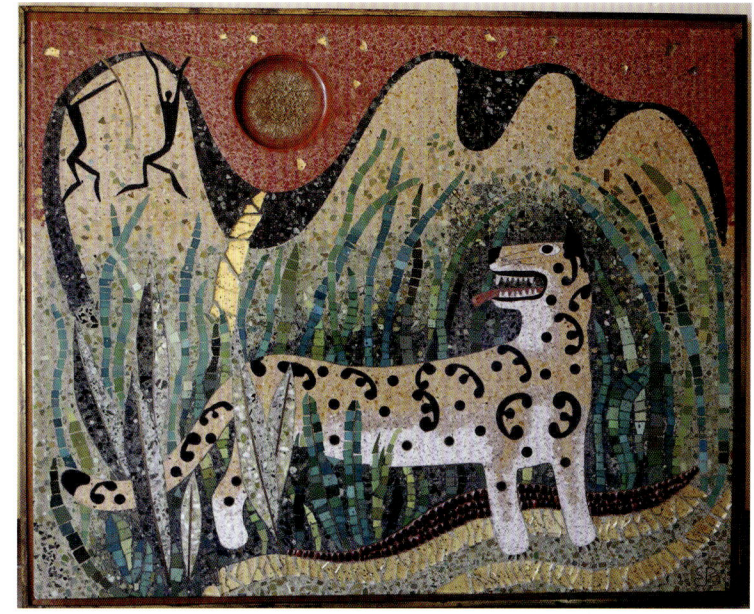

Leopard mosaic, by Esther Bruton (ca. 1935)

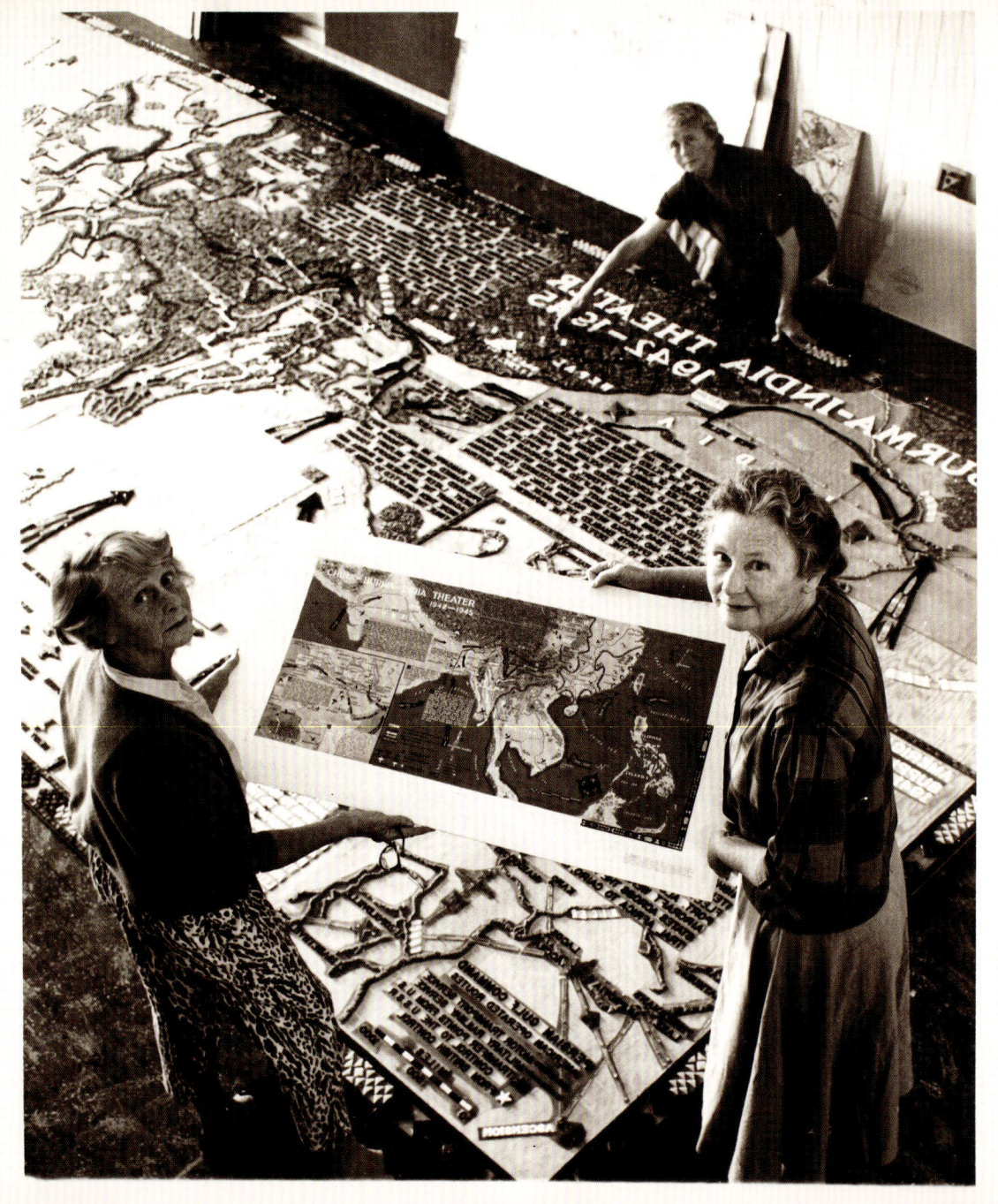

CHAPTER TEN

"A Truly Monumental Art Project"
(1950s)

The Bruton sisters experienced several painful losses during the 1950s. The first was the death of their good friend C.S. Price in May 1950. The Portland Art Museum and the Walker Museum of Art in Minneapolis organized a memorial exhibition of Price's work—543 pieces from 117 owners—that traveled to several venues. The Brutons and Ina Perham owned works by Price which they loaned to the exhibition. Esther wrote in 1951 that she and her sisters would be going to the Orange County Museum of Art in Newport Beach for "a memorial exhibition of the work of our old Monterey friend C.S. Price... We are all happy that he gained recognition before he died."

The Brutons' letters from this period are filled with reports about the declining health of their mother. "We have to stick pretty close to home these days," Margaret wrote in 1955, "as Mama has been laid up since the middle of June. Had a bad spell." A few months later she summarized to friends, "The complications of Mama & [our dog] Bo are more than we can cope with at this time... Mama has had a series of mishaps." The Brutons lost their mother on July 23, 1956. She is buried at the Monterey City Cemetery with their father, who had died almost thirty years earlier. The Bruton daughters decorated their parents' headstone with a colorful mosaic depicting a bouquet of flowers.

A few years later, in January 1959, Esther's husband passed away. Esther remained in Ojai, where she continued to update her home and studio, and she and her sisters visited each other as much as they could. Nearly in their sixties, all three sisters undertook many large and successful projects in the 1950s.

The Brutons' 1949 mosaic and terrazzo decorative arts exhibition at Gump's Gallery was so successful that they were offered a second group show there in 1952. When asked for a publicity statement, the self-effacing Brutons replied, "We just keep inchin' along and have been inchin' along for quite a while now." This exhibition was also extremely well received. Alexander Fried, who had criticized Helen's mosaics in 1949, felt that her work now surpassed that of her sisters. He stated that, in his opinion, this group show was superior to the one three years prior "particularly because Helen Bruton's mosaics now strike a happier, freer note than ever before." He described her mosaics as the "most vigorous of all—in their earthy, or stony look... Her mosaics have a delightful fancy and humor." Critic Alfred Frankenstein pointed out that Helen's mosaics of people and animals were full of "humor and brilliance," while Esther and Margaret's non-objective forms "have a kind of flow to them, and the whole thing is rich, complex and alive."

Along with Esther's new success with terrazzo, her mural paintings were still in demand. In 1952, she was hired to decorate Cafe Drake, a restaurant in San Francisco's elegant Sir Francis Drake Hotel that was undergoing alterations by architect Gardner Dailey. Esther's murals depicted places "Drake touched during pursuit of the gold-laden Manila

The Bruton sisters working on the mosaic maps for the Manila American Cemetery, photo by Dennis Rowedder (1959)

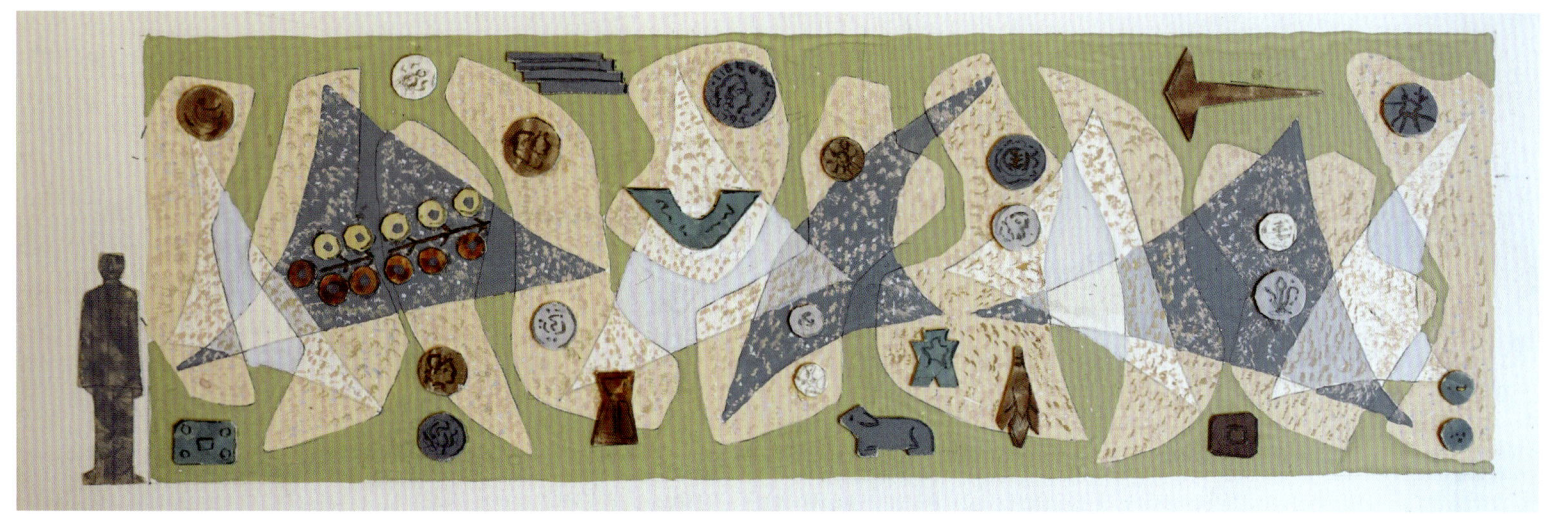

A plan for *Money Mural*, by Margaret Bruton (1953)

galleons." Unfortunately, Esther's murals were destroyed during later renovations of the hotel. At around the same time, Helen bid on a job to design a mural for the lobby of the Standard Federal Savings and Loan Association building at the corner of Grand Avenue and Wilshire Boulevard in Los Angeles. The architects rejected her proposal, saying that "the sketches do not exactly reflect what we had in mind." Helen likely passed the project on to Margaret, whose designs appealed to the architects. Since the mural would decorate the lobby of a bank, Margaret included abstract representations of the evolution of currency; she incorporated images of tobacco, cobs, a money tree, and coins. The enormous twelve-foot-by-thirty-two-foot terrazzo mural, which came to be known as the *Money Mural*, was "rich in warm hues of green and yellowish brown, laced with gold." An advertisement claimed that the mural, "designed by the internationally famous muralist

Margaret Bruton... is most certainly destined to become an outstanding point of cultural interest in Southern California." Sadly, Margaret's terrazzo mural is gone, and there is no record of what happened to it. Yet the work has not been lost forever. In 2021, the current owners of the building recreated Margaret's mural in the lobby.

Margaret's work for designer Frances Elkins continued well into the 1950s. Her coffee tables appeared in countless upscale homes across the country, including the Schlesinger and Crocker homes in San Francisco, the Coleman and Griffin houses in Pebble Beach, and the Gunst home in Vallejo, where her tables with terrazzo work in shells and with a seaweed motif shared space with lamps designed by Salvador Dalí and Alberto Giacometti. Margaret's reputation as a premier mid-century modern designer was firmly established when her work was paired with the architecture of Frank Lloyd Wright. Like many of the homes that Wright designed, the

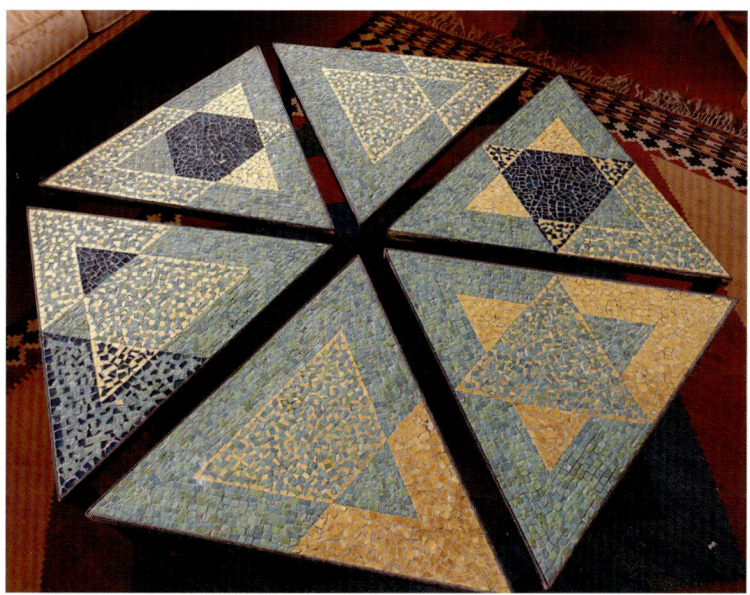

Coffee table in the Walker House, by Margaret Bruton (ca. 1952)

There is no evidence that Frank Lloyd Wright knew the Brutons, but they were friends with one of his protégés, Carmel architect Mark Mills. Having come to Carmel to assist with the construction of the Walker house, Mills settled there when Della Walker asked him to design two more homes on speculation. Much like the Brutons, Mills was humble, unassuming, and incredibly talented. The Brutons thought he might be a good match for Barbara Jenkins, the daughter of their good friend Louisa Jenkins, a mosaicist from Big Sur. Margaret and Helen held a dinner party in their Monterey home to introduce Barbara and Mark. The matchmaking dinner proved successful—Mark Mills and Barbara Jenkins became a couple and were married for more than fifty years until Mills's death in 2007.

Although the Bruton sisters were not devoutly religious—Esther once described the family as "backsliding Episcopalians"—some of their artwork took on distinctly religious themes during the 1950s. Helen contributed *Lot's Wife*, a "skillfully fashioned and humorous glass mosaic" to a show at the Pebble Beach Art Gallery in 1952. In November 1952, her mosaic of a nativity scene, *Nativity*, was displayed in the de Young Museum's exhibition of "Contemporary Religious Art by California Artists." Helen later donated the piece to Saint James Episcopal Church in Monterey, where it is still on display in the sanctuary. Margaret, too, experimented with religious themes in the 1950s. Her terrazzo *Twelfth Station of the Cross*, which depicts the crucifixion of Jesus against an abstract background, was exhibited at the 1952 de Young exhibition as well as a "Liturgical and Religious Arts" exhibition held in Denver in 1955. This phase of liturgical art was short-lived, and there is no evidence that the sisters had any kind of religious or spiritual awakening during this period. As they were always

Della Brooks Walker house—which sits dramatically on the beach in Carmel, California—blends seamlessly into its natural surroundings. It resembles the prow of a boat surging into the surf, its low profile and stone foundation harmonizing with Carmel's white sand beach. Wright's design for the 1952 home incorporates repeating geometric patterns; the hexagonal living room, topped with a hexagonal roof, is one of the home's most notable features. Della Brooks Walker, who studied at the Pratt Institute and was an artist herself, undoubtedly knew about the famous Bruton sisters. The mosaic coffee table Margaret made for Walker harmonizes with Wright's designs for the home; it consists of six separate triangular tables—in shades of green, gold, and black—that fit together to form a hexagon.

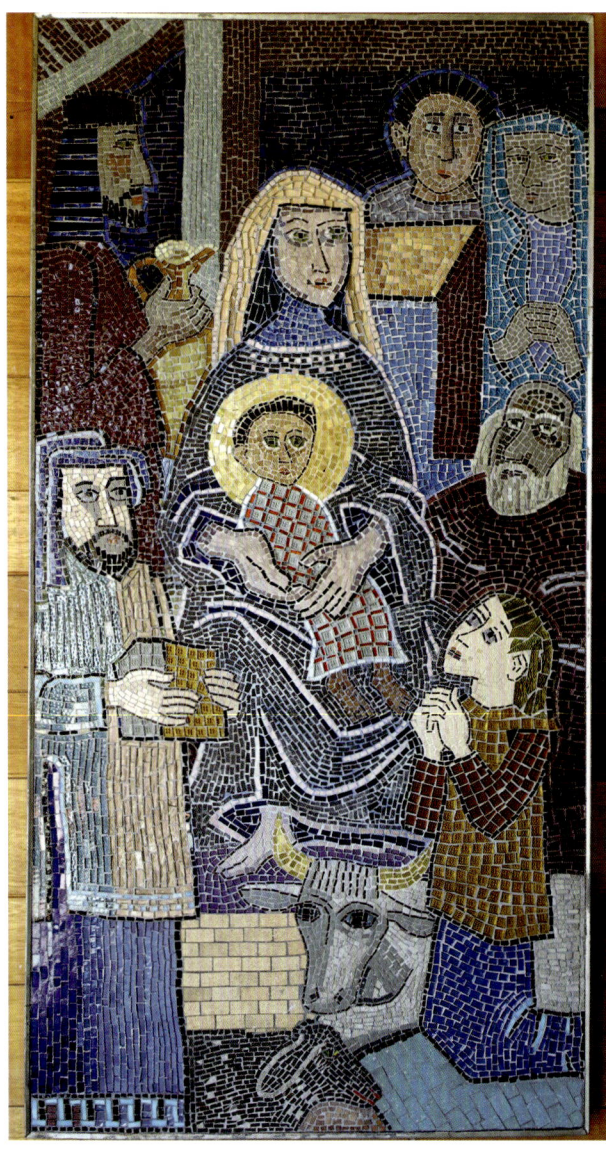

looking for new inspiration, perhaps this was just another avenue to explore.

As premier American decorative arts designers, the Brutons were once again receiving national attention with their work appearing in lifestyle magazines including *Sunset* and *House Beautiful*. In 1953, Esther's mosaic *Ghost Tree* was included in a traveling exhibition sponsored by the American Craftsmen's Education Council, and was seen in nine museums throughout the country. In 1954, Helen and Esther traveled to Dallas for the opening of a show of the Brutons' mosaic and terrazzo pieces at a Neiman Marcus department store. A representative from the store told Helen that the Brutons' exhibition was "by far the most successful we've ever had. We are so anxious to have a repeat performance." Both Helen and Esther had their work selected for "Pace Setter Houses," annual exhibition houses sponsored by *House Beautiful* magazine that featured modern design and architecture. Helen's mosaic *Pastoral*, a depiction of a reclining flutist done in blues and greens, was hung in the courtyard of the Pace Setter House at the 1954 Dallas State Fair. The following year, it was exhibited at the Dallas Museum of Art and acquired by the museum for their permanent collection. Two years later, one of Esther's terrazzo pieces was selected for the 1956 Pace Setter House in San Francisco; the work was also featured in the July 1956 edition of the magazine. A mosaic tabletop by Helen was on the cover of the October 1953 *House Beautiful*; a second table by Margaret and one of Esther's fireplace surrounds were featured inside the issue.

In 1954, Helen wrote an article, "How to Make Pebble Mosaics," for the July edition of *House Beautiful*. In addition to providing advice and step-by-step instructions for making

Nativity, by Helen Bruton (ca. 1952)

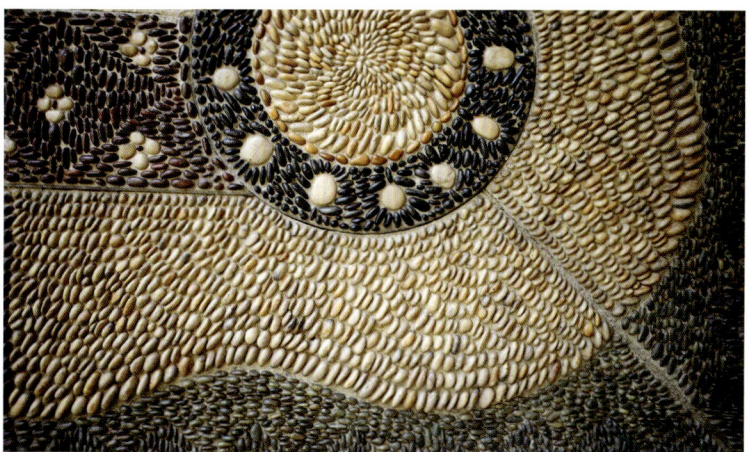

Pebble mosaic from her home in Ojai, by Esther Bruton (ca. 1946)

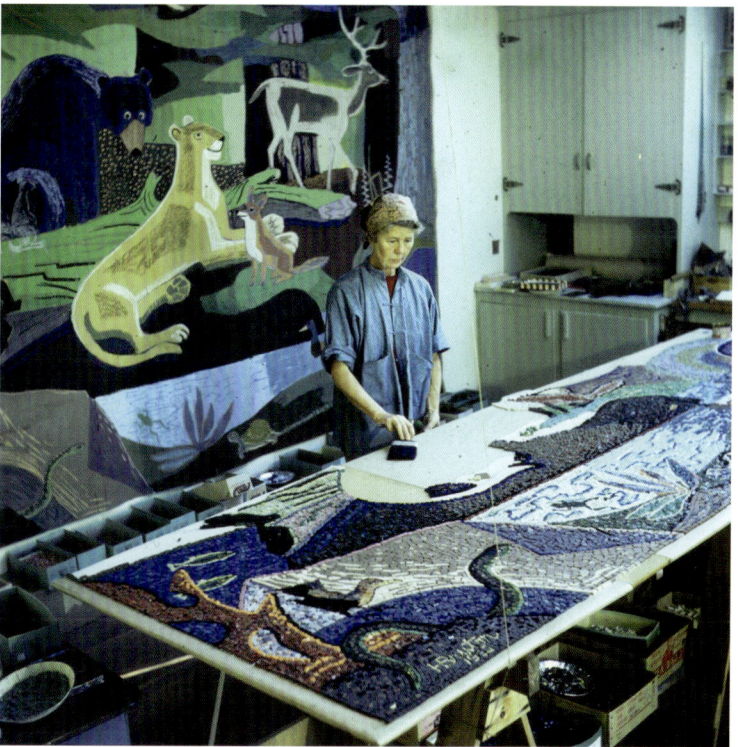

Helen Bruton in process of creating a mosaic for the Starr King Elementary School in San Francisco, 1954

decorative stepping stones for exterior paths and walkways, the article also reveals much about Helen's spiritual approach to materials:

> Pebble mosaics appeal anew to our feeling today for primitive as well as abstract forms, for the texture of natural materials, the impulse to try our own hands at creativity... Just to take a river stone and turn it in your hand is to get a sense of its possibilities... Each stone and pebble offers a distinct character, yet each is solidly related to all the others. A group of pebbles invites you to make a design, to draw spirals or lazy curves with them, perhaps to make boldly outlined figures of animals or tightly knit abstract forms.

In 1954, Helen was one of a number of artists hired to create artwork for the Starr King Elementary School in the Potrero Hill neighborhood of San Francisco. The Brutons'

friend Ruth Cravath made a sculpture of the school's namesake, Thomas Starr King. Helen's preliminary drawings suggest that she considered many different designs for the mosaic she was commissioned to make; eventually, she settled on animals and birds of California. Her eight-by-eleven-foot mosaic is a "strikingly decorative design" featuring "a graceful deer, a somnolent bear, sly fox, and tawny lion, a busy chipmunk and loitering turtle... quail, ducks, bluebird,

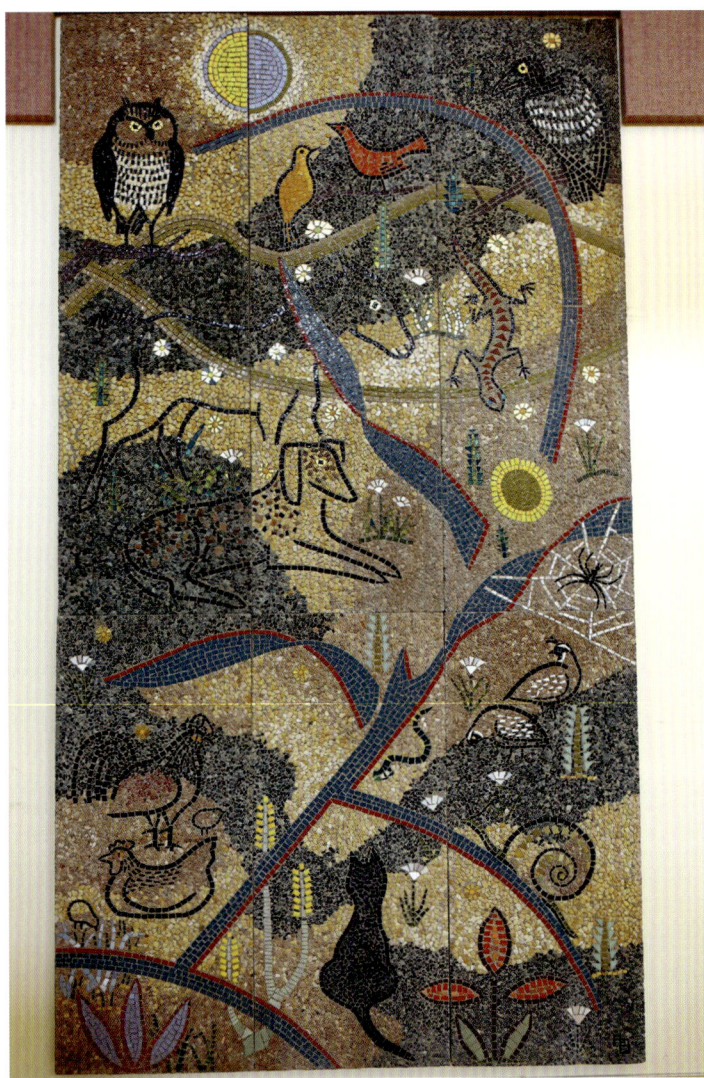

Mosaic at the SPCA Monterey County, by Helen Bruton (ca. 1967)

and slithering snake." Cravath's statue was vandalized a number of times over the years and eventually had to be removed from the school grounds. Helen's mosaic, which is mounted on the wall just outside the entrance to the school, remains in excellent condition.

The Starr King Elementary School mosaic was not the first time, and certainly not the last, that Helen would turn to the subject of animals; in fact, they were a recurring theme in her artwork. The Brutons had several beloved pets over their lifetimes, including a dog named Bo and a cat named Lulu. Helen's passion for animal welfare was second only to her passion for art. As early as 1926, the *Carmel Pine Cone* reported that Helen was a "prominent" member of the Monterey County's Society for the Prevention of Cruelty to Animals (SPCA), and she had "made a vigorous defense of homeless dogs of the Peninsula through the publication of several communications to the [*Peninsula Daily*] *Herald*." She was also concerned about preserving wildlife, including sea otters, coyotes, and wolves. On one occasion, Helen expressed her outrage about the use of animals for scientific experimentation. "Did you see this extraordinary picture of the space monkey[?]" she wrote in a letter to her cousin. "It seems like an indictment against the whole human race—at least the so-called 'developed' part and the direction we are taking. It took two hours to get the poor creature out of all its wiring." Helen's papers include several large posters with different designs, perhaps made for the SPCA, that all include the text "Be Kind To Animals."

Helen was good friends with Claude, the Countess of Kinnoull, a Carmel author and artist who was a major benefactor of the SPCA Monterey County. Lady Kinnoull's financial assistance made it possible for the organization to purchase a large piece of property on Highway 68, which became the new location for the animal shelter in 1967. Helen designed and executed a large mosaic for the exterior of the shelter building that features domestic animals such as a dog, a cat, a horse, and chickens, and wild animals such as an owl, a spider, a lizard, a snake, and several quail. An undated Christmas card sent to Helen by the SPCA Monterey County includes the message, "You, dear Miss Bruton, so faithful and so generous, are one of the members whose kindness warms our hearts." Helen remained a generous supporter of the SPCA Monterey County and left them a large bequest in her will.

In the late 1950s, Helen and Esther began moving in new directions with their art. The two began using smooth pieces of wood as their base medium, embedding pieces of glass, shell, and bone of varying sizes and shapes into the wood's surfaces. They called their technique "mosaic intarsia." These new designs were simple and clean, and perfectly complemented contemporary architecture of the period. The Brutons' use of organic materials and abstract forms demonstrated their sensitivity to the trends of mid-century modern design and marks a distinct evolution in their artwork.

The Brutons put this new style and technique into practice when they earned several exciting commissions from the Matson Navigation Company, an ocean-shipping services company. The sisters had begun their long and productive relationship with the company back in 1946, when Margaret created forty-seven terrazzo tabletops for the Matson-owned Royal Hawaiian Hotel. As Matson's luxury liners resumed their pre-war itineraries to the South Pacific—with stops in Hawaii, Tahiti, Fiji, New Zealand, and Australia—they began to update and renovate their ships. These luxury liners boasted state-of-the-art technology, luxurious accommodations, and the finest art and furnishings. The modern, streamlined ships, described

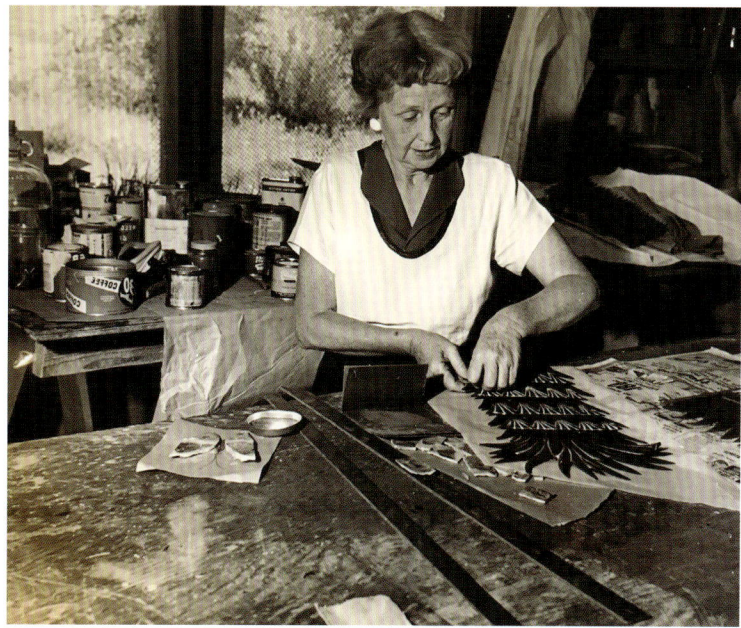

Esther Bruton creating her *Making of Kahilis* mural for the Princess Kaiulani Hotel, 1955

as "floating museums of contemporary fine and applied arts," boasted mid-century modern pieces and were styled with a Polynesian flair that complemented their South Pacific service.

The Matson Company also built hotels at their cruise ships' destinations, with the goal of creating package experiences for their passengers. One of these new hotels was the Princess Kaiulani Hotel, built in Honolulu in 1955. San Francisco architect Gardner Dailey, who had redesigned the Royal Hawaiian Hotel in 1946, was the supervising architect for the project. The style of the Princess Kaiulani was mid-century modern meets the Pacific Islands. The hotel commissioned dozens of prominent artists to decorate the property and even published a brochure with photographs and biographies of the contributors. Helen was hired to make mosaic tabletops for the "Sky Level" of the Princess Kaiulani. According to the hotel's art brochure, the design of her mosaic tables was constellations of the Southern Hemisphere against a background of Hawaiian colors. And Esther was hired to make two murals, including one for the "Kahili Room" cocktail lounge. She quipped later in life, "I have done so many bars that one would think they were my specialty."

Esther designed and executed her two commissioned murals in her Ojai studio. As she had never been to Hawaii, she began by conducting careful research to make sure that her work accurately and sensitively depicted Hawaiian culture. Matson Company staff in Honolulu also did extensive research at the Bishop Museum, which they passed on to Esther. A Honolulu newspaper wrote that "Mrs. Gilman has worked with care and pains to depict authentic scenes for the new hotel." One of her murals, *Making of Kahilis*, depicted different versions of feathered kahili—long staffs with ornate feathered tops that are symbols of Hawaiian royalty. The second mural, in two parts measuring eighteen feet by five feet and twelve feet by five feet, was called *Early Pacific Voyages*. This mural features four types of Polynesian canoes—Tongan, Hawaiian, Tahitian, and Maori—manned by royal-looking figures, some wearing feathered helmets and rich red capes. Fanciful, striped fish swim in the ocean below the canoes, and large "frigate birds" fly above. Despite her careful research, Esther didn't want to make a mistake when depicting the animals of Hawaii, so she made a point of using only extinct birds and fish in her work. Esther described this mural project as "experimental"— it was the first time she had started with a plywood base and then layered contrasting textures and grains of wood in muted

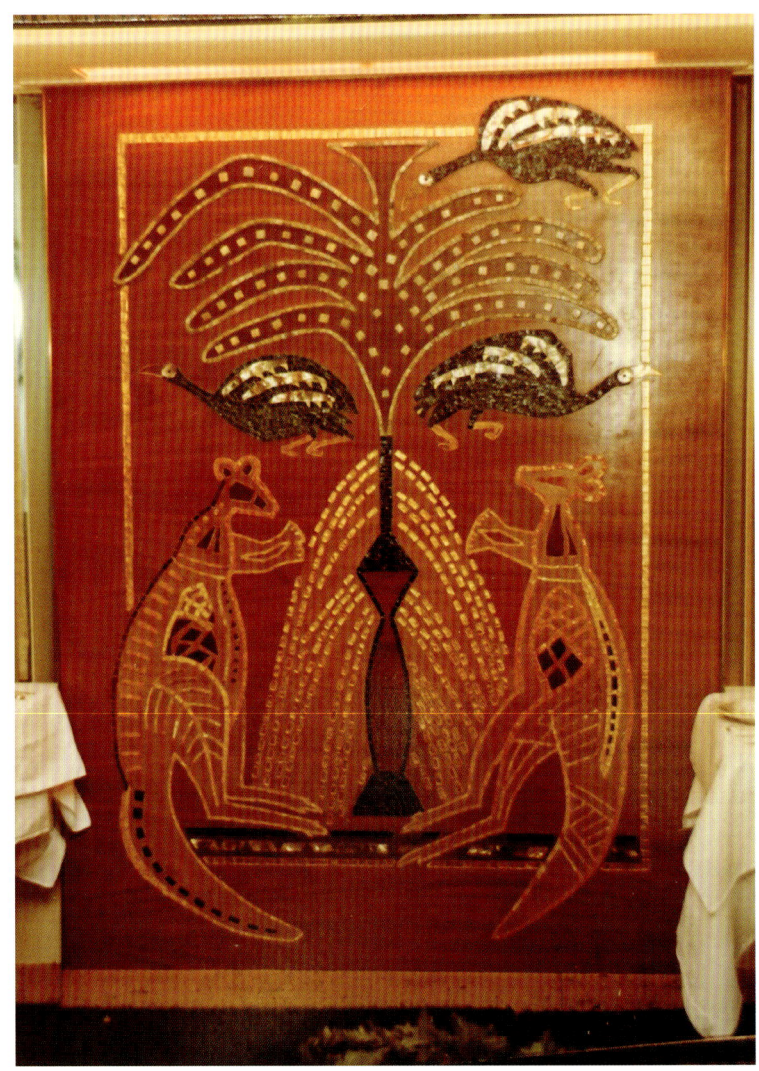

A mural in the dining room of the SS *Monterey*, by Esther Bruton (1956)

shades of black, brown, and terra-cotta. She attached fiberboard cutouts of boats and figures to the base, and then embedded pieces of bone, stone, and abalone shell into the wood. Esther had a party at her Ojai studio to exhibit her murals for the Princess Kaiulani Hotel before they were sent to Honolulu. Even before they were shipped, she had begun to worry about how they would be lit once they were in place at the hotel; evidently at her party "she hoped aloud that the usual gloomy bar lighting would be spared her masterpieces."

On June 11, 1955, the *Honolulu Star-Bulletin* dedicated six pages to the grand opening of the Princess Kaiulani Hotel, and an entire article to Esther's murals. By all accounts, the works were stunning. The newspaper noted that Esther's incorporation of natural materials in the murals honored "the ancient craft ways of the Polynesians." Unfortunately, although it was lengthy and full of praise, the article does not mention Esther by name or recognize her as the artist of these highly praised works. Today, the Princess Kaiulani Hotel is owned by Sheraton, the Kahili Room cocktail lounge is long gone, and there is no record of what happened to Esther's murals.

The following year, both Esther and Helen were back at work for the Matson Company. This time, they were hired to provide mosaics for the SS *Monterey* and the SS *Mariposa*, cruise ships that would travel between San Francisco and Sydney with stops in the South Pacific. Helen and Esther jointly negotiated the terms for their contract, which paid them $8,000 for their work—nearly $80,000 in today's dollars. This sum suggests that their work was still in high demand and that the Brutons continued to command significant respect within the art world.

Esther was hired to create six mosaic panels, each five by seven feet, for the dining room of the *Monterey*. In line with the ship's route, Esther chose to depict the flora and fauna of Australia—including kangaroos, frigate birds, and devil fish—set in walnut and accented with shards of abalone and "cat's eyes" (sea snail shells) from Tahiti.

Helen was hired to create a mural for the Southern Cross Lounge in the *Mariposa*. Helen's enormous mural—it measured twenty-five feet across and ten feet high—depicted the constellations of the Southern Hemisphere that would have been visible from the ship. The mosaic was "made of walnut, laminated in one section to form a graceful curve... [and] inlaid in glass and tesserae in intense as well as subdued tiles ranging in color from turquoise to shell pearl gray." Helen's complex design featured "pale pinks, purples, blues, and gold encrusted in mosaic and stone on sleek, rich wood" and included more than a dozen figures representing different constellations spread across an abstract background like stars across the night sky. The piece simultaneously brings to mind cave drawings, Aboriginal paintings, and works by European modernists such as Miró or Picasso. Through its color and forms, Helen succeeded in capturing a sense of timelessness with the mural, which looks simultaneously ancient and modern.

Passengers on the *Mariposa's* maiden voyage delivered high praise for the Southern Cross Lounge, describing it as "one of the high points... with many compliments for the gorgeous inlaid murals." One reporter said that the Southern Cross Lounge was "the most beautiful of the rooms [on the ship]... [it] glows, like stained glass only softer." *Constellations of the Seven Seas* was quite different from anything Helen had done before; the work clearly demonstrates that she had rediscovered her confidence and artistic footing. Compared to the rigid and primitive design of her *Ulysses and the Sirens* mural on the *Lurline*, this unique, exciting, and sophisticated mosaic was a redemption.

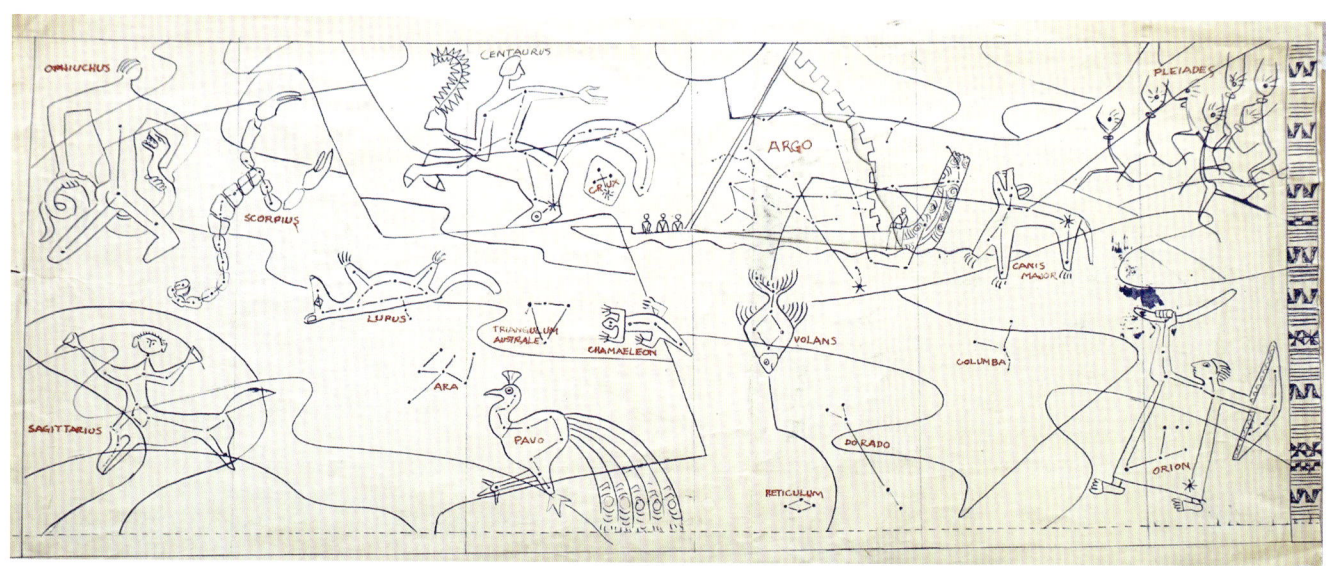

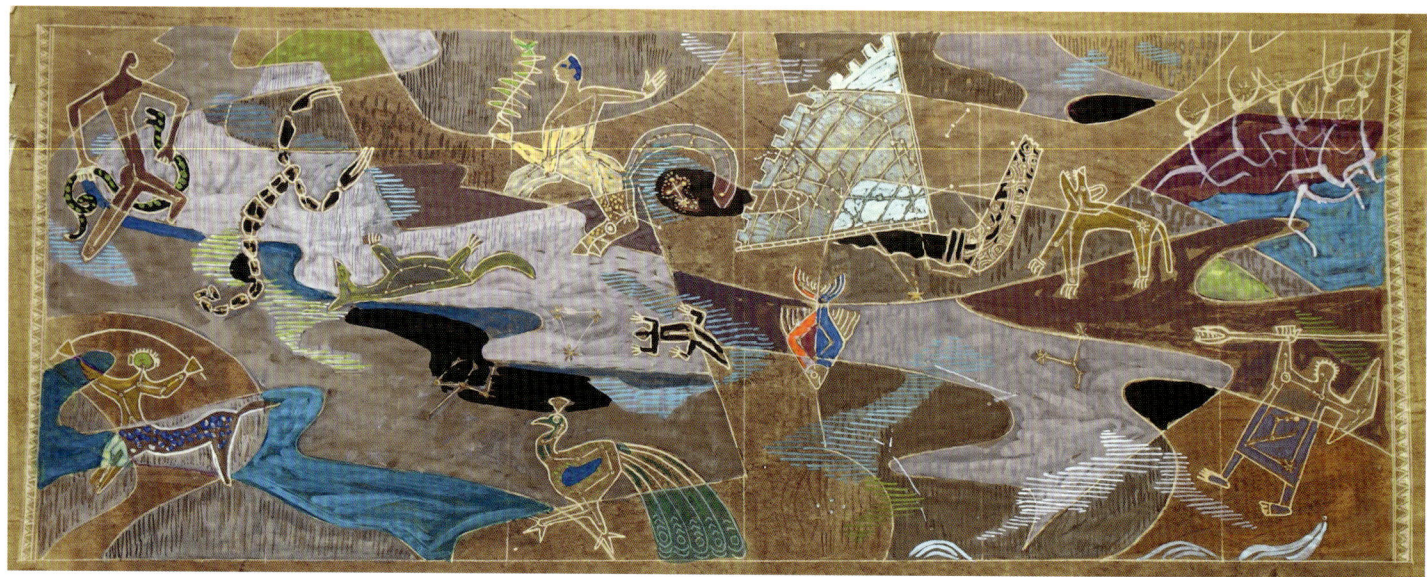

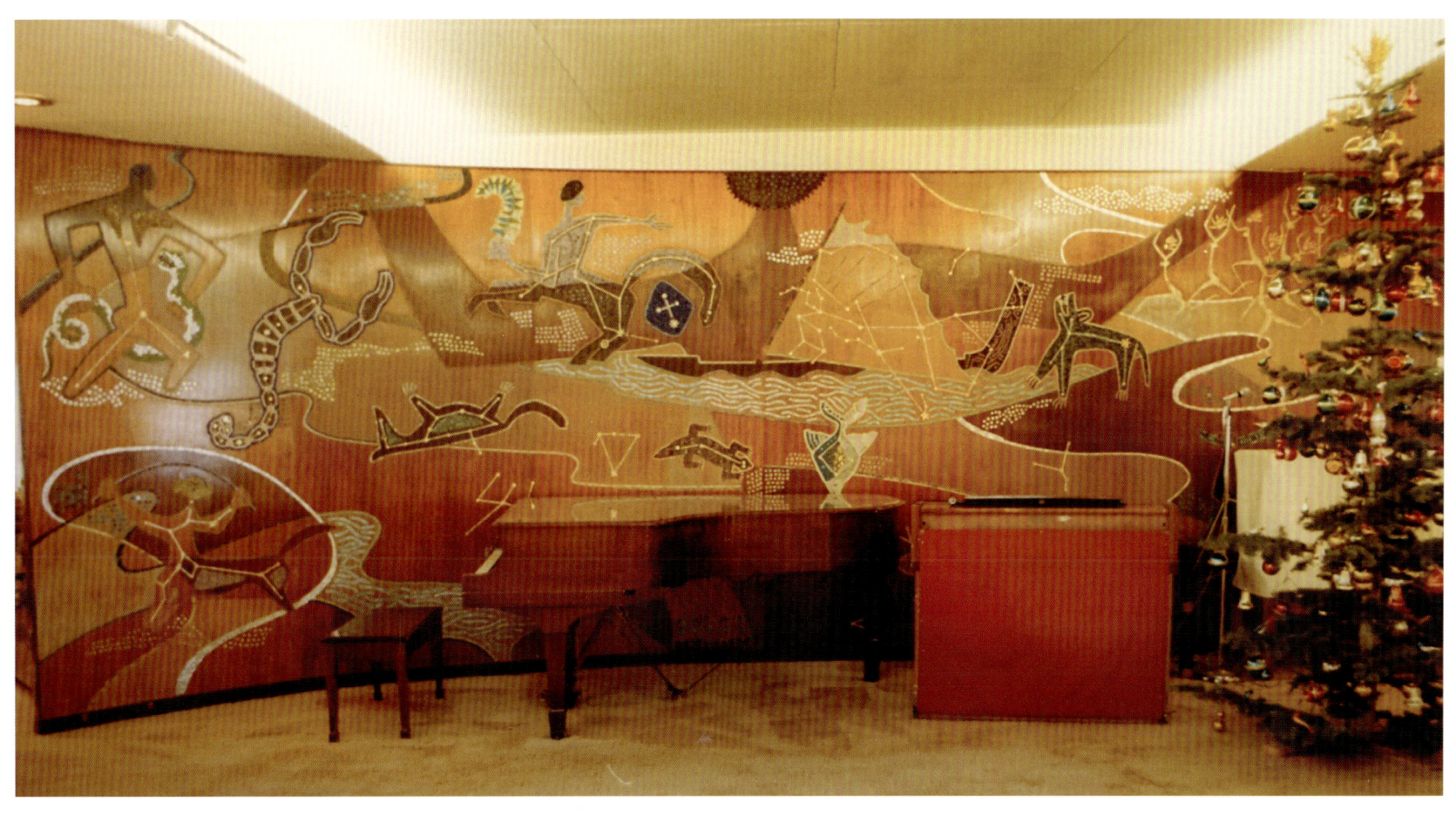

Left: Preliminary drawing and pastel for *Constellations of the Seven Seas*
Above: *Constellations of the Seven Seas* in the Southern Cross Lounge of the SS *Mariposa*,
by Helen Bruton (1956)

Helen experimented further with her new technique of mosaics on wooden panels in a 1956 commission for the chapel at St. Joseph's Seminary in Mountain View, California. The work, described as a "monumental altar screen of mosaic intarsia," began with five panels of beautifully grained hardwood, each seven feet high. Helen selected figures from the Bible, created them out of mosaic, and inlaid the mosaics into the wooden panels. Helen created the works in her Monterey studio, transferred them to Mountain View in a pickup truck, and supervised their placement on the chapel wall behind the altar. The finished work was dedicated in April 1956. Unfortunately, because St. Joseph's campus was severely damaged in the 1989 Loma Prieta earthquake, all of its buildings, including the chapel with Helen's mosaic altarpiece, had to be demolished.

Helen continued to perfect her mosaic technique, in a much subtler way, when she was called back to the UC Berkeley campus for a job. Gardner Dailey had been hired to design Hertz Memorial Hall, a new music building for the Berkeley campus. Dailey's striking, mid-century modern structure, completed in 1958, includes an auditorium with an enormous organ behind the stage. The design included sliding oak panels that could hide the organ from view and Helen was hired to decorate these panels. She came up with the idea of embedding small squares of gold Italian glass into the wood in abstract, geometric patterns meant to resemble musical notes. The work as a whole, which she called *Variations on a Theme*, is spare, modern, elegant, and sophisticated. Helen's mosaics provide visual interest without overwhelming the clean lines and simplicity of Dailey's architectural design. UC Berkeley has since replaced the original organ, but the wooden screens featuring Helen's gold mosaics are still in the hall, looking just

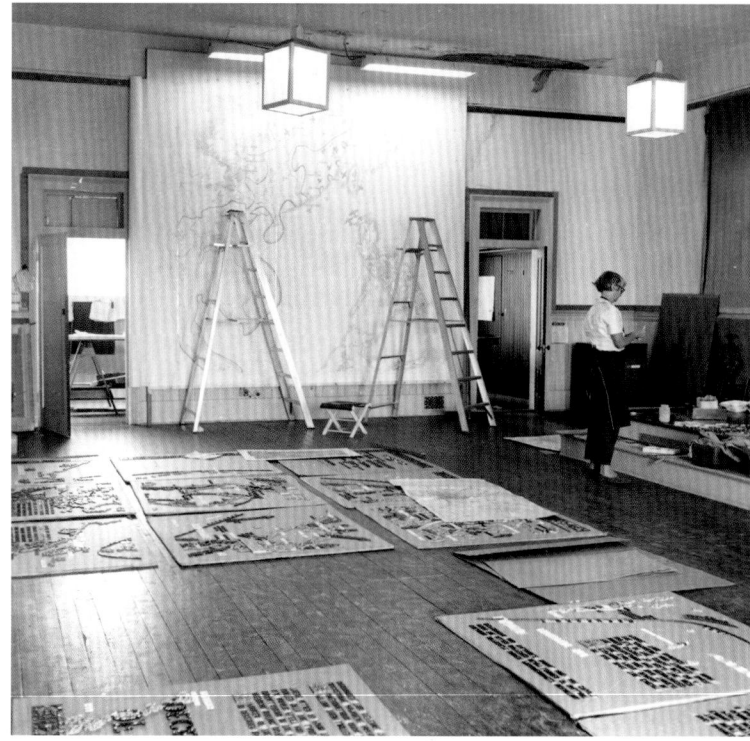

The studio used for work on the mosaic maps for the Manila American Cemetery

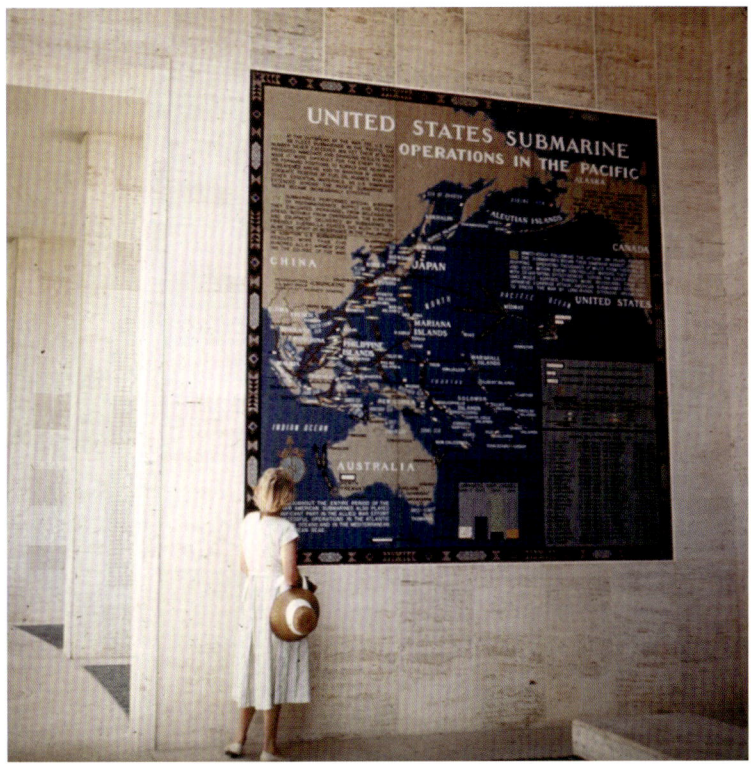

Esther Bruton viewing one of the mosaic maps at the Manila American Cemetery, 1961

as modern and fresh as the day they were installed.

Gardner Dailey and the Brutons would work together again on one the largest projects of the sisters' careers. Dailey had been hired to design a monument for a large cemetery located on the Fort William McKinley military reservation in Manila. The monument was to honor the more than 17,000 American soldiers buried on the site, as well as the more than 36,000 American soldiers missing in action in the Pacific. In 1954, Dailey's plan for an "Italian marble memorial" was approved at a projected cost of three million dollars, although the final expense was closer to five million.

Dailey's design is impressive; the monument includes a one-hundred-acre garden with flowering trees, a half-mile-long mall leading from the main gate, and a fifty-foot-tall chapel tower sitting on a small plateau. Curved colonnades, which Dailey called "hemicycles," form half circles around the main walk. The pillars of the colonnades are engraved with the names of soldiers missing in action. At the end of each hemicycle are "battle museums" that house a total of twenty-two maps of the major battles in the Pacific. Dailey wisely decided that the battle maps, which would be exposed to the elements, should be made in mosaic, an extremely durable medium that would last in the humid, tropical climate of the Philippines. Having worked with Margaret Bruton before, Dailey knew she was both dependable and capable of executing a large project: "She's the only one I know of that can do exactly what we have in mind."

Margaret was clearly pleased to be selected for this important commission. As she later recalled, "I had done quite a lot of work for [Dailey]... and he had confidence in us... It was really extraordinary that they accepted me." Dailey was likely well aware that by selecting Margaret, he was getting three artists for the price of one, and he was correct in his assumption. Although Margaret was in charge and did all the preliminary work during the first year, Helen and Esther spent countless hours on the project.

As with all the large projects they had worked on, this one had its limitations and frustrations. Margaret did all of her work in California and corresponded with staff of the American Battle Monuments Commission in Washington, D.C., who supplied her with battle map information and data. As the maps were incredibly complex and exact, she initially thought that she would have very little opportunity to use her own designs or imagination. As she felt she "had to take [the government-provided] drawings and make them a little interesting," there was some creativity involved in making the mosaic maps. In order to experiment with materials and colors, Margaret made several practice mosaics. These small sample pieces reveal her early attempts to depict airplanes, ships, parachutes, anchors, islands, and the curved arrows marking troop movements that would be featured so prominently in the maps.

When the preliminary work was done and it was time to begin the construction of the actual maps, Margaret relied heavily on her sisters. Esther's husband had recently died, and Esther was glad to come up to Monterey to assist Margaret. The Brutons were in their early sixties as they began the most time-consuming and physically strenuous project they would ever undertake. Each of the twenty-two maps was ten feet high and between ten and thirty feet long. The sisters needed a large space to work, and they were fortunate to find a loft in Monterey where they could spread the maps across the floor. A local newspaper wrote, "A truly monumental art project is underway in Monterey."

The Brutons followed the same procedure for mosaic-making they had been using for more than twenty-five years: they worked from a miniature drawing that was approximately one-tenth of the size of the finished product and created the mosaic in sections. With their extensive experience, they had modified and streamlined their process. When they began making mosaics in the 1930s, the terra-cotta tiles they used all looked identical on the back, regardless of the color on the face. Later, they started using tiles with color that showed through, allowing them to arrange the tiles face down. Helen has stated that this process "was really simpler—you could paste down a face as you went along, so that really was very much easier." It is remarkable that the Brutons considered it "easier" to make their mosaics upside down and in reverse, especially since the battle maps included copious amounts of text. They did make their share of mistakes; even after considerable attention to detail, they would sometimes finish a panel only to realize they had placed one letter backward.

As each mosaic map was completed, the sisters would take it to the P. Grassi American Terrazzo Company in South San Francisco. The workers there took the mosaics and filled in the background with cement; the finished boards were two inches thick and each weighed nearly two hundred pounds. Once a piece was cast, it was photographed, and the images were sent to Washington, where "they'd go over it all with a fine-tooth comb and look for any defect in lettering." Once the boards received final approval, they were crated, shipped to Manila, and installed on the site. Despite the complexity of the project, Margaret stated that it went very smoothly, saying, "I just can't get over how fortunate I was, because such terrible things could've happened but didn't. Even when it was erected over there, they had no difficulty—everything went out perfectly."

The Manila American Cemetery was dedicated on December 8, 1960. Articles about the event, which discussed the Bruton sisters' work on the mosaic maps, appeared in newspapers around the world. Many military dignitaries were in attendance for the elaborate opening ceremonies, but the Brutons remained at home in Monterey. It wasn't until the following year that Margaret and Esther traveled to Manila to see the installed mosaics for the first time. "I saw it soon after it was put up," Margaret said, "...and it's just perfect, and it's semi-exposed to the weather... [but] there hasn't been any fading." In 1973, Margaret returned to Manila, this time with Helen. "Seeing the Memorial itself, and the maps in place, makes the trip worthwhile," Helen said. "It's truly impressive— and hard to believe that we actually did it."

Fifteen years after its dedication, Margaret still felt that she had asked too much of her sisters in asking for their help with the mosaic battle maps for the Manila American Cemetery: "It just threw us all off. It was such a confining job and it was very hard for Helen and Esther both, and I feel guilty ever since that I let them do it, but they wanted to, and of course I just couldn't have done without them." She worried that the project "turned them off" from making mosaics. While it is true that the Bruton sisters each took a long break after completing this monumental art project, they were not interested in retirement. Within a few years they were back at work, together again, on another large commission.

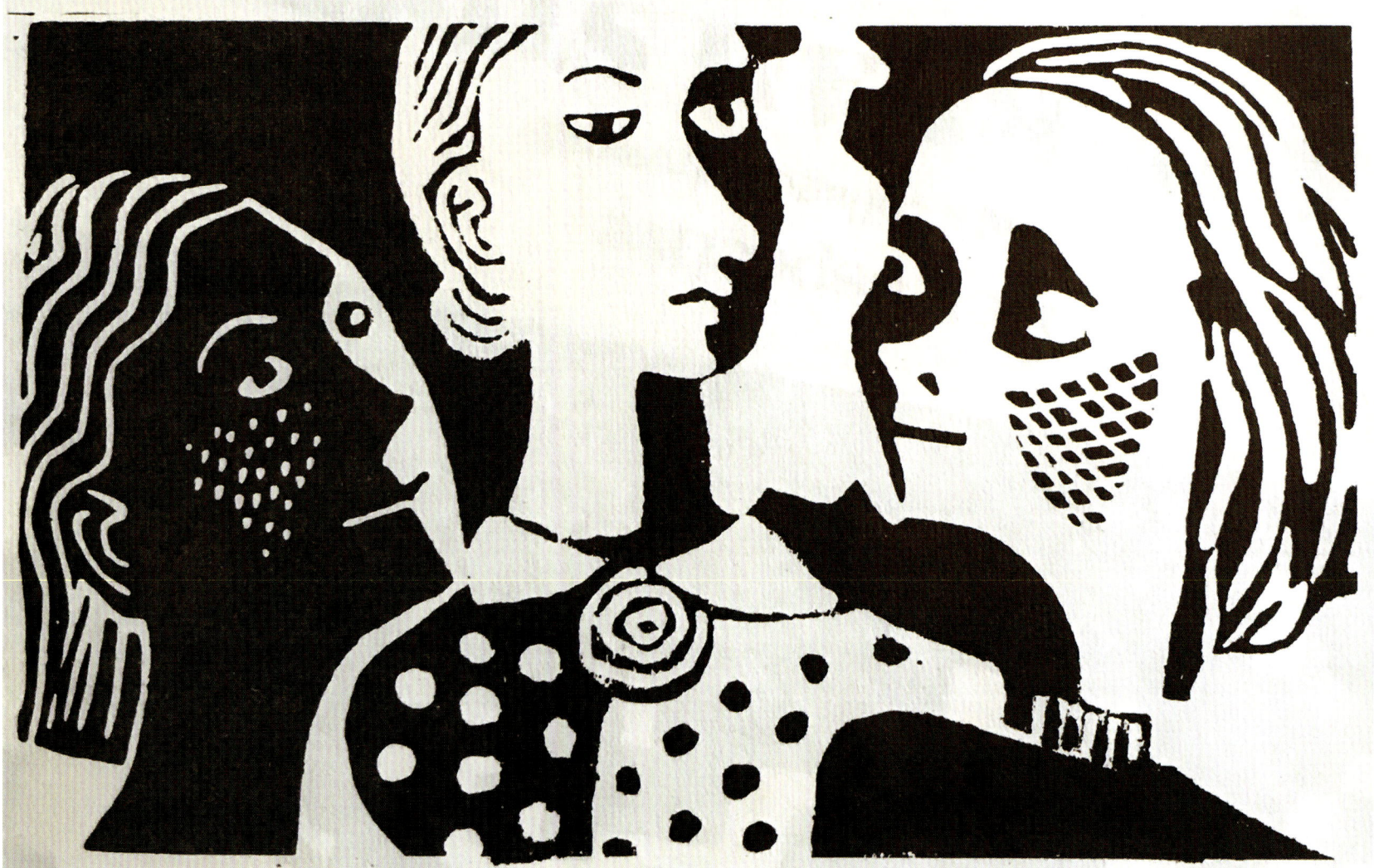

CHAPTER ELEVEN

"A Little Like Rip Van Winkle"
(1960–1992)

Twenty years after the Bruton sisters made *The Peacemakers* for the 1939 Golden Gate International Exposition, they were commissioned to create three large mosaics for Buddha's Universal Church in San Francisco. This project was the last major commission undertaken by the Brutons, who were in their sixties at the time.

Buddha's Universal Church has a fascinating history. It was built from scratch entirely by volunteers, including many San Franciscans outside the congregation. This incredible community effort took more than eleven years to complete. As the *Oakland Tribune* reported, "by the time the church was completed, Bay Area residents of every race and creed had contributed to its success." The church has five levels, including a tranquil rooftop garden that serves as a quiet oasis for contemplation. The minimalist style of the church is a blend of Asian aesthetics and mid-century modern architecture.

When it came time to design the church's vitally important representations of the Buddha, it was Helen Fung, wife of church leader Dr. Paul Fung, who reached out to the Brutons. She had heard about their work on the mosaic maps for the Manila American Cemetery and was impressed. Fung contacted the sisters and asked if they would create three mosaic Buddhas to be focal points for the new church. "We were thrilled at the opportunity," Esther is quoted in the church's press release as saying. "And, although we had little background in the Buddhist faith, or the teachings of Buddha,

Flyer (detail) advertising one of the Brutons' exhibitions in Monterey (1966)

Dr. Paul Fung told us exactly what he wanted, and taught us the symbolism of images." Helen also remarked that the congregation was quite persuasive: "These people have the faith that moves mountains." The Brutons were extremely proud to contribute to the church, and they volunteered their time just like everyone else involved in the project.

The sisters began gathering ideas and conducting research for their Buddha mosaics as early as 1959. When Margaret and Esther traveled to Manila to finally see their newly installed mosaic maps at the Manila American Cemetery, they also visited Thailand, Singapore, Sri Lanka, India, and Japan. They carefully studied the Buddha imagery they saw during their travels, and they used this insight and inspiration when creating their mosaics at Buddha's Universal Church.

The three Buddhas—each depicting a different stage of his life and completed one at a time over a four-year period—are located in different areas of the church. Helen's mosaic, located in an instruction room known as the general assembly area, was completed first. Her work depicts Buddha at age thirty, sitting on a lotus flower under the Bodhi tree, about a year after reaching enlightenment. He holds a lotus flower in his right hand, below the heart, and the second and third fingers of his left hand are pointed toward his thumb, symbolizing "the thoughts that come out of the heart (one finger) and the words that come out of the mouth (another finger) should be as one (the thumb)." This traditional mosaic, approximately five feet high by four feet wide, is made of thousands of pieces

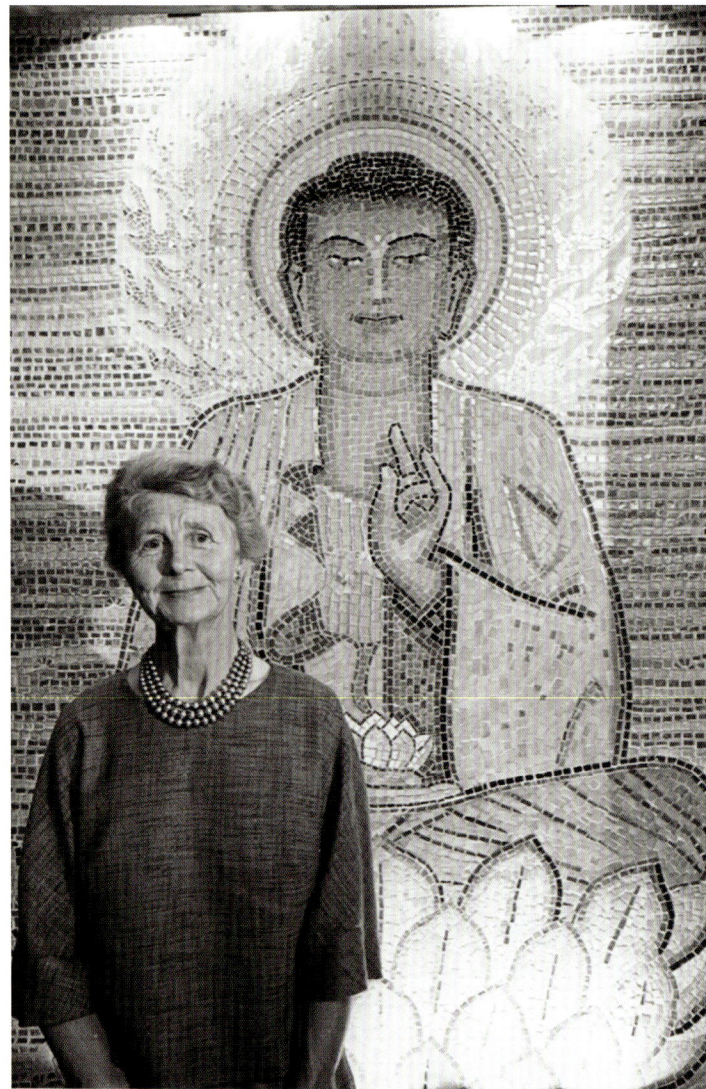

Helen Bruton in front of her Buddha mosaic at Buddha's Universal Church, 1963

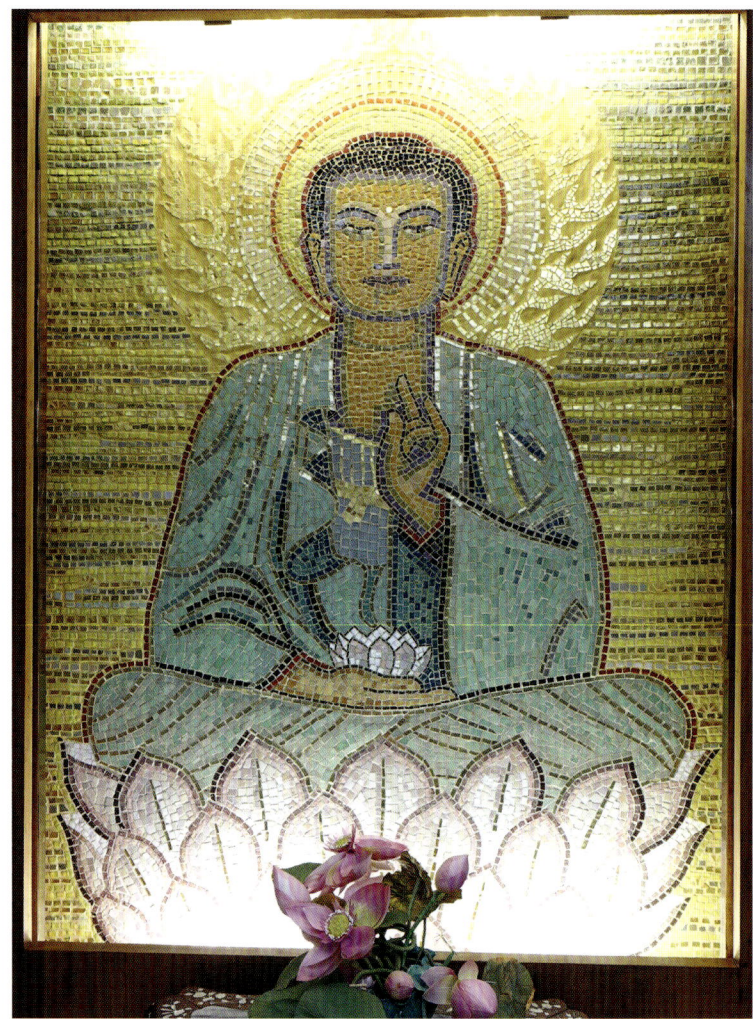

Helen Bruton's mosaic created for Buddha's Universal Church

of colorful glass and ceramic and is reminiscent of Helen's early mosaic work. A sliding screen closes over the work to protect it when the room is not in use.

The next Buddha to be completed was Margaret's, located behind the altar of the church's main auditorium. Nearly two stories high, it is made of ceramic, crushed quartz aggregate, and cement with gold leaf. This mosaic represents Buddha in his forties, sitting on a large white lotus flower. His gold leaf aura is the largest of the three, symbolizing that he has reached full enlightenment. He holds a lotus flower in his right hand, and his left hand sits in his lap, second finger and thumb touching. The extended fingers represent the mind of the past, the present, and the future, while the circle formed by the thumb and the second finger symbolizes non-attachment.

The final Buddha to be completed was Esther's—the centerpiece of the church's Chapel of the Bamboo Grove. The mosaic, closer to human scale at about four feet by ten feet, is made of glass, gold leaf, and abalone shell set into a smooth walnut panel. It portrays a youthful Buddha in his twenties, when he gave his first discourses. His left hand is held near his heart, symbolizing that an individual should acquire, cherish, and develop the teachings from within the heart and the mind. The right hand is held palm upward in a gesture of welcome and guidance. Dr. Fung called the church's three spectacular mosaics the "Bruton Buddhas," and they are reportedly the first images of Buddha to be made in mosaic. The works remain in pristine condition and are cherished by the congregation of Buddha's Universal Church.

When the mosaics were dedicated, numerous articles about the Brutons appeared in Bay Area newspapers. Descriptions of the sisters read like ones that appeared in the press decades earlier; they were described as "vivacious, humorous and

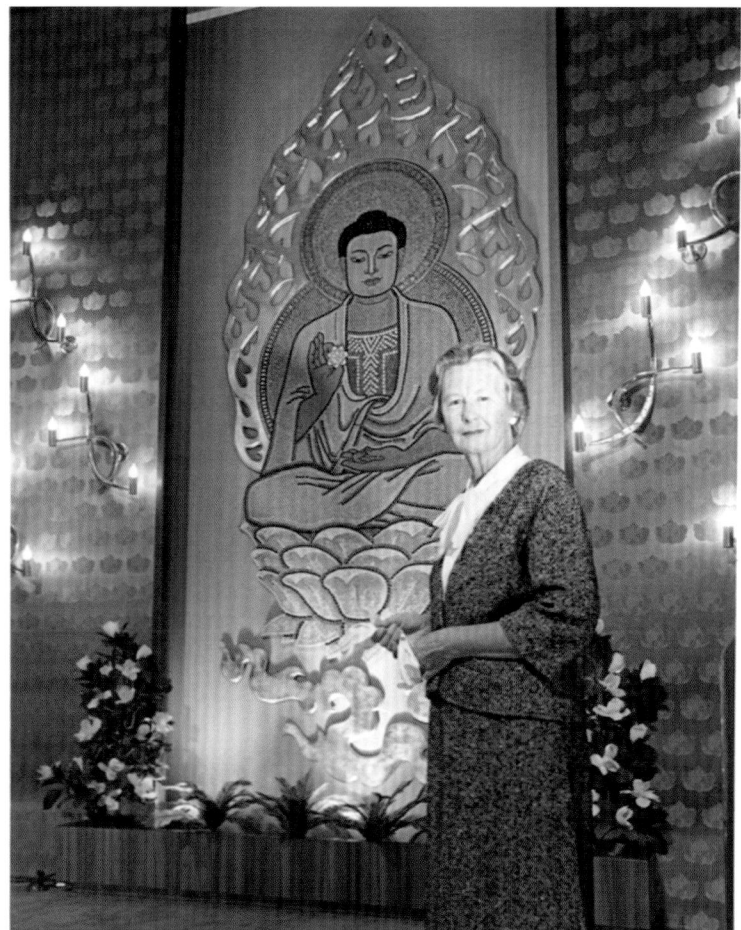

Margaret Bruton in front of her Buddha mosaic at Buddha's Universal Church, 1963

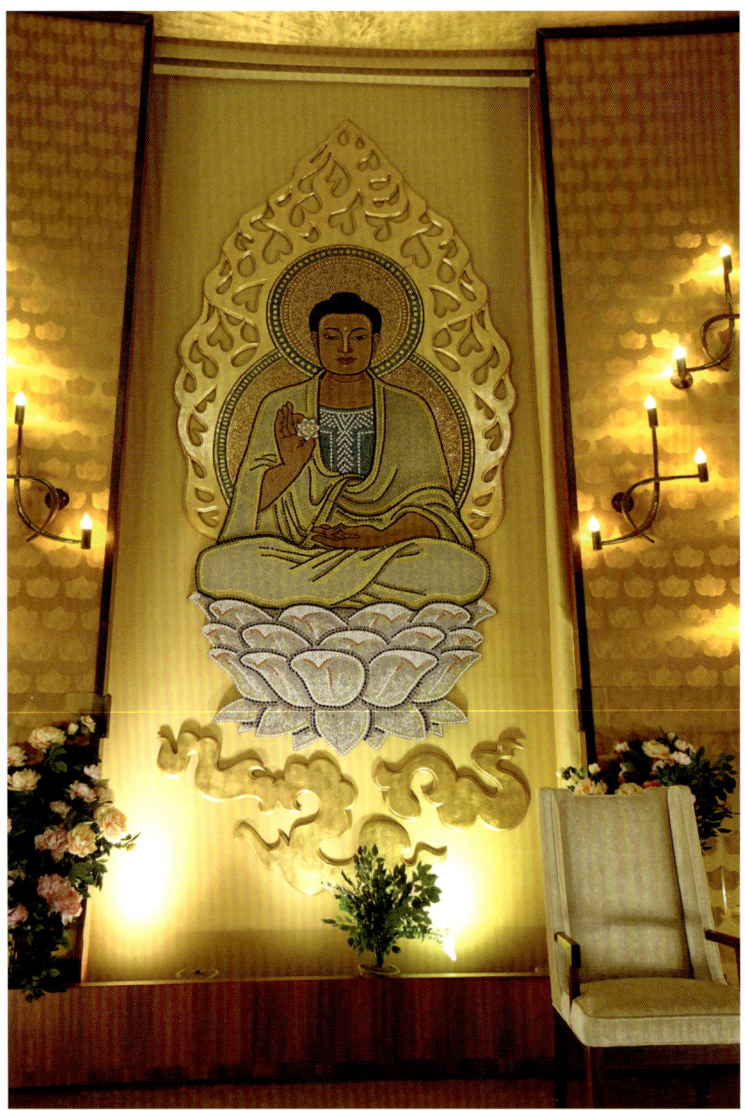

Margaret Bruton's mosaic created for Buddha's Universal Church

outspoken" and "tall, slender blondes with merry blue eyes and artistic talents 'that don't like to be tabbed.'" A 1963 photograph of the Brutons attending the church dedication shows three elegantly dressed and coiffed older women, sitting closely together and all looking away from the camera. According to family members, they preferred not to make eye contact with photographers. An iconic 1930 photograph taken by Imogen Cunningham backs this story up, with Margaret looking away from the camera and Helen gazing downward. Only Esther looks straight into the camera lens.

During the late 1960s and 1970s, the Brutons' pace finally began to slow down. Though they continued to exhibit sporadically in local venues, in most cases they showed older works. In 1967, Margaret exhibited her Virginia City paintings at Carmel Valley Manor, a senior citizens' residence, and Helen exhibited her drawings there a few years later. In December 1966, the Brutons held a ten-day group exhibition at the gallery of the New Monterey Neighborhood Center. A charming handmade flyer advertising the exhibition features a modernist woodblock portrait of the three sisters. The show consisted of photographs of the Brutons at work on the mosaic battle maps accompanied by color reproductions of the maps themselves. It also included photographs of many works that no longer survive, such as their cruise ship mosaics, Helen's altar screen at St. Joseph's Seminary, and Margaret's *Money Mural* at the Standard Federal Savings and Loan Building in Los Angeles. The exhibition traveled to the Community Art Center in Esther's hometown of Ojai.

Eventually, Margaret decided to stop making her terrazzo tables because it was very slow and heavy work. She took on a small, local project in 1965, providing the mosaic work for a harbor monument erected by the Monterey History

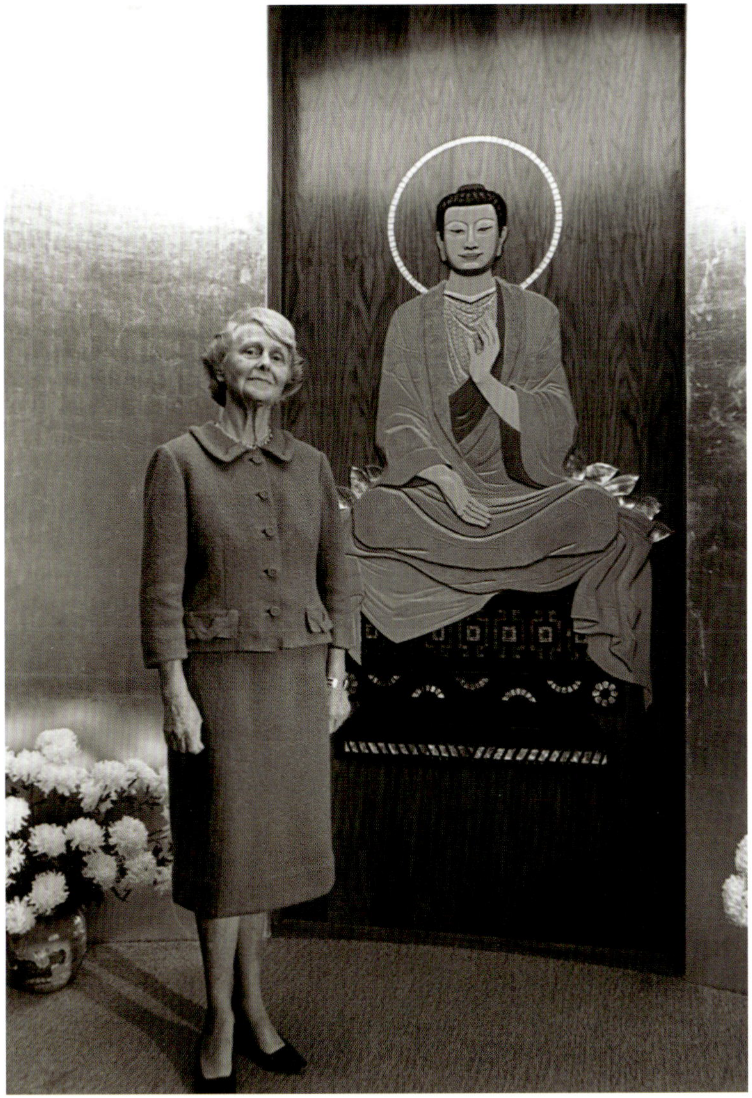

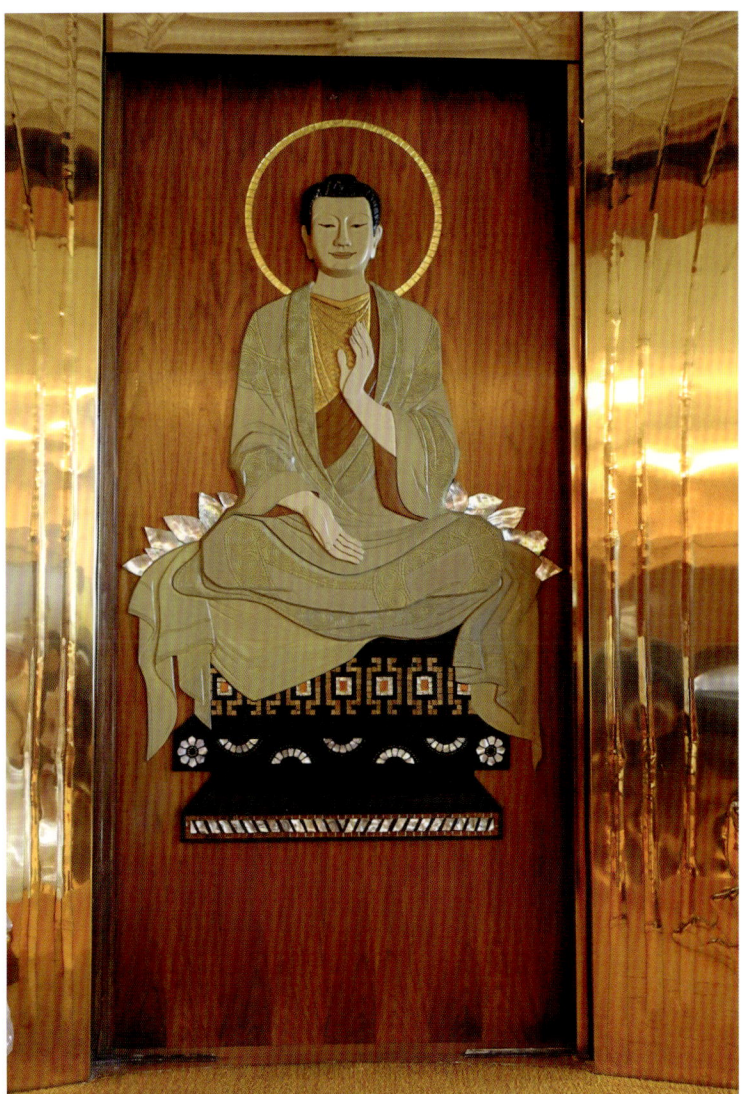

Esther Bruton in front of her Buddha mosaic at Buddha's Universal Church, 1963

Esther Bruton's mosaic created for Buddha's Universal Church

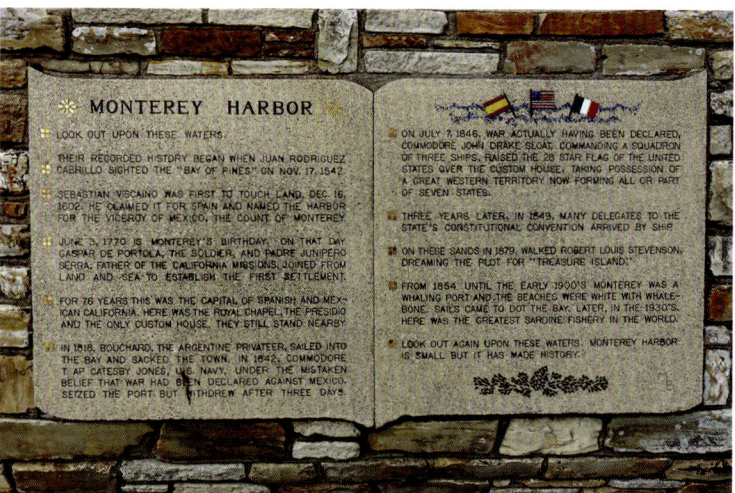

Harbor Monument near Fisherman's Wharf in Monterey with mosaic by Margaret Bruton (1965)

and Art Association, which still stands near the Fisherman's Wharf pier on Monterey's waterfront. For this piece, Margaret drew from her experience making the maps for the Manila American Cemetery since they incorporate large areas of text. The Monterey mosaic, which tells the history of the city, consists of more than two hundred words fashioned from black metal letters together with decorative gold pieces and the flags of Spain, Mexico, and the United States. These elements are set into a piece of concrete aggregate shaped like an open book that is mounted onto a stone edifice constructed by Myron Oliver, another Monterey artist and friend of the Brutons.

Well into her seventies, Margaret continued to make interesting new strides in her artwork. In 1971, she had a solo show of her "Mineral Mosaics" at the Pacific Grove

Museum of Natural History. She was experimenting with new materials such as broken glass, pottery shards, polished stone, coins, and keys, all of which began to appear frequently in her artwork. A review of the show described Margaret's range of colors as "astonishing... These mosaics are sensitively arranged in terms of color, pattern, and texture." The review goes on to say that Margaret had "a forward-thinking attitude toward her work... The majority of the mosaics in the current show are abstract, but are closely related in theme to today's concerns with ecology and space exploration." The titles of her works—*Oil Spill*, *Moon Shots*, *Fault*, *Opposing Factions*, and *Stellar Disintegration*—suggest that Margaret was concerned about the environment and the effect of human impact on it. It was perhaps the first time she had expressed a political point of view in her artwork, one underscored by a short statement that she prepared for this exhibition. "Being very aware during this atomic era of the extraordinary discoveries in the universe," she wrote, "[I am] finding the use of natural things like stones, shells and metals most appropriate and satisfying as [a] means of expressing the message of timelessness." At the age of seventy-seven, Margaret had reached yet another level of sophistication and poignancy in the art of terrazzo.

At the end of the exhibition, Margaret donated two of her terrazzo pieces to the Pacific Grove Museum of Natural History with the intention that they would be incorporated into a new addition planned for the museum. The pieces were never used, and they remain in storage at the museum as of this writing. One of the works, titled *Equation*, spells out Einstein's equation for his theory of special relativity—"$E=mc^2$"—in wire and features one of Margaret's distinctive house keys incorporated into the terrazzo.

As for Esther, she continued to win prizes for her artwork,

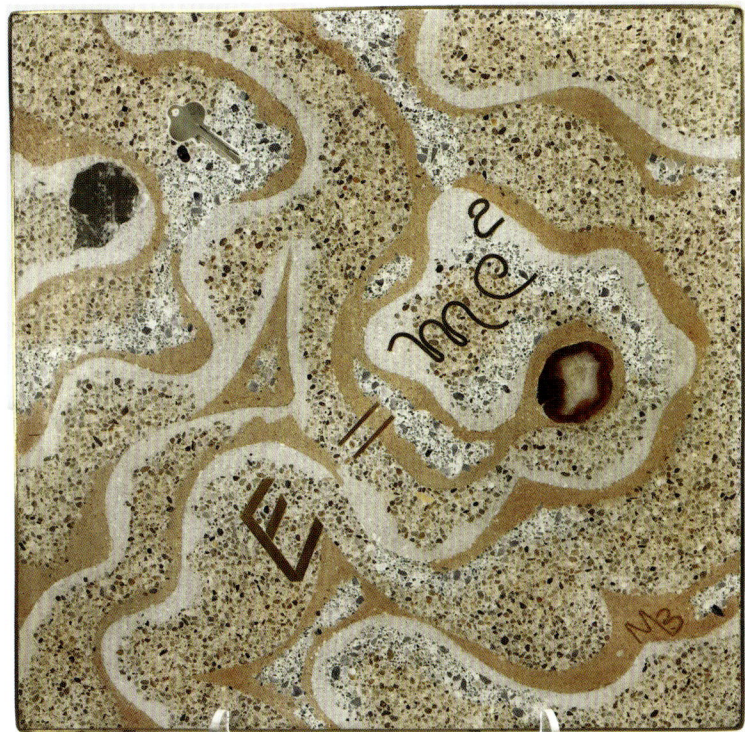

Equation, by Margaret Bruton (ca. 1971)

and her design became the official symbol for Monterey's Bicentennial.

In 1975, Helen had a solo exhibition of her drawings and prints at the Monterey Museum of Art. She called it a "Depression Show," as it featured drawings and prints from 1930 and 1931 when she and Esther were in New York. A typed guest list, likely prepared for the exhibition opening, reveals the Brutons' circle of friends in the 1970s. Names on the list include old friends such as Imogen Cunningham, Jeanette Maxfield Lewis, Ina Perham, Marjorie Eaton, Marcelle Labaudt (Lucian Labaudt's widow), Eleanor Pickersgill (their assistant during construction of *The Peacemakers*), and Frode Dann (the husband of their good friend Katy Skeele Dann, who had passed away in 1963). Also on the list were local friends Dick Bird, Lady Claude Kinnoull, and architect Mark Mills and his wife Barbara, as well as artists James and Jean Kellogg Dickie, Phil Paradise, Bob Skiles, and Emile Norman. Ansel and Virginia Adams were also on the guest list. The Brutons knew Adams well enough to tease him about "selling out" when he appeared in a 1973 Datsun automobile commercial. Perhaps in reaction to the good-natured ribbing he received from the Brutons, Imogen Cunningham, and others over his choice, Adams never allowed his work to be associated with a commercial project again.

As the years went by, the changing art scene became discouraging and baffling to the Brutons. In 1964, Helen already called the art world fickle: "Fashion in art seems to carry so much weight here in this country, and the trend that it's taken is so subjective in its mood. I mean artists nowadays—sometimes you feel that it's been reduced to such complete anarchy." Unable and unwilling to keep up with trends, the Brutons rarely exhibited or produced new work in the 1970s.

as she had been doing since the age of nineteen. In 1968, she entered a competition to design the official symbol for the Old Monterey Bicentennial, which was to be celebrated in 1970. Esther's drawing featured the Carmel Mission, crossed swords, and the dates of the bicentennial set in a checkerboard design. Originally, Esther took second place in the contest, but somewhat mysteriously, the first-place design became "a subject of community controversy" and was later rejected. This meant that Esther, at the age of seventy-two, had won the contest,

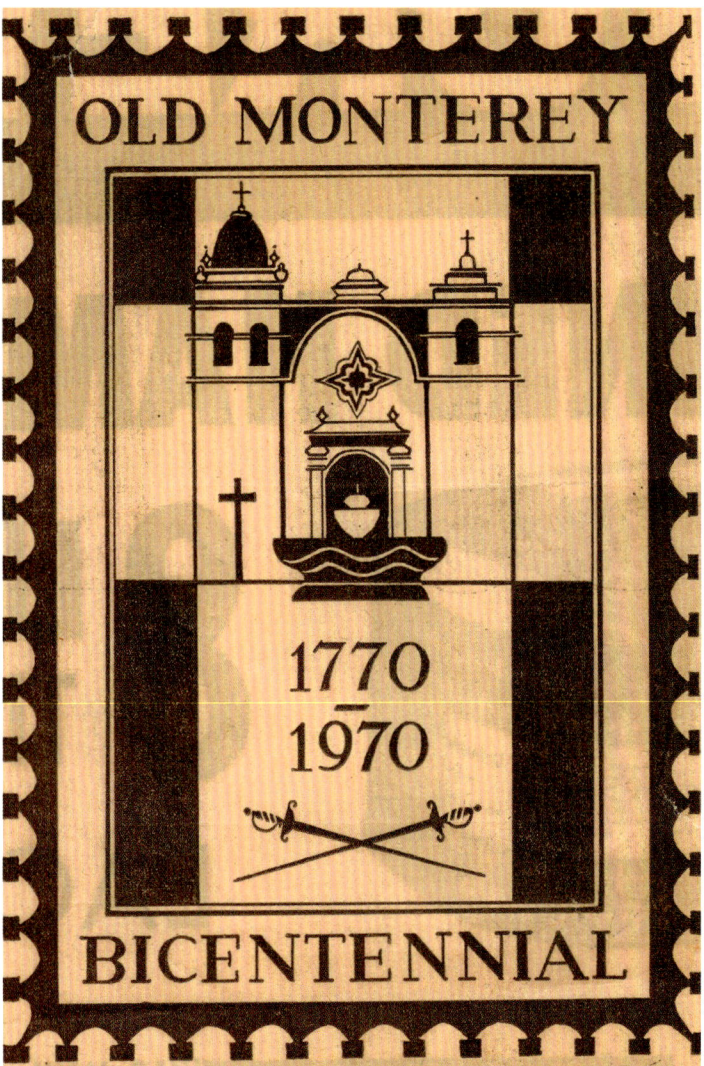

Esther Bruton's design for the official symbol of the Old Monterey Bicentennial (1968)

In 1975, Margaret summarized the pressure that artists felt, saying that if "you expect to be considered alive, you've got to be producing all the time." She stated that she made art only "when she wish[ed] to express an idea," and by the mid-1970s, she was doing very little work at all. Helen, too, was not producing much in the way of art. In 1968, she reported that she was "still suffering from severe constipation of the brain as far as 'creative' function goes. It really worries me."

Before long, the fame and accomplishments of the Bruton sisters had faded. Although their art had been exhibited in world-class museums and galleries nationwide, it was now relegated to displays in community centers and senior citizen homes. These once-acclaimed artists, who had shunned the limelight when popular, no longer had to avoid publicity—they were largely ignored by the press. In 1970, Alfred Frankenstein, when reviewing an exhibition of Imogen Cunningham's photographs at the de Young Museum in San Francisco, discussed many of the well-known people Cunningham had photographed and wondered why some of her once-famous sitters had been forgotten: "What has happened to... Marian Simpson, Joseph Sheridan, the Bruton sisters? They were major figures in the Bay Region art [scene] thirty years ago. Today one remembers them almost solely through the fact that they posed for Imogen Cunningham." In 1976, when the Brutons were included in an exhibition of New Deal art at the de Saisset Art Gallery and Museum at Santa Clara University, Frankenstein again pointed out that the Bruton sisters were no longer relevant; by this time they could only "stir nostalgia."

As they approached the end of their lives, the Bruton sisters were not particularly surprised nor bothered by the fact that they were no longer famous artists. In their collective opinion, whatever notoriety they had achieved was destined to be fleeting because their art was always evolving; as soon as they became recognized for their accomplishments in a particular style or medium, they moved on to something new. When interviewed in 1975, Helen seemed unconcerned that she was no longer part of the current art scene, proclaiming, "There are so many artists now, why worry about it? Since I'm fortunate enough that I don't have to... keep on [making art]. It doesn't matter to me." She did, however, reminisce about the 1920s, when the Brutons were at the epicenter of everything new and modern in the art world. "We do miss the contact with people who are thinking along the same lines, who like to talk art, and do it," she said. "Of course, there are many in Carmel... It's just crawling with artists now, but I'm afraid that we're a little like Rip Van Winkle. We've sort of lost touch with [the art scene]; we don't really seem to have much contact with it."

Even though they were no longer famous artists, nothing suggests that the Brutons were depressed, bitter, or in any way disengaged from life; in fact, quite the opposite was true. They spent time with family and friends, traveled extensively, and seemed to find the world endlessly fascinating. Into their sixties and seventies, they maintained their good humor and sense of fun. They resumed their passion for travel, including a Greek cruise in 1962 and a lengthy European tour in 1964, during which Helen visited Denmark and reconnected with her old friend, artist Kirsten Kjaer. In the early 1970s, Margaret and Esther traveled to Tahiti and Australia; Margaret and Helen visited Micronesia, Manila, and Portugal; and Esther went to Africa. Their photograph collection includes pictures of their travels to Cambodia, Singapore, Guam, India, Japan, the Philippines, Hong Kong, Johannesburg, Victoria Falls, Botswana, and the Bahamas.

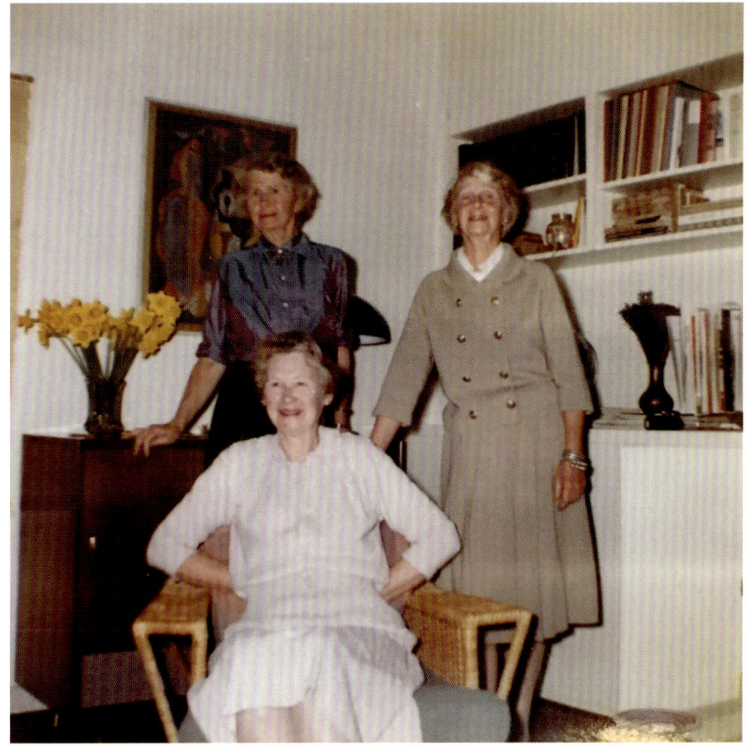

The Bruton sisters in their home in Monterey, 1963

Although they could have afforded luxury cruises, the Brutons frequently traveled by freighter ship. During the 1950s and 1960s, traveling on a cargo ship wasn't necessarily Spartan; in fact, the service could be refined and elegant. As there were rarely more than a dozen passengers aboard, they dined with the captain and crew. With no entertainment supplied, it was a quiet and restful way to travel to exotic places, which would have appealed to the Brutons. The sisters stopped traveling on freighters only when passengers above a certain age were no longer allowed, since there were no medical facilities on board.

During the 1970s, the Brutons also continued to get behind the wheel, driving into the city of San Francisco, as well as to destinations with natural appeal including Big Sur, the Sierra Nevada mountains, the desert resort town of Borrego Springs, and Kings Canyon and Sequoia National Parks. With Esther still living in Ojai, there were many trips up and down the coast to visit with each other. The sisters also loved to camp, and Helen and Esther took a camping trip to Taos in 1975 when they were in their late seventies. Helen and Margaret traveled in a Studebaker wagon with a sliding roof, while Esther had a Chevrolet Corvair "Greenbrier" camper van that she called the "Paddy Wagon II."

Later in life, the Brutons kept in touch with their good friends from the past, including Ina Perham, Lucy Pierce, Cecilia Graham, and Kirsten Kjaer. They remained especially close to their good friend Imogen Cunningham. In 1975, Margaret wrote, "Imogen is a wonder. We saw her about a week ago. She was down for a wedding. Ansel's secretary was the bride." Cunningham was, indeed, a wonder—her letters to the Brutons reveal that she was extraordinarily busy and productive well into her nineties. "I have so much to do," she wrote, "and am only half able to do it." In a 1972 letter, Cunningham discusses two different exhibitions of her work, a film being made about her, plans for her eighty-ninth birthday party—and also gives a nod to her enduring friendship with the Brutons. "My life is a frenzy," she wrote to Margaret, "[but] I get a great feeling of serenity from you gals even tho' you are always accomplishing something."

At the time, Cunningham was living in San Francisco. The Brutons visited her there, and Cunningham would stay with them whenever she came to Monterey for one of her frequent exhibitions or workshops. In April 1970, Cunningham stayed in Helen's studio, and afterwards Helen wrote her an apologetic letter:

> IMOGEN! You really are a double-barreled rascal... That you could use the studio for a few days—without even a decent coffee pot—and no attempt on my part to make it a little habitable before you got here—it embarrasses me... You don't know how often in the past I have wanted to do some little thing to repay you for all the work you did for us long ago!

Apparently, Cunningham didn't mind the state of Helen's studio, as she asked to stay there again when she returned to Monterey a few months later to conduct a seminar.

Helen had a close enough relationship with Imogen Cunningham that she was willing to share that, even in her early seventies, she sometimes lacked inspiration or a sense of direction with her art career. "Wish I did know better what I wanted to do—in the art line," Helen wrote in a 1971 letter. Similarly, despite her accomplishments, Cunningham had doubts and insecurities about her work; after photographing Helen's mosaic at the Monterey SPCA, with the intention of making postcards to raise money for the shelter, she told Helen, "You may easily get better [photographs]... I'm sure someone [else] will do a better view." In 1973, Helen attended Cunningham's ninetieth birthday in Carmel, where she shared her memories about the San Francisco artist parties of the 1930s and 1940s. Her stories must have been particularly saucy, as the local newspaper mentioned that Helen "did not describe the parties of old in the words she could have used for the sedate style of Imogen Cunningham's official Carmel ninetieth birthday."

Cunningham was close to all three Bruton sisters, and she would stay with Esther when she was in the Santa Barbara area. In 1974, Cunningham took a number of photographs of Esther, who was seventy-eight at the time. Esther was both flattered and embarrassed by the attention, saying,

> With all the work you have to do—to spend time on me makes me feel quite guilty. I do appreciate it however, and am most delighted to have the prints. They are very fine honest photos, but isn't it true that the camera doesn't lie—and I really look my age!... my face doesn't do for close-ups... Thank you, Imogen, for all you have done for me and for your visit which was a delight for me.

In addition to their circle of friends, the Brutons had extended family on the West Coast. They remained close to their younger cousin, Jack Stackable, and his wife, Helen Margaret. The Stackables had three daughters, June, Helen Margaret (Peggy), and Barbara, resulting in a confusing number of Helens and Margarets across two branches and three generations of the family. The Brutons often exchanged letters with Jack and his wife, and they visited each other regularly, especially during the holidays. When Jack passed away in 1976, Esther wrote to his widow, "I cherish, as one of my happiest times—the visit here with dear Jack and you all, just a year ago at this time. How we all miss Jack. I feel so fortunate to have had this visit with him."

The three Stackable daughters, all born in Berkeley, were the Brutons' first cousins once removed. They were, on average, fifty years younger than the Brutons, and although they were aware that these older women in the family were famous artists, they had no concept of the scope and depth

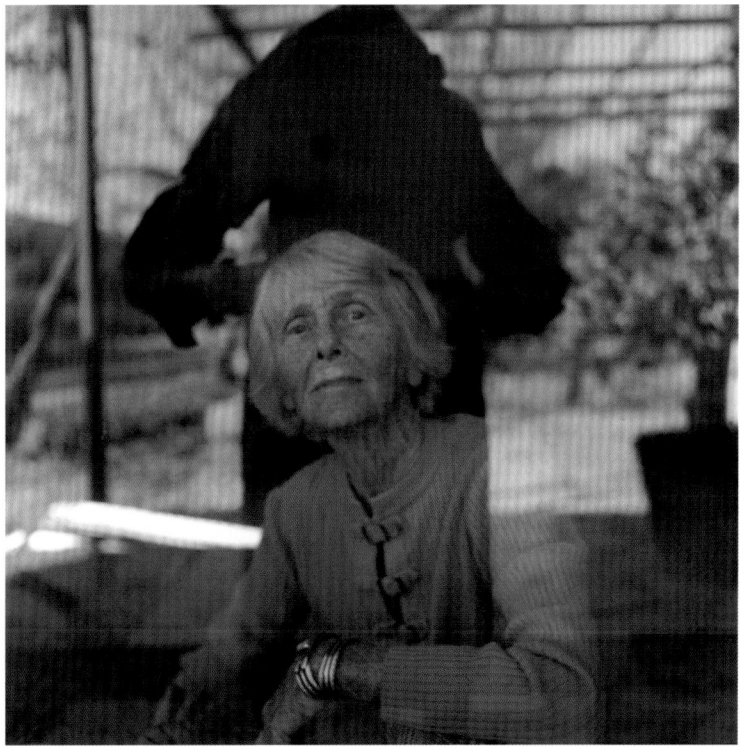

Self Portrait with Esther Bruton, by Imogen Cunningham (1974)

of their careers. The Stackable girls loved Margie, Ecky, and Helen because they were unique, fascinating, and quirky. The Brutons had a unique way of interacting with young people; rather than being authoritative or patronizing, they respected children and treated them as equals. The youngest daughter, Barbara, has many fond memories of the sisters, who were like "favorite aunts." "They were bigger than life," she recalled. "It was a very special relationship and a unique relationship." Helen, in particular, shared her love of nature and animals with her much younger cousins. They went on walks near Helen's studio where she would feed the quail and leave food scraps for the "varmints." Barbara recalled, "We'd go to the tidepools... Helen would start drawing mermaids in the sand for us. As little kids, this was just the greatest." Helen was always observing the world around her, picking up objects, and turning them in her hand as she weighed their artistic possibilities. Once, while on a walk, she found a bleached vertebra of a small animal. Thinking that it had potential to become something more, Helen brought it home and carved and painted the bone until it was transformed into the head of a cow; Helen presented the charming sculpture to Barbara, who still treasures it today.

After she graduated from college in 1970, Barbara lived with Helen and Margaret in Monterey while she worked as a teacher. Barbara's friends were puzzled by her desire to live with "old ladies," but, as she explained, these were "the coolest old ladies in the known world." She found the Brutons to be engaged in life: "They were so open and interested in what was going on in the world and not threatened by it." Whereas many people their age would have disapproved of "hippie" culture, the Brutons were fascinated by it. In 1969, Margaret wrote, "There are young people of all varieties on the road, heading

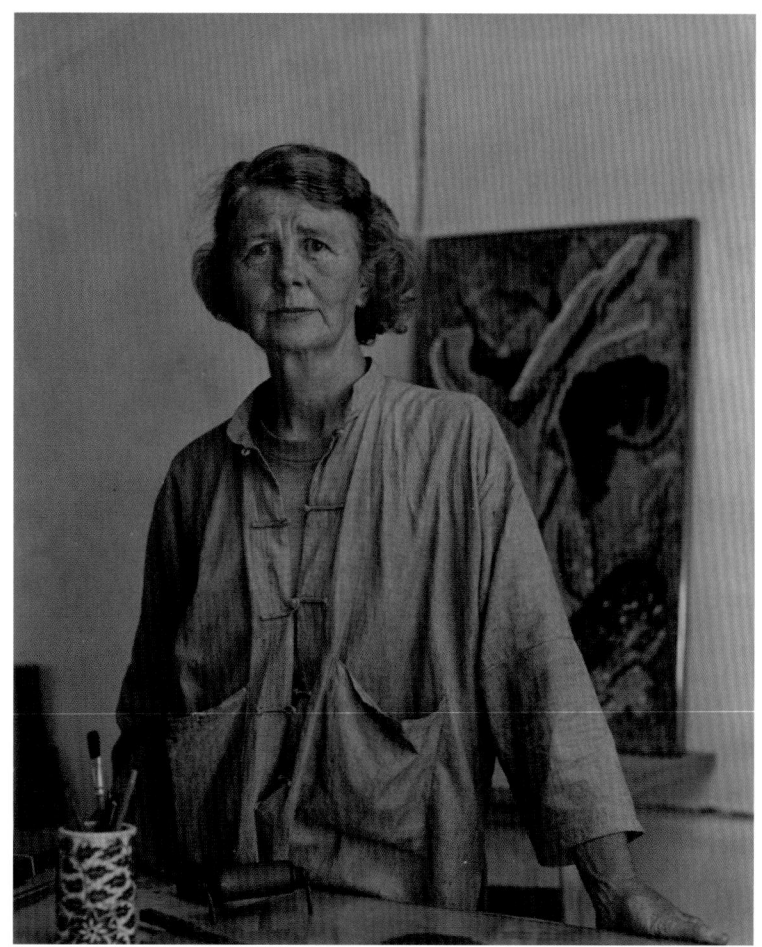

Helen Bruton, photo by Larry Colwell (ca. 1960s)

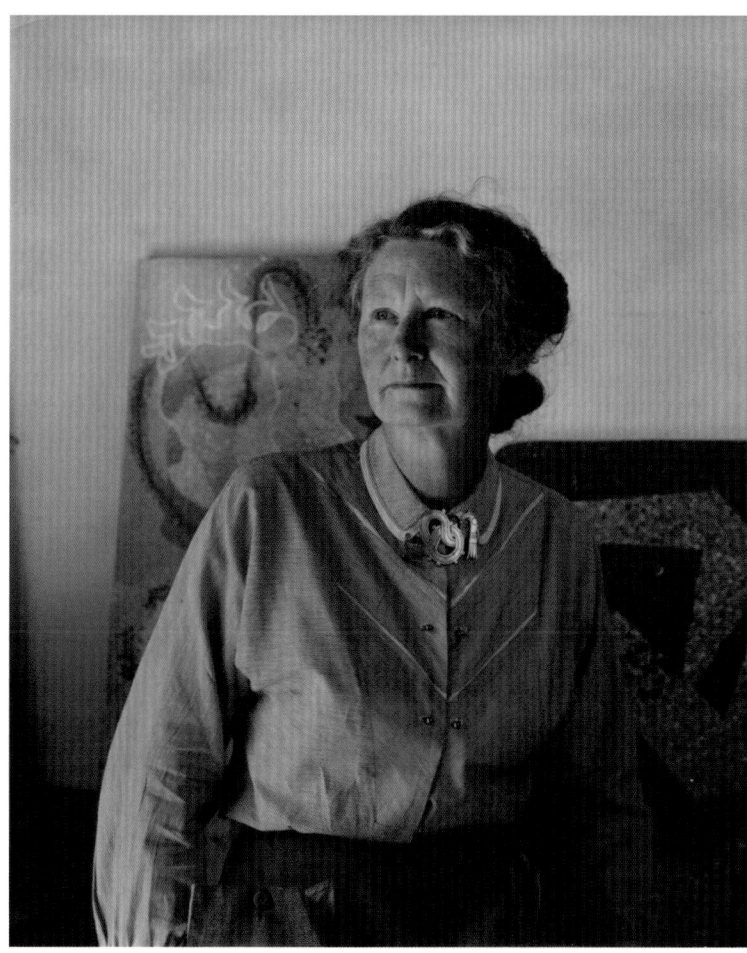
Margaret Bruton, photo by Larry Colwell (ca. 1960s)

for the south coast and around here, hitch-hiking. Goodness knows where they stay... They are not very welcome, and I feel sorry for them."

In 1981, the sisters were surprised and thrilled to learn that Esther's murals in the Cirque Room at the Fairmont Hotel—which they thought had been destroyed—had, in fact, survived. The Fairmont was reopening the bar and restoring the murals, and the Brutons were invited back to assist with the renovation. Helen and Esther attended a party celebrating the reopening of the Cirque Room in January 1982, where they hobnobbed with VIPs and were interviewed and photographed by the press. The sparkling Art Deco–style Cirque Room, embellished by Esther's circus murals, remains a jewel of the Fairmont Hotel.

As the sisters grew older, they began to part with some of their artwork. In 1967 Margaret gave twenty-seven of her watercolors of Virginia City to the California Historical Society in San Francisco, and in 1973 she gifted her award-winning 1925 painting *Monterey Landscape* (which she had renamed *Barns on Cass Street*) to the Monterey Museum of Art. Helen donated two versions of her print *Cass Street* to the Monterey Museum of Art in 1975. They also sold many of their works to Oakland art collectors Walter Nelson-Rees and James Coran, who began buying early twentieth-century California art in the 1980s, when underappreciated works of art could be obtained at reasonable prices. By 1991, these savvy collectors had acquired nearly 1,000 early California paintings.

Nelson-Rees first contacted Margaret in early May 1982, a particularly chaotic time in the sisters' lives. They were in the process of building an addition on Helen's studio so that Esther, who was selling her house in Ojai and moving back to Monterey, could live there. Nelson-Rees asked Margaret if she would be willing to sell any of her artwork. Given the sisters' uncertainty about their legacy and future relevance as artists, they must have been flattered by his interest. At Nelson-Rees's request, Margaret compiled a list of her works with prices, although it is unclear how she came up with these figures. From their correspondence, Margaret—who was eighty-eight and in ill health—seemed uncomfortable with the pace of the negotiations. Nelson-Rees tried assuage her concerns: "*Of course* I understand that transactions of this sort need to be worked out slowly," he wrote, "and I do not mean to be pushy—perhaps anxious only... thanks for your patience with this eager beaver." By the end of the month, Nelson-Rees and Coran paid $10,000 for eighteen of her works as well as nine works by other prominent artists from her collection, including etchings and paintings by August Gay, Armin Hansen, and C.S. Price. They purchased another nine items from Margaret a few months later. In the end, Margaret sold some of her most important works to the young collectors, including her modernist portraits of her parents and her prize-winning paintings from Virginia City: *Mining Mountains* and *On the Comstock Lode*.

Shortly after contacting Margaret, Nelson-Rees also reached out to Helen, asking her to provide a "shopping list" of works she would sell to them. Like Margaret, Helen was reticent at first: "You will have to forgive me, but I just can't seem to face putting prices on your shopping list... It's a real bind and I'm worried. Maybe it's because I'm not used to anybody being really interested in my work." She eventually came up with a list and prices, and in July 1982 Nelson-Rees and Coran acquired thirty-two of Helen's works for $4,145, including the iconic *Beach Picnic*—a work some consider her "masterpiece"—for which they paid $1,500.

It is difficult to say whether Nelson-Rees and Coran paid fair prices, but they clearly appreciated the Brutons' work at a time when few other collectors did. In a 2019 email, Coran said that the Brutons "were very appreciative of our purchases and with those funds they added on to the studio." Coran further claimed that he and Nelson-Rees had a close and sincere friendship with the Brutons: "We were guests many time[s] to the home they built... We were invited to be house sitters when they wanted to go drive down to visit their sister." But the Bruton sisters' family members see this relationship differently. They suggest that Nelson-Rees and Coran took advantage of the Brutons by pressuring them to sell works they didn't really want to sell for considerably less than they were worth. "We felt that the sisters had been beguiled," a cousin stated. It does seem out of character for the Brutons to sell some of their favorite works, especially ones with strong sentimental value—such as Margaret's portraits of their parents—when the sisters were financially secure and had no real need for the money.

In 1991, the home where Nelson-Rees and Coran stored their massive art collection burned to the ground in the Oakland Hills wildfires. Everything was destroyed, including the pieces they acquired from the Brutons. Fortunately, Nelson-Rees and Coran had published a catalog of their favorite works from their collection just two years before the fire. Color images of four of the Brutons' lost works survive in this catalog.

As the Brutons reached their eighties, these active, vigorous women were beginning to show signs of their age. Early in 1983, Esther sold her house in Ojai and moved back to Monterey to be with her sisters. Margaret was having numerous health problems; she suffered from heart disease and Paget's disease of bone, a condition that causes arthritis and joint pain. "Altho' nothing was found in my tests," she wrote in February 1983, "I still feel lousy and in no condition to travel or visit... I don't know why everything seems so complicated these days... 'Old Man River' has caught up with us, I guess." Margaret died six months later from congestive heart failure at a convalescent home in Monterey on August 29, 1983 at the age of eighty-nine.

In November 1983, just a few months after Margaret's death, Esther and Helen were involved in a serious car accident. According to Helen, they were traveling through Greenfield, California, about an hour south of Monterey, when Esther's car struck an object in the road and flipped over. Both women spent the night in the hospital, but despite the severity of the crash they were not seriously injured. James Coran and Walter Nelson-Rees, who were housesitting for the Brutons in Monterey at the time, drove down to the hospital to pick them up the following day. "To think of how well you got off is to start believing in miracles," Nelson-Rees wrote to Esther. "We were glad to have been able to help out and be with you." At around the same time, Esther gifted two paintings by C.S. Price to the collectors, perhaps in recognition of their assistance in the aftermath of the car accident.

Two years later on November 15, 1985, eighty-seven-year-old Helen had a heart attack and died at her home in Monterey. By this time, Esther was suffering from Alzheimer's disease and was no longer able to live independently; she spent her final years at an assisted living facility in Carmel Valley. When Barbara Mills visited Esther there in 1987, she reported that "[Esther is] well. Except for missing her family 'who've gone camping,' she seems quite happy." Esther died of a stroke at the Community Hospital of Monterey on August 31, 1992, at the age of ninety-five.

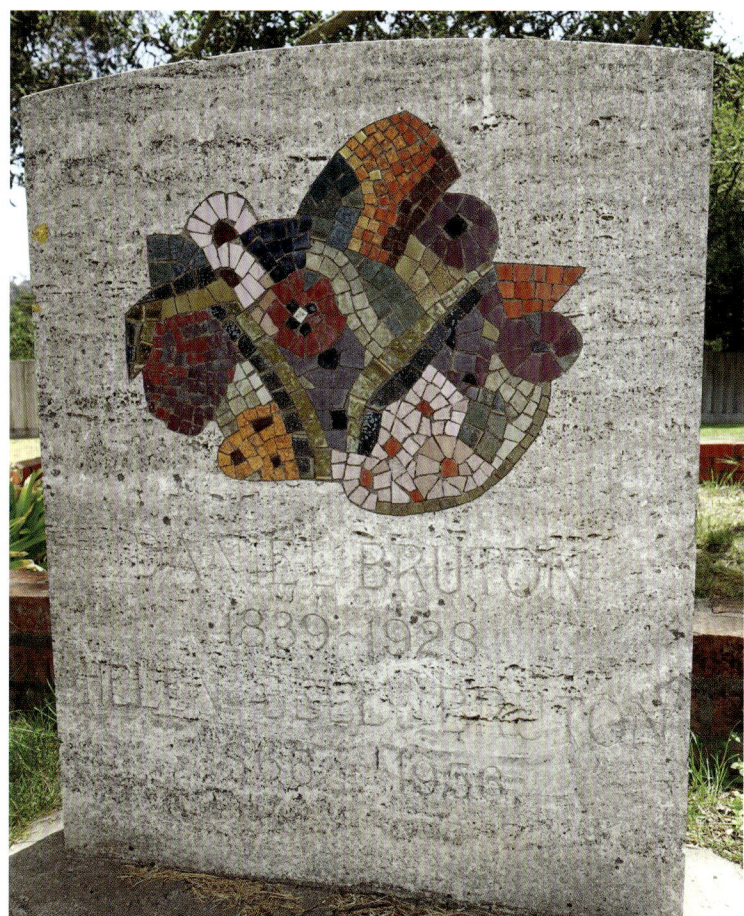

Margaret, Esther, and Helen created the mosaic work on the headstone for their parents, Daniel and Helen Bruton

In 1988, the Brutons' house on Cass Street in Monterey was purchased by Eric and Teresa Del Piero, who intended to renovate the building and use it as an office. Unfortunately, because the structure that Margaret designed "in about one day or two flat" had a crumbling foundation, it was condemned by the city of Monterey and had to be demolished. Prior to the demolition, the Del Pieros became intrigued by items they discovered on the property, including a backyard kiln, a kitchen backsplash made from Solon & Schemmel tile, and a pebble mosaic of a dog that included the intriguing phrase "Quickly but cautiously" and was found just outside Margaret's studio. A pass over the backyard with a metal detector revealed that plain stepping stones had beautiful mosaic decorations on their reverse sides. The Del Pieros salvaged what they could before the house was torn down, including a mosaic house number from above the front door. Having known nothing about the Bruton sisters when they purchased the house, they became increasingly curious about the creative women who had lived there and appreciative of the artwork they had left behind. Already collectors of early twentieth-century California art, the Del Pieros began to seek out works by the Brutons.

The once-famous Bruton sisters, who had hundreds of newspaper and magazine articles written about them during their lifetimes, died with little notice; there were no obituaries published for Helen or Esther. The ashes of all three sisters are buried alongside their parents in the family plot at the Monterey City Cemetery. Years earlier, the sisters had made a headstone for their parents and decorated it with a mosaic of flowers. After Margaret died, Helen and Esther hoped to mark their sister's grave with a large, natural rock to which they could attach a plaque, but they couldn't agree on the perfect stone, and as the years passed and their health declined, nothing was ever done. As a result, there are no markers or gravestone on the family plot to indicate that this is the final resting place of three very accomplished California artists.

Perhaps this is what the unassuming Bruton sisters would have wanted. Based on their comments and attitudes toward the end of their lives, they may not have expected their art careers to be reexamined or resurrected in any meaningful way after their deaths. They had wonderful lives, full of adventure, travel, close friendships, deep sisterly bonds, and successful art careers. For them, this was enough. They probably never thought that their art would be of any particular interest to future collectors, art historians, museum curators, or the general public. Fortunately for us, they were wrong.

Right: The Bruton sisters working on the Berkeley mosaic, photo by Imogen Cunningham (1936)
Next pages: *Pastoral*, by Helen Bruton (ca. 1954). Collection Dallas Museum of Art

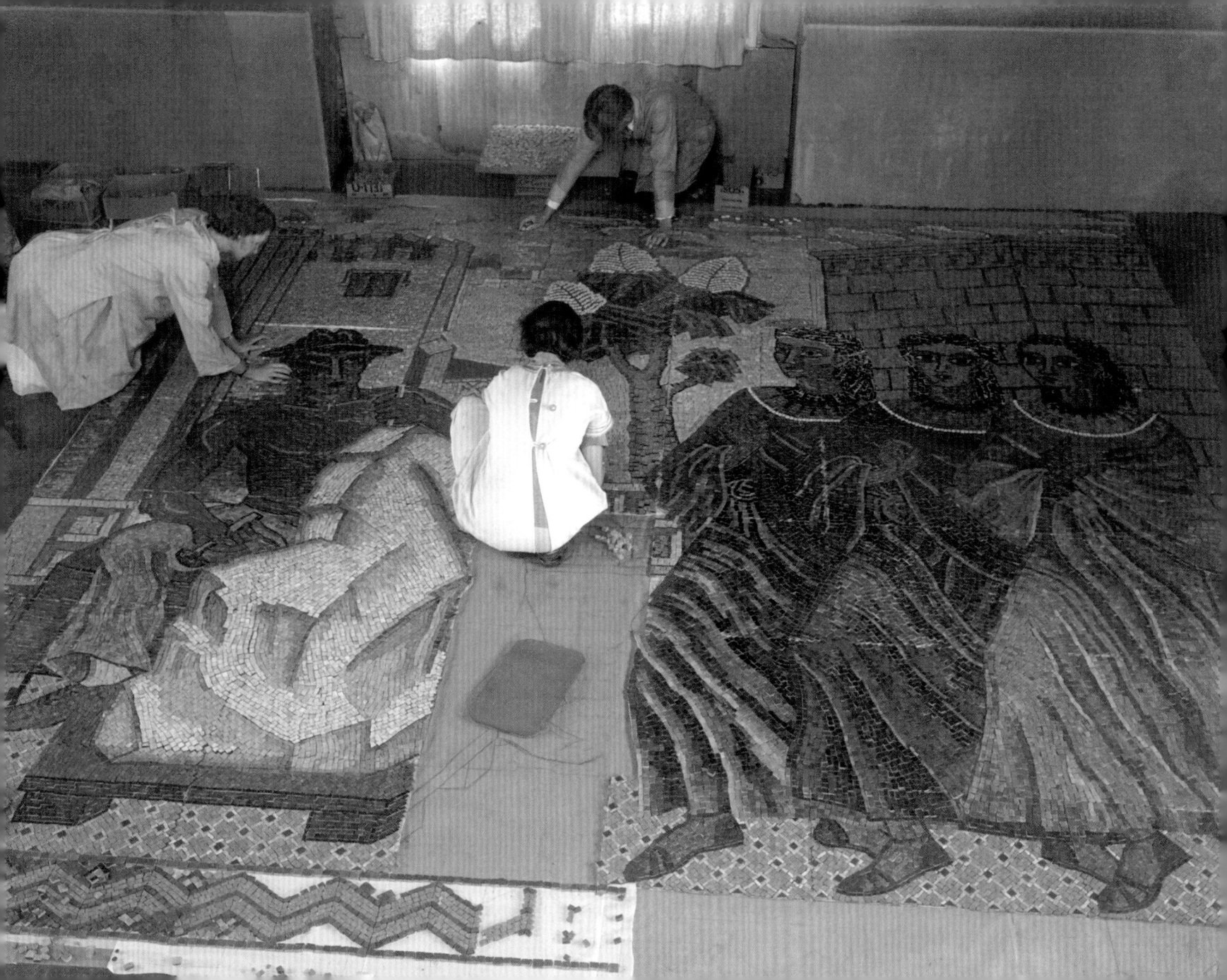

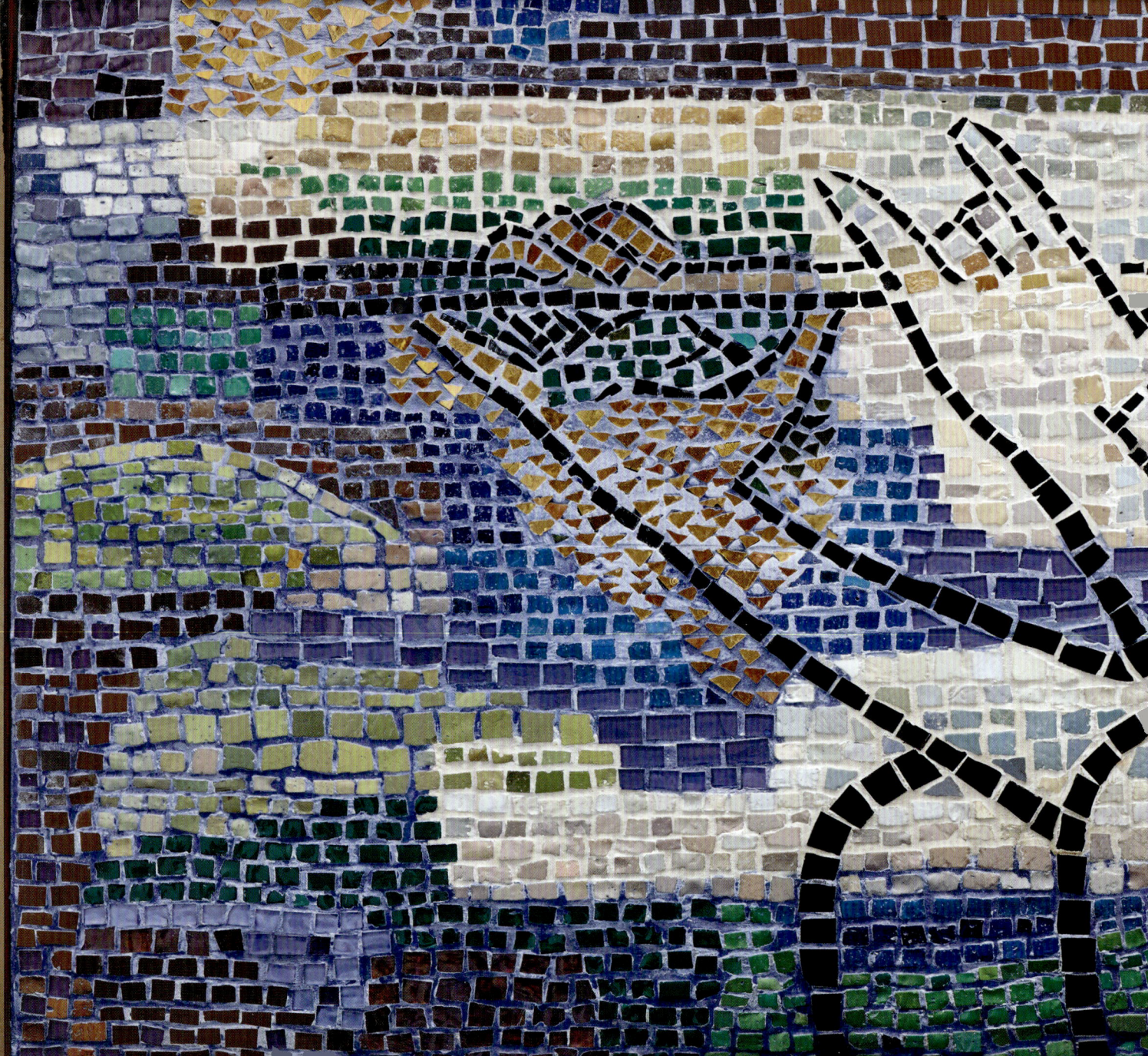

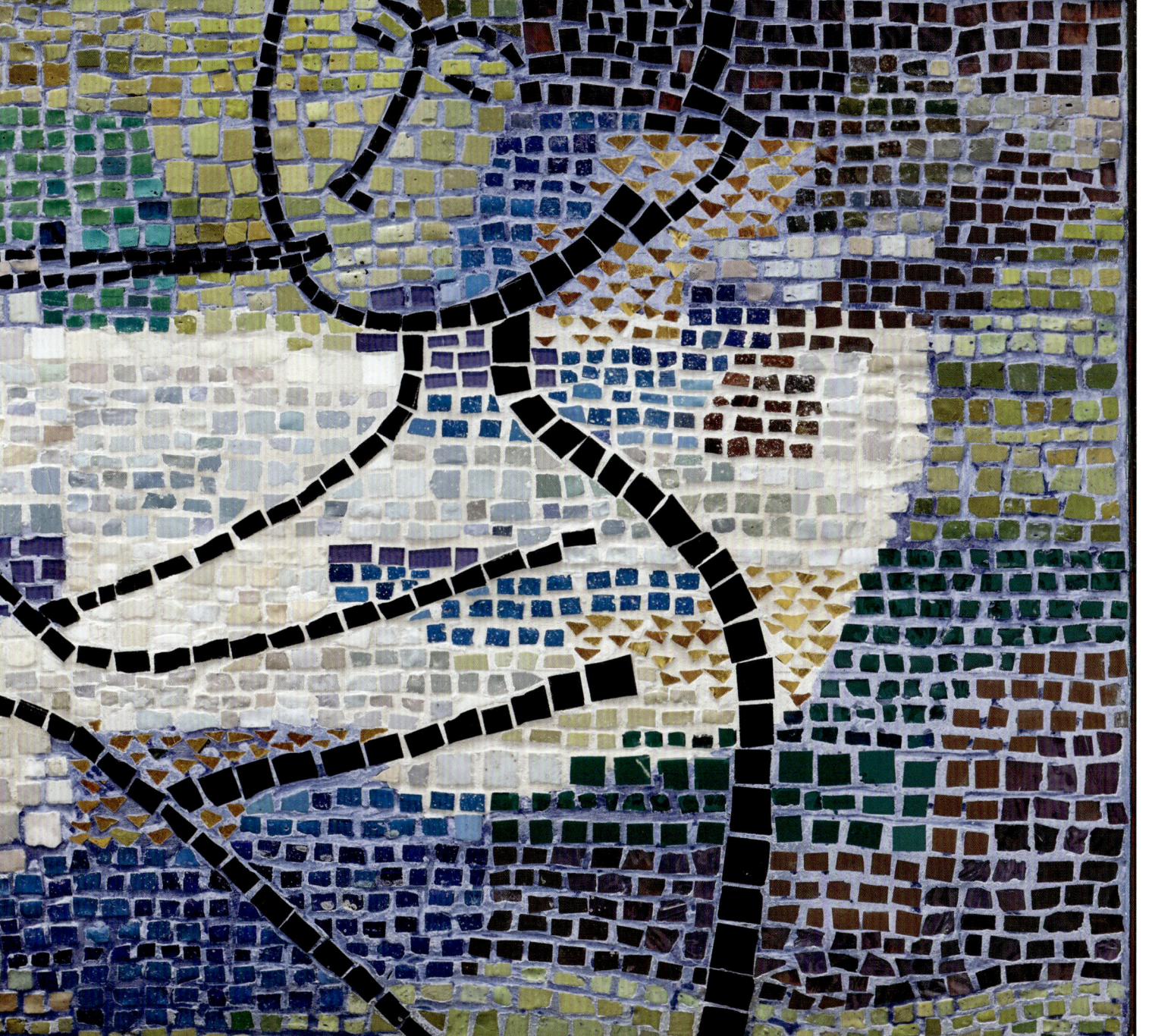

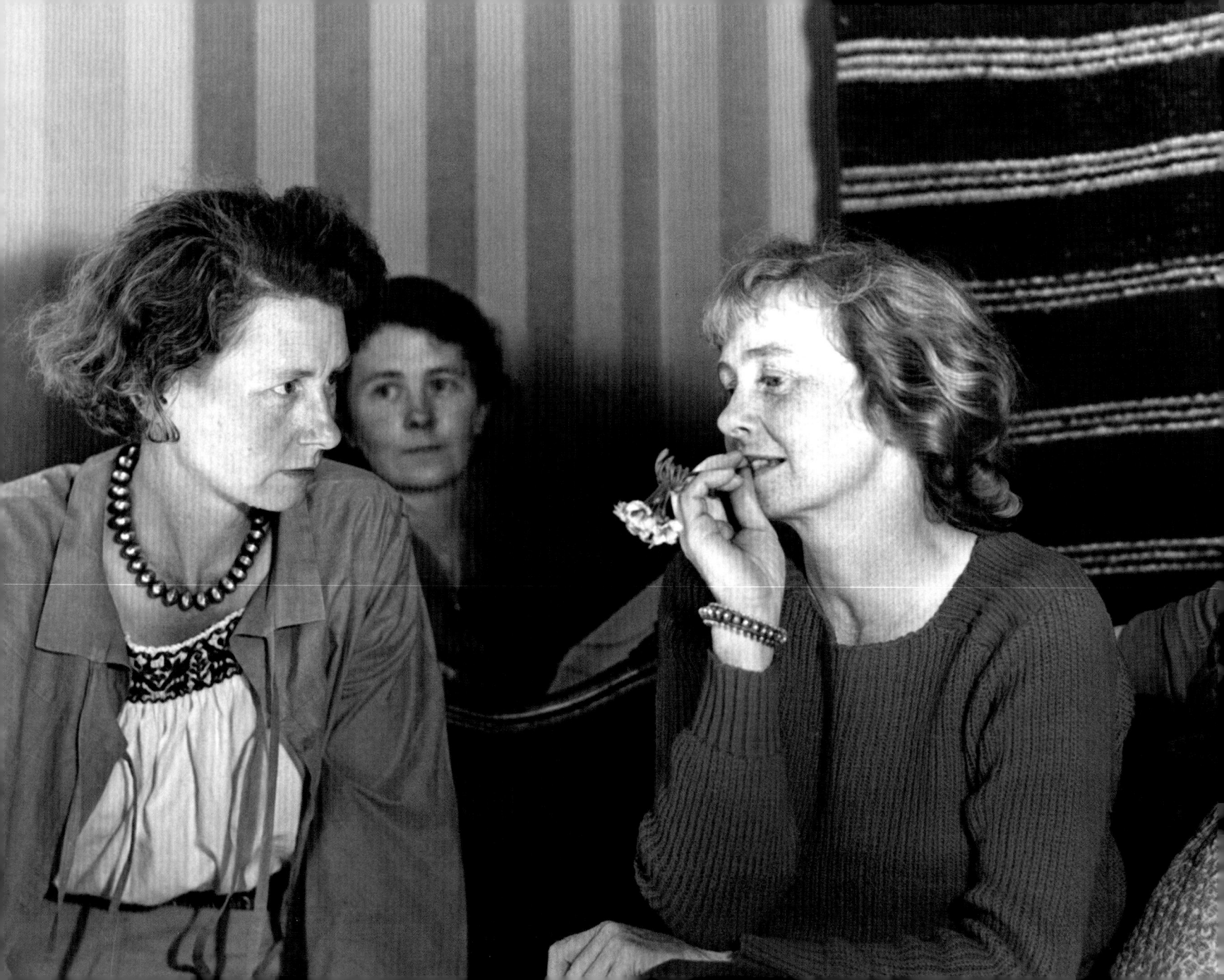

Epilogue: A Legacy Restored

The Indian coastal city of Alang is the world's largest ship graveyard and the final destination for many retired cruise ships. When these formerly glamorous hotels-on-the-sea are no longer profitable or seaworthy, they end up in ship-breaking yards like the one in Alang. The humbled behemoths are unceremoniously dismantled, stripped of any raw materials that can be sold. In November 2006, after decades of service, the SS *Monterey* docked for the last time on the ghostly shores of Alang. This former jewel of the Matson Line, which once featured beautiful mosaic murals by Esther Bruton, has since been destroyed. Her sister ship, the *Mariposa*—and Helen Bruton's innovative mosaic *Constellations of the Seven Seas*—met a similar fate in 1996. These unique artworks are gone forever.

The Bruton sisters' artworks have been vulnerable to the march of time and changing tastes, and few of their works have found their way to the protected walls of museum galleries. The Brutons' greatest triumph, *The Peacemakers*, existed for less than two years before it was dismantled along with the rest of the art and architecture at the Golden Gate International Exposition. Their works for cruise ships were destroyed, as were many other commercial commissions. As fashions and styles evolved, hotels and office buildings renovated and updated their spaces, painting over 1930s-era murals and removing mosaics that did not complement revamped architecture. Two notable exceptions have implausibly survived: Esther's murals in the Cirque Room at the Fairmont Hotel and Helen's mosaics at the Hotel Union Square. Margaret's mosaic maps in Manila are by all accounts in excellent condition, and the "Bruton Buddhas" at Buddha's

Universal Church in San Francisco have been meticulously preserved by the congregation since their installation almost sixty years ago. But even works by the Brutons that have held up beautifully, such as the mosaics on the Mothers Building at the San Francisco Zoo and the Old Art Gallery on the Berkeley campus, are in jeopardy; both these buildings are in desperate need of renovation and are currently closed to the public due to their condition.

Like many women artists of the early twentieth century, the Brutons "achieved national and international fame, only to vanish from view in the postwar period." A number of factors contributed to their disappearance from museums, galleries, and the media, including discrimination against women artists, changing tastes in art, and the sisters' unwillingness to document their accomplishments. The art world of the 1940s and 1950s belonged to Abstract Expressionism and, for the most part, to male artists. In addition to the gender biases women artists faced in this period, the Brutons' style of art no longer seemed relevant in the changing post–World War II art scene. Government-funded art projects of the 1930s—with their focus on the American scene and emphasis on social realism—seemed technically unsophisticated and "artistically insignificant." WPA-era mosaics and murals were no longer considered "good" art, and as a result, they were "denigrated and ignored... painted over, lost, or literally dumped." Accordingly, the reputation of artists from this era suffered. Even the Brutons' terrazzo and mosaic work from the 1940s and 1950s—once considered fresh and original—was rarely of interest to museums, galleries, or collectors.

The Bruton Sisters, photo by Imogen Cunningham (ca. 1930)

Another reason the Brutons' art fell out of fashion could be attributed to their unwillingness to take any steps to preserve their legacy. As early as the 1950s, when the Brutons' art careers were still going strong, they were reluctant to talk about themselves or their art—in their own words, they were "sort of diffident about it." In 1956, a student writing a thesis about mosaic reached out to Helen with a number of questions, and received this reply:

> Please forgive me for seeming so uncooperative. I'm not really lazy, or reluctant to part with precious secrets for I don't know any... But truly, and I now speak for my sisters also, we do not feel qualified, or care to be quoted as authorities on the subject of mosaic. We have no final answers to your technical questions. And as for the aesthetic ones all we can say is mosaic is still only a medium... I think all this to-do about mosaic is a bore and has nothing to do with art. Like everything else in this country, it will probably be "promoted" into an early grave, which will be a pity. About our work, it will have to speak for us, for better or worse, in mosaic or any other medium. We have no talent at all for words.

The Brutons were recognized by their colleagues and the broader art community as inventive pioneers and experts in their fields, yet they still felt uncomfortable talking about their art, much less acknowledging their impressive abilities and accomplishments.

Even with their own relatives, the Brutons preferred not to relive the past. Family members repeatedly tried to conduct interviews in order to preserve the Brutons' thoughts and memories on tape, but the sisters refused. Helen seemed to think that a recording of her words "would make her seem too important." Their cousin Barbara Carroll recalls that the sisters downplayed their fame: "They showed us [their works] but they never crowed about them. No self-aggrandizement at all... Margie in particular was very private." When asked to elaborate on their accomplishments, the sisters would demur. "That was years ago," they would say. "That was no big deal."

The Brutons' art-world colleagues, too, tried to get them some well-deserved publicity in their later years. Gardner Dailey felt they should be included in a dictionary of American women artists and nominated them for an award, but they couldn't be bothered to fill out the application. Helen recalled, "We didn't have any ambition to be in *Who's Who*... We got looking at all the questions... [about] what we did and what we didn't do and how old we were, and we said, 'Well, the hell with it.'" Helen did worry that they had hurt Dailey's feelings by not following through. Perhaps they had, but more long term, their inaction kept them out of a publication that would have provided documentation and recognition of their careers.

Helen, as business manager and spokesperson for the trio, was usually the main point of contact with the outside world. Yet sometimes she seemed to go out of her way to be uncooperative, even when serious scholars showed a sincere interest in the Bruton sisters' work. In 1975, Helen was contacted by Phil Kovinick, who requested biographical information so he could include the Brutons in *An Encyclopedia of Women Artists of the American West*. At first Helen ignored his request, largely because she didn't think of the Brutons as "Western" artists. However, she eventually replied to Kovinick, "We have all of us been careless about getting out any kind of detailed biographical accounts, and am afraid never did have a proper professional attitude... And now it is a little too late to care." A few years later, while preparing her landmark work *American Women Artists from Early Indian Times to the Present*, author Charlotte Rubenstein wrote to Helen asking for biographical information about the Brutons. Helen was reluctant to provide anything of use. All she was willing to concede was to say, "I can now say without embarrassment, 'yes, we were artists.'" Helen is briefly mentioned in Rubenstein's book and Margaret and Esther do not appear at all.

While the Brutons seemed unconcerned about their legacy, they cared very deeply about the caliber of their art. Without considerable ambition and a drive for excellence, they could not have produced such high-quality work, nor could they have had such long and successful careers. The Brutons had what artist Alice Neel described as "sensitivity and tremendous will-power... the power to stick with what you believe." The Bruton sisters were strong-willed and resilient; rejection and failure didn't stop them from producing art. Nor did they slavishly commit themselves to a medium or technique once they had mastered it. All three of the Brutons had restless appetite for experimentation, regardless of the result; their resilience and confidence were crucial aspects of their personalities that enabled them to keep evolving and maturing as artists.

Where did this resilience and confidence come from? Perhaps from the way the Brutons were raised—the encouragement they received from their mother and the freedom and space they had to experiment artistically, even as children. Perhaps it came from the extremely close and supportive lifelong bond that existed between the sisters. Perhaps both, with another, more practical factor also in play: they always had the financial means to be self-sufficient. They could pursue their art full-time and didn't depend on it

to make a living. Knowing that their income and livelihood did not depend on good reviews, commissions, or sales must have been incredibly liberating; the Brutons could be bold and experimental without jeopardizing their lifestyle. Their financial independence was an important advantage that many of their peers didn't have, and it was a significant factor in their development as artists.

Despite the slow decline of the Brutons' reputations over the years, there were instances in which art historians became interested in them again. In 1964, Lewis Ferbraché from the Smithsonian Institution's Archives of American Art interviewed Margaret and Helen at their home in Monterey. They were interviewed again in 1975 by Lydia Modi-Vitale and Steven Gelber in conjunction with the *New Deal Art: California* exhibition at the de Saisset Art Gallery and Museum at Santa Clara University. When Gelber inquired if the Brutons would agree to a videotaped interview, they were at first reluctant to participate. Helen wrote to Gelber, explaining, "What little I have of remaining relics I hesitate to bring out into the cold light of contemporary criticism... I am almost pathologically camera shy and my sister Margaret extremely reticent." Eventually, Margaret and Helen allowed Gelber to videotape the interview, giving additional fascinating insight into Margaret's and Helen's personalities.

In both interviews, Helen takes charge and does almost all the talking; her vitality, enthusiasm, and wry sense of humor are on full display. Margaret, on the other hand, hangs back, speaking only occasionally when prodded for a response. She resisted participating in these interviews and didn't want to talk about the past. Margaret "was terrible—she was really awful," Helen remarked. "She hates to go back... She didn't like this idea at all. She didn't like my idea of even showing this old stuff." For Helen, decades' worth of artwork, once lauded by the press and hung in the finest museums and galleries, was now simply "old stuff." The only time Margaret speaks at length in this interview is when she is pulled aside by the interviewer and asked directly about her experiences making the battle maps for the Manila American Cemetery in the Philippines.

In 1977, the *Monterey Peninsula Herald* featured a multi-page article about the Brutons, appropriately titled, "The Bruton Sisters Look Back, Reluctantly." The reporter interviewed Helen and Margaret, who were "living quietly" at their home on Cass Street. The article featured numerous photographs, including one with a caption that read, "In spite of a long, eventful past, [Helen Bruton] lives very much in the present." When asked to share their memories of their storied art careers, both Helen and Margaret "protested that they don't really like to talk about other times." As Margaret explained, "That's all in the past."

Perhaps the Brutons—or at least Helen and Margaret—were reluctant to relive their achievements because they believed they were no longer relevant in the late-twentieth-century art scene. They were never self-promoters, even at the height of their fame, and they were perhaps even less likely to assert themselves toward the end of their lives when their artistic reputations were in question. Yet, by repeatedly refusing to tell their stories, they again did themselves a disservice; the overall lack of documentation about the Brutons and their careers ensured the continued decline of their reputations and their near disappearance from the annals of art history. As time went on, many of their contributions—particularly Helen's— were forgotten. Even as recently as 2019, Helen's mosaics at the University of Southern California were misattributed to the male architect of the building, her mosaic at University of California at Berkeley was obscured by vegetation, her *Nativity* mosaic was identified as the work of Louisa Jenkins, and staff members at the Hotel Union Square were telling guests that her *City* and *Country* mosaics were by Diego Rivera. None of these errors are intentionally malicious or disrespectful; they occurred because the Brutons' vital roles in American art have been underappreciated.

The late twentieth century brought about renewed interest in the Brutons' work, at least among collectors. Gerald Buck, who amassed a vast collection of California art, was an early collector of the Bruton sisters' work, acquiring twenty-five pieces during the late 1980s. These works are now in the collection of the Institute and Museum of California Art at the University of California at Irvine. In the 1990s, the mid-century modern collector Steve Cabella also began acquiring works by the Brutons. "A large part of my collection is work by women artists whose contributions to Modernism and 1950s design is only now being recognized," stated Cabella in a 1994 interview. "I search for their work [and try] to interview [the artists] and preserve their accomplishments." Eric and Teresa Del Piero, who purchased the Brutons' Monterey home in 1988, also began to acquire their work. Notable acquisitions by the Del Pieros were Margaret's paintings *The Harmonica* circa 1935 and *Nudes (She's Not Happy)* circa 1930. Over the years they have formed one of the largest private collections of the Bruton sisters' works.

The Bruton sisters' reputations continue to rebound nearly one hundred years after the height of their popularity. In 2012, the Brutons' childhood home, the birthplace of their artistic careers, was designated an Alameda Historical Monument. Maurine St. Gaudens's four-volume work on California women artists, *Emerging from the Shadows*, devotes a full twenty pages to the sisters and their art. Works by the Brutons have been appearing in recent exhibitions in California—at the San Francisco Museum of Modern Art and the Pasadena Museum of History—and outside of California, at the Wolfsonian–Florida International University in Miami and the Honolulu Museum of Art. The Monterey Museum of Art and the Chaffey Community Museum of Art both own a number of artworks by the Brutons and have been displaying them with increasing frequency. The Brutons' work has appeared in traveling exhibitions celebrating women's art, California art, and mid-century modern design. In 2019, when one of Esther's terrazzo fireplace surrounds was exhibited at the Salon Art + Design Expo in New York—an art fair with booths representing fifty-six art galleries from thirteen countries—*Architectural Digest* called it one of the "eight standouts" at the show. The Bruton sisters are even prominently featured in *Ina's Circle*, a 2020 film documentary about their good friend Ina Perham.

Looking back at the long and productive careers of Margaret, Esther, and Helen Bruton, there is much to appreciate and admire. They were smart and funny, and didn't take themselves too seriously; they liked to play, in life and in art. They were unfailingly loyal to each other and could never have achieved alone what they accomplished together, yet each sister was also a fiercely independent and unique talent. Perhaps most impressive is their lifelong dedication to art. From the time they were toddlers playing with dough, until they were in their seventies and could no longer keep up with the physical demands of their work, they were always dedicated artists. Decade after decade, they each remained open to their creative, imaginative spirit and followed it wherever it led them. They were non-competitive, yet ambitious; humble,

yet fearless; sensitive, yet resilient. They were constantly experimenting and evolving—for the Brutons, it was always about the journey rather than the destination. Helen Bruton once remarked, "About our work, it will have to speak for us." The art the Brutons left behind is so inventive and inspired that it will continue to speak eloquently for them for decades to come.

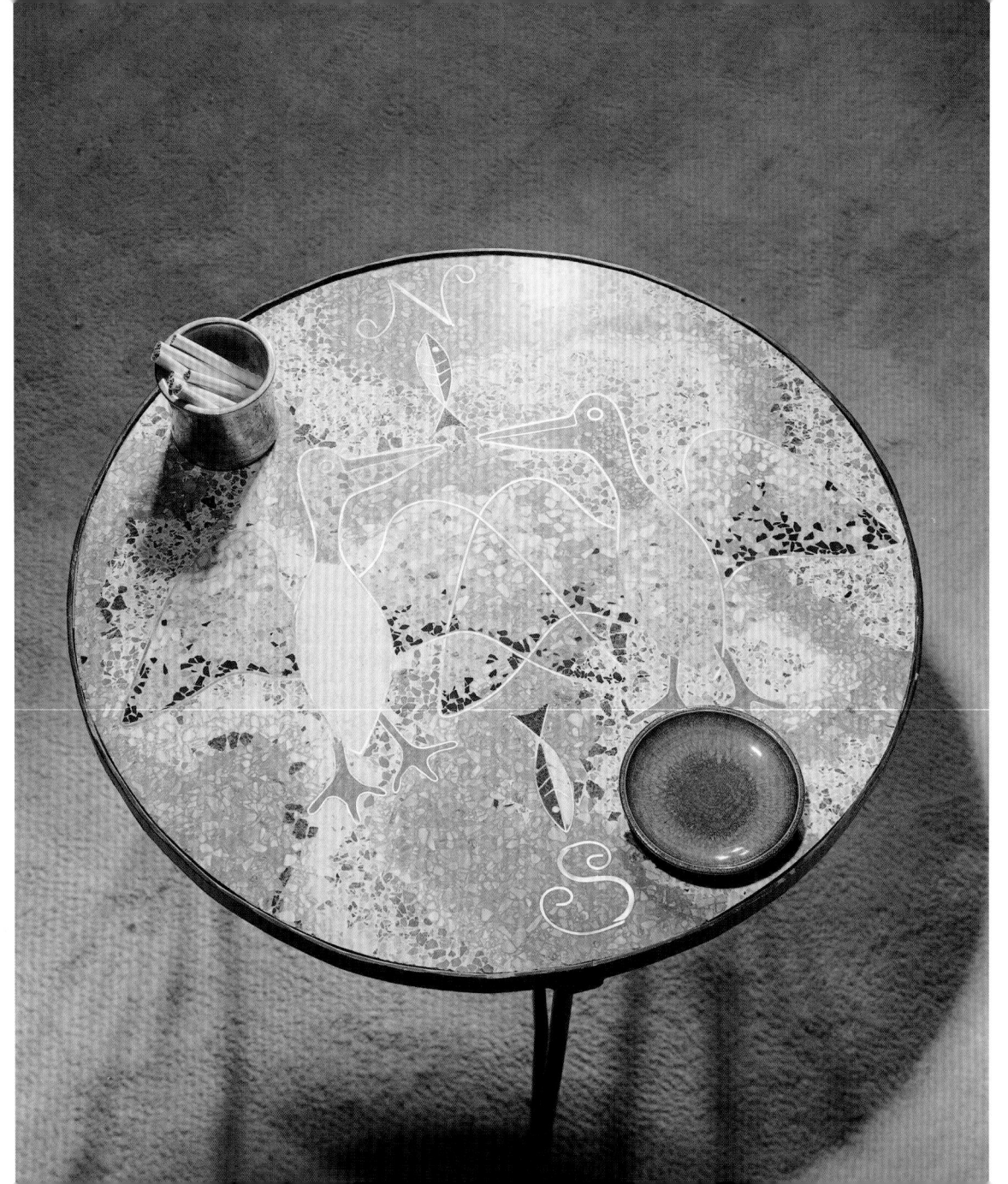

Author's Note

I first became interested in the Bruton sisters when I saw photographs of the modernist coffee tables Margaret Bruton created for the interior designer Frances Elkins in the 1940s and 1950s. The tables were bold, fresh, and exciting, and I became curious about the artist, especially when I learned that she was from a family of women artists. Who were the Bruton sisters, and why were they frequently referred to as one unit? How did they develop their unique styles and techniques? What was their connection to my home, the Monterey Peninsula?

As a reference librarian and archivist, I began digging. I found pieces of information that gave me a sense of the scope and length of their careers. All three sisters had been famous and critically acclaimed artists of their time. Why didn't they get more recognition today? I had an overwhelming feeling that these women were special and deserved to be remembered. I am not an art historian—nor had I ever written a book before— but I felt that I had to share their stories.

As it turns out, documenting the lives and careers of the Bruton sisters has been challenging. With the exception of the biographies published in *California Art Research* in the 1930s and two interviews they conducted later in life, there wasn't a lot to go on. My big break came when I tracked down the Brutons' closest surviving family members—their first cousins once removed on their mother's side—who for years had been quiet caretakers of an extensive archive of the sisters' papers. Most of the material had been in storage since the Brutons' deaths and hadn't been seen in decades. This newly discovered archive includes letters, photographs, preliminary

Terrazzo table, by Margaret Bruton (1954)

work, sketches, clippings, and biographical information that the sisters wrote themselves. I am grateful that the Brutons' cousin Peggy Stackable—who passed away during the writing of this book—had the foresight to preserve these materials. Another Bruton cousin, Barbara Carroll, and her husband Jim, went beyond the call of duty to uncover and literally bring to light this fascinating and significant archive. They welcomed me into their home, shared their memories, and gave me full access to the Bruton archive. I could not have written this book without their kindness, generosity, and support.

Tracking the movements of Margaret, Esther, and Helen Bruton from decade to decade was a mammoth task. Over the years, their professional and personal lives intersected, separated, and then intersected again. All three had extremely long and productive careers that resulted in multiple large-scale projects, hundreds of artworks, dozens of exhibitions, and extensive travel. The artworks I describe in the book are those that I have seen in person or can document through photographs, articles, reviews, or catalogs. When possible, I explain where the artwork is currently located, whether in a museum, a private collection, or a public space. In some cases, the titles of the Brutons' works have changed over time, and the sisters occasionally gave the same, or similar, titles to different works. Ultimately, when it came to naming and identifying their artwork, I made my best guess and, when appropriate, I provide alternate titles in the endnotes. Any errors in this book are mine alone.

Countless people have helped, encouraged, and supported me in this project. First, I offer my sincere thanks to the amazing team at West Margin Press. Jennifer Newens believed in this book and gave me the incredible opportunity to share the Bruton sisters' story. The careful reading of editor Emily Bowles kept the manuscript focused and accurate. Olivia Ngai and Rachel Metzger expertly and patiently guided a first-time author through the editorial and design process, and Angie Zbornik enthusiastically promoted and publicized the book. Thanks for taking a chance on me and helping me to bring this important part of women's history to light.

I am extremely grateful to my fellow librarians and archivists, as well as the authors, historians, museum curators, gallery owners, and collectors who have so generously shared their resources, photographs, and significant knowledge. This includes Anthony Barboza; Abby Bridge and Peggy Tran-Le from the San Francisco Museum of Modern Art Archives; Sean Briscoe from the California History Room, Monterey Public Library; Nancy Boas; Beth Brookhouser from the SPCA Monterey County; Steve Cabella; Stephanie Cassidy at the Art Students League of New York; Gala Chamberlain of The Annex Galleries; Thomas Carey, Katherine Ets-Hokin, and Jeff Thomas at the San Francisco History Center, San Francisco Public Library; Nancy Chan and Chris Conners from the San Francisco Zoo; Tyler Chisman from the Office of History at the Defense Language Institute; Dennis Copeland; James Coran; Sauli Danpour; John Crosse; Nancy DeDiemar and Jenelle Lowry at the Chaffey Community Museum of Art; Eric and Teresa Del Piero; Zachary Diaz; Robert Edwards; Simon Elliott from UCLA Library Special Collections; Scott Hahn from ARG Conservation Services; Jann Haynes Gilmore; Jeannie Graham; Jeff Gunderson from the San Francisco Art Institute Archives; Steve Hauk of Hauk Fine Arts; Harvey Helfand; Chuck and Kit Henderson; Jolene Hoffman from the Humane Society of Ventura County; Michael Horikawa of Michael D. Horikawa Fine Art; Peter Huestis from the National Gallery of Art; Rick Janick; Nate King from the Pacific Grove Museum of Natural History; Father Jeff Kohn from St. James Episcopal Church, Monterey; Lynn Krantz from the Matson Company Archives; Raphael Marchand from the Fairmont, San Francisco; William Maynez of the Diego Rivera Mural Project; Melissa Miller, Ruth Wallach, and Christina Snider from the University of Southern California; Matthew Nye from Special Collections at the San Diego Public Library; Katie O'Connell from Harrison Memorial Library; James Oles; Victoria Pearson; Scott Powell; Alan Renga from the San Diego Air and Space Museum; Shoshana Resnikoff and Amy Silverman at The Wolfsonian-Florida International University; John Rexine at the Monterey Museum of Art; Katie Riddle from the Environmental Design Archives, UC Berkeley; Richard Rothman; Dennis Rowedder; Kent Seavey; Maurine St. Gaudens and Joseph Morsman; Terry St. John; Morgan Schlesinger from the de Saisset Museum, Santa Clara University; Andrew Shanken from UC Berkeley; Michael Sturtevant; Ron Solorzano from the Ventura County Library; Jenny Swadosh from the New School Archives and Special Collections; Mary Tehranchi and Liz O'Brien of Liz O'Brien, New York; Paul Totah; Terry Trotter of Trotter Galleries; Richard Guy Wilson; and Nina Zurier.

Art historian Hanne Abildgaard from Denmark reached out from across the Atlantic to give me fresh insight into the friendship between Helen Bruton and the Danish artist Kirsten Kjaer.

Very special thanks to the congregation of Buddha's Universal Church, in particular Dr. Alan Chan, Dr. Daphne Chan, and Noreen Sandino, who welcomed me into their church and from the beginning expressed their encouragement and enthusiasm for this book.

Special thanks to Meg Partridge of the Imogen Cunningham Trust who generously allowed me to use her grandmother's remarkable photographs of the Bruton sisters, in particular the iconic photo on the cover of the book.

My sincere thanks to Erin Stout, Julianne Gavino, Dawn Minegar, Amy Lim, Kevin Appel, and Kim Kanatani at the Institute and Museum of California Art at the University of California, Irvine, for their interest, enthusiasm, and support of this project.

I am grateful to Sally Chavez, Susan Clark, and Ann and George Perham—the descendants of Ina Perham—who shared their family photographs and correspondence. The filmmaker William Lorton, also a descendant of Ina Perham, was one of the first people who shared my interest in these forgotten women artists. Most of the people who were close friends of the Bruton sisters are no longer with us, although I was able to find a few individuals who knew the sisters and were kind enough to share their memories with me, including Barbara and Jim Carroll, James Coran, Barbara Mills, George Perham, and Ann Stocker.

I must, of course, thank my family and friends, who were always by my side on this journey and were endlessly forgiving of my single-minded pursuit of all things Bruton. Thanks to my parents, William and Wiesje Van Wyck, who have encouraged my writing since I was a girl and never complained when I decided to become an English major. My mother-in-law Bonnie Good—who passed away during this project—was one of my biggest fans, and I think she would be pleased to see how the book turned out. Thanks also to my sisters, Lauren Dowling and Christine Adams, who taught me about the bonds of sisterhood. My friends Chris Zimmerman, Alondra Valdez Klemek, and Kathleen Finn listened to my stories, accompanied me on research trips, and provided housing. Special thanks to my children, Andrew and Christopher, for their enthusiasm, sound advice, and editorial assistance, and thanks to my husband, Duane, for his endless patience, encouragement, and support.

ENDNOTES

PROLOGUE

"Totally out of control." Federal Emergency Management Agency, *The East Bay Hills Fire: Oakland-Berkeley California*, U.S. Fire Administration Technical Report Series, October 1991, 24, http://www.usfa.fema.gov/downloads/pdf/publications/tr-060.pdf.

"Most of the victims apparently didn't realize..." Tracy Wilkinson, "Speed of Flames Took Victims By Surprise," *Los Angeles Times*, October 23, 1991, http://www.latimes.com/archives/la-xpm-1991-10-23-mn-174-story.html.

Tragically, twenty-five people lost their lives... Federal Emergency Management Agency, *The East Bay Hills Fire*, 45.

A knowledgeable and savvy collector... Suzanne Muchnic, "$45-Million Art Collection Destroyed," *Los Angeles Times*, October 23, 1991, http://www.latimes.com/archives/la-xpm-1991-10-23-mn-212-story.html.

In 1991, Nelson-Rees and Coran were preparing for a major museum exhibition... Iona M. Chelette, *California Grandeur and Genre: From the Collection of James L. Coran and Walter A. Nelson-Rees* (Palm Springs, CA: Palm Springs Desert Museum, 1991).

"I couldn't believe..." "Oakland Fire Ravaged Collections of Priceless Art, Books, Furniture," *Deseret News*, November 3, 1991, http://www.deseret.com/1991/11/3/18949684/oakland-fire-ravaged-collections-of-priceless-art-books-furniture.

"They had No. 1 [sic] works by so many artists that can't be replaced, this is a major lost to the American art world." Muchnic, "$45-Million Art Collection Destroyed."

The press emphasized their lithe beauty and sharp wit... Esther eventually married in her mid-forties, when her art career was well established.

CHAPTER ONE

"In the old family home in Alameda..." Beatrice Judd Ryan, "Brutons-3," *Women's City Club Magazine* (July 1932): 16.

"Valiantly experiment in new media and manners." Gene Hailey, "Margaret Bruton," in *California Art Research* (San Francisco: Abstract from WPA Project 2874, 1937), Vol. 16, 1.

There may have been another pressing reason... Ryan, "Brutons-3." Although Ryan suggests that John Bruton was a member of the left-wing republican political party, Sinn Fein, this organization was not formed until 1905, long after the Bruton family had already immigrated to the United States.

Daniel had been fascinated with the West Coast... Ryan, "Brutons-3."

Alameda's best-known resort... "Alameda History," Alameda Museum, accessed December 15, 2020, https://alamedamuseum.org/news-and-resources/history/.

"Charming and accomplished." "Personal and Social," *Alameda Daily Argus*, May 25, 1893, 3.

According to the local paper, Daniel Bruton didn't set eyes... "Personal Mention," *Alameda Daily Argus*, October 19, 1895, 1.

The Brutons' second daughter was born in Alameda on October 18, 1896. The California Death Index incorrectly lists Esther's birth date as October 17.

"Daniel Bruton is having a very fine house built on St. Charles Street." "News in Brief Form," *Alameda Daily Argus*, August 27, 1897, 4.

Nearly three months later, the newspaper noted the family's arrival in the neighborhood. "Personal," *Alameda Daily Argus*, November 17, 1897, 4.

They vacationed at Howell Mountain... "Personal Notes," Oakland Tribune, June 20, 1905, 12; "Misses Bruton Return from Summer Outing," *Alameda Daily Argus*, July 25, 1911, 8.

They also visited their seventy-seven-acre hay ranch... "Death of Mrs. Bruton," *Alameda Daily Argus*, March 24, 1896, 1.

The Brutons spent considerable time on the Monterey Peninsula... Barbara Carroll, telephone interview by Wendy Good, May 19, 2019.

The family was in Pacific Grove... Elise Jerram, "Bruton Sisters Look Back, Reluctantly," *Monterey Peninsula Herald*, December 18, 1977, C1.

According to family legend, she was turned away... It is also possible that Helen was turned away because the Presidio hospital treated only military personnel, not the general public.

Since there were no other medical facilities in the area... Carroll, interview, May 19, 2019; Helen Bruton graph paper chronology [ca. 1981], Bruton Sisters Archive.

Although they had planned to stay only for the summer... "To Tour South in Automobile," Oakland Tribune, April 23, 1907, 4; "Mr. and Mrs. Bruton and Family Will Winter in New York," *Alameda Daily Argus*, September 20, 1907, 8.

According to Margaret, she attended classes... "Margaret Bruton: Biographical Listing," [ca. 1981], Bruton Sisters Archive.

When the Brutons returned to their home on St. Charles Street... "Mr. and Mrs. Daniel Bruton and Family Return Home," *Alameda Daily Argus*, April 11, 1908, 8.

"Amateur actress of undoubted ability." "Will Return to Honolulu," *Alameda Daily Times*, September 4, 1908, 3.

"We really got along remarkably well..." Helen Bruton and Margaret Bruton, interview with Lydia Modi-Vitale and Steven Gelber, February 27, 1975, video 1, 26:12–26:50, New Deal Art Video Collection, de Saisset Museum, Santa Clara University, Santa Clara, California. https://archive.org/details/castcdsm_000002/castcdsm_000002_t01_access.HD.mov.

"Drawing animals with colored crayons on the window shades." "Mural for Peace," Christian Science Monitor, *Weekly Magazine Section*, December 14, 1938, 15.

"The earliest artwork that I can remember..." Helen Bruton and Margaret Bruton, oral history interview with Lewis Ferbraché, December 4, 1964, transcript, Archives of American Art, Smithsonian Institution. https://www.aaa.si.edu/collections/interviews/oral-history-interview-helen-and-margaret-bruton-11725#transcript.

Margaret received a medal... "Pet Exhibition a Huge Success," *Evening Times-Star* (Alameda, CA), December 5, 1910, 4.

An article about her achievement... "Ad-Masque Poster Contest Closes; Esther Bruton Awarded First Prize," *San Francisco Chronicle*, January 22, 1916, 4.

"The Brutons, being practical little girls..." "Sensitivity to the demands of material." Dorothy Puccinelli, "The Brutons and How They Grew," *California Arts & Architecture* 57:10 (October 1940), 18.

William Bruton, who contributed... "News in Brief," *Brooklyn Union*, January 8, 1885, 2.

He died of consumption... "Personal," *Alameda Daily Argus*, November 19, 1887, 3; "Death of a Journalist," *Daily Alta California*, November 18, 1887, 1.

"Encouraged them, cared for their home..." Hailey, "Margaret Bruton," 2–3.

"Who became resigned early in our lives to having the place messed up." "Mural for Peace."

In 1885, the San Francisco Art Association... Susan Landauer, "Searching for Selfhood: Women Artists of Northern California," in *Independent Spirits: Women Painters of the American West, 1890–1945*, ed. Patrician Trenton (Berkeley: University of California Press, 1995), 10–11.

In 1912, she began taking classes... Blue and Gold (Berkeley: University of California at Berkeley, 1912), 488.

"Embodied a spirit of experimentation..." "SFAI History," San Francisco Art Institute, accessed December 15, 2020, http://sfai.edu/about-sfai/sfai-history.

"Frank Van Sloun is the one I remember..." Helen Bruton and Margaret Bruton, interview, 1964.

"West Coast legacy of radical innovation." "SFAI History."

"Strongly drawn, carried remarkably well..." T. L. Fitz Simons, "The Competition of the Art Students' League," Arts and Decoration 3:8 (June 1913), 283.

"Mother let Margaret go to art school..." Jerram, "The Bruton Sisters Look Back."

In reality, Mrs. Bruton traveled with her daughter... "Many Gay Functions to Enliven the Week for Trans-Bay Folks," *San Francisco Chronicle*, August 31, 1913, 29.

During her second year in New York... "To Resume Art Studies," *Oakland Tribune*, August 19, 1914, 12.

"It nearly ruined me!" Jerram, "The Bruton Sisters Look Back." Margaret might have been suggesting that her formal art training almost destroyed her natural, instinctual talent.

Helen remembered being particularly jealous... "Like a bat out of hell..." Helen Bruton and Margaret Bruton, interview, 1975, video 1.

"I didn't really know... what I wanted to do..." Helen Bruton and Margaret Bruton, interview, 1964.

"Very ambitious," "a college dropout." Helen Bruton, interview by Nancy Boas, April 5, 1983, copy in possession of author.

"I couldn't copy anything..." Helen Bruton and Margaret Bruton, interview, 1975, video 1.

"I never studied painting..." Helen Bruton and Margaret Bruton, interview, 1964.

An estimated eighteen million visitors... "The Panama-Pacific International Exposition," National Park Service, last updated October 17, 2016, http://www.nps.gov/goga/learn/historyculture/ppie.htm.

"One who has not kept abreast..." Compared to Impressionist paintings' idealized and colorized scenes... "bone of contention among the critics," "was the greatest of Norwegian painters," "won the Grand Prix at Rome and awards in every other European capital." Ben Macomber, *The Jewel City* (San Francisco: John H. Williams, 1915), 116, 121, 109.

"A vital moment..." "Jewel City: Art from the Panama–Pacific International Exposition," Fine Arts Museums of San Francisco, accessed December 15, 2020, http://www.famsf.org/press-room/jewel-city-art-panama-pacific-international-exposition.

"Surprisingly keen and is a very good index..." "Current Notes," *Arts and Decoration* 6:3 (January 1916), 150.

Family photographs taken on the grounds... These photographs are in a scrapbook in the Bruton Sisters Archive.

"New penchant for meatier subject matter and style experimentation." Al Morch, "S.F.'s Rich Heritage of Art by Women," *San Francisco Examiner*, December 12, 1983, B13.

CHAPTER TWO
"Felt that the Academy's instruction..." "An Unparalleled Impact on American Visual Arts," The Art Students League of New York, accessed December 15, 2020, http://www.theartstudentsleague.org/mission/#history.

Margaret's teacher in San Francisco... "Frank Joseph Van Sloun," Annex Art Galleries, accessed March 1, 2021, https://www.annexgalleries.com/artists/biography/2429/Van%20Sloun/Frank.

"Among the most outstanding educators in American art history." "The Influence of Frank Vincent Dumond," Ridgewood Art Institute, accessed December 15, 2020, http://www.ridgewoodartinstitute.org/our-history-looking-back/frank-vincent-dumond.

Perhaps because Fortune was more conservative... Helen Bruton and Margaret Bruton, interview by Terry St. John, July 21, 1972, copy in possession of author.

The leader of a group of nonconformist artists... "The Eight and American Modernisms," Milwaukee Art Museum, accessed December 31, 2020, https://mam.org/american/the_eight.php.

He eventually became a prominent art instructor... "About Robert Henri," Robert Henri Museum and Art Gallery, accessed March 1, 2021, https://www.roberthenrimuseum.org/about-robert-henri. The women students of Robert Henri are discussed in the book *American Women Modernists: The Legacy of Robert Henri, 1910–1945*, ed. Marian Wardle (New Brunswick, NJ: Rutgers University Press), 2005.

Henri's ideas about art were revolutionary... Marian Wardle, "Thoroughly Modern: The 'New Woman' Art Students of Robert Henri," in *American Women Modernists*, 6.

"Beauty was everywhere..." "full fledged artists..." Sarah Burns, "Fabricating the Modern: Women in Design," in *American Women Modernists*, 30.

"Esther was exposed to Bridgman briefly, but... she escaped!" Helen Bruton and Margaret Bruton, interview, 1975, video 1, 02:13–02:18.

"Industry is the nation's life..." "Our Legacy," Parsons School of Design, accessed December 15, 2020, http://www.newschool.edu/parsons/history.

In May 1918, at the end of her first year... "Practical Designs Shown," *New York Herald*, May 15, 1918, 9.

After completing the two-year program... Helen Bruton and Margaret Bruton, interview, 1975, video 2, 22:18–22:44.

Helen, who had completed one year at Berkeley... Helen Bruton, application for United States Civil Service Commission, [ca. 1942], Bruton Sisters Archive.

Women were allowed to join the Navy... Nathaniel Patch, "The Story of the Female Yeomen During the First World War," *Prologue Magazine* 38:3 (Fall 2006), http://www.archives.gov/publications/prologue/2006/fall/yeoman-f.html.

In October 1918, Helen enlisted... "Miss Gordon to Take Canteen Work," *San Francisco Examiner*, October 26, 1918, 9.

She worked as a stenographer... "United States, Veterans Administration Master Index, 1917–1940," FamilySearch, accessed December 15, 2020, https://familysearch.org, citing NARA microfilm publication 76193916, St. Louis: National Archives and Records Administration, 1985; Helen Bruton, application for United States Civil Service Commission.

Margaret, who had returned to California... Anna Cora Winchell, "Artists and Their Work," *San Francisco Chronicle*, August 4, 1917, 6S; "Margaret Bruton: Biographical Listing."

The hospital cared for more than 18,000 soldiers... "Letterman Hospital Complex," Presidio of San Francisco, National Park Service, last updated February 28, 2015, http://www.nps.gov/prsf/learn/historyculture/letterman-complex.htm.

Margaret worked as an occupational therapist... Lieutenant Colonel Myra L. McDaniel, "Occupational Therapists Before World War II (1917–40)," United States Army Medical Department, Office of Medical History, accessed December 15, 2020, http://history.amedd.army.mil/corps/medical_spec/chapteriv.html.

"First formal attempt at studying art." Helen Bruton and Margaret Bruton, interview, 1964.

She traveled to New York to join Esther... Enrollment records from The Art Students League reveal that Helen took classes from October through May in 1920-1921 and 1921-1922.

It is unsurprising that all three sisters... Betsy Fahlman, "The Art Spirit in the Classroom: Educating the Modern Woman Artist," in *American Women Modernists*, 105.

At the League, Helen decided to become a sculptor... A. Stirling Calder was part of a dynasty of American sculptors that had begun with his father, Alexander Milne Calder, who sculpted the iconic thirty-seven-foot statue of William Penn that tops the tower of Philadelphia's City Hall. Stirling's son, Alexander Calder, became a famous artist whose modernist mobiles are displayed in museums around the world.

"He was the world's worst sculptor..." Helen Bruton and Margaret Bruton, interview, 1975, video 1.

He had studied art in Rome and Bologna... "Leo Lentelli: A Sculptor of the City Beautiful," San Francisco Public Library Art, Music and Recreation Center, June 18, 2007, http://sfplamr.blogspot.com/2007/06/leo-lentelli-sculptor-of-city-beautiful.html.

Helen's experience with Lentelli was disappointing... Helen Bruton and Margaret Bruton, interview, 1975, video 1.

In November 1926, the Carmel Pine Cone announced... "Helen Bruton Off For New York To Study Sculpture," *Carmel Pine Cone*, November 5, 1926, 6; Helen later claimed, "I don't think [Boardman Robinson] influenced me very much... I don't know why that is." Helen Bruton and Margaret Bruton, interview, 1975, video 1.

"I was the housekeeper..." Helen Bruton and Margaret Bruton, interview, 1975, video 1.

In November 1922, Esther and Helen returned to Alameda. "Stewart-Millar Wedding Cards Already Issued," *Oakland Tribune*, November 13, 1922, 10.

While in Papeete, they lived next door... "Papeete Charm Felt by Women of America," *San Francisco Chronicle*, August 30, 1924, 10.

Photographs from the trip show them traveling... These photographs are in the Bruton Sisters Archive.

"We watched every day from under our sun porch..." "Papeete Charm."

Esther's story is both comical and mischievous... The young man Esther saw was actually Paul Gauguin's son, Emile, whom she described as "an indolent, dreamy man who showed little interest in art." Gene Hailey, "Esther Bruton," *California Art Research* (San Francisco: Abstract from WPA Project 2874, 1937), Vol. 16, 33.

"Tahiti is full of French girls..." "Girls Fail to Find Romance," *San Francisco Examiner*, August 11, 1924, 8.

"I'm going back there someday..." "Papeete Charm."

Tahiti's tropical settings did influence... Betty Wentworth, "Travels in South Pacific Islands Influence the Work of Ojai Artist," *Ventura County (CA) Star-Free Press*, July 8, 1953, 6.

But for the serious artist of the era... "With the Artists," *All Arts Gossip*, June 1925, 5. The article mistakenly reports that Helen, instead of Esther, traveled to Europe with Margaret. While they had planned to be abroad for two years,

in August 1926, a little more than a year after their departure, Margaret, Esther, and Ina returned to California. "Art Notes," *Carmel Pine Cone*, August 6, 1926, 11.

Their trip included sketching expeditions... "Margaret Bruton: Biographical Listing"; Hailey, "Margaret Bruton," 5.

Margaret and Esther enrolled in classes... Académie de la Grande Chaumière, accessed December 15, 2020, http://www.academiegrandechaumiere.com.

The value of the French franc had plunged... "Foreign Exchange Rates 1913–1941 #2: The Currency Upheavals of the Interwar Period," New World Economics, April 6, 2014, http://newworldeconomics.com/foreign-exchange-rates-1913-1941-2-the-currency-upheavals-of-the-interwar-period.

This exhibition was likely a seminal event... Eric Del Piero and Teresa Del Piero, "Monterey Modernism," Monterey Museum of Art, May 5, 2012, http://www.youtube.com/watch?v=-rg7mklLZ4s, 02:32–03:00.

"There was not so much conflict..." "there was absolutely no feeling..." Eleanor Munro, *Originals: American Women Artists* (New York: Simon and Schuster, 1982), 46, 148.

Yet this sense of liberation... Erika Doss, "Complicating Modernism: Issues of Liberation and Constraint Among the Women Art Students of Robert Henri," in *American Woman Modernists*, 128.

Opportunities for women professional artists... Carmel artist Henrietta Shore... Landauer, "Searching for Selfhood," 12, 25.

Painter Eugenia McComas... Many women artists continued to make gender-neutral or male-sounding professional name choices well beyond the 1920s.

CHAPTER THREE

The hotel was the starting and finishing point... "Historic Hotel Del Monte," Naval Postgraduate School, accessed December 28, 2020, https://library.nps.edu/hotel-del-monte.

"Never married and remained free..." Landauer, "Searching for Selfhood," 23.

In 1907, the Hotel Del Monte... Barbara J. Klein, "The Carmel Monterey Peninsula Art Colony: A History," *Resource Library*, April 21, 2005, 1, http://www.tfaoi.com/aa/5aa/5aa300.htm.

The most prominent artist in the town of Monterey... Chase, who personified the Gilded Age... Robert W. Edwards, *Jennie V. Cannon: The Untold History* (Oakland: East Bay Heritage Project, 2012), 185, 132–133. Chase's criticism of modernism resulted in his exclusion from a list of twelve American painters who were given their own galleries at the 1915 Panama–Pacific Exposition. http://www.tfaoi.com/aa/10aa/10aa557.htm.

She first came to the area in the summer of 1921... Helen Bruton and Margaret Bruton, interview, 1964. Although Margaret didn't recall coming down to Monterey until 1922, she exhibited with the Carmel Arts and Crafts Club in the summer of 1921. Edwards, *Jennie V. Cannon*, 189-190.

She attended Hansen's painting and sketching classes... "Margaret Bruton: Biographical Listing."

"Was more of a mutual association..." Monterey: The Artist's View: 1925-1945 (Monterey, CA: Monterey Museum of Art, 1982), 12.

Helen later called this period the "Hansenian era"... Helen Bruton and Margaret Bruton, interview, 1975, video 1. Although Helen says in this part of the interview that Hansen "was going strong, and he was quite an influence among the students," she adds, "although I don't think on us," meaning her and her sisters.

"A great many of our local people..." "Many Fine Pictures Being Displayed at Studio," *Monterey Daily Cypress*, December 11, 1921, 4.

Reflecting on the period later in life... Helen Bruton and Margaret Bruton, interview, 1972.

"As a conduit between the bohemian moderns..." Nancy Boas, *Society of Six: California Colorists* (San Francisco: Bedford Arts, 1988), 136.

In the summer of 1921, several Monterey artists... Edwards, *Jennie V. Cannon*, 189-190.

"One of the greatest exhibitions of painting..." "Artists of Monterey Arrange Exhibition for the Exposition," *Monterey Daily Cypress*, September 2, 1922, 1.

Margaret was in good company... "Monterey Show Proves Success," *San Francisco Chronicle*, September 8, 1922, 7.

"Margaret Bruton's 'The Old Timer'..." "Peninsula Artists' Exhibit Draws Much Real Appreciation," *Peninsula Daily Herald*, September 2, 1922, 1. A painting by Margaret Bruton called *The Old Timer* is in the collection of the Institute and Museum of California Art at the University of California, Irvine.

"The finest works in the exhibition." "Armin Hansen dominates his gallery... All of [her works]..." "Peninsula Again Proves Title to 'Art's Workshop,'" *Peninsula Daily Herald*, December 4, 1922, 1, 5.

Helen, Margaret, and Ina Perham lived in the attic... Helen Bruton graph paper chronology; Helen Spangenberg, *Yesterday's Artists on the Monterey Peninsula* (Monterey: Monterey Peninsula Museum of Art, 1976), 58.

"Designed that house in about one day or two flat..." Helen Bruton and Margaret Bruton, interview, 1975, video 1.

Helen's linoleum block print... When preparing a price list for a 1975 exhibition, Helen described *Cass Street* as a linoleum block print. "Prices – Helen Bruton's Show, Monterey Museum of Art, Jan. 11 – Jan. 20, 1975," Bruton Sisters Archive.

As was often the case with Helen's work... "Monterey Street Scene," *Monterey Peninsula Herald*, October 29, 1960, A17.

In addition to Gay, the group included... Boas, *The Society of Six*, 9.

"Modernizers bringing a much-needed breath of fresh air to the regional art scene." Julianne Burton-Carvajal, "Gus and the Gang: Communities of Artists and the Career of August Gay (1890–1948)," *Noticias de Monterey* 54: 3 (Summer 2005), 7.

"Cookouts and beach parties... spaghetti feeds and dance sessions." Burton-Carvajal, "Gus and the Gang," 8. The hotel—which provided lodging for local fishermen before artists moved in—was popularly known as the Stevenson House because Robert Louis Stevenson stayed there for a few months in 1879 while recovering from an illness and courting his future wife, Fanny Osbourne. Burton-Carvajal, "Gus and the Gang," 8.

"It was a wonderful group..." "Crazy twenties." Boas, *The Society of Six*, 136.

"When dawn finally dispersed..." "costumed in the manner..." "Artists Revive 'Idle Forties' in Monterey Fete," *San Francisco Chronicle*, November 11, 1923, 8S.

A posted photograph from that evening shows Margaret and Helen... This photo is in the Bruton Sisters Archive.

"A center for lively discussion..." Spangenberg, *Yesterday's Artists*, 58.

"Avidly studied reproductions..." John Cunningham, "Clayton Price Laid Foundation Here for His Later Fame," *Monterey Peninsula Herald*, October 31, 1950, 12.

"Some of us would wander down..." Albert Barrows, "Personal Letters and Interviews," in Frances Price Cook and Patrick J. Leach, eds., *The Life and Art of C.S. Price: In Pursuit of the One Big Thing* (North Charleston, SC: CreateSpace, 2012), chap. 16, Kindle.

Despite Price's quiet demeanor and love of solitude... Spangenberg, *Yesterday's Artists*, 58.

"A warm welcome form the artists who lived there." William Johnstone, *Points in Time: An Autobiography* (London: Barry & Jenkins, 1980), 134.

"Their work was brilliant..." Johnstone, *Points in Time*, 129–130. Johnstone also recalled that the Brutons had played a role in encouraging Paul Klee and Wassily Kandinsky to exhibit their works at the Oakland Art Gallery in 1926, although no additional evidence has surfaced to support this claim.

"On the fringe," "a very interesting lively period." Helen Bruton and Margaret Bruton, interview, 1964; Helen Bruton and Margaret Bruton, interview, 1975, video 1, 17:41–17:44.

Her linoleum block print The Party... The *San Francisco Chronicle* described *The Party* as a woodblock print ("California Society of Etchers Picks Work by Millier," September 23, 1928, D7). Yet when preparing a price list for a 1975 exhibition, Helen described *The Party* as a linoleum block print. "Prices – Helen Bruton's Show, Monterey Museum of Art, Jan. 11 – Jan. 20, 1975," Bruton Sisters Archive.

Pictured in the work are C.S. Price and Ina Perham... Boas, *Society of Six*, 136.

"'The Party' is full of the restless..." Junius Cravens, "Prints from Private Presses," *The Argus*, October 1928, 11.

Like The Party, friends of Helen's circle from Monterey... James L. Coran and Walter A. Nelson-Rees, *If Pictures Could Talk: Stories About California Paintings in Our Collection* (Oakland: WIM, 1989), 263.

"One of the best things here..." Arthur Millier, "San Francisco Painting Takes Sabbatical Year," Los Angeles Times, October 2, 1932, 18.

"Strong, socially symbolic." Morch, "S.F.'s Rich Heritage of Art by Women." *Beach Picnic* was destroyed in the Oakland Hills fire.

"A modest amount of publicity and a lukewarm reception," "by far the best portrait of the group," "little more than a colored drawing [yet[much is expressed by these simple means." Edwards, *Jennie V. Cannon*, 204; "Interesting Colors, Lines Are Found in Carmel Exhibit," Peninsula Daily Herald, May 16, 1925, 1, 5. The current location of *Luzina* is unknown.

"Languished and quickly closed." Edwards, *Jennie V. Cannon*, 204.

"Vital painters," "pleasing to both conservative and radical." Gene Hailey, "Art News of the Week," *San Francisco Chronicle*, May 15, 1927, D7.

"Do not show the qualities which one knows she has." Jehanne Bietry Salinger, "The Monterey Group," *The Argus*, June 1927, 1.

"Zeal to be modern at all costs..." Junius Cravens, "Art Notes," *Argonaut*, May 14, 1927, 16. Armin Hansen did not participate in this exhibition, and Cravens pointedly remarked, "We can hardly say we blame him."

"Dangerous," "I don't think Armin got anywhere with his painting..." Helen Bruton and Margaret Bruton, interview, 1972.

A few stragglers, including Margaret Bruton... "Among the Artists," *Carmel Pine Cone*, February 10, 1928, 4.

"This aesthetic beauty..." Antony Anderson, "Sixth Exhibition by Native Artists," *Los Angeles Times*, April 12, 1925, 34. The current location of the *The Bar Maid* is unknown.

"Of nationwide renown," "the best artists of North and South America." Margaret's co-exhibitors were Lucy Valentine Pierce, Armin Hansen, Julian Greenwell, and William Ritschel. "Monterey Artists to Exhibit Work," *San Francisco Chronicle*, November 9, 1925, 15.

"Happy design," "glorious color," "captures your heart[s]..." Arthur Millier, "First Impressions at Museum's Annual," *Los Angeles Times*, April 11, 1926, 28.

"The neighboring paintings... appear anemic." Arthur Millier, "Three Talented Sisters: Esther, Helen, and Margaret Bruton, Californians, Impress by Intelligence of Their Art," *Los Angeles Times*, February 2, 1930, 18. As of 1982, *Carmel Valley*, renamed *Pastoral and Natives*, resided at the home of Gertrude Noyes Croxton in Walnut Creek, California (photo of the work, August 1982, Bruton Sisters Archive). Croxton was the sister of the Brutons' friend Harriet Noyes (Helen Bruton, Christmas card list, 1965, Bruton Sisters Archive).

"Its bold handling and brilliant coloring is a delight..." "Exhibition by Bruton and Cram Notably Excellent," *Carmel Pine Cone*, September 3, 1926, 11.

"I wish I were more modern..." H.L. Dungan, "Artists and Their Work," *Oakland Tribune*, January 23, 1927, 8M.

"Strongly and crisply handled..." Gene Hailey, "'Rosie' of Tahiti Comes to Town," *San Francisco Chronicle*, January 30, 1927, D7.

The painting was awarded second prize... Arthur Millier, "Art and Artists," *Los Angeles Times*, April 10, 1927, 32.

"One of the stronger works... suggestive of Gauguin." Florence Wieben Lehre, "Artists and Their Work," *Oakland Tribune*, July 24, 1927, 4S. A painting called *Rosie* was purchased from Margaret Bruton by the art collectors Walter Nelson-Rees and James Coran in 1982. Walter Nelson-Rees, letter to Margaret Bruton, July 13, 1982, Bruton Sisters Archive. Its current location is unknown.

"Is by far the best I have seen of her..." Jehanne Bietry Salinger, "The Forty-Ninth Annual Exhibition of the San Francisco Art Association," *The Argus*, April 15, 1927, 2.

"Solid and convincing," "simple, forceful and altogether admirable." Alberta Spratt, "Palette Scrapings," *The Carmelite*, April 25, 1928, 7; Junius Cravens, "Odious Comparisons," *Argonaut*, May 12, 1928, 5. These portraits of the Bruton sisters' parents were destroyed in the Oakland Hills fire in 1991.

Sunning is a more traditional impressionistic work... Sunning (My Mother) is in the collection of the Monterey Museum of Art.

"A real jewel," "If Cézanne, the mentor..." Coran and Nelson-Rees, *If Pictures Could Talk*, 28–29.

"Modern type of art... impressively painted... 'modern' in its bold masses..." Hazel E. Marcen, "Local Canvasses Vie With Best in State at Fine Display in Beach Auditorium," *Santa Cruz Evening News*, January 31, 1928, 7; H.L. Dungan, "Artists and Their Work," *Oakland Tribune*, February 12, 1928, S7; Florence Wieben Lehre, "Artists and Their Work," *Oakland Tribune*, February 5, 1928, S5. *Monterey Landscape* is probably the painting known as *Barns on Cass Street* in the collection of the Monterey Museum of Art.

"Similarities in color, shape, subject, and even brush strokes." Hansen's *Before the Storm* is in the collection of the Monterey Museum of Art.

"That the teacher can sometimes learn..." Karen Crews Hendon, "Modernism in Monterey," AFA News, May 10, 2012, http://www.afanews.com/articles/item/1190-modernism-in-monterey#.XqtaCJNKgb0.

"One feels the force of originality..." Junius Cravens, "Art Notes," *Argonaut*, January 29, 1927, 16.

"Quite exceptional..." Edwards, *Jennie V. Cannon*, 28.

"The golden age of Monterey..." Helen Bruton and Margaret Bruton, interview, 1964.

CHAPTER FOUR

In the summer of 1929... "Margaret Bruton: Biographical Listing." They might have made the trip in the family's four-passenger "Little Marmon Speedster," which Mrs. Bruton purchased for $2,000 in 1927. Purchase receipt, August 9, 1927, Bruton Sisters Archive.

"Put in at least six or seven hard years... until she couldn't stand it any longer." Helen Bruton and Margaret Bruton, interview, 1975, video.

"The sun shines with its peculiar desert brightness..." Rose Henderson, "Art That Blooms at the Desert's Rim," *The Outlook*, August 1, 1923, 506–507.

"Seems to rain like globules on the earth." Will Irwin, "The Land of the Little People," *Saturday Evening Post*, April 7, 1923, 109.

"The sun made everything luminous..." Mabel Dodge Luhan, *Edge of Taos Desert: An Escape to Reality* (Albuquerque: University of New Mexico Press, 1987), 55–56.

"Full of pianists, painters, pederasts, prostitutes and peasants... Great material." Patricia Leigh Brown, "The Muse of Taos, Still Stirring," *New York Times*, January 16, 1997, http://www.nytimes.com/1997/01/16/garden/the-muse-of-taos-stirring-still.html.

"Legendary gathering of modernistas." John Crosse, "Miguel Covarrubias in Taos, 1929," Southern California Architectural History (blog), April 2, 2017, http://socalarchhistory.blogspot.com/2017/04/miguel-covarrubias-in-taos-1929.html.

"A different kind of color from any I'd ever seen... The world is so wide up there, so big." Roxana Robinson, *Georgia O'Keeffe: A Life* (New York: Harper & Row, 1987), 327.

A young Ansel Adams... Elmo Baca, *Mabel's Santa Fe and Taos: Bohemian Legends, 1900-1950* (Salt Lake City: Gibbs-Smith, 2000), 132. The text for Adam's first book, *Taos Pueblo* (1930), was written by author and former Carmel resident Mary Austin, who had been living in Santa Fe since 1924. Arrell Morgan Gibson, *The Santa Fe and Taos Colonies: Age of the Muses, 1900-1942* (Norman, OK: University of Oklahoma Press, 1983), 204.

Mexican artist Miguel Covarrubias... "Miguel Covarrubias: Drawing a Cosmopolitan Line," Georgia O'Keeffe Museum, September 2014, http://www.okeeffemuseum.org/installation/miguel-covarrubias-drawing-a-cosmopolitan-line/.

"Esther and Marge are still enthusiastic, but Mama is bored to death." Helen Bruton, letter to Kirsten Kjaer, August 7, 1929, Kirsten Kjaer Papers.

Meanwhile, Helen had been living in the Montgomery Block... Helen Bruton and Margaret Bruton, interview, 1964; Helen Bruton graph paper chronology. Constructed in 1853 as one of the first fire- and earthquake-resistant buildings, it lived up to its promise in 1906—it was one of the few structures that remained standing after the San Francisco earthquake.

Originally home to writers... Harvey Smith, "The Art Culture of the New Deal in the San Francisco Bay Area," FoundSF, accessed March 1, 2021, https://www.foundsf.org/index.php?title=New_Deal_Artists_and_Programs_During_the_Depression.

"Part of a lively arts scene..." Smith, "The Art Culture of the New Deal."

Esther had a studio in the Montgomery Block... "Burnished Belles at Parilia Ball to Honor New Queen," *San Francisco Call*, December 31, 1935. Smith, "The Art Culture of the New Deal." The Montgomery Block was torn down in 1959 to make way for a parking lot, and later, the Transamerica Pyramid building.

By 1929, Helen had decided that she wanted to be a ceramicist. Helen Bruton and Margaret Bruton, interview, 1972.

Helen had been employed as a designer... "Items," All Arts Gossip, October 1925, 15; Helen Bruton and Margaret Bruton, interview, 1975, video 1.

"They were frightfully busy..." Helen Bruton and Margaret Bruton, interview, 1964.

Out of the twenty-five tile draftsmen... Helen Bruton and Margaret Bruton, interview, 1975, video 1.

"It's all very novel and exciting..." Helen Bruton, letter to Ina Perham and Lucy Valentine Pierce, June 13, [1929], Perham Private Collection. Helen's car "Lizzie" might have been a Model T or "Tin Lizzie." Mrs. Bruton traded in the family's 1922 Ford when she purchased a new "Little Marmon Speedster" in 1927 (purchase receipt dated August 9, 1927, Bruton Sisters Archive). It is possible that the affluent family owned two automobiles in the late 1920s.

Helen's letter refers to two of her good friends... Interestingly, Kjaer and Skeele would end up married to the same man. Kjaer left her husband—the Danish artist Frode Nielsen—in 1929, when she returned to Denmark. Nielsen, who remained behind in California, began to pursue Katy Skeele. More than two decades later, Nielsen—who later changed his name to Frode Dann—and Katy Skeele were finally married.

"I mis you more than I can say... Somehow, you had a way of inspiring me..." "found a quiet place." Helen Bruton, letter to Kirsten Kjaer, August 7, 1929, Kirsten Kjaer Papers.

"I like the work I'm doing..." Helen Bruton, letter to Ina Perham, June 13, [1929], Perham Private Collection.

"I'm really a bit disgusted with my own work..." Helen Bruton, letter to Kirsten Kjaer, August 7, 1929, Kirsten Kjaer Papers.

"All I could think of..." "I put the dogs up." Helen Bruton and Margaret Bruton, interview, 1975, video 1.

"The philosophers are finished at last..." Helen Bruton, letter to Ina Perham, December 17, [1929], Perham Private Collection. Paul Rockwood was a graphic artist, printmaker, and lithographer originally from Southern California. He lived in San Francisco in the 1930s. "Paul Clark Rockwood," Nevada Fine Art, accessed January 4, 2021, https://www.nevadafineart.com/heritage/paul-clark-rockwood.

"Darned good party." "After dinner we gathered roung..." Esther Bruton, letter to Ina Perham, [ca. December 1929], Perham Private Collection. It is unclear who "Peter" was, although Esther later mentions Peter's wife, Julia, and their two children.

About a decade older than the Brutons, Stackpole had studied... "Ralph Stackpole," U.S. Commission of Fine Arts, accessed December 17, 2020, http://www.cfa.gov/about-cfa/who-we-are/ralph-stackpole.

"It was great to see Ralph..." "Who is busy on the library murals..." Esther Bruton, letter to Ina Perham, [ca. December 1929], Perham Private Collection.

"Subdued, tonal colors," "flattened, decorative forms." "Sketch For a Mural Decoration, 1925," Crocker Art Museum, accessed January 4, 2021, https://www.crockerart.org/collections/american-art-before-1945/artworks/sketch-for-a-mural-decoration-1925.

The show was a sampling of their diverse body of work... Esther Bruton, letter to Ina Perham, [ca. December 1929], Perham Private Collection.

"These three sisters go their separate ways..." Junius Cravens, "Exemplary Effort," *Argonaut*, December 7, 1929, 5.

"It was easier to tell them apart by the characteristics of their work..." Aline Kistler, "Bruton Sisters Exhibit Work at Galerie," *San Francisco Chronicle*, December 1, 1929, 4D.

"If Helen and Margaret are extremes of humor and pathos, then Esther is a happy combination of both." Prudence Woollette, "Art and Artists," *Los Angeles Saturday Night*, February 1, 1930, 19.

"The most sophisticated and erudite of them all." Gobind Behari, "Sign of New Art Energy in S.F.," *San Francisco Examiner*, December 1, 1929, 10E.

"An outstanding canvas... an exceptionally expressive work." Cravens, "Exemplary Effort." A painting by Margaret Bruton called *Taos Woman* was purchased by Walter Nelson-Rees and James Coran in 1982. Walter Nelson-Rees and James Coran, letter to Margaret Bruton, May 28, 1982, Bruton Sisters Archive. A painting with the same title and the same dimensions is in the collection of the Institute and Museum of California Art at the University of California, Irvine.

"A vividly dramatic picture..." Gobind Behari, "First Prize Won by Miss Bothwell," *San Francisco Examiner*, November 10, 1929, 10E. Margaret painted two works called *Augustine*, one with the subject seated and another with the subject standing with a wrap ("Margaret Bruton 1929 Taos," May 1982, Bruton Sisters Archive). The latter work is in the collection of the Institute and Museum of California Art at the University of California, Irvine.

"All staked on clean, modern methods..." Millier, "Three Talented Sisters."

"A workable combination of aesthetics..." Florence Wieben Lehre, "Artists and Their Work," *Oakland Tribune*, December 8, 1929, 4B.

"It is in two decorative screens that we see..." Cravens, "Exemplary Effort."

"Originally conceived and faultlessly made..." Behari, "Sign of New Art Energy in S.F." *Corn Dance* is in the collection of the Wolfsonian at Florida International University in Miami, and as of this writing, *Rabbit Hunt* is for sale at the Annex Galleries in Santa Rosa, California.

"Broad mental range," "extraordinarily elastic mind." Cravens, "Exemplary Effort."

"I expect and certainly hope to make..." "The height of the screen..." Esther Bruton, letter to Ina Perham [ca. December 1929], Perham Private Collection. According to the gallery that currently owns the work, Esther originally made the screens using aluminum leaf and Dutch metal and redid them in 1934 when she first learned to work with gold leaf. Maurine St. Gaudens, *Emerging*

from the Shadows, Volume 1, (Atglen, PA: Schiffer Publishing Ltd., 2015), 137.

"An interesting and well executed decoration." H.L. Dungan, "Award Juries Always Face Hard Problem," *Oakland Tribune,* May 15, 1932, 6S.

"Unsurpassed for sheer decorativeness." Nadia Lavrova, "Many Noted Easterners in Show," *San Francisco Examiner,* April 24, 1932, 8E.

Later that year, Eagle Dance was one of thirty-five works... H.L. Dungan, "Artists Select 35 Canvases for Exhibition," *Oakland Tribune,* June 12, 1932, 8S. Esther's *Eagle Dance* is in a private collection.

"Capable and strong," "bold, clear, and full of humor, "highly imaginative [and] amusing." Lehre, "Artists and Their Work," December 8, 1929; Millier, "Three Talented Sisters"; Cravens, "Exemplary Effort."

"This expressionistic canvas..." Behari, "Sign of New Art Energy in S.F."

"Somewhat crude," "rendered with extreme simplicity..." Cravens, "Exemplary Effort."

"Singularly interesting... [and] beautifully handled." Kistler, "Bruton Sisters Exhibit Work at Galerie."

"Collectively and individually, the sisters triumph..." Millier, "Three Talented Sisters."

"For genuine vigor, see what the Bruton sisters have mustered." Woollette, "Art and Artists," 19.

"Three California girls who are making a stir with their paintings and prints." "Moderns Blend With Antiques," *Los Angeles Times,* October 26, 1930, 16.

"Positively devastating." Phil Townsend Hanna, letter to Esther Bruton, February 6, 1930, Bruton Sisters Archive.

Several newspapers stated that the group exhibition... Millier, "Three Talented Sisters"; "Bruton Sisters Send Work to New York," *San Francisco Chronicle,* March 9, 1930, D5.

"We have sent some prints in..." Esther Bruton, letter to Ina Perham, [ca. February 1930], Perham Private Collection.

Although the Weyhe Galleries... Frank E. Washburn Freund, "Guide Through New York Art Land," *Pittsburgh Post-Gazette,* January 3, 1931, 11.

"Both a collective and an individual triumph." "Three Sisters Hold a Joint Exhibition," *Art Digest,* mid-February 1930, 15.

"That was the big trouble..." Helen Bruton, interview, 1983.

"Just now there is a dee lightful... The three B's had a little show..." "although the sales did not mount up..." "the gallery advertises and pushes..." "We are each so sick of our

own work..." Esther Bruton, letter to Ina Perham, [ca. December 1929], Perham Private Collection.

The Brutons had known Cunningham for years and had even babysat her sons. Carroll, interview, May 19, 2019.

CHAPTER FIVE

August Gay remained in Monterey... Esther remarked that "Gay has a suite de Luxe now in the Stevenson House—the whole upstairs in fact, and he sails around it like Robert Louis [Stevenson] himself. He even has a guest room— the little one where Price used to sleep." Esther Bruton, letter to Ina Perham, [ca. December 1929], Perham Private Collection.

The Monterey artists came from a wide variety... Burton-Carvajal, "Gus and the Gang," 8, 11; Spangenberg, *Yesterday's Artists,* 62.

Neither earned their livings from painting alone... Barrows, "Personal Letters and Interviews."

"Worried that he didn't have enough to eat." Nancy Boas, "August Gay: California Modernist," in *Wonderful Colors! The Paintings of August Francois Gay,* ed. Jo Farb Hernandez (Monterey: Monterey Museum of Art, 1993), 19.

"Considerable wealth." Kent Seavey, *Monterey: The Artist's View,* 6.

Ina Perham's family made their money... Edwards, *Jennie V. Cannon,* 571.

"They lived a very simple life." Carroll, interview, May 19, 2019.

They cared little for fashion... Lucy Valentine Pierce, letter to Ina Perham, January 3, 1930, Perham Private Collection.

For Helen, a necklace made of natural materials... Carroll, interview, May 19, 2019.

In letters written to her husband... Ina Perham, letter to Fred Story, [ca. September 1932], Perham Private Collection.

"Reluctant to sell [his works]..." Barrows, "Personal Letters and Interviews."

He must have considered the Brutons good friends... Cunningham, "Clayton Price Laid Foundation Here.".

Even so, what Price earned... C.S. Price, letter to Arch Price, December 27, 1925, "Personal Letters and Interviews."

"Gave more to the WPA..." Helen Bruton and Margaret Bruton, interview, 1964.

"The most famous painter..." "top ten in the United States." Cunningham, "Clayton Price Laid Foundation Here."

Today he is recognized as one of the most creative minds... Edwards, *Jennie V. Cannon,* 191.

"Gus was a real artist to the core..." Boas, "August Gay: California Modernist," 13.

"Great sensitivity," "was about the most talented person [in Monterey]." Helen Bruton and Margaret Bruton, interview, 1972; Helen Bruton and Margaret Bruton, interview, 1964.

"Came right out of him." "You couldn't help but like Gay." Helen Bruton and Margaret Bruton, interview, 1972.

"Nest." Frode Dann, letter to Kirsten Kjaer, October 1934, Kirsten Kjaer Papers.

"The Bruton sisters... have finally forsaken the fogs..." Lehre, "Artists and Their Work," December 8, 1929.

"An exuberantly female refuge," "The walls of the home..." Burns, "Fabricating the Modern," 51.

The sisters renewed their connections... "Margaret Bruton: Biographical Listing"; "Biographical Chronology, 1930–1939," Hans Hofmann, accessed December 17, 2020, http://www.hanshofmann.org/1930–1939. There is no evidence that the Bruton sisters ever studied with Hofmann.

"Very noisy and boisterous..." "Gee, it was a thrill..." Esther Bruton, letter to Ina Perham, [ca. early 1930], Perham Private Collection.

"Master-etcher." Burton-Carvajal, "Gus and the Gang," 9.

"Butting into what the other fellow was doing..." Helen Bruton and Margaret Bruton, interview, 1975, video 1.

"One of her first loves." "Famed Woman Artist Whose Murals Adorn Ships and Hotels Takes Up Her Residence in Mobile," Mobile Press Register, May 18, 1941, 10.

This is not to suggest, however... "Famed Woman Artist."

"Truthful and sensitive..." "Monterey Art Shown in Monrovia Studio," Los Angeles Times, July 14, 1929, 18.

"One of the most promising of the younger artists." "Etchings by Californians," San Francisco Chronicle, pictorial section, September 16, 1928, 3.

"Charming humor," "an evident piece of sophisticated art." Aline Kistler, "Prize Prints Show Modern Art Trend," San Francisco Chronicle, September 22, 1929, D5.

"Seriously and splendidly organized design..." "California Etchers Hold Their Annual Show," Art Digest, October 1, 1929, 22.

"A gathering of the intelligentsia..." "California Society of Etchers Opens Annual Exhibition," San Francisco Chronicle, September 21, 1930, 4D.

In the same competition, Esther won first prize... Although some sources say Top of the Tent received second prize, Art Digest (November 1, 1930, 24), the San Francisco Chronicle (September 21, 1930, 4D), and the Sacramento Bee (October 4, 1930, 2) all reported that the work was awarded first prize.

"Contemporary in feeling." Christian Science Monitor, October 1929, as quoted in Hailey, "Esther Bruton," 38.

"One seldom sees cut with more charm..." Cravens, "Prints from Private Presses."

"Acrid humor." "Helen Bruton's Drypoint Wins in Etchers Annual," San Francisco Examiner, September 27, 1931, 8E.

"Spark of hope for the future..." Junius Cravens, "The Art World," Argonaut, October 2, 1931, 7.

Their prints were also exhibited... "Society of Etchers Exhibit Many Works At Arts Academy," Honolulu Advertiser, April 20, 1930, 12; Freund, "Guide Through New York Art Land"; Arthur Millier, "Brush Strokes," Los Angeles Times, August 28, 1932, 16; Elisabeth Luther Cary, "The Virtue of Woodcut," New York Times, August 7, 1932, 7.

"Alive and sparkling..." Franz Geritz, "Western Wonders: Presented Seriously and Satirically in the Block Prints by the Sisters Bruton," Touring Topics, April 1930, n.p.

"The Bruton humor does not slapstick..." "Art Exhibitions Reviewed," Los Angeles Times, June 4, 1933, 4.

"Some clever Negro character sketches by Esther Bruton." "Golden Gate Bridge Plans To Be Shown," Oakland Tribune, August 5, 1934, 8S.

While spending time in Natchez... These portraits are in the Bruton Sisters Archive.

"Spent one very happy evening..." Helen Bruton, letter to Kirsten Kjaer, February 26, 1929, Kirsten Kjaer Papers.

"It was the year they were selling apples..." Helen Bruton and Margaret Bruton, interview, 1964.

Esther and Helen had only ten days to complete nine drawings. Hailey, "Esther Bruton," 37.

The book, published in 1931... Wolcott Gibbs, Bird Life at the Pole (New York: Morrow & Co., 1931), frontispiece.

"A tremendous vogue..." Hailey, "Esther Bruton," 37.

"Grand and clever spoof..." "'Bird Life at the Pole' Just a Grand Continuous Spoof," Philadelphia Inquirer, February 28, 1931, 10.

"The illustrations are funnier than the text." "A Little Nonsense," The Courier-Journal (Louisville, KY), March 15, 1931, 4.

"It was just people that interested me... I didn't ever develop a style." Helen Bruton and Margaret Bruton, interview, 1975, video 2.

"I never followed any school..." Munro, *Originals*, 128. Alice Neel, like Margaret Bruton, was a student of Ashcan School artist Robert Henri.

"Decided she would rather go hungry in San Francisco than in New York." Helen Bruton and Margaret Bruton, interview, 1964.

"The freight trains go by..." Helen Bruton, interview, 1983.

"Good sized mirror..." "merchandise, edible or wearable." H.L. Dungan, "Art and Artists," *Oakland Tribune*, June 4, 1933, 8S.

The Brutons' co-exhibitors included... "Work of 36 Artists Shown in Carmel Art Group Exhibition," *Carmel Pine Cone*, December 9, 1932, 1.

"Drawn with acrid humor and appreciation," "she has done more appealing work, but it is not here." Marjorie Tait, "Bruton Sisters at Denny Watrous Gallery," *Carmel Pine Cone*, May 6, 1932, 7.

"Motoring through the 'Ghost Cities' of the State's old mining regions." "Miss Charlot to Marry Dr. L.K. Born," *San Francisco Chronicle*, August 7, 1932, B.

At its peak, Virginia City... "Virginia City Historic District, Nevada," National Park Service, accessed December 17, 2020, http://www.nps.gov/places/virginia-city-historic-district.htm.

During their stay in Virginia city... Coran and Nelson-Rees, *If Pictures Could Talk*, 272.

The bathtub was located in a corner of the kitchen... "Life is much as it was in Taos..." Ina Perham, letter to Fred Story, September 8, 1932, Perham Private Collection.

"It is one of those places where we all feel we 'belong'..." Esther Bruton, letter to Fred Story [ca. September 1932], Perham Private Collection.

"A very fertile period." Helen Bruton and Margaret Bruton, interview, 1964.

"A Garden of Eden," "a Hell hole." Helen Bruton, letter to Fred Story [ca. September 1932], Perham Private Collection.

"A magnet for artists..." Ronald M. James, *The Roar and the Silence: A History of Virginia City and the Comstock Lode* (Reno: University of Nevada Press, 1998), 258.

"A vein which now seems to be exhausted, if not actually overworked." Junius Cravens, *San Francisco News*, April 20, 1935, as quoted in Hailey, "Margaret Bruton," 21.

"The old Virigina City ruins..." H.L. Dungan, "3 Brutons Exhibit in J. Danysh Galleries: Alameda Sisters Display Oils, Drawings, Prints, Other Work in S.F.," *Oakland Tribune*, January 13, 1935, S7.

"In the modern manner." H.L. Dungan, "First Annual at Gump's is Good Exhibit," *Oakland Tribune*, March 19, 1933, 8S. The current location of *Mansion in Ruins* is unknown.

"Life is one glad and glorious spectacle..." Arthur Millier, "Women Again Lead Field in Art Exhibits of the Week: The Bruton Sisters Paint Gayly," *Los Angeles Times*, October 8, 1933, 5.

In 1934, she exhibited On the Comstock Lode... "Western Oil Painting at the Legion Palace," *San Francisco Chronicle*, October 7, 1934, D3.

"The best painting I have seen..." H.L. Dungan, "James A. Holden Leads in Vote for Best Painting on Exhibition at Oakland Art Gallery Annual," *Oakland Tribune*, October 21, 1934, 8S. A painting by Margaret Bruton called *On the Comstock Lode* was purchased by Walter Nelson-Rees and James Coran in 1982. Walter Nelson-Rees and James Coran, letter to Margaret Bruton, May 28, 1982, Bruton Sisters Archive. Its current location is unknown.

"A warm, color view of Virginia City's mining dumps..." H.L. Dungan, "Wm. Gaw and Miss M. Bruton Lead for Prize," *Oakland Tribune*, March 25, 1934, 10S.

"In the home stretch Miss Bruton forged ahead." H.L. Dungan, "First Prize in Art is Awarded to Miss Bruton," *Oakland Tribune*, April 8, 1934, 12S.

Mining Mountains won other awards... "Record Throng Sees Opening of State Fair," *Oakland Tribune*, September 1, 1935, 4A.

Margaret was one of just ten... "Art Exhibit at Berkeley City Club," *Oakland Tribune*, January 22, 1937, 10; Alfred Frankenstein, "Ten Bay District Artists Exhibit Work in National Show at N.Y.," *San Francisco Chronicle*, May 17, 1936, 10. Frankenstein's article mistakenly lists Helen Bruton as being selected for this exhibition instead of Margaret. The number of works each state could contribute to the exhibition was based on population, and California was allowed ten works. "State Art To Be On Display," *Charleston (WV) Daily Mail*, May 10, 1936, 17.

Mining Mountains was one of Margaret's own favorite works... A photo of Margaret in her Monterey home with *Mining Mountains* in the background appeared in the *Monterey Peninsula Herald* on December 18, 1977, C1. The painting was purchased from Margaret by Walter Nelson-Rees and James Coran in 1982. Walter Nelson-Rees, letter to Margaret Bruton, May 28, 1982, Bruton Sisters Archive. It was destroyed in the 1991 Oakland Hills fire.

"Acknowledged as one of the most distinguished artists on this Coast." "Art Exhibit at Berkeley City Club."

"Employed elements of the Cubist aesthetic." Edwards, *Jennie V. Cannon*, 342–343.

"Numerous houses remind us of Cubist post-Impressionism." Reginald Poland, "Some Western Oils," *Christian Science Monitor*, April 7, 1932, 8.

Cubism's influence on Margaret... The Harmonica (ca. 1935) is in the collection of Eric and Teresa Del Piero.

Resembling a worker during the Great Depression... Karen Crews Hendon, "Modernism in Monterey." In Hendon's opinion, Margaret's modernist painting style makes her the most influential of all the Bruton sisters.

"Radical." H.L. Dungan, "Many Paintings Submitted for Oakland Annual," *Oakland Tribune*, February 26, 1933, 8S.

"The old theory that a family can have only one genius..." "Three Artist Sisters Upset One Genius to Family Idea," *Oakland Tribune*, August 18, 1932, D15.

"The Brutons three, are modern in their viewpoit on art..." Ryan, "Brutons-3."

"The Bruton show is neither great nor profound..." Junius Cravens, *San Francisco News*, January 12, 1935, as quoted in Hailey, "Margaret Bruton," 23.

"Those three amazing Bruton sisters of Alameda..." Dungan, "3 Brutons Exhibit."

"Some very amusing rearranged advertisements..." Lucy Valentine Pierce, letter to Ina Perham, January 3, 1930, Perham Private Collection.

"Spare parts shop," "Hiccough Common, Pierce Desert Towns, and Mexico Preferred," "all kinds of terrible looking pills." Helen Bruton, letter to Ina Perham, January 27, 1932, Perham Private Collection.

Like many of the sisters' parties, costumes were part of the fun... "Diamond Lil," *Encyclopedia Britannica*, accessed February 15, 2021, https://www.britannica.com/topic/Diamond-Lil.

"You are invited to participate..." Invitation to "Brutons' Burlesque," [ca. December 1935], Bruton Sisters Archive.

"Tobogganed like ten-year-olds," "we knocked a few years off our calendars and a few wrinkles off our brows." Esther Bruton, letter to Ina Perham, [ca. February 1930], Perham Private Collection.

"Open car of ancient vintage." Hailey, "Margaret Bruton," 21-22.

In 1934, two newspapers reported that Esther... "Mexican Players of Padua to Entertain at L.A. Dedication," *Pomona (CA) Progress-Bulletin*, November 2, 1934, 12; "L.A. Society Will Fete Race Opening," *San Francisco Chronicle*, October 7, 1934, 2S.

In October, her oil painting Mexican Street Scene... "Women Artists Given Prizes," *San Francisco Chronicle*, October 30, 1936, 13; "'Night Fiesta,' by Margaret Bruton, Is Winner of First Prize," *San Francisco Examiner*, November 15, 1936, E7.

"World trip." Helen Bruton graph paper chronology.

Sales remained strong during the worst years of the Depression... Barrie A. Wigmore, *The Crash and Its Aftermath: A History of Securities Markets in the United States, 1929–1933* (Westport, CT: Greenwood Press, 1985), 274.

Later in life, at least one of the sisters must have felt guilty... Family members don't remember any of the Bruton sisters as smokers, although there is at least one photograph of Esther holding a cigarette.

Another advantage that carried the Brutons... Their parents had purchased the property at 1060 Buchanan Street—near the corner of Golden Gate Avenue and Buchanan Street—in 1909 for just ten dollars. The property was put in Mrs. Bruton's name only, perhaps because she was so much younger than her husband and likely to outlive him. Property deed, May 27, 1909, Bruton Sisters Archive.

"Depended largely." Helen Bruton and Margaret Bruton, interview, 1975, video 2. The Brutons' San Francisco apartment building was requisitioned during the city's post-World War II urban renewal program.

"The trouble with us..." Helen Bruton, letter to Ina Perham, January 27, 1932, Perham Private Collection.

"We were very fortunate..." Helen Bruton and Margaret Bruton, interview, 1975, video 2.

CHAPTER SIX

Photographs from this period reveal that they made a striking group... Ann Stocker, telephone interview by Wendy Good, May 27, 2019.

"Blonde and buoyant," "blonde and slender and tall." "Mural for Peace"; Ruth Cravath, oral history interview by Archives of American Art, Smithsonian Institution, September 23, 1965, 107.

At 5'7", Esther was sometimes referred... This was Esther's height according to her 1924 passport application, FamilySearch, accessed December 18 2020, https://familysearch.org, "United States Passport Applications, 1795-1925," citing NARA microfilm publications M1490 and M1372. Washington, D.C.: National Archives and Records Administration, n.d. In 1929, Kistler also refers to Margaret as "the tall one." Kistler, "Bruton Sisters Exhibit Work at Galerie." Helen listed her height as 5'10" in her application for the United States Civil Service Commission.

"Tawny-headed women..." Ryan, "Brutons-3."

"With an air." "Mural for Peace."

"Wild women." Eric Del Piero, telephone interview by Wendy Good, May 1, 2018. Del Piero recalls that Jay Hannah described the Brutons as "wild women."

"One very wild night..." "lower than a snake..." Helen Bruton, letters to Kirsten Kjaer, February 10, 1929, and August 7, 1929, Kirsten Kjaer Papers.

"Were extremely private." Carroll, interview, May 19, 2019.

"The last time she was in love." Peggy kept notes about what Helen told her. "The Loves of Helen Bruton As Told To Peggy," October 7, 1983, Bruton Sisters Archive.

"Was a bit in love with [Rockwood]..." Helen Bruton, letter to Kirsten Kjaer, August 7, 1929, Kirsten Kjaer Papers.

"They were raised to be very independent..." Carroll, interview, May 19, 2019.

Another factor in their individual decisions... Barbara Carroll, written statement, September 26, 2020, in the possession of the author.

"Wish it were possible for a fellow..." Frode Dann, letter to Kirsten Kjaer, October 1934, Kirsten Kjaer Papers.

"For the female of the species..." "acutely aware of how motherhood..." Doss, "Complicating Modernism," 128, 129.

"I have not regretted being childless." Munro, Originals, 183.

"Immediately saw in the work of the three sisters more imagination..." Jehanne Bietry-Salinger, "Three Decorators," Opera and Concert, October 1949, 33.

"He was such a favorite with artists..." Helen Bruton and Margaret Bruton, interview, 1975, video 1.

He hired Esther Bruton, one of his favorite artists, to paint them. Therese Poletti, Art Deco San Francisco: The Architecture of Timothy Pflueger (New York: Princeton Architectural Press, 2008), 176.

"The decision on Bruton paintings is unanimous, so go to it." Timothy Pflueger daybook, 1935, Timothy L. Pflueger Papers.

"Did such a terrible job on the first day..." Helen Bruton and Margaret Bruton, interview, 1964.

Helen considered it a lovely room... Helen Bruton and Margaret Bruton, interview, 1975, video 1.

"The Fairmont Circus Lounge... is an artistic achievement..." Junius Cravens, "Artist's Decorations Prove Delightfully Humorous Caricatures," San Francisco News, May 11, 1935.

"Nothing can increase the pleasure of drinking..." "The New Cocktail Room in the Fairmont Hotel San Francisco," California Arts & Architecture, June 1935, 20.

Esther's murals were such a hit... Cravens, "Artist's Decorations Prove Delightfully Humorous Caricatures."

"The Bruton sisters painted the new cocktail room." The Dowager, "Easter Ball at Burlingame Saturday Night May Continue Through to Sunrise Services," San Francisco Examiner, April 18, 1935, 11.

"The entire credit for this work belongs to Esther." "Mural for Peace."

"We were lucky we didn't lose those paintings," "were thrilled." Karen Liberatore, "The Circus is Back in Town," San Francisco Chronicle, This World, January 31, 1988, 6.

Esther earned another commercial commission... The Hawaiian Pineapple Company was founded in 1901 by James Dole and was the predecessor of the Dole Food Company. "James Drummond Dole," Dole Plantation, accessed December 18, 2020, https://www.doleplantation.com/resources/#resources-tabs%7C||resources-tabs|8.

Over the years, a number of other respected artists... Enrique Limon, "Hawaiian Topic: New Exhibit at the Georgia O'Keeffe Exudes Island Feel," Santa Fe Reporter, February 25, 2014, http://www.sfreporter.com/arts/artsvalve/2014/02/26/hawaiian-topic/. Unlike Esther, O'Keeffe travelled to Hawaii, where she painted two floral artworks that were used in Dole's 1939 advertising campaign.

The figures are embraced by circular patterns... The Three Graces, which is very similar to a screen that appears in one of the advertisements, has been on display several times at the Hawaii Museum of Art and was, at the time of this writing, for sale at a gallery in Honolulu. Michael D. Horikawa Fine Art, accessed December 28, 2020, https://www.mdhfineart.com/.

Also in the mid-1930s, Esther was hired... According to Gene Hailey, C&H also hired Esther to paint murals in their corporate offices located on the fifteenth floor of the Matson Building in downtown San Francisco ("Esther Bruton," 44). The building is currently owned by Pacific Gas & Electric Company, and it is not known whether these murals still exist.

Its text was written by Neill C. Wilson, a minor novelist... Therese Thau Heyman, "Photography and the Group f.64," in On the Edge of America: California Modernist Art, 1900–1950, ed. Paul J. Karlstrom (Berkeley: University of California Press, 1996), 257.

His photograph of her captures... This photograph is in the Bruton Sisters Archive.

"Sunshine and blue water combine to make Crockett's setting one of tonic healthfulness and beauty." Neill C. Wilson, Behind Your Sugar Bowl: The Story of Sugar in Words and Pictures (San Francisco: The California and Hawaiian Sugar Refining Corporation, 1936), 13.

In 1937, she was hired to paint murals for the Golden State Hotel... Located at 114 Powell Street at Ellis, it is now the Hotel Union Square. The hotel was built in

1913, largely to provide lodging for tourists visiting the 1915 Panama-Pacific International Exposition. Hotel Union Square, accessed December 18, 2020, https://hotelunionsquare.com.

"Daring modernistic design." "Revive Powell Promenade," *San Francisco Examiner*, September 11, 1937, 6.

"I finished the Golden State bar murals..." Esther Bruton, letter to Ina Perham, September 8, [1937], Perham Private Collection.

"Done in delicate tones and blend[ing] effectively..." "Tier Mosaics Praised," *San Francisco Examiner*, September 25, 1937, 6.

"I was so thrilled by the beautiful effect..." Lee Randolph, letter to Esther Bruton, October 27, 1937, Bruton Sisters Archive.

"Wiped out... by tobacco smoke... [they were] too delicate." Helen Bruton, letter to Phil Kovinick, January 7, 1976, Bruton Sisters Archive.

A second mural features vaqueros... These blueprints are in the Bruton Sisters Archive.

"Inter-tribal ceremonial," "purely Indian..." "From there we headed up into the Navajo and Hopi country..." "Hope I love that desert country..." Esther Bruton, letter to Ina Perham, September 8, [1937], Perham Private Collection.

"Pewter colored Chinese paper..." Puccinelli, "The Brutons and How They Grew," 18.

"Painted on luminous metal foil..." "$3,000,000 Magnin Home Epitome of Beauty," *Los Angeles Evening Citizen News*, February 11, 1939, 13.

The center mural is a desert scene... Esther's large signature is visible on the lower right corner of the center mural.

A photograph of Esther's murals appeared in Vogue magazine. Ruby Ross Wood, "A Decorator Looks at California," *Vogue* 93 (April 15, 1939), 92.

Hundreds participated in the pageant and thousands attended the event... "Quinn Denies Conducting Probe of Parilia Police," *San Francisco Examiner*, February 7, 1937, 3. A $2.50 ticket purchased in 1937 is equivalent to a $45 ticket today.

"Bizarre and scanty." "Angkor Vat [sic] Scene of Ball," *San Francisco Examiner*, January 17, 1936, 17.

"Going in for more modesty, less nudity this year." "Parlia Costume?" *San Francisco Examiner*, February 16, 1938, 34.

A "menu" for one of them... Parilia menu, [n.d.], Timothy L. Pflueger Papers.

"Remove a few dozen 'bodies'..." "Games All Over, Gay Parilia Goes to Dogs at Dawn," *San Francisco Examiner*, January 21, 1934, 19.

The 1937 party made the front page... "13 Injured, 15 Jailed in Parilia," *San Francisco Examiner*, February 7, 1937, 1.

In their defense, party-goers explained... "Quinn Denies Conducting Probe."

"The following year, the newspaper reported... "Parilia Tame, Only 21 Drunks Land in Jail," *San Francisco Examiner*, February 27, 1938, 18.

The king of the Parilia was another of Pflueger's favorite artists, Victor Arnautoff. Poletti, *Art Deco San Francisco*, 176. At the time, Arnautoff was working on his murals at George Washington High School in San Francisco.

"Prominent and popular younger artists of San Francisco." "Parilia Pageant King Selected," *San Francisco Chronicle*, January 2, 1936, 19. The *San Francisco Examiner* misspelled both artists' names in its initial announcement. "Miss Esther Brunton will reign as queen of Parilia with Mr V. Arnatoff as king," December 31, 1935, 15. The error was corrected the following day when the newspaper printed a photograph of Bruton and Arnautoff in costume.

At the 1936 Parilia... "One of the most resplendent pagents..." "Cambodian Pageant: Artists Ball Colorful and Resplendent," *Architect and Engineer*, February 1936, 33–35.

"Beads and very little more." Carolyn Anspacher, "S.F. Art Association Makes Merry from 9 Until Dawn," *San Francisco Chronicle*, January 18, 1936, 5.

"One of the most interesting goings on of that decade..." Helen Bruton and Margaret Bruton, interview, 1975, video 2.

CHAPTER SEVEN

"A polite lady sculptress." Helen Bruton and Margaret Bruton, interview, 1964. The building has since been torn down.

In 1925 she won an honorable mention... "Prizes Awarded in S.F. Exhibition," *All Arts Gossip*, June 25, 1925, 9.

"To fiddle around..." "By the time I would get a plate..." Helen Bruton and Margaret Bruton, interview, 1964.

"The aesthetic preoccupations of the 1920s..." "were required to follow an equal opportunity..." Charlotte Streifer Rubenstein, *American Women Artists from Early Indian Times to the Present* (Boston: G.K. Hall & Co., 1982), 215.

"There was no discrimination against women..." "a great thing for most artists..." Munro, *Originals*, 108, 174. Krasner worked for the WPA in New York.

"Felt a great sense of camaraderie and equality with their male colleagues." Rubenstein, *American Women Artists*, 215.

"We didn't often collaborate actually..." Helen Bruton and Margaret Bruton, interview, 1964.

The family still had considerable assets... Bay Area PWAP director Walter Heil may have had some latitude in choosing his artists. Museum director Juliana Force, who was in charge of selecting PWAP artists in New York, was roundly criticized for hiring "established gallery artists -- many of whom were not in need of assistance." Nicolas Lampert, *A People's Art History of the United States: 250 Years of Activist Art and Artists Working in Social Justice* (New York: The New Press, 2013), 158.

"Extreme destitution..." United States, Federal Works Agency, *Final Report On the WPA Program, 1935-43* (Washington, DC: U. S. Govt. print. off, 1947), 16.

Mothers Building at the San Francisco Zoo. Also known as the Mothers House.

The ornate Italian Renaissance–style stone building... "The original idea was for a place with restrooms, nurseries, and clinical rooms where medical advice would be given. There would be provision for supplying distilled water and milk for the children and refreshments for the mothers... At one time, tea was served from the Mothers House and picnic lunches were provided for those who wished to eat outside in the play area adjacent to the building." The document notes that males over the age of six were not allowed to enter the Mothers Building. United States Department of the Interior, "National Register of Historic Places - Nomination Form, Delia Fleishhacker Memorial Building / Mothers House," July 30, 1979. https://npgallery.nps.gov/GetAsset/1a754185-c760-434a-aff7-d46ac5190fa3.

"Hardly knew what [Margaret] was talking about..." Helen Bruton and Margaret Bruton, interview, 1975, video 1.

"Except for some little experiments that I had made..." Helen Bruton and Margaret Bruton, interview, 1964.

"Some of the earliest, if not the first, public mosaics to be executed in San Francisco." St. Gaudens, *Emerging from the Shadows*, 140.

"The only ones so far in this country..." Ada Hanafin, "Tile Mosaics Completed by Bruton Trio," *San Francisco Examiner*, August 5, 1934, 6S.

"Nobody at that time was doing anything very much with mosaic." Helen Bruton and Margaret Bruton, interview, 1975, video 1.

"Among the earliest pioneers..." J. Mellentin Haswell, *Von Nostrand Reinhold Manual of Mosaic* (London: Thames and Hudson, 1973), 176. Haswell also mentions Margaret Bruton, Louisa Jenkins, Mary Bowling, and Frans Wildenhain as early innovators in the medium.

"Somebody else, probably Esther or Margaret, might have suggested the subject matter." Helen Bruton and Margaret Bruton, interview, 1964.

"Gentle harmonious scenes [that] exemplify the hopeful nature of the New Deal." Nancy Acord, "The Women of the WPA Art Projects: California Murals, 1933–1943," in *Yesterday and Tomorrow: California Women Artists*, ed. Sylvia Moore (New York: Midmarch Arts Press, 1989), 17.

"[We were] almost more fortunate..." Helen Bruton, "Mosaic as a Modern Expression," *San Francisco Art Association Bulletin*, December 1936, 4.

The Brutons found much-needed advice... According to Barbara Carroll, Falcier might have helped the sisters procure some leftover tiles from the floor-to-ceiling mosaic work done for the Roman-style swimming pool at Hearst Castle.

"If it hadn't been for Mr. Falcier..." This resulted in a fair amount of waste and seconds... *"fawn color... strong ochre... deep Mars violet."* Helen Bruton and Margaret Bruton, interview, 1964.

"Helen's mosaics made with these..." Puccinelli, "The Brutons and How They Grew," 18.

"The juxtaposition of little cubes..." Hanafin, "Tile Mosaics Completed by Bruton Trio."

Fortunately, the Brutons could work in their expansive attic studio in Alameda. Helen Bruton and Margaret Bruton, interview, 1964.

A preliminary drawing of one of the mosaics reveals... This preliminary drawing is in the Bruton Sisters Archive.

The design was then filled in with mosaic tiles... A decade later, the sisters described a slightly different method, saying they would "take a piece of light cloth, cover it with wallpaper paste and smooth the cloth over the top of the mosaic." "Mosaics... and their Use in Western Homes and Gardens," *Sunset Magazine*, October 1947, 40.

"Concentrated hard work... jealous personal interest..." Helen Bruton, "Mosaic as a Modern Expression."

"To see that there was not going to be anything offensive slipped in." Helen Bruton and Margaret Bruton, interview, 1964.

For two exhausting weeks... Helen Bruton and Margaret Bruton, interview, 1975, video 1.

"It made me nervous..." Helen Bruton and Margaret Bruton, interview, 1964.

"Terribly nice, gentle young man... was a nice enough man but I simply could not..." Helen Bruton and Margaret Bruton, interview, 1975, video 1.

"The section that you were mounting..." Helen Bruton and Margaret Bruton, interview, 1964.

"It knocked off a couple of years off my life getting it up there on the wall." Helen Bruton and Margaret Bruton, interview, 1975, video 1.

"Representational but not naturalistic." Burns, "Fabricating the Modern," 49.

Despite the help they provided... The Bruton Sisters Archive includes lists of artworks compiled by the sisters for publicity purposes. Margaret and Esther's lists of works do not include the mosaics on the Mothers Building.

"I can't see that there's been any deterioration at all." Helen Bruton and Margaret Bruton, interview, 1964.

Tapped to create mosaics for the niches on either side... Campus Public Art + Architecture Map, self-guided tour pamphlet (Berkeley: University of California, [2020]) 18, https://artsdesign.berkeley.edu/sites/default/files/2020-08/FINAL_BerkTourBookSpread.pdf.

"It was more or less decided, I think, by Mrs. Swift, and maybe Mr. Neuhaus." Helen Bruton and Margaret Bruton, interview, 1964.

The artists included buildings from the Berkeley campus... Campus Public Art + Architecture Map, 18.

Swift's seated woman is a portrait... A Century of Art: Outdoor Art at the University of California, Berkeley, self-guided tour pamphlet (Berkeley: University of California, 2001), n.p., https://capitalstrategies.berkeley.edu/sites/default/files/publicartcollectionbrochure-2001.pdf. This brochure mistakenly lists Esther Bruton as the artist of the mosaic.

"Similarity to the slender Bruton sisters." Henry Helfand, "Mosaic Murals of Music & Art," California Magazine, Fall 2011, 86; Helen Bruton and Margaret Bruton, interview, 1964.

"Gendered divisions of the art world," "a genre under male control." Katherine H. Adams and Michael L. Keene, Art, Women, and the New Deal (Jefferson, NC: McFarland, 2016), 35.

"Had significance in relation to the building." Helen Bruton and Margaret Bruton, interview, 1964.

"Neutral earth colors..." Acord, "The Women of the WPA Art Projects," 17.

Helen's mural also shows the influence... Helen Bruton and Margaret Bruton, interview, 1975, video 1.

Early Byzantine art... "Byzantine Art," Ancient History Encyclopedia, accessed December 19, 2020, https://www.ancient.eu/Byzantine_Art/.

Helen Bruton's mosaic mural at Berkeley... "Large Mosaics Given U.C. to be Dedicated," Oakland Tribune, November 1, 1936, 6A.

The mosaics were dedicated in a ceremony... "Art Projects Murals Throughout U.S. Being Filmed," San Francisco Examiner, December 27, 1936, E7. The film can be viewed on YouTube: "Work Pays America," Works Progress Administration, [ca. 1930s], YouTube, accessed December 20, 2020, https://youtu.be/Cx3FVJhF1YY.

"Rich in color..." "Mosaics Are Accepted at U.C. Ceremony: Works of Helen Bruton and Florence Swift Dedicated," Oakland Tribune, November 8, 1936, 6B.

"The murals will be an outstanding adaptation..." Junius Cravens, San Francisco News, May 6, 1936, as quoted in Gene Hailey, "Helen Bruton," California Art Research (San Francisco: Abstract from WPA Project 2874, 1937), Vol. 16, 61. Cravens wrote many positive reviews of the Brutons' work, but this was one of his last. Just two months after writing about the Berkeley mosaics, the body of this respected Bay Area art critic was discovered washed up on the beach not far from San Francisco. "Junius Cravens Murdered; Body Discovered On Beach Identified as S.F. Art Critic," San Francisco Examiner, July 5, 1936, 1. At first foul play was suspected, but in the end it was determined that the forty-two year old Cravens had fallen from a cliff and drowned; it is unknown whether the fall was accidental or intentional. Ellen Schwartz, "California Art Research: An Historical Essay," California Art Research (La Jolla, CA: Lawrence McGilvery, 1987), vi.

Both [mosaics] will tumble soon... "Mosaics Are Accepted at U.C. Ceremony."

"They undoubtedly will pull it down..." Helen Bruton and Margaret Bruton, interview, 1964.

At times, the mosaics have been neglected and obscured by vegetation. After a visit to the UC Berkeley campus, Helen reported that the murals had both gotten "quite covered over with ivy." Helen Bruton and Margaret Bruton, interview, 1964.

But despite the Oakland tribune's dire predictions, the Old Art Gallery has been spared. At the time of this writing, the Old Art Gallery building remains closed as it awaits restoration and renovation "as an intimate musical performance and rehearsal space." University of California Berkeley, Disability and Access Compliance, accessed November 30, 2020, https://dac.berkeley.edu/old-art-gallery.

"Finest mosaics." Acord, "The Women of the WPA Art Projects," 17.

"I'd much rather tell you..." "An enlarged kind of beadwork..." Helen Bruton, "Mosaic as a Modern Expression."

"Pretty different in feeling... striking anything like a similar note." Helen Bruton, letter to Inslee A. Hopper, June 28, 1939, Bruton Sisters Archive.

"I feel a little sad, for Miss Davis's sake..." Helen Bruton, letter to Edward B. Rowan, July 6, 1939, Bruton Sisters Archive.

Helen was paid $1,400 to create both works. Federal Works Agency, Public Buildings Administration, Public Voucher for Purchases and Services, December 28, 1940, Bruton Sisters Archive.

The molds were used to fabricate... Helen Bruton and Margaret Bruton, interview, 1964.

"What I wanted to do..." Helen Bruton, letter to Forbes Watson, November 14, 1939, Bruton Sisters Archive.

Helen believed that the Native Americans of the area... Helen Bruton and Margaret Bruton, interview, 1975, video 2.

Helen Forbes and Dorothy Puccinelli, the artists... Puccinelli's mural is called *Vacheros* and Forbes' is called *Jedediah Smith Crossing the Merced River*. The post office is now the Merced Federal Building. "Post Office—Merced, CA," The Living New Deal, accessed January 2, 2021, https://livingnewdeal.org/projects/post-office-merced-ca/.

"Jobs that didn't jell." This envelope is in the Bruton Sisters Archive.

"I'd break my heart over trying..." When asked which WPA art project... "Work like everything to get a job..." Helen Bruton and Margaret Bruton, interview, 1975, videos 1 & 2.

"Was always happiest in the process..." Helen Bruton, letter to Ellen Schwartz, November 22, 1981, Bruton Sisters Archive.

"You are supposed to deliver..." *"the fact that you have to please somebody else..."* *Toward the end of her life...* Helen Bruton and Margaret Bruton, interview, 1975, videos 1 & 2.

In 1937, in between her Berkeley mosaic... Helen Bruton, letter to Fred Schell, February 20, 1937, Bruton Sisters Archive.

"They are just symbolic of the West..." *"I can't talk to you very much..."* "Free as a Breeze, This Girl," *San Francisco News*, May 21, 1937, 25.

"The very limitations of [mosaic]..." Helen Bruton, "Mosaic as a Modern Expression."

"Mosaics do not belong to a time but a human need of exceptional duration." Munro, *Originals*, 178.

"As the artist who created it..." Helen Bruton, letter to Frank Lembi, November 2, 1974, Bruton Sisters Archive. Helen Bruton, letter to Robert Gallagher, January 22, 1975, Bruton Sisters Archive.

Labaudt immortalized the Brutons... Masha Zakheim Jewett, *Coit Tower, San Francisco: Its History and Art* (San Francisco: Volcano Press, 1983), 108.

"The absence of adequate information..." Gene Hailey, "Introduction," *California Art Research*, Vol. 1, 1–2.

"The modern artistic counterpart..." Hailey, "Margaret Bruton," 1.

After her biography was first published... These corrected pages are in the Bruton Sisters Archive.

Fifty years later, Ellen Schwartz prepared... Ellen Schwartz and Gene Hailey, *California Art Research: Handbook, Microfiche Edition* (La Jolla, CA: Lawrence McGilvery, 1987).

The original artist biographies were untouched and the errors about the Brutons remained. Helen used graph paper to prepare chronologies for herself and her sisters with the hope that their biographies would be corrected and updated in the new edition; this didn't happen and the material was never used.

"Were not accurate..." Helen Bruton, interview, 1983.

"Would give you much better technical information than I could... When it comes right down to it..." Helen Bruton, letter to Emanuel M. Benson, August 18, 1939. WPA Artists' Essays, 1936-1939, Box 6, Folder 144, Francis V. O'Connor Papers, 1920-2009, Archives of American Art, Smithsonian Institution.

"This is hardly important. Let's see other mosaic articles." WPA Artists' Essays, 1936-1939, Frances V. O'Connor Papers.

This collection of essays about WPA-era art... Frances V. O'Connor, *Art for the Millions: Essays from the 1930s by Artists and Administrators of the WPA Federal Art Project* (Boston: New York Graphic Society, 1973).

"A very happy and busy time..." Helen Bruton, letter to Steven Gelber, September 5, 1974, Bruton Sisters Archive.

"I think they were wonderful..." Helen Bruton and Margaret Bruton, interview, 1975, video 2.

"Although there is a great deal..." Helen Bruton and Margaret Bruton, interview, 1964.

"Provided the opportunity to work on sizable projects..." Helen Bruton, biographical statement prepared for exhibition at Monterey Museum of Art, [1975], Bruton Sisters Archive.

CHAPTER EIGHT
"Gave off melodious sounds as it fluttered gently in the breeze." Eugen Neuhaus, *The Art of Treasure Island* (Berkeley: University of California Press, 1939), 31; Jack James and Earle Weller, *Treasure Island: "The Magic City," 1939-1940* (San Francisco: Pisani Printing and Publishing, 1941), 35.

Though the sisters were by nature modest and humble... Carroll, interview, May 19, 2019.

"Largest of the contracts." "$40,000 Worth of Murals," *Arts Magazine*, October 15, 1937, 16.

"Flabbergasted." "Mural for Peace."

"The longest single suspension span in the world... the largest structure of its kind in the history of man." "In keeping with the magnitude of the projects it was to celebrate." James, *Treasure Island*, 3.

"The most beautiful World's Fair in history." H.L. Dungan, "$1,000,000 Spent on Art at '39 Fair," *Oakland Tribune*, January 22, 1939, B7.

The subtitle of the fair's name... "'Golden Gate' Chosen Name for S.F. Fair," *San Francisco Examiner*, June 4, 1936, 16.

"Mysticism of the East with the vision and vigor of the West." "1,000,000 Spent on Murals, Statuary," *San Francisco Examiner*, February 15, 1939, 3.

"A new mood in decorating." Wendy Kaplan, *California Design, 1930–1965: Living in a Modern Way* (Los Angeles: Los Angeles County Museum of Art, and Cambridge, MA: MIT Press, 2011), 51.

Pflueger was put in charge of the Court of Pacifica... Official Guide Book: *Golden Gate International Exposition on San Francisco Bay* (San Francisco: The Crocker Company, 1939), 31-32.

"One wishes the entire Fair..." Alfred Frankenstein, "Art on Treasure Island: The Obituary of an Art Era," *San Francisco Chronicle, This World*, October 29, 1939, 25.

"Professed to be very sad about it..." Helen Bruton and Margaret Bruton, interview, 1964.

"One of the most significant murals ever conceived." "'Peacemakers' Mural to Set Fair Theme," *San Francisco Chronicle*, August 5, 1938, E6.

"It is the general feeling among the artists' colony..." Glenn Wessels, "The Art World," *Argonaut*, May 13, 1938, 20.

In one photo, Helen and Margaret manage... "Sisters Win $20,000 Fair Contract," *San Francisco Chronicle*, May 7, 1938, 13.

"Working out the technical parts..." Helen Bruton and Margaret Bruton, interview, 1964.

"A beautiful array of special problems." Puccinelli, "The Brutons and How They Grew," 41.

"We spent weeks and months..." Helen Bruton and Margaret Bruton, interview, 1964.

Although the sisters had assistants... Helen Bruton, letter to Mrs. Salanave, June 15, 1939, Bruton Sisters Archive.

Their attic studio in Alameda couldn't possibly accommodate... "Bruton Sisters Collaborate in Murals and Other Fields of Art," *Monterey Peninsula Herald*, November 1, 1946, 7.

"The most interesting job I think that I've done." Helen Bruton and Margaret Bruton, interview, 1964.

"I'm always wobbly..." Helen Bruton, letter to Timothy Pflueger, February 15, 1940, Timothy L. Pflueger Papers.

The sisters worked from 9 a.m. to 5 p.m... "Mural for Peace."

They were assisted by a young woman... Thirty years later, Pickersgill was on the guest list for Helen Bruton's 1975 exhibition at the Monterey Museum of Art (Bruton Sisters Archive).

They carefully planned out the mural in advance... Golden Gate International Exposition, press release, [ca. 1938], Bruton Sisters Archive.

"One side was..." Helen Bruton, interview, 1983.

According to early plans... Golden Gate International Exposition, press release. Perhaps in the end the sisters felt that carving the detailed lettering was simply too time consuming.

"Slow march of mankind toward peaceful ideas of East and West." Official Guide Book, 32. The fair's guidebook also describes the mural's ocean waves as representing the "transitory quality of our material civilization."

Makes clear just how much the Pacific..." "perfectly expressed the attitude of the fair."* Andrew M. Shanken, *Into the Void Pacific: Building the 1939 San Francisco World's Fair* (Oakland: University of California Press, 2014), 97.

"Exacting scholars will find plenty to criticize." Helen Bruton, letter to Mrs. James, April 6, 1939, Bruton Sisters Archive.

"Some critics have scoffed..." "We'll have to wait as patiently as we can..." "Mural for Peace."

"As beautiful as it was massive," "new and spectacular." Nicholas and Betty Veronico, *Depression-Era Sculpture in the Bay Area* (Charleston, SC: Arcadia Publishing, 2017), 76; "'Peacemakers' Mural to Set Fair Theme," *San Francisco Chronicle*, August 5, 1938, E6.

"A technical innovation as been made..." Neuhaus, *The Art of Treasure Island*, 108, 111.

"One of the most outstandingly successful mural decorations at the fair," "outstanding artistic achievement." Puccinelli, "The Brutons and How They Grew," 41; James, *Treasure Island*, 34.

"I expect the stunning Bruton bas-relief to advertise Coca Cola any minute!" Shanken, *Into the Void Pacific*, 97.

"The Bruton sisters' doubly-colossal..." Kevin Wallace, "Treasure Island Tales," *San Francisco Examiner*, January 26, 1939, 15.

"Looks to be nine miles high..." "Notes in Passing," *California Arts & Architecture*, October 1940, 15.

"They were about six feet." Helen Bruton, interview, 1983.

"Given a few sticks and stones..." "Led b y a mouthy young guy..." "Notes in Passing."

"I am convinced..." Helen Bruton, letter to Eugene Prince, February 14, 1939, Bruton Sisters Archive.

According to their contract with Exposition organizers... Golden Gate International Exposition, contract with Margaret, Esther, and Helen Bruton, April 6, 1938, Bruton Sisters Archive.

By mid-February, nearly a month after... Golden Gate International Exposition, press release. This press release describes Helen as "the business manager for the trio."

"Most of [the money]..." Helen Bruton, letter to Eugene Prince, February 14, 1939, Bruton Sisters Archive.

"If we do not receive the balance..." Helen Bruton, letter to H.C. Bottorff, February 23, 1939, Bruton Sisters Archive.

"The year 1939 would go down in history..." "America's role as a peacemaker..." James, *Treasure Island*, 56, 269.

"Unprecedented in the history of art display." "'Art in Action' at S.F. Fair," *Honolulu Star Bulletin*, May 25, 1940, 11.

"If you still haven't got a better person..." Helen Bruton, letter to Timothy Pflueger, February 15, 1940, Timothy L. Pflueger Papers.

"Miss Bruton in Charge." H.L. Dungan, "Artists to Work While Others Watch," *Oakland Tribune*, April 28, 1940, B7.

"My brain has been ticking so loud..." Helen Bruton, letter to Timothy Pflueger, February 11, 1940, Timothy L. Pflueger Papers.

"We expect it to be quite a circus..." Mildred Rosenthal, "Fine Arts in the 1940 Fair: Active Arts Section to Present Artists at Work," *San Francisco Art Association Bulletin*, April 1940, 2.

"If these letters don't scare you off me..." Helen Bruton, letter to Timothy Pflueger, February 15, 1940, Timothy L. Pflueger Papers.

"Particular brand of excitement." Helen Bruton, letter (draft) to Alexander Calder, [ca. February 1940], Timothy L. Pflueger Papers.

"What are our chances of having..." Helen Bruton, letter (draft) to Salvador Dali, [ca. February 1940], Timothy L. Pflueger Papers. Dali's designs for Bacchanal included a woman in a fish head, a hoop skirt covered in teeth, male dancers with sexually suggestive red lobsters on their thighs, and a ballerina that appeared to be dancing in the nude. See Tina Sutton, "Goodbye Dali: A Surreal Experience at the Ballet," *The Making of Markova*, August 16, 2013, https://themakingofmarkova.com/tag/bacchanale/.

"Right hand man." "Ben Sharpsteen," Walt Disney Archives, accessed December 21, 2020, https://d23.com/walt-disney-legend/ben-sharpsteen/.

"Nothing like asking for plenty..." Helen Bruton, letter (draft) to Benny Sharpsteen, [ca. February 1940], Timothy L. Pflueger Papers.

"We all think your court idea..." Esther Bruton, letter to Timothy Pflueger, [ca. February 1940], Timothy L. Pflueger Papers.

"Practically none of the artists made anything..." Timothy Pflueger, letter to William Monahan, September 21, 1940, Timothy L. Pflueger Papers.

"Wasn't really running it at all... I never had more fun in my life." Helen Bruton and Margaret Bruton, interview, 1975, video 1.

"I am curious to know if Mrs. Bruton's attitude is justifiable." Arne Ingels, letter to Timothy Pflueger, July 30, 1940, Timothy L. Pflueger Papers.

"I have the utmost confidence..." Timothy Pflueger, letter to Arne Ingels, August 6, 1940, Timothy L. Pflueger Papers.

The Brutons' good friend Katy Skeele... "They Like Portraits," *Los Angeles Times*, January 5, 1941, 8.

"Construction of murals." Hazel Holly, "Bay Region Clubs to Observe Women's Day at Fair Today," *San Francisco Examiner*, September 18, 1940, 16.

Esther also joined in, constructing a mosaic bird bath... "Fair Art in Action!" *Petaluma Argus-Courier*, August 30, 1940, 8. The newspaper failed to identify Esther by name, identifying her only as "one of a score of artists."

"Several wild-looking female artists..." Fred Clark, "San Francisco World's Fair," *Placer Herald (Rocklin, CA)*, September 21, 1940, 2.

"Helen Bruton, one of the able workers..." H.L. Dungan, "Workers Tell Non-Workers About Work," *Oakland Tribune*, May 19, 1940, B7.

"The three famous muralists, Helen, Margaret, and Esther Bruton." Hazel Holly, "Women Artists at Fair Will Be Honored Tomorrow," *San Francisco Examiner*, July 25, 1940, 14.

Altogether, eighty-one artists came through... Timothy Pflueger, letter to William Monahan, September 21, 1940, Timothy L. Pflueger Papers.

"A small blonde cyclone of energy, with freckles." Charles Lindstrom, "News and Comment on Art," *Architect and Engineer*, March 1941, 8.

Since there was no money to pay the artists... "All's Fair," *California Arts & Architecture*, June 1940, 16–17.

"They all had such a good time..." Helen Bruton and Margaret Bruton, interview, 1975, video 1.

On one interior wall of the Fine Arts building... This mosaic is now located at San Francisco City College's Science Hall. "City College of San Francisco Mosaic," The Living New Deal, accessed December 20, 2020, https://livingnewdeal. org/projects/city-college-san-francisco-organic-inorganic-science-mosaic-san-francisco-ca/.

"We would have to devise a way..." Helen Bruton, letter to Timothy Pflueger, February 15, 1940, Timothy L. Pflueger Papers.

The Bruton sisters probably knew Kahlo... A signed print of this portrait is in a private collection. Frida used the alternate spelling of her name, "Frieda," in the late 1930s. "Biography of Frida Kahlo," Frida Kahlo Foundation, accessed March 3, 2021, https://www.frida-kahlo-foundation.org/biography.html.

Diego Rivera commuted daily... "Golden Gate International Expo," Diego Rivera Mural Project, accessed March 3, 2021, https://riveramural.org/ggie/

"We had the most terrible time with him." Helen Bruton and Margaret Bruton, interview, 1975, video 1.

"One of the most interesting and successful innovations..." Clark, "San Francisco World's Fair;" "'Art in Action Proved Feature of Great Display," *Oakland Tribune*, September 29, 1940, B7.

"The 'Art in Action' project so dominates..." Jane Watson, "'Art in Action' at San Francisco," *Magazine of Art*, August 1940, 462.

"Batch of artists actually drawing pictures..." Ernie Pyle, "Roving Reporter," *Clarion-Ledger* (Jackson, MI), July 15, 1940, 4.

"What a show! This is..." "Rivera 'In Action' for Fair Visitors," *Oakland Tribune*, June 16, 1940, B7.

"Set a pattern for all exhibitions of the future." Dungan, "Workers Tell Non-Workers."

The program was so successful that after the close of the fair... "'Art in Action' To Be Museum Event," *San Francisco Examiner*, November 3, 1940, D11.

"We have been so frantically busy..." Esther Bruton, letter to Helen and Jack Stackable, September 22, 1940, Bruton Sisters Archive.

"Come as a picture from the Fine Arts Show..." Invitation, September 1940, Timothy L. Pflueger Papers. The final line of the poem refers to the Society for Sanity in Art, a group of artists that rejected all forms of modern art. This ultra-conservative group had tried to exert its influence on the committee that selected the artwork for fair. Unsurprisingly, the Society was ridiculed by Helen and her modernist peers.

Esther came as a portrait of Frida Kahlo. Ruth Cravath, interview, 1965. Cravath, who was dressed as Frida Kahlo, was surprised and somewhat embarrassed to run into Diego Rivera. Rivera put Cravath at ease and assured her that she "looked like Frida." It seems that Kahlo herself did not attend the party.

Helen and Margaret, who called themselves the "Picket Sisters"... "The News Goes To a Party," *San Francisco News*, September 23, 1940, 9.

Although the work ended up being almost twice as big... After the viewing, the fresco was disassembled, crated, and stored for almost two decades. In the interim, Rivera became a controversial and unpopular figure due to his political views and membership in the Communist Party. In addition, the public became uncomfortable with the mural's depictions of Hitler, Mussolini, and Stalin. It wasn't until 1961 that Rivera's *Pan American Unity* mural was finally installed at the City College of San Francisco. "Public To See Rivera Mural," *The Times* (San Mateo, CA), November 25, 1940, 12.

"Great success," "silent memorial service." "Diego Rivera Mural Preview Turns Into Memorial for Fair," *San Francisco Examiner*, December 2, 1940, 8.

"Board-and-plaster illusions that had passed for palaces under the floodlights." "Fair II, The End," *San Francisco Chronicle, This World*, October 6, 1940, 5.

Fair buildings were razed... After the fair closed, the plans to develop Treasure Island into an airport were abandoned; in wartime, the land had greater value as a base for the United States Navy. In 1941 the Navy took over the island and it became a training and education center. By the time the war ended in 1945, Treasure Island was no longer a viable location for an airport, given the larger planes and complexities of modern aviation. The Navy remained there until 1997, when the land was leased back to the city of San Francisco. "Island History," Treasure Island Museum, accessed December 21, 2020, http://www. treasureislandmuseum.org/island-history.

"The exhibit places, the exotic buildings..." Ernest Lenn, "Gala Farewell Marks Fair's Last 2 Days," *San Francisco Examiner*, September 28, 1940, 1.

"Everybody thought it was very sad, but I never missed it..." Helen Bruton and Margaret Bruton, interview, 1964.

"What a pity it couldn't stay up." Helen Bruton, interview, 1983.

CHAPTER NINE

"Their friends are extending a warm welcome..." "Misses Bruton Are Back in Monterey to Make Their Home," *Monterey Peninsula Herald*, February 24, 1941, 6. The sisters' move to Monterey did not become permanent until 1944.

"Motoring to New Orleans. The date of their return is indefinite." "Margaret Bruton Dines at Club," *Monterey Peninsula Herald*, April 7, 1941, 12.

Margaret is not in the family wedding photos... "Margaret Bruton: Biographical Listing." Esther's wedding photos are in the Bruton Sisters Archive.

"First operation." Margaret Bruton, graph paper chronology.

He and Esther had met in Haiti... "Haiti Romance Culminates in Marriage," *Monrovia (CA) News-Post*, April 19, 1941, 3.

"Marry an engineer and see the world." Anson B. Cutts, "San Francisco Muralist Now Exhibits Skill, Imagination At Experimental Plane Riveting," *Tribune Sun* (San Diego, CA), April 19, 1944, X3.

"Looked like a Bruton..." Ruth Cravath, interview, 107.

She also put her artistic talents to good use... Stocker, interview.

"Mr. Esther Bruton." Cutts, "San Francisco Muralist Now Exhibits Skill."

The first occurred in 1940... "Artists for New Liners Chosen," *San Francisco Chronicle*, August 12, 1940, 15.

"Glazed gold and palladium [silver] leaf." "Artists Selected To Decorate Ships Being Built Here," *Daily Press* (Newport News, VA), August 11, 1940, 2. The *President Garfield* went into service in April 1941, but its life as a luxury liner was brief. Following the attack on Pearl Harbor just eight months later, it was converted into a troop transport ship and renamed the *USS Thomas Jefferson*. After seeing significant action in both World War II and the Korean War, the ship was scrapped in 1973. "Thomas Jefferson II (AP-60)," Naval History and Heritage Command, October 27, 2015, http://www.history.navy.mil/research/histories/ship-histories/danfs/t/thomas-jefferson-i.html.

"One of the country's most outstanding women artists." "Famed Woman Artist."

"Sparkling, spirited, and sensitively created." Alfred Frankenstein, "Solving Group Show Problems," *San Francisco Chronicle*, *This World*, July 26, 1942, 11.

The plant, which employed... Bob Dutton, "The Story of Kaiser Steel," August 31, 2017, YouTube, https://youtu.be/c4DHPF5qIF0.

"I usually go around looking for subjects..." "Famed Woman Artist."

These watercolors... David Allen, "These Paintings of Kaiser Steel Construction in Fontana Are a Blast," *Inland Valley Daily Bulletin* (Rancho Cucamonga, CA), August 9, 2018, http://www.dailybulletin.com/2018/08/09/these-paintings-of-kaiser-steel-construction-are-a-blast/.

"I guess I couldn't help doing them..." Julia G. Andrews, "Guild Will Honor Esther Bruton At Art Gallery Reception Today," *San Diego Union*, April 16, 1944, 7C.

"Brilliant... They have enthralled art lovers..." "Noted Artist Here Takes Pride in Her Riveting Skill," *Consolidated News*, Official Publication of Consolidated Vultee Aircraft Corporation, San Diego Division, July 13, 1944, 6.

"A revelation of the exquisite beauty..." Andrews, "Guild Will Honor Esther Bruton."

"The transformation of a pig farm..." Anson B. Cutts, "Triple-Barreled Treat Offered at San Diego Gallery of Fine Arts Display of Paintings," *Tribune Sun* (San Diego, CA), April 11, 1944, A8.

"Just as keen about her bench-riveting assignment..." Cutts, "San Francisco Muralist Now Exhibits Skill."

A photograph accompanying the article... "Noted Artist Here Takes Pride in Her Riveting Skill."

"I must say I make a better farmer..." Esther Bruton, letter to Marion Stackable, July 4, 1945, Bruton Sisters Archive.

By 1946, Esther and Carl returned... Wentworth, "Travels in the South Pacific Islands."

"Ultra-modern." Henry J. Seldis, "Esther Bruton Gilman Does Her Ancient Terrazzo Work in Modern Ojai Studio," *Santa Barbara News Press*, July 2, 1950, A10.

"A multitude of fine work..." "Artists of the Ojai," *Los Angeles Times*, June 7, 1953, 13.

Esther loved having guests at her home in Ojai... Esther Bruton, letter to Jack and Helen Stackable, [ca. March 1955], Bruton Sisters Archive; "Ojai Art Exhibit," *Press-Courier* (Oxnard, CA), April 13, 1955, 16. Esther made all the arrangements for a surprise wedding between Katy Skeele and Frode Dann, who were married in Ojai in June 1946. Esther and Carl hosted the wedding supper at their home. "More Or Less Personal," *Monrovia (CA) News-Post*, June 27, 1946, 4.

"Those who view women artists..." Janet Turpin, "Know Your Ojai Neighbor," *Ventura County Star-Free Press*, July 12, 1947, 2.

"Slight, unpretentious, energetic..." Alice Harris, "Esther Bruton Gilman Brings New Beauty To Medieval Art of Terrazzo," *Ojai Valley News*, March 1, 1951.

"Golden Gate Park and Fleishhacker Zoo in 1903," "America's most novel cocktail bar..." "Cocktails to Relax," *San Francisco Chronicle*, February 19, 1950, 5.

"But they put on a brave front..." Mildred Brown Robbins, "From Where I Sit," *San Francisco Chronicle, Women's World*, April 11, 1947, 12.

In its final week, on Christmas Eve... "Fire Closes Fairmont Bar Prematurely," *San Francisco Chronicle*, December 25, 1951, 3.

The former site of the Merry-Go-Round Bar... Dan Levy, "Fairmont's Makeover Leaves Hotel Less Fussy, More Regal," *SF Gate*, updated August 6, 2012, https://www.sfgate.com/news/article/Fairmont-s-Makeover-Leaves-Hotel-Less-Fussy-More-2812753.php.

"Master craftsman." "Wounded Learning Arts, Crafts; Need Materials," *San Francisco Examiner*, August 15, 1943, 5.

Helen and Margaret were both employed... "Margaret Bruton: Biographical Listing."

Regardless, younger family members have enjoyed... Barbara Carroll, interview by Wendy Good, August 24, 2019.

In January 1944... "The Noyes Sisters Are New Homeowners," *Monterey Peninsula Herald*, January 21, 1944, 7.

With two sisters in Monterey... Woodruff Minor, *Alameda Historical Monument Case Report: Bruton House* (Alameda: Historical Advisory Board, 2011), 13.

"WARNING–Anyone in Alameda..." Classified advertising section, *Oakland Tribune*, May 10, 1944, 15.

After the war, Helen returned to the home... Carroll, interview, May 19, 2019.

In 1947, Helen's studio was built... Esther Bruton, graph paper chronology, [ca. 1981], Bruton Sisters Archive.

The Brutons owned a large piece of land... "First Presbyterian Church Site Acquired," *Monterey Peninsula Herald*, April 11, 1959, 6. Helen's studio, which had "a cantaloupe-colored exterior highlighted by gold and avocado trim" remained nearby. Steve Hauk, "Artists on the Mesa, 1826-1960," in *The Monterey Mesa: Oldest Neighborhood in California*, ed. Julianne Burton-Carvajal (Monterey: City of Monterey, 2002), 33.

Helen thought the church and its congregation... Carroll, interview, August 24, 2019. Helen's Mesa studio was demolished in 1999. Hauk, "Artists on the Mesa," 33.

Tensions rose when local artists... Sara Rubin, "A Century After Monterey Bought It, Fisherman's Wharf Comes Full Circle," *Monterey County Weekly*, October 3, 2018, http://www.montereycountyweekly.com/news/831_tales/a-century-after-monterey-bought-it-fisherman-s-wharf-comes/article_0d4ca8d4-2b91-11e3-944c-0019bb30f31a.html.

"Whether one resents it..." "News Comments," *Monterey Peninsula Herald*, January 16, 1946, 1.

"It was the artists long ago..." Helen Bruton, letter to the editor, "Letter Box," *Monterey Peninsula Herald*, January 18, 1946, 2.

"It is my personal opinion..." Helen refers to an event in September 1924, when the Associated Oil Company tanks near the Presidio were struck by lightning and caught fire. Pat Hathaway, "Oil Fire, Monterey, California, September 14, 1924," California Views: The Pat Hathaway Photo Collection, accessed December 21, 2020, http://www.caviews.com/Oil.html.

"It's artistic... It's unique..." Angelo's advertisement, *Monterey Peninsula Herald*, February 28, 1946, 14.

"Inlaid table and mobile birds." "Bruton Sisters Collaborate in Murals and Other Fields of Art," *Monterey Peninsula Herald*, November 1, 1946, 7.

"Attractive use of brilliantly colored clay animals against a gold backdrop." "Palace Stationery Window Wins Yule Display Contest," *Monterey Peninsula Herald*, December 24, 1946, 2. The judges of the competition were the Brutons' friends Myron Oliver and Bruce Ariss.

In 1947, Helen was paid $2,800... John W. Saunders, letter to Helen Bruton, February 20, 1947, Bruton Sisters Archive; Michael L. Grace, "Matson Line's SS Lurline 'Was' Hawaii in the 1950s," Cruiseline History, November 11, 2014, http://www.cruiselinehistory.com/the-ss-lurline-was-hawaii/.

"The most challenging medium available, both for color and texture." Photo caption, *Monterey Peninsula Herald*, Art Edition, October 31, 1947, 12.

"Sparkling colors..." "Local Artist Completes Huge Mosaic Mural," *Monterey Peninsula Herald*, January 14, 1948, 12.

"Marge had her easel set up..." Helen Bruton, letter to Ina Perham Story, January 27, 1932, Perham Private Collection.

Despite the prizes she had won... Carroll, interview, May 19, 2019.

"'Samples' of what could be done to a wall..." "Mural Conceptualism Show Offers Suggestions," *Oakland Tribune*, November 21, 1937, n.p.

"Many mosaics, most of them bad..." Alfred Frankenstein, "Academy Oils at Legion Palace," *San Francisco Chronicle*, This World, November 21, 1937, 15.

"A turning point..." "Margaret Bruton: Biographical Listing."

"So radical that it must give pause..." "Women Artists Go Modern in Show," *Oakland Tribune*, November 12, 1939, B9.

"Seeking mediums suitable for architectural work." Wentworth, "Travels in the South Pacific Islands."

Esther exhibited her first terrazzo piece... Esther's work, a terrazzo coffee stand, was a preview of the technique she would master in the 1940s: "[T]he top of the table [is] fascinating. The design is modern, shot with brass, copper, and Monel metal wires and strips to separate the colors." "Berlandina Water Colors Shown in S.F.," *Oakland Tribune*, April 15, 1934, 12S.

One of her first attempts was a terrazzo dog... Wentworth, "Travels in the South Pacific Islands."

"After making her design, she uses..." "Esther Bruton Gilman Prepares Her Terrazzo Pieces for Exhibit in S.F.," *The Ojai* (CA), August 19, 1949, 2.

"Chicken scratch, Coca Cola bottles..." "County Party Line," *Ventura County Star-Free Press*, September 6, 1952, 5.

"We're working completely in the dark..." Wentworth, "Travels in the South Pacific Islands."

"Without my husband's help..." "Esther Bruton Gilman Does Her Ancient Terrazzo Work in Modern Ojai Studio," *Santa Barbara News-Press*, July 2, 1950, A10.

They were more than willing to work... Helen Bruton, letter to Graham Miller, [ca. May 1956], Bruton Sisters Archive.

Yet, over time, the work took its toll... Helen Bruton, letter to Esther Bruton, [ca. 1950s] Bruton Sisters Archive.

"Nothing short of a sledgehammer..." Alfred Frankenstein, "Around the Local Art Galleries," *San Francisco Chronicle, This World*, September 18, 1949, 24.

"One is apt to find all sorts of things..." Puccinelli, "The Brutons and How They Grew," 41.

"Terrazzo tables have drawn the attention..." "Local Artists Exhibit Work," *Monterey Peninsula Herald*, November 23, 1954, 16.

From 1927 to 1947... "Frances Adler Elkins (1888-1953)," Monterey State Historic Park, sign posted at Stevenson House.

Through this project, Elkins gave Margaret... Photo caption, *Monterey Peninsula Herald*, Art Edition, October 31, 1947, 12.

The Sonoma County house's grounds... The Donnells commissioned... Kaplan, *California Design*, 47, 51.

"Did too many," "put a terrible lot..." "was so pleased to think..." Helen Bruton and Margaret Bruton, interview, 1964.

In 1948, she received the Decorate Arts Award... H.L. Dungan, "U.C. Professor Wins Medal in National Art Contest," *Oakland Tribune*, November 14, 1948, C11.

In the same show and competition... Photo caption, *San Francisco Chronicle*, December 3, 1950, 3L.

"Since any consideration of mosaics brought up..." "Mosaics... and Their Use in Western Homes and Gardens," 38.

In January 1949, Margaret wrote... Margaret Bruton, letter to Richard Freeman, January 18, 1949, Bruton Sisters, Artist Files Collection, SFMOMA Library.

"I have admired your work greatly..." Richard Freeman, letter to Margaret Bruton, February 16, 1949, Bruton Sisters, Artist Files Collection, SFMOMA Library.

"Unfortunately, by the time Margaret received Freeman's response... Margaret Bruton, letter to Richard Freeman, February 18, 1949, Bruton Sisters, Artist Files Collection, SFMOMA Library.

"I am more sorry than I can tell you..." Richard Freeman, letter to Margaret Bruton, February 24, 1949, Bruton Sisters, Artist Files Collection, SFMOMA Library.

"For a long time the possibilities of using marble..." Esther, Margaret, and Helen *Bruton: Exhibition of Mosaics*. [San Francisco: Gump's Gallery, 1949].

"Since they are all sisters, all blondes..." Puccinelli, "The Brutons and How They Grew," 18.

"Would be more or less in charge..." "We wouldn't criticize it..." Helen Bruton and Margaret Bruton, interview 1975, video 1.

"Somewhat modern, somewhat primitive, but wholly delightful." Harris, "Esther Bruton Gilman Brings New Beauty."

The Hunt was purchased by Helen Woodring... Paul C. Faria, letter to Mrs. Harry Woodring, November 10, 1953, Invaluable (online auction record), accessed December 22, 2020, http://www.invaluable.com/auction-lot/esther-bruton-american-1896-1992-inlaid-terrazo-m-1491-c-27240c0b88#. Esther's fireplace surround owned by the Woodrings eventually made its way to Dallas, where it was purchased by a New York designer in 2019. Wendy Goodman, "Magical Thinking at the Park Avenue Armory," Curbed, October 9, 2020, https://www.curbed.com/2020/10/salon-art-design-park-avenue-armory.html.

"Polished, elegant, well-wrought," "striking individuality, ingenuity and charm." H.L. Dungan, "Bruton Sisters Hold Mosaics Exhibition," *Oakland Tribune*, September 18, 1949, 10C; Alexander Fried, "Bruton Sisters' Mosaics Carry Individual Charm," *San Francisco Examiner*, September 18, 1949, n.p.

"There is nothing piddling or miniature..." Frankenstein, "Around the Local Art Galleries."

"Brilliantly fine and delicate, and rich in decorative values." "Victorian coarseness or heaviness," "primitive rigidity." Fried, "Bruton Sisters' Mosaics Carry Individual Charm."

"Monotonous rows of pictures..." Louisa Jenkins, "Bruton Sisters Exhibit Mosaics and Terrazzo," *Monterey Peninsula Herald*, October 4, 1949, 7.

"The forties, fifties, and sixties..." Rubenstein, *American Women Artists*, 268.

"An all-male, all-white enclave..." Jeanne Willette, "Post-War Culture in America," Art History Unstuffed, January 21, 2012, http://arthistoryunstuffed.com/post-war-culture-in-america/; Landauer, "Searching for Selfhood," 37.

"Their work was marginalized..." Daniela Salvioni, "Introduction: Art in Context," in Diana Burgess Fuller and Daniela Salvioni, eds., *Art, Women, California 1950-2000: Parallels and Intersections* (Berkeley: University of California Press, 2002), 4.

"They got to do things, whatever they wanted to do..." Carroll, interview, May 19, 2019.

CHAPTER TEN

The Portland Art Museum and the Walker Museum of Art... "C.S. Price," Portland Art Museum, accessed January 5, 2021, http://portlandartmuseum.us/mwebcgi/mweb.exe?request=record;id=5643;type=701.

"A memorial exhibition..." Esther Bruton, letter to Jack Stackable, February 21, [1951], Bruton Sisters Archive.

"We have to stick pretty close..." Margaret Bruton, letter to Helen Stackable, July 21, 1955, Bruton Sisters Archive.

"The complications of Mama..." Margaret Bruton, letter to Jack and Helen Stackable, December 11, 1955, Bruton Sisters Archive.

A few years later, in January 1959, Esther's husband passed away. California Death Index, 1940-1997, Family Search, accessed December 22, 2020, https://search.ancestrylibrary.com/cgi-bin/sse.dll?indiv=1&dbid=5180&h=2685653&tid=&pid=&queryId=2981a1a57dd80d52361063ec556a86c8&usePUB=true&_phsrc=HnX1&_phstart=successSource.

"We just keep inchin' along..." Alfred Frankenstein, "Artist Tony Duquette Works With Everything from Beads to Bones," *San Francisco Chronicle, This World*, September 21, 1952, 30.

"Particularly because Helen Bruton's mosaics now strike..." Alexander Fried, "Three Bruton Sisters Hold Unusual Decorative Exhibit," *San Francisco Examiner, Pictorial Review*, September 28, 1952, 19.

"Humor and brilliance..." Frankenstein, "Artist Tony Duquette Works With Everything from Beads to Bones."

In 1952, she was hired to decorate Cafe Drake... Advertisement for the re-opening of Café Drake, *San Francisco Examiner*, March 20, 1952, 13.

"Drake touched during pursuit of the gold-laden manila galleons." "The San Francisco Dining Out Directory," *San Francisco Chronicle, Gourmet Guide*, May 17, 1954, 32.

"The sketches do not exactly reflect what we had in mind." Maynard Woodard, letter to Helen Bruton, August 19, 1952, Bruton Sisters Archive.

"Rich in warm hues of green and yellowish b rown..." "Bruton Sisters Add Luster to Monterey Name," *Monterey Peninsula Herald*, November 2, 1953, A15.

"Designed by the internationally famous muralist Margaret Bruton..." Advertising supplement, *Los Angeles Times*, September 22, 1953.

In 2021, the current owners of the building... Sauli Danpour, email to Wendy Good, January 12, 2021.

Her coffee tables appeared in countless upscale homes... Grace Oddie, "House Tour of an Old Home Made New," *San Francisco Chronicle*, April 16, 1950, 14S.

Having come to Carmel to assist with the construction... Mark Mills obituary, *Monterey County Herald*, June 10, 2007, http://newsbank.com.

The matchmaking dinner proved successful... Barbara Mills, telephone interview by Wendy Good, March 28, 2020.

"Backsliding Episcopalians." "Buddhas of the Three Sisters," *San Francisco Chronicle*, September 29, 1963, 30.

"Skillfully fashioned and humorous glass mosaic." "Abel Warshawsky Portrait of Martin Flavin Now on Exhibit," *Monterey Peninsula Herald*, July 1, 1952, 2.

In November 1952, her mosaic of a nativity scene... "Bruton Sisters Add Luster." This mosaic also goes by the name *Nativity*.

Helen later donated the piece... "Youth Pageant at St. James'," *Monterey Peninsula Herald*, December 22, 1956, 4. Over time, the history of the piece was lost and, understandably, the congregation believed it to be the work of mosaicist Louisa Jenkins. The author corrected this error in 2019 and wrote a new label for the piece.

Her terrazzo Twelfth Station of the Cross... Liturgical and Religious Arts Lenten Season Dallas –1955, 9.

In 1953, Esther's mosaic Ghost Tree... "Prizewinner," *Monterey Peninsula Herald*, November 18, 1953, 16. Helen Bruton also made a mosaic called *Ghost Tree*. "Helen Bruton Mosaics" (typescript page), Bruton Sisters Archive.

"By far the most successful..." Maggie Murchison, letter to Helen Bruton, [ca. 1952], Bruton Sisters Archive.

Both Helen and Esther had their work selected... Monica Michelle Penick, "Pace Setter Houses: Livable Modernism in Post-War America," Thesis, University of Texas at Austin, December 2007, https://repositories.lib.utexas.edu/handle/2152/3628.

The following year, it was exhibited at the Dallas Museum of Art... "New Laurels Won by That Talented Trio of Brutons," *Monterey Peninsula Herald*, Art Edition, October 29, 1955, 26.

Two years later, one of Esther's terrazzo murals... "Art News," *Monterey Peninsula Herald*, June 27, 1956, 19.

A mosaic tabletop by Helen... "Biggest Style News: Glitter, Glitter, Everywhere," *House Beautiful*, October 1953, 179.

"Pebble mosaics appeal anew..." Helen Bruton, "How to Make Pebble Mosaics," *House Beautiful*, June 1954, 70.

The Brutons' friend Ruth Cravath made a sculpture of the school's namesake, Thomas Starr King. "Entertainment Planned for Visiting Artists," *San Francisco Examiner*, March 22, 1956, 20.

"Striking decorate design..." "New Laurels Won."

The Brutons had several beloved pets... Carroll, interview, May 19, 2019.

"Made a vigorous defense of homeless dogs..." "Helen Bruton Off To New York."

She was also concerned about preserving wildlife... Helen's papers include newsletters from animal rights organizations, including the SPCA, the Otter Raft, and Howl.

"Did you see this extraordinary picture..." Helen Bruton, letter to Helen and Jack Stackable, Bruton Sisters Archive. This letter might have been written in 1959, when a monkey first survived a trip into space.

Helen's papers include several large posters... These posters are in the Bruton Sisters Archive.

Helen was good friends with Claude... Mills, interview.

Lady Kinnoull's financial assistance... "Carmel Countess Dies at Age 80," *Carmel Pine Cone*, July 25, 1985, 23; "Our History," SPCA Monterey County, accessed December 22, 2020, https://www.spcamc.org/about/about.html.

Helen designed and executed a large mosaic... The mosaic is currently located inside the SPCA building. Beth Brookhouser, email to Wendy Good, July 29, 2020.

"You, dear Miss Bruton..." SPCA, Christmas card to Helen Bruton, n.d., Bruton Sisters Archive.

Helen remained a generous supporter... Carroll, interview, May 19, 2019.

"Mosaic intarsia." Helen Bruton, letter to James Watrous, January 14, 1957, Bruton Sisters Archive.

"Floating museums of contemporary fine and applied arts." Dorothy Walker, "2 New Liners," *San Francisco News*, September 15, 1956, 6.

Helen was hired to make mosaic tabletops for the "Sky Level"... Art of the Pacific in the Princess Kaiulani (brochure), Matson Company, June 1955.

And Esther was hired to make two murals... "New Laurels Won."

"I have done so many bars that one would think they were my specialty." Turpin, "Know Your Ojai Valley Neighbor." Helen also designed cocktail napkins and coasters for the hotel. Purchase order, Matson Navigation Company, July 5, 1955, Bruton Sisters Archive.

"Mrs. Gilman has worked with care..." Drue Lytle, "Kaiulani Hotel Murals Given Send-Off in Ojai," *Honolulu Advertiser*, May 11, 1955, A8.

Despite her careful research, Esther didn't want to make a mistake... Betty Wentworth, "Betty Wentworth Reporting," *Ventura County Star-Free Press*, April 1, 1955, 7.

She attached fiberboard cutouts... Audrey Hoyt, "Carved Mural by Esther Gilman to Decorate New Hawaiian Hotel," *The Ojai*, April 7, 1955, Sec. 3, 1.

"She hoped aloud that the usual gloomy bar lightning would be spared her masterpieces." Lytle, "Kaiulani Hotel Murals Given Send-Off in Ojai." It seems unlikely that Esther herself would have referred to these works as her "masterpieces."

By all accounts, the works were stunning. Margaret Bruton, letter to Helen Stackable, July 21, 1955, Bruton Sisters Archive.

"The ancient craft ways of the Polynesians." "Kahili Room is Exotic in Its Decor," *Honolulu Star Bulletin*, June 11, 1955, 30.

This sum suggests that their work... Helen Bruton, letter to Graham Miller, [ca. May 1956], Bruton Sisters Archive.

"Cat's eyes." SS Mariposa SS Monterey, [San Francisco: Matson Navigation Company, ca. 1956]; "Matson Liners Are Setting for Works by Local Artists," *Monterey Peninsula Herald*, Art Edition, November 3, 1956, p A7.

"Made of walnut, laminated in one section..." Lois Stewart, "Air Lanes – Sea Lanes," *Honolulu Advertiser*, October 27, 1956, A8.

"Pale pinks, purples, blues..." Marjorie Trumbull, "The Mariposa's Interior Is a Touch of Hawaii," *San Francisco Chronicle*, October 26, 1956, 25.

"One of the high points... with many compliments for the gorgeous inlaid murals." Roby Gemmell, "Bib 'n' Tucker," *The Press Democrat* (Santa Rosa, CA), October 28, 1956, 2B.

"The most beautiful of the rooms..." Blanche Hixson Smith, "Matson Line's Magnificent Mariposa Is Ship of Rare Beauty and Luxury," *Meriden (CT) Record*, December 1, 1956, 6.

"Monumental altar screen of mosaic intarsia." "Matson Liners Are Setting for Works by Local Artists."

Helen created the works in her Monterey studio... Frank Slattery, "New St. Joseph's College Chapel Abounds in Religious Art," *The Monitor* (San Francisco), April 27, 1956.

The work as a whole, which she called Variations on a Theme... "Helen Bruton Mosaics in Hertz Memorial Hall," *Monterey Peninsula Herald, Art Edition*, November 1, 1958, A5.

The monument was to honor the more than 17,000 American soldiers... "Battle Memorial for Hawaii Said in Thought Stage," *Honolulu Star-Bulletin*, February 19, 1954, 3.

"Italian marble memorial." "G.I. Memorial Plan Drafted by S.F. Man," *San Francisco Examiner*, April 4, 1954, 16; "U.S. Military Cemetery is Dedicated," *Wilkes Barre (PA) Times Leader*, December 8. 1960, 13.

"She's the only one I know of that can do exactly what we have in mind." "G.I. Memorial Plan Drafted by S.F. Man."

"I had done quite a lot of work..." As maps were incredibly complex and exact... "Had to take [the government-provided] drawings..." Helen Bruton and Margaret Bruton, interview, 1975, video 2.

These small sample pieces reveal her early attempts... These test pieces reside in private collections.

When the preliminary work was done... Helen Bruton and Margaret Bruton, interview, 1975, video 2.

"A truly monumental art project is underway in Monterey." "Monumental Art Project by Artist Sisters," *Monterey Peninsula Herald*, Oct 31, 1959, A11.

"Was really simpler..." Helen Bruton and Margaret Bruton, interview, 1975, video 1.

They did make their share of mistakes... Stocker, interview.

"They'd go over it all with a fine-tooth comb..." "I just can't get over how fortunate I was..." Helen Bruton and Margaret Bruton, interview, 1975, video 2.

It wasn't until the following year that Margaret and Esther... "Margaret Bruton: Biographical Listing."

"I saw it soon after it was put up..." Helen Bruton and Margaret Bruton, interview, 1975, video 2.

"Seeing the Memorial itself..." Esther Bruton, letter to Helen and Jack Stackable, January 26, 1973, Bruton Sisters Archive. Seven years after the dedication of the Manila American Monument and Cemetery, on October 24, 1967, Gardner Dailey committed suicide by jumping from the Golden Gate Bridge. Although the seventy-two-year-old Dailey was in poor health, his wife was stunned by his suicide. Dailey was an internationally known architect at the time, and his death was widely covered in newspapers across the nation. "Architect Dailey is Bridge Suicide," *Oakland Tribune*, October 25, 1967, 22. Margaret made a donation in Dailey's memory to the Audubon Canyon Ranch, a nature preserve in Marin County. *The Gull*, Marin Audubon Society, January 1968, 5.

"It just threw us all off..." Helen Bruton and Margaret Bruton, interview, 1975, video 2.

CHAPTER ELEVEN

This incredible community effort took more than eleven years to complete. Additional information about the history of Buddha's Universal Church is available on their website, https://www.bucsf.com/history/.

"By the time the church was completed..." "Buddhist Church Dedication Slated," *Oakland Tribune*, February 28, 1963, 30.

"We were thrilled at the opportunity..." "California Artists Make Buddha Mosaics for San Francisco Church," Buddha's Universal Church, press release, October 1963, Bruton Sisters Archive.

"These people have the faith that moves mountains." "Buddhas of the Three Sisters," *San Francisco Chronicle*, September 29, 1963, 30.

The sisters began gathering ideas... "3 Sisters Build Images for Church," *Oakland Tribune*, September 25, 1953, 14D.

They carefully studied the Buddha imagery... "California Artists Make Buddha Mosaics."

"The thoughts that come out of the heart..." The extended fingers represent the mind... The right hand is help palm upward... Buddha's Universal Church, press release, [ca. September 1963], Bruton Sisters Archive.

"Bruton Buddhas." "Buddhas of the Three Sisters"; Irene Alexander, "Monterey Sisters Do Mosaics," *Monterey Peninsula Herald*, May 22, 1963, 10.

"Vivacious, humorous and outspoken," "tall, slender blondes..." "Buddhas of the Three Sisters"; Mildred Schroeder, "A Trio of Image Makers Decorates Buddhist Church," *San Francisco Examiner*, September 25, 1963, 24.

A 1963 photograph of the Brutons... Schroeder, "A Trio of Image Makers Decorates Buddha's Church."

According to family members, they preferred not to make eye contact with photographers. Carroll, interview, May 19, 2019.

In 1967, Margaret exhibited her Virginia City paintings... "Margaret Bruton Paintings Shown in Carmel Valley," *Monterey Peninsula Herald*, September 29, 1967, 13; Margot Hyatt, "Several Generations Spanned in Art Shows," *Monterey Peninsula Herald*, April 27, 1970, 5.

In December 1966, the Brutons held... Today the space is known as the Scholze Park Community Center.

It also included photographs of many works that no longer survive... Irene Alexander, "Bruton Sisters Works Shown," *Monterey Peninsula Herald*, December 14, 1966, 41.

Eventually, Margaret decided to stop making... Helen Bruton and Margaret Bruton, interview, 1964.

"Astonishing..." "A forward-thinking attitude toward her work..." Gay Weaver, "P.G. Enjoying Mosaic Display," *Monterey Peninsula Herald*, November 25, 1971, 35.

"Being very aware during this atomic era..." Margaret Bruton, handwritten personal statement, [ca. 1971], Bruton Sisters Archive. It is likely that Margaret prepared this statement in connection with her "Mineral Mosaics" exhibition.

"A subject of community controversy." "Official Symbol," Monterey Peninsula Herald, May 29, 1968, 9.

She called it a "Depression Show"... Irene Lagorio, "American Watercolor Society Paintings Displayed at Museum," *Monterey Peninsula Herald*, January 19, 1975, 5C.

Also on the list were local friends Dick Bird... Both Barbara Mills and Barbara Carroll mentioned that Dick Bird, an architect, was a close friend of the Brutons. Mills, interview; Carroll, interview, May 19, 2019.

"Selling out." Carroll, interview, August 24, 2019. In Adams' defense, he felt he was doing a good deed by promoting the company's "Drive a Datsun, Plant a Tree" program; for every test drive, Datsun donated money to the United States Forest Service to plant a tree in a national forest. Ansel Adams and Mary Street Alinder, *Ansel Adams: An Autobiography* (Boston: Little Brown, 1985), 178.

Perhaps in reaction to the good-natured ribbing... Adams, *Ansel Adams*, 361.

"Fashion in art seems to carry..." Helen Bruton and Margaret Bruton, interview, 1964.

"You expect to be considered alive, you've got to be producing all the time." Helen Bruton and Margaret Bruton, interview, 1975, video 2. Helen is quoting Margaret in this part of the interview.

"When she wish[ed] to express an idea." Margaret Bruton, handwritten personal statement; "Margaret Bruton: Biographical Listing."

"Still suffering from severe constipation of the brain..." Helen Bruton, letter to Kirsten Kjaer, October 29, 1968, Bruton Sisters Archive.

"What has happened to... Marian Simpson, Joseph Sheridan, the Bruton sisters?..." Alfred Frankenstein, "A History of Photography," *San Francisco Chronicle*, November 19, 1970, 48.

"Stir nostalgia." Alfred Frankenstein, "New Deal Art on Exhibition," *San Francisco Chronicle*, February 22, 1976, 31.

In their collective opinion, whatever notoriety they had achieved... Carroll, interview, May 19, 2019.

"There are so many artists now..." Helen Bruton and Margaret Bruton, interview, 1975, video 2.

"We do miss the contact with people who are thinking..." Helen Bruton and Margaret Bruton, interview, 1964.

As there were rarely more than a dozen... Michael L. Grace, "Freighter Travel in the 1950s and 1960s," Cruise Line History, March 24, 2013, http://www.cruiselinehistory.com/freighter-travel-in-the-1950s-and-1960s/.

The sisters stopped traveling on freighters only... Carroll, interview, May 19, 2019.

The sisters also loved to camp... Helen Bruton, graph paper chronology.

"Paddy Wagon II." The Brutons' friend Cecilia Graham owned "Paddy Wagon I." Esther Bruton, letter to Helen Stackable, [n.d.], Bruton Sisters Archive.

"Imogen is a wonder..." Margaret Bruton, letter to Helen Stackable, November 17, 1975, Bruton Sisters Archive.

"I have so much to do..." Imogen Cunningham, letter to Margaret and Helen Bruton, [ca. 1974], Imogen Cunningham Papers, 1903–1991, Archives of American Art, Smithsonian Institution.

"My life is a frenzy..." Imogen Cunningham, letter to Margaret Bruton, February 11, 1972, Imogen Cunningham Papers.

The Brutons visited her there, and Cunningham would... Carroll, interview, May 19, 2019; Margaret Bruton, letter to Helen Stackable, February 4, 1974, Bruton Sisters Archive.

"IMOGEN! You really are a double-barreled rascal..." Helen Bruton, letter to Imogen Cunningham, April 9, 1970, Imogen Cunningham Papers.

"Wish I did know better what I wanted to do—in the art line." Helen Bruton, letter to Imogen Cunningham, January 22, 1971, Imogen Cunningham Papers.

"You may easily get better [photographs]..." Imogen Cunningham, letter to Helen Bruton, June 18, 1971, Imogen Cunningham Papers.

"Did not describe the parties of old..." Catherine Healy, "Imogen Cunningham Has 90th birthday at Workshop," *Carmel Pine Cone*, April 19, 1973, 28.

"Cunningham was close to all three Bruton sisters..." Imogen Cunningham, letter to Esther Bruton, January 17, 1974, Imogen Cunningham Papers.

"With all the work you have to do..." Esther Bruton, letter to Imogen Cunningham, September 26, [ca. 1974], Imogen Cunningham Papers.

"I cherish, as one of my happiest times..." Esther Bruton, letter to Helen Stackable, May 7, 1977, Bruton Sisters Archive.

"They were bigger than life..." Carroll, written statement, September 26, 2020.

"We'd go to the tidepools..." "They were so open and interested..." Whereas many people their age... Carroll, interview, May 19, 2019.

"There are young people of all varieties on the road..." Margaret Bruton, letter to Helen Stackable, March 23, 1969, Bruton Sisters Archive.

Helen and Esther attended a party celebrating the reopening... Kate Berenson, letter to Esther Bruton, February 2, 1982, Bruton Sisters Archive.

The sparking Art Deco–style Cirque Room... As of this writing, the Cirque Room is open for private functions. It has also been used as a cocktail lounge during the holiday season.

By 1991, these savvy collectors had acquired... Michael Taylor, "Walter Nelson-Rees, UC Berkeley Geneticist, Dies," SF Gate, January 28, 2009, https://www.sfgate.com/bayarea/article/Walter-Nelson-Rees-UC-Berkeley-geneticist-dies-3253182.php.

At Nelson-Rees's request, Margaret compiled a list... These lists are in the Bruton Sisters Archive.

"Of course I understand that transactions..." Walter Nelson-Rees, letter to Margaret Bruton, May 20, 1982, Bruton Sisters Archive.

"You will have to forgive me..." Helen Bruton, letter to Walter Nelson-Rees and James Coran, June 8, 1982, Bruton Sisters Archive.

She eventually came up with a list and prices... Purchase receipt, July 13, 1982, Bruton Sisters Archive; Hauk, "Artists on the Mesa," 35.

"Were very appreciative of our purchases..." "We felt that the sisters had been beguiled." Barbara Carroll, email to Wendy Good, September 17, 2020.

Fortunately, Nelson-Rees and Coran had published a catalog... James L. Coran and Walter A. Nelson-Rees, *If Pictures Could Talk: Stories About California Paintings in Our Collection* (Oakland: WIM, 1989).

Early in 1983, Esther sold her house in Ojai... Margaret Bruton, letter to Helen Stackable, February 1, 1983, Bruton Sisters Archive.

Margaret was having numerous health problems... Margaret Bruton, death certificate, August 31, 1983, certificate no. 2700-1286, Monterey County Recorder's Office, Monterey, California, copy in possession of author.

"Altho' nothing was found in my tests..." Margaret Bruton, letter to Helen Stackable, February 1, 1983, Bruton Sisters Archive.

Margaret died six months later... For a while, Helen kept Margaret's ashes on a shelf in her studio. Barbara Carroll, email to Wendy Good, June 10, 2020.

According to Helen, they were traveling through Greenfield... The Brutons' cousin Peggy Stackable recorded the details of this accident in her notebook on December 4, 1983.

"To think of how well you got off..." Walter Nelson-Rees, letter to Esther Bruton, December 4, 1983, Bruton Sisters Archive.

At around the same time, Esther gifted two paintings... Walter Nelson-Rees, letter to Esther Bruton, December 4, 1983, Bruton Sisters Archive.

Eighty-seven-year-old Helen had a heart attack and died at her home in Monterey. Helen Bell Bruton, death certificate, November 20,1985, certificate no. 2700-001853, Monterey County Recorder's Office, Monterey, California, copy in possession of author.

By this time, Esther was suffering from Alzheimer's disease... Esther Bruton Gilman, death certificate, September 1, 1992, certificate no. 39227-001315, Monterey County Recorder's Office, Monterey, California, copy in possession of author.

"[Esther is] well..." Barbara Mills, letter to Helen Stackable, April 6, 1987, Bruton Sisters Archive.

"In about one day or two flat." Helen Bruton and Margaret Bruton, interview, 1975, video 1.

A pass over the backyard with a metal detector... Del Piero, "Monterey Modernism."

The Del Pieros salvaged what they could... The Del Pieros incorporated the mosaic number into a low stone wall on the Cass Street side of the property.

After Margaret died, Helen and Esther hoped to mark... Carroll, email, June 10, 2020.

EPILOGUE
The Indian coastal city of Alang... "5 Killed in Alang Port Shipbreaking Yard Blast in Gujarat," *Biharprabha*, June 28, 2014, http://news.biharprabha.com/2014/06/5-killed-in-alang-port-shipbreaking-yard-blast-in-gujarat/.

In November 2006, after decades of service... Reuben Goossens, "SS Monterey," SS Maritime, accessed December 28, 2020, http://ssmaritime.com/matson-msc-monterey.htm.

This former jewel of the Matson Line... "SS Mariposa (II)," Great Ships, accessed December 28, 2020, http://greatships.net/mariposa2.

"Achieved national and international fame..." Landauer, "Searching for Selfhood," 10.

"Artistically insignificant." Connie W. Kieffer, "New Deal Murals: A Legacy for Today's Public Art and Art Education," *Art Education*, March 2000, 40–45.

"Denigrated and ignored..." Rubenstein, *American Women Artists*, 215.

"Sort of diffident about it." Helen Bruton and Margaret Bruton, interview, 1975, video 2.

"Please forgive me for seeming so uncooperative..." Helen Bruton, letter to Mrs. Robert E. Matson, December 14, 1956, Bruton Sisters Archive.

"Would make her seem too important." "They showed us [their works]..." Carroll, interview, May 19, 2019.

"We didn't have any ambition to be in Who's Who..." Helen Bruton and Margaret Bruton, interview, 1975, video 2.

In 1975, Helen was contacted by Phil Kovinick... Phil Kovnick and Marian Yoshiki-Kovinick, *An Encyclopedia of Women Artists of the American West*. (Austin: University of Texas Press, 1998).

"We have all of us been careless..." Helen Bruton, letter to Phil Kovinick, January 7, 1976, Bruton Sisters Archive.

A few years later, while preparing her landmark work... Charlotte Streifer Rubenstein, *American Women Artists from Early Indian Times to the Present* (Boston: G.K. Hall & Company, 1982).

"I can now say without embarrassment, 'yes, we were artists.'" Helen Bruton, letter to Charlotte Rubenstein, February 15, 1980, Bruton Sisters Archive.

"Sensitivity and tremendous will-power..." Munro, *Originals*, 121.

"What little I have of remaining relics..." Helen Bruton, letter to Steven Gelber, September 5, 1974, Bruton Sisters Archive.

Eventually, Margaret and Helen allowed Gelber to videotape the interview... Unfortunately, Esther was living in Ojai at the time and was unable to participate in either interview.

"Was terrible—she was really awful..." Helen Bruton and Margaret Bruton, interview, 1975, video 2.

"In spite of a long, eventful past..." Jerram, "The Bruton Sisters Look Back."

"I search for their work [and try]..." Accession records, Institute and Museum of California Art at the University of California, Irvine.

"A large part of my collection is work..." Diane Dorrans Saeks, "Back to the 50s," *San Francisco Chronicle*, Home Section, October 26, 1994, 6.

Maurine St. Gaudens's four-volume work... Maurine St. Gaudens, *Emerging from the Shadows: A Survey of Women Artists Working in California, 1860–1960*, Volume 1 (Atglen, PA: Schiffer Publishing Ltd., 2015).

The Brutons' work has appeared in traveling exhibitions... Works by the Bruton sisters were in the following exhibitions: *California Design, 1930–1965: Living in a Modern Way*, Los Angeles Museum of Art, October 1, 2011 – March 25, 2012; *California's Designing Women, 1896-1986*, at the Autry Museum of the American West, August 10, 2012 – January 6, 2013; and *Something Revealed; California Women Artists Emerge, 1860-1960*, Pasadena Museum of History, September 29, 2018 - April 13, 2019.

"Eight standouts." Nicole Anderson, "8 Salon Art + Design Standouts," *Architectural Digest*, November 16, 2019, http://www.architecturaldigest.com/story/8-salon-art-design-2019-standouts.

Adams, Ansel and Mary Street Alinder. *Ansel Adams: An Autobiography*. Boston: Little Brown, 1985.

Adams, Katherine H., and Michael L. Keene. *Women, Art and the New Deal*. Jefferson, NC: McFarland, 2016.

Art of the Pacific in the Princess Kaiulani. San Francisco: Matson Navigation Company, 1955.

Baca, Elmo. *Mabel's Santa Fe and Taos: Bohemian Legends, 1900–1950*. Salt Lake City: Gibbs-Smith, 2000.

Benét, James. *A Guide to San Francisco and the Bay Region*. New York: Random House, 1966.

"Biggest Style News: Glitter, Glitter, Everywhere." *House Beautiful*, October 1953, 179.

Boas, Nancy. *David Park: A Painter's Life*. Berkeley: University of California Press, 2012.

———. *The Society of Six: California Colorists*. San Francisco: Bedford Arts, 1988.

Bruton, Helen. "How to Make Pebble Mosaics." *House Beautiful*, July 1954, 70.

———. "Mosaic as a Modern Expression." *San Francisco Art Association Bulletin*, December 1936, 4.

Burton-Carvajal, Julianne. "Gus and the Gang: Communities of Artists and the Career of August Gay (1890–1948)." *Noticias de Monterey* 54, no. 3 (Summer 2005).

Campus Public Art + Architecture Map. Self-guided tour pamphlet. Berkeley: University of California 2020. https://artsdesign. berkeley.edu/sites/default/files/2020-08/FINAL_ BerkTourBookSpread.pdf.

Cook, Frances Price, and Patrick J. Leach, ed. *The Life and Art of C.S. Price: In Pursuit of the One Big Thing*. North Charleston, SC: CreateSpace, 2012. Kindle.

Coran, James L., and Walter A. Nelson-Rees. *If Pictures Could Talk: Stories About California Paintings in Our Collection*. Oakland: WIM, 1989.

Dawdy, Doris Ostrander. *Artists of the American West: A Biographical Dictionary*. Chicago: The Swallow Press, 1974.

Del Piero, Eric, and Teresa Del Piero. "Monterey Modernism." Monterey Museum of Art. May 5, 2012. http://www.youtube. com/watch?v=-rg7mklLZ4s.

Edwards, Robert W. *Jennie V. Cannon: The Untold History of the Carmel and Berkeley Art Colonies, Vol. One*. Oakland: East Bay Heritage Project, 2012.

Esther, Margaret, and Helen Bruton: Exhibition of Mosaics. San Francisco: Gump's Gallery, 1949.

Federal Emergency Management Agency. *The East Bay Hills Fire: Oakland-Berkeley California*. U.S. Fire Administration Technical Report Series, October 1991. http://www.usfa.fema.gov/ downloads/pdf/publications/tr-060.pdf.

Fuller, Diana Burgess and Daniela Salvioni, ed. *Art, Women, California 1950-2000: Parallels and Intersections*. Berkeley, CA: University of California Press, 2002.

Geritz, Franz. "Western Wonders: Presented Seriously and Satirically in the Block Prints by the Sisters Bruton." *Touring Topics*, April 1930, n.p.

Gibbs, Wolcott. *Bird Life at the Pole*. New York: William Morrow & Co., 1931.

Gibson, Arrell Morgan. *The Santa Fe and Taos Colonies: Age of the Muses, 1900–1942*. Norman: University of Oklahoma Press, 1983.

Goodwin, Jean. "California Mosaics." *In Art for the Millions: Essays from the 1930s by Artists and Administrators of the WPA Federal Art Project*, edited by Frances V. O'Connor, 56–59. Greenwich, CT: New York Graphic Society, 1973.

Hailey, Gene, ed. *California Art Research*. Vol. 16, First series. Abstract from WPA Project 2874; C.P. 65-3-3632. San Francisco: Works Progress Administration, 1937.

Haswell, J. Mellentin. *Von Nostrand Reinhold Manual of Mosaic*. London: Thames and Hudson, 1973.

Hauk, Steve. "Artists on the Mesa, 1826–1960." *In The Monterey Mesa: Oldest Neighborhood in California*, edited by Julianne Burton-Carvajal, 27–36. Monterey: City of Monterey, 2002.

Helfand, Harvey. "Mosaic Murals of Music & Art." In *California Magazine* (Fall 2011), 86.

Hendon, Karen Crews. "Modernism in Monterey." AFA News, May 10, 2012. http://www.afanews.com/articles/item/1190-modernism-in-monterey#.XqtaCJNKgb0.

Hernandez, Jo Farb. *Wonderful Colors!: The Paintings of August Francois Gay.* Monterey: Monterey Museum of Art, 1993.

Heyman, Therese Thau. "Photography and the Group f.64." In *On the Edge of America: California Modernist Art, 1900–1950*, edited by Paul J. Karlstrom, 243-270. Berkeley: University of California Press, 1996.

Hughes, Edan M. *Artists In California 1786–1940*. Third edition. Sacramento: Crocker Art Museum, 2002.

James, Jack, and Earle Weller. *Treasure Island: "The Magic City" 1939–1940*. San Francisco: Pisani Printing and Publishing, 1941.

James, Ronald M. *The Roar and the Silence: A History of Virginia City and the Comstock Lode*. Reno: University of Nevada Press, 1998.

Jewett, Masha Zakheim. *Coit Tower, San Francisco: Its History and Art*. 50th Anniversary Edition. San Francisco: Volcano Press, 1983.

Johnstone, William. *Points in Time: An Autobiography*. London: Barry & Jenkins, 1980.

Kaplan, Wendy, ed. *California Design, 1930–1965: Living in a Modern Way*. Los Angeles: Los Angeles County Museum of Art, and Cambridge, MA: MIT Press, 2011. Published in conjunction with an exhibition of the same title, organized by and presented at the Los Angeles Museum of Art, October 1, 2011–March 25, 2012.

Kieffer, Connie W. "New Deal Murals: A Legacy for Today's Public Art and Art Education." *Art Education* 53, no. 2 (March 2000), 40–45.

Klein, Barbara J. "The Carmel Monterey Peninsula Art Colony: A History." Reprinted in *Resource Library*, April 21, 2005. Traditional Fine Arts Organization (website). www.tfaoi.com/aa/5aa/5aa300.htm.

Kovinick, Phil, and Marian Yoshiki Kovinick. *An Encyclopedia of Women Artists of the American West*. Austin: University of Texas Press, 1998.

Lampert, Nicolas. *A People's Art History of the United States : 250 Years of Activist Art and Artists Working in Social Justice*. New York: The New Press, 2013.

Langa, Helen, and Paula Wisotzki, eds. *American Women Artists, 1935–1970: Gender, Culture, and Politics*. London: Routledge, 2016.

Luhan, Mabel Dodge. *Edge of Taos Desert: An Escape to Reality*. Albuquerque: University of New Mexico Press, 1987.

Macomber, Ben. *The Jewel City*. San Francisco: John H. Williams, 1915.

Minor, Woodruff. *Alameda Historical Monument Case Report: Bruton House*. Alameda: Historical Advisory Board, 2011. City of Alameda (website). http://alameda.granicus.com/MetaViewer.php?view_id=2&clip_id=930&meta_id=32516

Monterey: The Artist's View, 1925–1945. Monterey: Monterey Museum of Art, 1982.

Moore, Sylvia, ed. *Yesterday and Tomorrow: California Women Artists*. New York: Midmarch Arts Press, 1989.

"Mosaics... and their Use in Western Homes and Gardens." *Sunset Magazine*, October 1947, 38–41.

Munro, Eleanor. *Originals: American Women Artists*. New York: Simon and Schuster, 1982.

Neuhaus, Eugen. *The Art of Treasure Island*. Berkeley: University of California Press, 1939.

O'Connor, Francis V., ed. *Art for the Millions*. Greenwich, CT: New York Graphic Society, 1973.

Official Guide Book: Golden Gate International Exposition on San Francisco Bay. San Francisco: The Crocker Company, 1939.

Outdoor Art at the University of California, Berkeley: Self-Guided Tour. "A Century of Art" pamphlet series. Berkeley: University of California, 2001. http://capitalstrategies.berkeley.edu/sites/default/files/publicartcollectionbrochure-2001.pdf.

Penick, Monica Michelle. "Pace Setter Houses: Livable Modernism in Post-War America." Thesis, University of Texas at Austin, December 2007, https://repositories.lib.utexas.edu/handle/2152/3628.

Poletti, Therese. *Art Deco San Francisco: The Architecture of Timothy Pflueger.* New York: Princeton Architectural Press, 2008.

Puccinelli, Dorothy. "The Brutons and How They Grew." *California Arts & Architecture* 57, no. 10 (October 1940), 18.

Robinson, Roxana. *Georgia O'Keeffe: A Life.* New York: Harper & Row, 1987.

Rubenstein, Charlotte Streifer. *American Women Artists from Early Indian Times to the Present.* Boston: G.K. Hall & Company, 1982.

Ryan, Beatrice Judd. "Brutons-3." *Women's City Club Magazine*, San Francisco, July 1932, 16.

Schwartz, Ellen. "California Art Research: An Historical Essay," in *California Art Research: Handbook, Microfiche Edition*, vi–ix. La Jolla, CA: Lawrence McGilvery, 1987.

Shanken, Andrew M. *Into the Void Pacific: Building the 1939 San Francisco World's Fair.* Oakland: University of California Press, 2014.

Snipper, Martin. *A Survey of Art Work in the City and County of San Francisco.* San Francisco: Art Commission, City and County of San Francisco, 1953.

Spangenberg, Helen. *Yesterday's Artists on the Monterey Peninsula.* Monterey: Monterey Peninsula Museum of Art, 1976.

SS Mariposa SS Monterey. San Francisco: Matson Navigation Company, ca. 1956.

St. Gaudens, Maurine. *Emerging from the Shadows: A Survey of Women Artists Working in California, 1860–1960.* Atglen, PA: Schiffer Publishing Ltd., 2015.

Trenton, Patricia, ed. *Independent Spirits: Women Painters of the American West, 1890–1945.* Berkeley: University of California Press, 1995.

United States. Federal Works Agency. *Final Report On the WPA Program, 1935-43.* Washington, D.C.: U. S. Govt. print. off, 1947.

Veronico, Nicholas A., and Betty S. Veronico. *Depression-Era Sculpture in the Bay Area.* Charleston, SC: Arcadia Publishing, 2017.

Wardle, Marian, ed. *American Women Modernists: The Legacy of Robert Henri, 1910–1945.* New Brunswick, NJ: Rutgers University Press, 2005.

Wells, Ed, ed. *Bohemian Crossroads: Art & Culture Collide Then Subside on the Monterey Peninsula.* Pacific Grove, CA: Guardian Stewardship Editions, 2014.

Wigmore, Barrie A. *The Crash and its Aftermath: A History of Securities Markets in the United States, 1929–1933.* Westport, CT: Greenwood Press, 1985.

Wilson, Neill C. *Behind Your Sugar Bowl: The Story of Sugar in Words and Pictures.* San Francisco: The California and Hawaiian Sugar Refining Corporation, 1936.

Young, Joseph L. *Course in Making Mosaics: An Introduction to the Art and Craft.* New York: Reinhold Publishing Corporation, 1957.

———. *Mosaics: Principles and Practice.* New York: Reinhold Publishing Corporation, 1963.

ARCHIVAL COLLECTIONS

Bruton Sisters Archive. Private collection.

Cunningham, Imogen. Papers, 1903–1991. Archives of American Art, Smithsonian Institution. Washington, D.C.

Dailey, Gardner A. Collection. Environmental Design Archives. College of Environmental Design. University of California, Berkeley. Berkeley, California.

Kjaer, Kirsten. Papers. Kirsten Kjaer Museum. Frostrup, Denmark.

O'Connor, Francis V. Papers, 1920–2009. Archives of American Art, Smithsonian Institution. Washington, DC.

Perham Private Collection [Ina Perham Papers]. Private collection.

Pflueger, Timothy L. Papers. The Bancroft Library. University of California, Berkeley. Berkeley, California.

INTERVIEWS

Albro, Maxine, and Parker Hall. Oral history interview with Mary McChesney, July 27, 1964. Archives of American Art, Smithsonian Institution. https://www.aaa.si.edu/collections/interviews/oral-history-interview-maxine-albro-and-parker-hall-12350#transcript.

Bruton, Helen. Interview by Nancy Boas, April 5, 1983. In the possession of Nancy Boas.

Bruton, Helen. Interview by Terry St. John, July 21, 1972. Copy in possession of the author.

Bruton, Helen, and Margaret Bruton. Interview with Lydia Modi-Vitale and Steven Gelber, February 27, 1975. New Deal Art Video Collection, de Saisset Museum, Santa Clara University, Santa Clara, California. https://archive.org/details/castcdsm_000002/castcdsm_000002_t01_access.HD.mov.

Bruton, Helen, and Margaret Bruton. Oral history interview with Lewis Ferbraché, December 4, 1964. Archives of American Art, Smithsonian Institution. https://www.aaa.si.edu/collections/interviews/oral-history-interview-helen-and-margaret-bruton-11725#transcript.

Cravath, Ruth. Oral history interview with Mary McChesney, September 23, 1965. Archives of American Art, Smithsonian Institution. https://www.aaa.si.edu/collections/interviews/oral-history-interview-ruth-cravath-12345#transcript.

IMAGE CREDITS

Cover, 84, 96, 169, 175, and 178: © 2021 Imogen Cunningham Trust

6-7, 109 and 110: Photos by Karl Jacob. Courtesy Paul and Kathryn Totah

10, 12 (left) 14, 15, 20, 23, 24, 37, 38, 54, 57 (left), 60-62, 64, 67, 77, 78, 90, 93, 94, 99, 101 (right), 107, 116, 121, 124, 125, 128, 137, 144, 147 (right), 152, 154, 155, 166 and 167: Bruton Sisters Archive

12 (right), 13, 42, 118: Courtesy Barbara Carroll

18: Photo by James David Givens

25: Courtesy Susan Clark

26: *Untitled [Bruton Sisters]* – Oil on canvas, 30½ x 92¼ x 1½ in. The Wolfsonian-Florida International University, Miami, Florida. The Mitchell Wolfson, Jr. Collection, TD1991.83.2. Photo by Lynton Gardiner

28: Collection Monterey Museum of Art. Gift of the artist, 1973.022

30: *The Old Timer* – Oil on canvas, 30 x 24 in. The Buck Collection at UCI Institute and Museum of California Art

31: *Helen at Sargent House Studio* – Oil on canvas, 40 x 34 in. The Buck Collection at UCI Institute and Museum of California Art

32: Collection Monterey Museum of Art. Gift of the artist, 1975.003.001

34: *The Party* – Linoleum block print, 10 5/16 x 12 7/8 in. The Buck Collection at UCI Institute and Museum of California Art

35: Courtesy James Coran and William Lorton

39, 40 (right), and 52: Courtesy James Coran

40 (left): Collection Monterey Museum of Art. Gift of Barbara and William Hyland, 1991.222

45: Photo by Christina Snider. Courtesy Hoose Library, University of Southern California

48: *Taos Woman* – Oil on canvas, 24 1/8 x 21 1/8 in. The Buck Collection at UCI Institute and Museum of California Art

50: *Corn Dance* – Wood, gold and aluminum leaf, 30¼ x 70½ x 11¼ in. The Wolfsonian–Florida International University, Miami, Florida. Purchase, 2017.16.1 Photo by Lynton Gardiner

51: Courtesy Annex Galleries

57 (right): Reba and Dave Williams Collection. Gift of Reba and Dave Williams, National Gallery of Art, Washington, D.C., 2008.115.1085

65 and 141: From the collection of Eric and Teresa Del Piero

68 and 71: Courtesy of the Fairmont, San Francisco

72 and 73: Photos by William Lorton. Courtesy of the Fairmont, San Francisco

75: Courtesy Michael D. Horikawa Fine Art

80, 81 and 184: Maynard L. Parker, photographer. Courtesy of The Huntington Library, San Marino, California

83 and 104: San Francisco History Center, San Francisco Public Library

87 and 88: Photos by Richard Rothman, San Francisco

95: Courtesy of the University of California, Berkeley

97: Photo by Richard Guy Wilson

100 and 101 (left): Courtesy Hotel Union Square, San Francisco

102: Courtesy ARG Conservation Services

113: Reba and Dave Williams Collection. Gift of Reba and Dave Williams, National Gallery of Art, Washington, D.C., 2008.115.1084

INDEX